TUBE OF PLENTY

By Erik Barnouw

MASS COMMUNICATION:
Television, Radio, Film, Press

THE TELEVISION WRITER

(with S. Krishnaswamy)
INDIAN FILM

A HISTORY OF BROADCASTING
IN THE UNITED STATES

1. A Tower in Babel
2. The Golden Web
3. The Image Empire

DOCUMENTARY:
A History of the Non-Fiction Film

THE SPONSOR:
Notes on a Modern Potentate

THE MAGICIAN AND THE CINEMA

TUBE OF PLENTY

The Evolution of American Television

SECOND REVISED EDITION

Erik Barnouw

New York   Oxford
OXFORD UNIVERSITY PRESS
1990

ress

ronto
dras Karachi
Kong Tokyo
pe Town
Melbourne   Auckland

and associated companies in
Berlin   Ibadan

Copyright © 1975, 1982, 1990 by Erik Barnouw

Published by Oxford University Press, Inc.,
198 Madison Avenue, New York, New York 10016-4314

Oxford is a registered trademark of Oxford University Press

Most of the material in this book has been derived from
the following books: *A Tower in Babel: A History of Broadcasting
in the United States to 1933*, copyright © 1966 by Erik Barnouw;
The Golden Web: A History of Broadcasting in the United States, 1933-53,
copyright © 1968 by Erik Barnouw; and *The Image Empire: A History of
Broadcasting in the United States from 1953*,
copyright © 1970 by Erik Barnouw.

Library of Congress Cataloging-in-Publication Data
Barnouw, Erik, 1908-
Tube of plenty: the evolution of American television / Erik
Barnouw.—2nd rev. ed.
p.   cm.   Includes bibliographical references.
ISBN 0-19-506483-6.—ISBN 0-19-506484-4 (pbk.)
1. Television broadcasting—United States—History.   I. Title.
HE8700.8.B37   1990
384.55'0973—dc20   89-78547

6 8 9 7
Printed in the United States of America

FOREWORD

When the study that has become *Tube of Plenty* was begun decades ago, the subject—television—was seen as offspring of an "entertainment" heritage devoted to enlivening idle hours. Not for one moment, in the intervening years, has the subject sat still for its portrait. Taking over all hours, it has seized jurisdiction over far more than entertainment. Its exponents have mushroomed into huge industries powered by arcane technologies addicted to sudden, quantum changes. The upheavals continue.

The patterns made in vacuum tubes by fusillades of electrons have meanwhile imprinted themselves on the lives and institutions of people, nations, and the world at large. The swirling dots have become an arena in which countless contending interests conduct symbolic shadow warfare in fable and song even as flesh-and-blood gladiators in parliament, battlefield, courtroom, and stadium continue their ceaseless struggles. Amid the phantasmagoria of shadow and substance, some see the planet working out its destiny.

Substantially updated as well as condensed, *Tube of Plenty* includes material originally presented in the three-volume *History of Broadcasting in the United States*. Readers wishing the more extensive account of the early decades should consult the original volumes with their ample footnotes, bibliographies, and appendices: *A Tower in Babel*, which carried the story to 1933; *The Golden Web*, on the years 1933-53; and *The Image Empire*, dealing with the years 1953-70. Further aspects of the story are covered in *The Sponsor: Notes on a Modern Potentate*.

Tube of Plenty, encompassing the full history in a more rapid chronicle, stresses the emergence of television as a dominant factor in American life and in American influence throughout the world.

Fair Haven, Vermont   E. B.
October 1989

CONTENTS

Contents

FOREBEARS

1

"Such is the stock I spring from."

PLAUTUS

1877 prophecy: "Terrors of the Telephone."   New York *Daily Graphic*

Long before television, long before the broadcasting era, some of their possibilities were glimpsed. When Alexander Graham Bell began exhibiting his telephone in 1876, his demonstrations provoked diverse and extravagant visions. An artist in the New York *Daily Graphic* depicted what he called "Terrors of the Telephone." He showed an orator at a microphone heard by groups of people around the world.

About the same time a popular song, "The Wondrous Telephone," published in St. Louis, described future delights in these terms:

You stay at home and listen
To the lecture in the hall,
And hear the strains of music
From a fascinating ball!

Almost immediately afterwards, others took a dramatic further leap. Bell had described the telephone as an apparatus for transmitting sounds "telegraphically," and had based his device on study of the ear. If people could hear "telegraphically," would they not soon

1879 prediction: televised sports—by Du Maurier.   *Punch*

also see "telegraphically"—by a device based on study of the eye? Instruments for doing so were soon imagined by many, and given various names, including *telephonoscope*—i.e., a telephone transmitting sound and picture. In 1879, in *Punch*, the artist and writer George du Maurier portrayed such an instrument. He showed a couple by a fireplace, watching a tennis match on a screen above the mantle; they could communicate vocally with the players.

Three years later the French artist Albert Robida drew a series of pictures that embodied more startling predictions. Families of the future would, as he saw it, watch a distant war from the comfort of the living room. In his imagination, the screen on the wall would also allow people to take courses taught by a faraway teacher. And it would enable the housewife to survey goods for sale, and her husband to watch a girlie show—all from the comfort of home.

Surprisingly, laboratory steps toward such ideas followed almost

1882 forecast: watching a war—by Robida.   Bettman Archive

at once. One step came in 1884, when the German Paul Nipkow devised the "Nipkow disk"—a rotating disk with perforations arranged in a spiral pattern. A beam of light shining through these perforations, as the disk revolved, caused pinpoints of light to perform a rapid "scanning" movement, like the movement of eyes back and forth across a printed page. The device was at once seen as a way of transmitting pictures by wire, in the form of a series of dots of varying intensity. The Nipkow disk remained for decades the basis for experiments in the transmission of images—both still pictures and moving pictures.

The company formed by Bell was rife with such visions, all seen as emanations of the telephone. The company soon concentrated on something more immediately profitable—providing facilities for two-way conversation. But the visions continued to stir investigators—at Bell laboratories and elsewhere—and won new voltage from related bursts of invention, such as the advent of the phonograph in 1878, the peepshow *kinetoscope* in 1894, the *cinématographe* in 1895; and, almost simultaneously, the invention of wireless, soon followed by that of radio.

Each of these had its meteoric rise; each also belongs in the prehistory of television. Television in the United States has been shaped to a considerable extent by events in these older, related media. The interrelationships are part of our story.

Individually, their histories show striking parallels. All stemmed mainly from work of individual experimenters—not corporation laboratories—and seem, in this respect, to reflect an age now vanishing. All won attention as toys, hobbies, or fairground curiosities. Yet the patents soon became corporation assets and the subject of violent patent wars and monopoly litigation. More than that, they became stakes in international struggles between military-industrial complexes. Each in turn was felt to have a pervasive and unsettling social impact, not readily defined.

The transition pattern is dramatically exemplified by the story of the boy-inventor Marconi, whose bedroom tinkerings led in a few short years, via entertainment ballyhoo, to the councils of armies and navies, the formation of the Radio Corporation of America, mammoth antitrust struggles, and the creation of worldwide television systems.

BLACK BOX NO. 1

Guglielmo Marconi, born in 1874, was the son of a well-to-do Italian gentleman and a much younger Irish girl who had run away from home to marry him. The boy grew up on his father's estate near Bologna—a thin, intense youth, spending hours in his thirdfloor room, experimenting. His father was annoyed by the boy's seclusiveness.

In 1894-95 his experiments concerned radio waves, then known as "Hertzian waves." The scientist Heinrich Hertz had shown how

1882 Visions: home-screen delights—by Robida.
Bettman Archive

to actuate such waves—with a spark leaping across a gap—and how to detect them. It was widely felt that the waves could, in some way, be used to communicate across large distances, but no one had figured out how. Guglielmo, an avid reader of electrical journals, knew that famous scientists throughout Europe were working on the problem—Oliver Lodge in England, Alexander Popov in Russia, Adolphus Slaby in Germany, Edouard Branley in France. The awareness drove Guglielmo on, like someone possessed. He failed to appear at meals. His mother took to leaving trays upstairs outside his locked door. The father fumed; Guglielmo seemed to be wasting irreplaceable years.

In due time he could, via radio waves, ring a bell across the room, or even downstairs. The family was properly amazed, but not sure of the significance. He then moved the experiments outdoors, to try for larger distances. He broke the emissions into short and long periods—dots and dashes, using a Morse telegraph key. After a time he devised something he called an "antenna," and a grounding at each end of the operation; these seemed to be valuable additions. At first, successful reception could be signaled by the wave of a handkerchief, but this was inadequate when the question became: would the messages pass through hills, woods, and other obstacles? For such tests, a local farmer and carpenter helped, lugging the antenna over a distant hill, armed with a rifle. After they had disappeared over the rim, Guglielmo began sending from his upstairs room. A rifle shot rang out from the distance.

The father began to take things seriously. With advice from a parish priest and the family doctor, a letter was written to the Italian Minister of Post and Telegraph about the invention. When the reply came, saying the government was not interested, his mother made a quick, remarkable decision: she and Guglielmo would take the invention to England. Perhaps she longed to visit her homeland; in any case, she could not have decided more shrewdly. For the scattered British empire, held together by thin lines of ships and threads of ocean cable, such a means of communication had obvious attractions. Britain's virtual control of ocean cables, important as it was, was of uncertain military value; what would become of them in time of war was not yet known.

Early in 1896 young Marconi carefully packed and locked the black box that held the invention, and they set sail. In England the black box at once stirred the suspicion of customs officials. Two years earlier the French President had been killed by an Italian anarchist. In the black box were wires, batteries, and tubes with metal filings. Smashing it seemed wisest, and this they did; Guglielmo had to begin his English visit by reconstructing his invention. But good fortune awaited him. The mother's relatives got him in touch with the chief engineer of telegraphs in the British Post Office, Sir William Preece, who had himself experimented with wireless and could appreciate what young Marconi had accomplished. Tests on Salisbury plain began at a hundred yards but soon went to nine miles. Marconi later recalled: "The calm of my life ended then."

In 1897 a British corporation was formed, backed by a powerful group and capitalized at £100,000. Marconi, aged 23, received half the stock and £15,000 in cash. He became one of six directors, in charge of development.

For years the pace of events did not slacken. Off the British coast, signals were sent long distances from ship to shore, and from ship to ship, penetrating fog and rain. The tests caused international excitement. Foreign observers arrived, especially army and navy observers—from France, Germany, Russia, Italy. The equipping of lighthouses and British warships began. The French navy became interested. But the Marconi directors had other priorities: they wanted first to approach the American navy.

An invitation from the New York *Herald* provided the occasion. The *Herald* wanted Marconi for a spectacular sports exploit: he was to provide a minute-by-minute account of the *America*'s Cup Race scheduled for October 1899. The *Herald* planned to have details of the race in print before the ships even returned to port; it would be the journalistic scoop of the year. Marconi accepted the

Marconi and his black box. Smithsonian

invitation. In the course of the sports gala, there would be military discussions.

It happened to be an ideal moment for such overtures. As Marconi landed in New York in September 1899, the city was preparing a welcome not for him—nor for Sir Thomas Lipton, the cup challenger, arriving with his *Shamrock*—but for the hero of Manila Bay, Admiral George Dewey. It was an hour bursting with manifest destiny. The Spanish-American War had suddenly made the United States an empire with overseas possessions. There were protesters, including William Jennings Bryan and the Anti-Imperialist League, but they were widely assailed for wanting a "small" instead of a "big" America. The prevailing mood was muscular; navy and army appropriations were sliding swiftly through Congress. People with overseas interests were not averse. Protected bases, harbors, coaling stations were needed by a great and expanding power, and such a nation would—like the British empire—have to think about communication. In the "splendid little war," as Secretary of State John Hay had called it, there had been difficulties in communication. According to navy annals, it had been splendid within naval squadrons but unsatisfactory between army and navy, and between the field forces and Washington. To inform Washington headquarters of his victory and subsequent actions at Manila, Admiral Dewey had had to send dispatch boats to Hong Kong, whence the news was telegraphed over British-controlled cables via the Indian Ocean, the Red Sea, the Mediterranean, and the Atlantic Ocean. Presumably London knew all the facts before Washington did. Somehow this didn't fit with the new world posture. At this juncture Guglielmo Marconi arrived in America.

The victory of the *Columbia* over the *Shamrock—"reported by wireless!"*—was duly proclaimed in *Herald* headlines. The hour seemed to belong to the sporting world, but other events were in process. After the races came special tests for the navy; also, historic legal business. On November 22, 1899, the Marconi Wireless Company of America ("American Marconi") was incorporated under the laws of New Jersey, to exploit Marconi patents in the United States and various possessions including Cuba. Authorized capital of $10,000,000 was covered by two million shares with a par value of $5. Many of these shares went back to England, 365,000 being held by the parent firm.

A United States boom in the manufacture of wireless equipment, for commercial and military shipping and shore installations, quickly developed. American Marconi inevitably led the way, but soon had rivals. The fact that it was a subsidiary of a British company was irksome to the navy. American Marconi was looked on as a British device for extending to wireless the control already exercised over ocean cables. Ideas for wresting American Marconi from British control were soon discussed in Washington. In due time they bore fruit.

VOICES IN THE ETHER

Wireless soon became a popular mania. Wireless clubs erupted. Wireless became a favorite theme of fiction and nonfiction. It was noisily demonstrated at fairs. Wireless amateurs or "hams" began to fill the air with code. The life-saving aspects of wireless were constantly discussed, but the excitement also dovetailed with the needs of trade, the zeal for empire, and the burgeoning of military budgets.

The spirit of the time was symbolized by the hasty departure of Marconi for England after his American triumphs. It was explained that he was needed for advice on wireless apparatus for the Boer War. It was soon learned that the British found the Boers also using wireless. Captured apparatus has apparently been made in Germany, and was similar in design to Marconi equipment.

In the United States, competitors challenging the Marconi leadership included two enterprises likewise stemming from individual experimenters. Both were obsessed with the desire to replace dots and dashes with the human voice.

One was Reginald Aubrey Fessenden, a Canadian who had taught electrical engineering in Pittsburgh, had worked for Westinghouse, and in 1900 began wireless experiments for the weather bureau of the U.S. Department of Agriculture. Backers then helped him start his own National Electric Signaling Company, experimenting at Brant Rock, Mass., and concentrating on voice transmission—designated by such terms as "wireless telephone," "radio telephone," "radiophone," and "radio." Instead of sending an interrupted wave or series of bursts, as Marconi did, Fessenden's idea was to send a continuous wave, on which voice would be superimposed as variations or modulations. This idea, at first seen as a heresy, became fundamental to radio.

Limited success came as early as 1901, but the experiments reached a climax on Christmas Eve, 1906. Ship wireless operators over a wide area of the Atlantic, sitting with earphones to head, alert to the crackling of distant dots and dashes, were startled to hear a woman singing; then a violin playing; then a man reading passages from Luke. It was considered uncanny; wireless rooms were soon crowded with the curious. The phenomenon was identified as coming from Brant Rock; those who heard it were asked to notify Fessenden. Later Fessenden tests were heard as far away as the West Indies, on banana boats of the United Fruit Company.

United Fruit, which found wireless valuable for coordinating far-flung plantations and directing cargoes to profitable markets, made equipment purchases from Fessenden, but later formed its own equipment subsidiary, and acquired a number of patents. It specialized in "crystal detectors"—utilizing the discovery that various kinds of crystals could, in some mysterious way, "detect" radio waves and turn them into electrical currents, if touched in the right spot with a thin wire or "cat's whisker"—as amateurs liked to call it.

Fessenden sold equipment also to the navy, but he was generally in financial straits. Navy officials considered him irascible and hard to deal with; he found them unreasonable. His company collapsed in a few years; his remaining patents were later acquired by Westinghouse.

Lee de Forest, like Fessenden, was dedicated to voice transmission. After his studies, which began with religion but switched to science, he got a job in Chicago with Western Electric, equipment subsidiary of the American Telephone and Telegraph Company, the heir to Bell's work. De Forest then began his own experiments in his rented bedroom. He eventually brought voice transmission to a new stage of development with his "Audion" tube, patented in

Fessenden and co-workers at Brant Rock.   Smithsonian

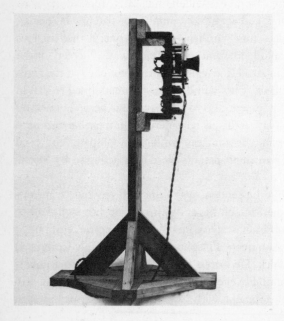

Fessenden micro-
phone—*ca.* 1907.
Smithsonian

1907. A glass-bulb detector of radio waves—also capable, as was later shown, of amplifying and generating radio waves—it was an extension of work done by John Ambrose Fleming for the Marconi company in England, and was ultimately descended from Edison's electric light bulb. The extraordinary Audion became the foundation of the electronics industry—a Pandora's tube of endless ramifications. As detector it outperformed the crystal, but was expensive. For most amateur experimenters, the crystal remained standard—the poor man's Audion.

De Forest, to demonstrate and refine his Audion, immediately began "broadcasts" in New York, using phonograph records and also inviting singers to his laboratory for tests. In 1908 he performed similar demonstrations from the Eiffel Tower in Paris. In 1910, back in New York, he broadcast Enrico Caruso from the Metropolitan Opera stage. By 1916 he was broadcasting in New York on a fairly regular schedule, which included several innovations: a broadcast speech by his mother-in-law, demanding votes for women; and the 1916 presidential election returns, read from newspapers and—based on their misinformation—announcing the election of Charles Evans Hughes as President.

De Forest, son of a minister, had a sense of mission about all this. From his college days on, he wrote a diary in florid, sometimes biblical style, rebuking himself for time lost. "The morning wasted, bitterly will its hours be craved, but no tears of remorse avail to bring back one golden moment." He seemed to see himself as a pilgrim, struggling upward through severe trials, occasionally triumphant. "Unwittingly then," he wrote after his early work on the Audion, "had I discovered an invisible Empire of the Air."

Like Fessenden, De Forest made sales to the navy, and at times appeared firmly established. But he too was underfinanced, and a constant prey to promoters who wanted him to stage spectacular demonstrations in order to sell stock. Their manipulations kept De Forest in legal as well as financial hot water. And his obsession with "broadcasting," which seemed to hold no economic promise, was

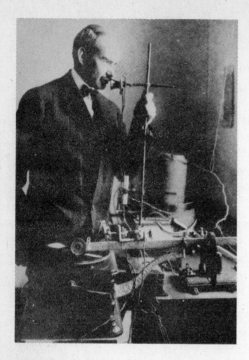

De Forest broadcasting in New York—1907.
Smithsonian

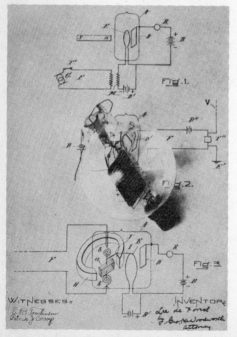

De Forest Audion patent—1907.

widely considered indicative of an impractical nature—although it roused the enthusiasm of the "hams."

On the eve of World War I, the air was a chaos of crackling codes, voices, and music. Under a 1912 law, transmission required a government license, but this had not reduced the chaos, and the law was in any case widely ignored. Much of the transmission was army and navy communication, relating to training and maneuvers. Another large part was contributed by the irrepressible amateurs, already numbering thousands, who were anathema to the military; their chatter was said to interfere with military communication. They were even accused of sending fake orders to navy ships, purportedly from admirals. Another part of the transmission was related to technical experimentation—by individual inventors, universities, government agencies, corporations. It already included experiments in the transmission of images, which, like radio, had acquired a variety of names: "visual wireless," "visual radio," "electric vision," and even "television"—a term used in an American journal—*Scientific American*—as early as June 1907. Most theories and experiments were based on the Nipkow disk. This was seen as the key to transmission of still pictures—"facsimile" transmission—and eventually to television, which was seen as a speeding-up of the same process.

Prominent among experimenting corporations was the American Telephone and Telegraph Company. Alarmed by the rise of American Marconi, which seemed to pose a threat to its own domain, AT&T bought various patents of De Forest, at a time when the latter was on the verge of bankruptcy. AT&T prepared for a possibly wireless telephonic era, and also became an early "visual wireless" experimenter.

But American Marconi still forged ahead. In 1912 it had won world attention when a young Marconi operator, 21-year-old David Sarnoff, picked up faint signals: "S. S. *Titanic* ran into iceberg. Sinking fast." He alerted other ships in the area, and informed the press. Accounts of how he stuck to his telegraph key, relaying news of survivors to countless anxious relatives, acquired over the years a legendary quality that seemed to fit his life story. Since the age of ten he had been the main support of his immigrant Russian family. Having won a foothold at American Marconi as an office boy, Sarnoff became within a few years its commercial manager. As American Marconi grew, he grew with it. He was, heart and soul, a company man. And the company was turning into big business, and winning government contracts—in spite of navy misgivings.

Other corporations increasingly active in experiments were General Electric and Westinghouse. By the time World War I began, both held significant patents. And with the outbreak of war, they suddenly emerged as dominant forces in the field—for a curious but compelling reason: they had assembly lines that could turn out electric light bulbs by the thousands—or, with modifications, glass vacuum tubes for radio. And the military suddenly needed vacuum tubes by the thousands. They wanted transmitters and receivers for ships, airplanes, automobiles. They wanted "pack transmitters" and "trench transmitters," using barbed wire as antennae. They wanted electronic submarine detectors, radio direction finders, and equipment for recording and study of code transmissions. And all this equipment required vacuum tubes.

A few years earlier, experimental radio tubes had been made one at a time by a glassblower, with others looking over his shoulder, offering suggestions. Now they were in mass production. At one point the Signal Corps placed a single order for 80,000 tubes.

The result of all this was a vast, coordinated production of radio equipment, with the navy as chief coordinator. Under its guiding hand, enormous technical progress was made. All patent claims were set aside for the duration of the war under government war powers, to be adjudicated later; as Assistant Secretary of the Navy, Franklin D. Roosevelt signed the order. With United States entry into the war, all amateurs were ruled off the air; their equipment

World War I radio receiver SCR 70—made by Westinghouse.
Signal Corps Museum, U.S. Army

was to be sealed. The bothersome interference was finally gone. The government took control of all privately owned shore installations—most of which were American Marconi stations.

In the official *History of Communications—Electronics in the United States Navy* the period of World War I is referred to as the "Golden Age." Radio was used for coordination and intelligence, and eventually for propaganda. As the war approached its climax, most parts of the world heard Wilson's Fourteen Points broadcast again and again from numerous transmitters, some of transoceanic power.

So euphoric was the navy about its wartime achievements that it announced, immediately after the armistice, a dramatic proposal. It recommended that there be a monopoly in radio—a navy monopoly.

WE NEED A MONOPOLY

The proposal took the form of legislation, submitted to Congress in the fall of 1918. Hearings began.

In many countries, government was taking control of the development of wireless and radio—including "visual radio." In many places the closeness of enemy borders, and the economic prostration left by war, were factors in the move. Although such factors were not decisive in the United States, the navy felt that the policy should be adopted here also, and that the navy was its natural custodian. At congressional committee hearings in December 1918, Secretary of the Navy Josephus Daniels testified:

> . . . the passage of this bill will secure for all time to the Navy Department the control of radio in the United States, and will enable the navy to continue the splendid work it has carried out during the war.

A return to the prewar free-for-all seemed to him unthinkable. The Secretary did not shrink, under questioning, from the monopoly implications of his proposal.

> . . . it is my profound conviction and is the conviction of every person I have talked with in this country and abroad who had studied this question that it must be a monopoly. It is up to the Congress to say whether it is a monopoly for the government or a monopoly for a company. . . .

The U.S. State Department enthusiastically endorsed the bill. The army also urged a government monopoly, though demurring at the idea of navy supervision.

In spite of this impressive backing, vociferous opposition developed. It came largely from the amateurs, who were beginning to unpack their sealed equipment and return to the air. In spite of their lowly status, they managed to stir up a hullabaloo. At the hearings their spokesman, Hiram Percy Maxim, president of the American

Radio Relay League, pointed out that the navy achievements in radio had been made possible by those same amateurs, who by tens of
thousands had poured into war communication. Now these men
were leaving the armed forces; the navy's expectations of continued
glory were therefore, said Maxim, illusory. The men needed for the
work would not be there. They would be back home, looking for
new ways to apply their special knowledge. "We block the ambi-
tion of over 100,000 of the best brains we possess to apply their efforts in that field in which they most want to work." In 1917, when
all amateur equipment had been sealed, 8,562 had held licenses to
transmit; but according to Maxim, 125,000 owned receiving equipment.

Congressman William S. Greene of Massachusetts was among
those joining Maxim's protests. By what right did the backers of the
bill so cavalierly flout the antitrust laws? "I have never heard before
that it was necessary for one person to own all the air in order to
breathe. . . . Having just won a fight against autocracy, we would
start an autocratic movement with this bill." Amid such protests the
bill was tabled and died.

But the navy was not finished. If its first choice, a navy monopoly, was ruled out, it would push for its second choice—a private
monopoly in congenial hands. This time it had greater success.

On October 17, 1919, a new corporation was formed: the Radio
Corporation of America. At first an empty shell, it became within
months the dominant power in the electronic world. It was, to begin with, American Marconi—expropriated and Americanized. But
it was also more: it represented virtually all important patents in the
field.

The phenomenon was accomplished by swift and skillful maneuvers. After urgent discussions between the U.S. Navy Department
and General Electric, mainly led by Rear Admiral W. H. G. Bullard of the navy and Owen D. Young of General Electric, arrangements were made to incorporate RCA—for the moment, a paper
creation. The articles of incorporation provided that only United
States citizens might be directors or officers; also, that not more than

20 per cent of the stock could be held by foreigners. A United States government representative was to sit with the board.

Now American Marconi was invited to transfer all its assets and operations to the new company. Individual stockholders would be asked to accept RCA shares in place of American Marconi shares. GE proposed to buy the approximately 365,000 shares held by British Marconi.

The Marconi interests had virtually no choice but to accept the plan. Almost all land stations of American Marconi were still in United States government hands. The attitude of the Navy Department indicated that they would not be returned to a British-dominated company. Nor could such a company expect future government contracts. On the other hand, a government-sponsored RCA could expect to be a government favorite. To individual stockholders this would be important. In addition, a strong RCA might in the long run be a more valuable ally to British Marconi than a weak American Marconi. Scarcely a month after the creation of RCA, American Marconi—with the approval of its stockholders—transferred all its assets and obligations to the new company. Owen D. Young became RCA board chairman; Admiral Bullard became the government representative who would sit with the board.

GE now replaced British Marconi as parent company, but within months three other American corporations became GE partners in the venture: AT&T, United Fruit, Westinghouse. Each placed its many patents in the common pool, which they would jointly control; it represented a total of some two thousand electronic patents. Each acquired a block of RCA stock and representation on the board. By 1921 they owned RCA stock in the following proportions:

	COMMON	PREFERRED	TOTAL	PER CENT
GE	2,364,826	620,800	2,985,626	30.1%
Westinghouse	1,000,000	1,000,000	2,000,000	20.6%
AT&T	500,000	500,000	1,000,000	10.3%
United Fruit	200,000	200,000	400,000	4.1%

A fabulous power concentration had thus emerged from the little black box of Guglielmo Marconi. It seemed certain to control future developments in the world of the ether, and all ramifications of the vacuum tube. The partners, insofar as they could foresee the future of the electronic world, divided it between them.

Through the cross-licensing arrangement each was fortifying its position in its own fields of interest; through RCA each would also share in the control of new dominions.

Even in its infancy, RCA took a leading role in international communication. Acquiring American Marconi shore installations, it began sending messages to England at 17 cents a word, undercutting the cable rate of 25 cents a word. It arranged a consortium of telegraph interests in Latin America, with ultimate authority in United States hands—an extension of the Monroe Doctrine, Owen D. Young called it. It began negotiating for rights in China and elsewhere. A dominant American role in international message services was thus an almost instant achievement.

It had been mainly for this that RCA—in 1919—had been created. That other electronic empires would immediately open before them was scarcely guessed by the incorporators. But even as they shaped their alliance, strange events exploded. With startling suddenness, the broadcasting era began. Touched off late in 1920, it became within a year a mania and a bonanza. The RCA allies, patent-rich, seemed in an unchallengeable position to control the development—in radio and soon afterwards in television.

Events did not quite follow this expectation—not precisely. Developments came so fast that the arrangements of the allies were soon obsolete. As unanticipated conflicts arose, the allies quarreled bitterly over their division of the world. At the same time, their very power made the alliance a target—for would-be competitors and government trust-busters. For although RCA had been formed with the prodding of high government officials, there was much about it that seemed to defy the Sherman and Clayton antitrust acts. Antimonopoly rumblings soon stirred.

Early in the negotiations that created RCA, Owen D. Young had

suggested to Secretary of the Navy Josephus Daniels that Congress
be asked to approve a government charter, specifically authorizing
a monopoly in radio. Daniels, though favoring the monopoly idea,
doubted that Congress would be sympathetic. A different strategy
was therefore adopted: the *fait accompli*. The issue would, if necessary, be faced some other day.

Perhaps soon. As the broadcasting fever spread, transmitter towers were shooting up throughout the country. Diverse receiving
equipment appeared on store counters, and eager crowds lined up
to buy. Television experimentation quickened. Behind all this was
that old anarchic force, the "more than 100,000" amateurs championed by Hiram Percy Maxim, most of whom were back from
military service. If they were aware that the RCA partners had divided up the electronic world, they showed no sign of it. They
were going vigorously into action. RCA and its corporate owners
felt their patents were being pillaged. They prepared for battle
with the trouble-makers—even while battling each other. Chaos
seemed likely, but one thing was clear. New levers of power were
in the making.

TODDLER

2

"It is a wise father that knows his own child."

SHAKESPEARE

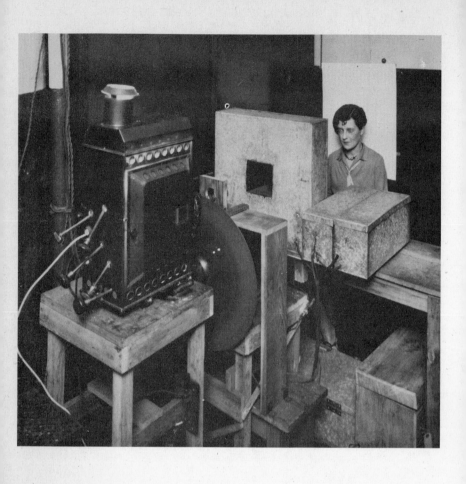

Scanner with "Nipkow disk"—as used by General Electric in experiments of 1920's.
Smithsonian

The excitement that exploded in 1920 was a nationwide eruption, but activities in Pittsburgh were especially decisive.

For the Westinghouse company, the halt in war production had created a bleak outlook. As government contracts for transmitters, receivers, and vacuum tubes ended, the company searched for ways to use its idled production equipment, but for a time found none. When its rival GE, by forming RCA, seemed set to take a dominant role in international communication, Westinghouse was not at first included in the venture. One Westinghouse researcher, Vladimir K. Zworykin, who had been a communication specialist in the Czarist army and had participated in television experiments in Russia, asked for permission to pursue these. Permission was given, but with reluctance; financial returns seemed remote.

A turn in the Westinghouse fortunes came from an unexpected quarter—the world of the amateur. Frank Conrad, a valued Westinghouse researcher, had been prominent in carrying out the government contracts: he had supervised manufacture of the SCR-69 and SCR-70, compact receivers made for the Signal Corps, as well as army and navy transmitters. After the war he had been transferred to making electrical switches. But Conrad was also a prewar amateur; even as the radio work collapsed at Westinghouse, he un-packed his amateur gear and resumed his hobby. From a workshop over his garage in Wilkinsburg, outside Pittsburgh, he broadcast phonograph music and talked with other amateurs, using his old call letters 8XK. Thanks to his war contract work, he now had up-to-date vacuum tubes. Letters from other amateurs praised the qual-ity of his transmissions, and sometimes requested particular musical numbers. Evening phonograph "concerts" from the Wilkinsburg garage became a regular feature—on Saturdays and sometimes week-days. Conrad's sons Francis and Crawford and various friends be-gan to participate. A newspaper item of May 2, 1920, mentioned a piano solo by Francis Conrad, for which a wire was stretched from the house to the garage so that the music could be "sent into the ether by the radiophone apparatus located there."

So far, the activity in Wilkinsburg was not new, nor unique. It followed prewar precedents set by De Forest and others, and simi-lar activities were going on elsewhere. In Madison, Wisconsin, a group headed by Professor Earle M. Terry was broadcasting music and weather bulletins with the call letters 9XM. In Hollywood, electrical engineer Fred Christian had a 5-watt transmitter in his bedroom and entertained nearby amateurs with concerts, using the call letters 6ADZ. In Charlotte, North Carolina, contractor Fred M. Laxton had a transmitter in a chicken coop behind his home, with up-to-date equipment derived from wartime employment with General Electric; using the call letters 4XD, he too broadcast phonograph concerts. In Detroit William E. Scripps, Detroit *News* publisher, having begun as a home experimenter, decided in 1920 to move the activity to his office; in August his 8MK, following De Forest's example, broadcast primary election returns along with "radio-phone" concerts.

Many such experimenters knew each other, and listened and talked to each other. They formed a close brotherhood. But the fol-lowing month a new element entered the situation.

Home and garage of Frank Conrad, site of 8XK—1920.   NBC

THE AMATEURS

"Concert" preparations at 8MK, of Detroit *News*—1920.
Detroit Historical Museum

MERCHANDISING CONCEPT

In the Pittsburgh *Sun*, on September 29, 1920, the Joseph Horne department store ran an advertisement for a $10 item on sale in its basement. The advertisement used a news-story format:

AIR CONCERT "PICKED UP" BY RADIO HERE

Victrola music, played into the air over a wireless telephone, was "picked up" by listeners on the wireless receiving station which was recently installed here for patrons interested in wireless experiments. The concert was heard Thursday night about 10 o'clock, and continued 20 minutes. Two orchestra numbers, a piano solo—which rang particularly high and clear through the air—and a juvenile "talking piece" constituted the program.

The music was from a Victrola pulled up close to the transmitter of a wireless telephone in the home of Frank Conrad, Penn and Peebles Avenues, Wilkinsburg. Mr. Conrad is a wireless enthusiast and "puts on" the wireless concerts periodically for the entertainment of the many people in this district who have wireless sets.

Amateur Wireless Sets, made by the maker of the Set which is in operation in our store, are on sale here $10.00 up.

—West Basement

The advertisement was seen by Harry P. Davis, Westinghouse vice president and Conrad's superior, and it gave him pause. Davis knew of Conrad's amateur activity and had never given it much thought, even when it received newspaper attention. But the advertisement, apparently reflecting a judgment on a merchandising value, had an entirely different effect on him.

The few hundred amateurs thought to be listening to Conrad's concerts in the Pittsburgh area were all technical-minded individuals who had themselves assembled their receivers. Since the turn of the century, receiving had been for those with technical knowledge. The practitioners themselves had woven a mystique around their activity, and surrounded it with arcane terminology. During the war the subject had become even more remote, mysterious, and legendary. But the Westinghouse receivers made for the Signal Corps, such as the SCR-70, were complete in one unit and easy to operate—on the insistence of the military. What suddenly dawned on Davis was the vision of a market—not of electrical wizards, nor of military forces, but of *everyone*. It seemed to him suddenly that this market might be virtually *limitless*, and that it could be activated merely by going on the air, and maintaining a regular program service.

The vision put the idea of broadcasting in an entirely new light. What had seemed an eccentric hobby, or a form of exhibitionism, or at best a quixotic enterprise pursued by visionaries like De Forest, was suddenly seen as a sound business concept that could yield rich profits through the sale of receivers.

On the very next day, September 30, Harry Davis conferred with Conrad. He wanted Conrad to build a transmitter at the Westinghouse works—like Conrad's 8XK, but stronger. Could Conrad have it ready by November 2, so that they could start a program schedule with maximum dramatic effect, via election returns? Conrad said he could.

On one of the taller buildings of the Westinghouse works in East Pittsburgh a shack was built, and a 100-watt transmitter assembled. An antenna ran from a steel pole on the roof to one of the powerhouse smokestacks. Throughout October the work went forward. On October 27 the U.S. Department of Commerce, which allocated licenses required by the radio law of 1912, assigned the call letters KDKA—commercial shore-station call letters. The Pittsburgh *Post* agreed to relay election information to the rooftop shack by telephone. From the shack Leo H. Rosenberg of the Westinghouse publicity department would broadcast the bulletins. A hand-wound phonograph was brought to the shack to fill periods between returns.

Westinghouse did not yet have complete sets in distribution, nor did other manufacturers. Equipment on sale at electrical stores

Rooftop shack, Westinghouse plant: first KDKA studio.   NBC

consisted mainly of the assortment of parts from which amateurs assembled their tangled contraptions. Most of these still used crystal detectors. Westinghouse promised complete sets in the near future. Such sets were also on view for listening groups organized at the plant and at other locations including a country club.

In all publicity, Westinghouse stressed ease of operation. Radio was pictured as a coming social delight for everyone. The one-time preserve of scientific genius, and more recently the guarded domain of the military, was being opened to the masses.

Preparations were completed barely in time for the November 2 debut. Conrad's 8XK was available in case of transmitter trouble, but was not needed. Broadcasting began at 8 p.m. and went on until after midnight. By then it was clear that the Republican nominee

Shack interior: broadcasting the election returns, 1920.   NBC

Warren G. Harding, U.S. Senator from Ohio, had been elected
President, defeating James M. Cox. The listening groups appeared
jubilant, both over the political turn and over their participation in
a historic occasion.

It was significant in more ways than they could realize. The
presidential contenders Harding and Cox were both newspaper
publishers. Their nomination had symbolized the place of the press
in the constellation of power—and also marked its zenith. KDKA
was the start of a dislocation, the extent of which could scarcely
be anticipated.

Skillfully promoted, the election broadcast received wide comment. But Westinghouse did not pause for self-congratulation. The
broadcast was the start of a daily schedule, at first offering only an

Tent for orchestra, KDKA, Pittsburgh—1920.   NBC

hour or so each evening—8:30-9:30—but soon expanding. This
called for much improvisation, which was sometimes bizarre. A
Westinghouse band was presented by wire from a hall, but the
reverberation was unendurable on the air, so the next musical group
was presented from the roof, where the acoustics were splendid.
Rainy weather came, so a tent was built on the roof; the acoustics
were still good. Then the tent blew down, and it was necessary to
move indoors again. The acoustical problem was now solved by
erecting the tent indoors. In time this arrangement gave way to
studios hung with burlap—which often had a tent-like look.

In January 1921 KDKA tried a remote broadcast from the Pittsburgh Calvary Baptist Church, with engineers disguised in choir
robes. Soon afterwards came pickups from a prizefight, a theater,
and the Duquesne Club—for a speech by Secretary of Commerce
Herbert Hoover.

Within weeks the 100-watt transmitter was replaced by a 500-
watt transmitter, and similar transmitters were shipped elsewhere

Tent-like studio, WHK, Cleveland—*ca.* 1923.   Smithsonian

to give birth to WJZ, Newark, N.J.; WBZ, Springfield, Mass.; and KYW, Chicago—all Westinghouse stations. Again, rooftop shacks served as temporary studios. At the Westinghouse plant in Newark, would-be broadcasters had to climb a vertical ladder, and were then hauled or pushed through a roof hatch. To end such indignities, a section of the ladies' "cloakroom" was partitioned to make a studio. In Chicago, the KYW 1921 schedule settled down to pickups from the Chicago Civic Opera, headed by Mary Garden. That winter all performances, afternoon and evening, six days a week, were broadcast.

These Westinghouse moves had rapid and numerous results. It was the KDKA debut that won for Westinghouse its invitation to join the RCA alliance, which thus became a GE-AT&T-United Fruit-Westinghouse partnership. It also changed the agenda for RCA. Broadcasting—and plans for the mass production and sale of receivers—suddenly won priority. At GE, researcher William C. White found himself "amazed at our blindness . . . we had every-

thing except the idea." He and others pushed plans for a General
Electric station, and soon initiated WGY, Schenectady, followed
by KGO, San Francisco, and KOA, Denver. RCA gave birth to
WJY, Jersey City; later to WRC, Washington.

At RCA, the turn of events gave new impetus to the rise of David
Sarnoff. Unlike most American Marconi holdovers, he had regarded
the prewar broadcasts of De Forest with interest. As early as 1916
Sarnoff was urging American Marconi to manufacture "Radio
Music Boxes," but the idea was rejected as harebrained by Edward
J. Nally, general manager of American Marconi. Early in 1920,
when the company had turned into RCA, Sarnoff mentioned the
idea again, this time to Owen D. Young, and followed with a merchandising plan, including sales predictions which later turned out
to be startlingly accurate. He estimated that Radio Music Boxes at
$75 would sell as follows:

1st yr.	100,000 Radio Music Boxes	$ 7,500,000
2nd yr.	300,000 Radio Music Boxes	22,500,000
3rd yr.	600,000 Radio Music Boxes	45,000,000*

But in the spring of 1920 the RCA leaders were not ready to believe. Tangled in worldwide diplomacy, they considered the Sarnoff suggestion a digression. They allotted him $2,000 to develop a
prototype of the Radio Music Box he had in mind. That got the
matter off the agenda for the moment. Then the success of KDKA
put it right back on. RCA had, in effect, missed the boat. Within
weeks the national excitement was boiling in a way that could not
be ignored. Early in 1921 the reorientation within RCA was under
way. Sarnoff, aged thirty, was made general manager. Edward
Nally, who had become RCA president, decided to retire; he was
confused by the turn of events.

* In 1922, the first year in which RCA sold complete radio sets, its sales
totaled about $11,000,000—substantially more than the prediction. For the
second year Sarnoff's prediction was exactly right. For the third, sales ran
to $50,000,000 or more than predicted.

Sarnoff was now RCA's most indispensable man. He knew everything about the company. At the very start of his career, as office
boy, he had filed letters—and read each one, studying executive
prose style. He carried a pocket dictionary and looked up unfamil-
iar words. Only he knew exactly who in the company did what,
and what commitments had been made. He took night courses, im-
proving himself. He hung around the company's experimental
workshops. When Marconi visited the United States, Sarnoff managed to talk to the great man, and ran errands for him. Whenever
there was a difficult job to do, Sarnoff volunteered to do it.

When the time came, in 1922, to choose a new RCA president to
succeed Nally, Sarnoff was not considered. A president, in the view
of board chairman Owen D. Young, had to have entree to government at its highest levels. It was no surprise when a general was
chosen—Major General James G. Harbord, recommended by former Secretary of War Newton D. Baker. He represented a continuation of the military influence under which radio had grown, and
under which RCA had been born. But there was no doubt who was
in charge of domestic operations as the company faced the broadcasting era—including the inevitable coming of television. It was
David Sarnoff.

In a way, the situation had the look of omnipotence. With two
thousand patents, including all patents relating to the vacuum tube,
the RCA group had a seemingly impregnable position. Yet there
were loopholes, that now came to plague the life of David Sarnoff.
Mostly, they concerned the "amateurs."

RAGGLE-TAGGLE MOB

Under agreements of the RCA allies, an effort had been made to
allocate everything. The making of receivers and parts would be
done by GE and Westinghouse; the marketing of these receivers
and parts would be done through RCA under RCA trademarks.

RCA would assign 60 per cent of all manufacturing to GE, 40 per cent to Westinghouse. The sale of transmitters would be mainly an AT&T concern; they would be manufactured by its subsidiary Western Electric. Telephony as a service, or involving any business aspect, belonged to AT&T, whether wired or wireless. RCA had the chief role in international communication. Government orders were exempted from the provisions of these agreements; any of the companies could fill government contracts in any field. There were innumerable other provisos and reservations, but in general the radio world had been divided along these lines—*except for the amateurs*.

De Forest, in selling his patents, had kept the right to sell equipment to amateurs. The same reservation had been made by another experimenter, young Edwin H. Armstrong, who as a Columbia University student had invented important circuits, and had later sold patents to Westinghouse and RCA. At the time the reservations were made, they seemed unimportant. The RCA partners could also sell equipment to amateurs; the reserved rights had not been exclusive. But just who was an amateur?

In 1922, as the RCA group went into high gear with its manufacture and sales, Americans spent $60,000,000 on receiving equipment. But only $11,000,000 of this—less than a fifth—went to the RCA group. To be sure, it was an impressive sum, and it immediately made the broadcasting field the chief source of RCA income —exceeding marine and transoceanic communication, the original objectives of RCA. This strengthened Sarnoff's position in the company. Yet the RCA group was outraged over its small share of total sales.

What was happening was clear. All over the country "amateurs" were buying parts and putting sets together. Millions of people suddenly wanted sets, so the "amateurs"—gradually metamorphosing into business entrepreneurs—were selling them and getting more parts and making more sets. Throughout the United States, hundreds of workshops were assembling sets.

"Amateurs" were also making transmitters. In 1922 more than 500 stations rushed to the air. Many had begun as amateur operations—in many cases using parts sold by RCA for amateur use. The "amateurs" then decided to use the transmitters for regular broadcasting, and applied for new call letters and wave lengths. Thus 8MK became WWJ, Detroit; 9XM became WHA, Madison; 6ADZ became KNX, Hollywood; 9ZJ became WLK, Indianapolis; W9CNF became KWCR, Cedar Rapids; 9CT became WDAP, Chicago; 1XZ became WCN, Worcester. Amateur-made transmitters were suddenly leaving garages, attics, and chicken coops, and some of them were turning up on the roofs of newspapers, department stores, hotels, factories. These transmitters were not being used for amateur purposes but—said AT&T—for telephony as a service. Under the patent-pool agreements, the sale of transmitters for such purposes belonged exclusively to AT&T's subsidiary, Western Electric. Yet of the first 600 stations to reach the air, only 35 had bought Western Electric transmitters. AT&T was up in arms.

The radio boom, said Secretary of Commerce Herbert Hoover—whose office continued to be flooded with applications for broadcasting licenses—had been created by "the genius of the American boy." The RCA allies no doubt approved of the American boy, but resented his taking what they regarded as their business.

The carefully built alliance of the titans, dividing the universe, seemed to be crumbling. In the words of Lawrence Lessing, biographer of Edwin Armstrong, a "raggle-taggle mob of free enterprisers was running away with the business." At RCA the pressure was on Sarnoff, to crack down. It could not possibly be a popular job. But he was a company man, and went into battle.

In August 1922 an RCA patent policy committee, in a meeting attended by Sarnoff as general manager, recommended:

That suits be brought . . . but that great pains be taken not to have a multiplicity of suits. Pains should, however, be taken to bring enough suits so that if one defendant goes out of business, time will not be lost.

RCA thus began a campaign to drive the upstart opposition out of business in an orderly manner.

But the troublemakers were no less indignant. They began to complain to their congressmen. The "radio trust" became a burning issue on Capitol Hill.

The public was scarcely aware of all this. It was trying, far into the night, to pick up Cleveland, Kansas City, Cincinnati, Denver, Detroit, Chicago. The mania mounted, even as the monopoly issue built up steam.

But if Sarnoff faced patent problems with hosts of small competitors, he faced even more formidable problems within the RCA group. An especially crucial issue was a 1922 innovation of AT&T, of large implications for television—the commercial.

COME INTO OUR PHONE BOOTH

When broadcasting began, it all seemed delightfully inexpensive. Talent budgets seemed unnecessary. Most broadcasters began with phonograph records; when they switched to live performers, it was because they came voluntarily, in droves. The main problem was to keep people in line.

At WWJ, Detroit, this was handled in 1922 by Edwin Tyson, a former forestry student who had somehow digressed into the radio boom. He lined up the performers in the WWJ reception room. They would tell Tyson what they could do. "We didn't rehearse them, we took their word for it." Tyson would take each into the studio, place him at the microphone, then return to the reception room to hear him on the loudspeaker—the only available monitor. If he seemed too loud or soft, Tyson would go in again to move the artist. After a suitable interval, he would rush a new artist in, and the other out. In this he was assisted by a former college football player, Lawrence Holland, who worked at a Detroit gas station but came in the evening to help out, for the pleasure of it. He was a good bouncer when necessary.

At WJZ, Newark, it was the same way, though the studio was in a hard-to-reach factory. Artists from New York had to come by Hudson tube or across on the ferry. Yet the processions came—the famous, not-so-famous, and amateur. They included John Charles Thomas, Lydia Lipkowska, Percy Grainger, Olga Petrova, Eddie Cantor, Milton Cross—and countless others. Vincent Lopez brought his orchestra. It was a pilgrimage to a new kind of shrine. It was a moment in history all wanted to share and savor. No one asked to be paid. At KYW, Chicago, a full season of opera involved not a single payment.

But this could not last. The parade gradually slackened. Stations began to find they had a recruiting problem.

With this came other troubles. Broadcasters had used music freely, and they often read from newspapers, magazines and books without considering copyright problems. When ASCAP—the American Society of Composers, Authors and Publishers—began to ask for payment and in 1923 followed the demand with lawsuits, broadcasters were outraged. In the case of music, a copyright owner's control over performance rights was limited, under copyright law, to public performance "for profit." WOR, Newark, when sued by ASCAP, said it was not broadcasting for profit; it was offering a free cultural service. But its listeners were periodically reminded that this service was emanating "from L. Bamberger and Company, one of America's great stores." The announcements were bringing crowds of the curious to the store. In August 1923 a court decided that this was not a charitable enterprise, but indeed involved a profit purpose. Broadcasters, dismayed and angry, began to pay ASCAP annual license fees—starting at $250 per year but rising rapidly in later years. Holders of literary copyrights prepared to follow the ASCAP example. Broadcasters saw a very different future before them.

Lydia Lipkowska, court singer
to former Czar, visits WJZ
"cloakroom" studio in Westinghouse factory, Newark, N.J.
Thomas Cowan collection

A new, more elegant studio on
ground floor of factory is ready
for Olga Petrova.
Thomas Cowan collection

All this precipitated intense debate on how broadcasting might eventually be financed. *Radio Broadcast*, a monthly magazine launched in 1922, predicted that equipment manufacturers would not remain willing to bear the cost of broadcasting services after the radio-buying boom subsided. So "a different scheme" would have to be found.

The magazine published several suggestions. One was "endowment" of stations by wealthy donors, following the precedent set by Andrew Carnegie in his gifts to libraries. The idea was applauded, but brought no rush of philanthropists.*

Another suggestion was support by local governments. The magazine conceded this might seem socialistic, but felt the idea was nonetheless plausible, since such governments also financed schools and museums.

Another proposal—which won a prize as the best idea submitted —called for a tax on each set ($2 per tube, or 50¢ for a crystal set) to provide operating funds for a central broadcasting organization. David Sarnoff was said to favor a plan of this sort—not unlike the system Britain was adopting.

But meanwhile another plan was winning attention. Early in 1922 AT&T had resolved to take up broadcasting in a special way, which it considered appropriate to its experience and service. It used what seemed to many an odd terminology. An executive who participated in the original decision, Lloyd Espenschied, later described it in these terms:

> We, the telephone company, were to provide no programs. The public was to come in. Anyone who had a message for the world or wished to entertain was to come in and pay their money as they would upon coming into a telephone booth, address the world, and go out.

In keeping with the telephone imagery, AT&T called this "toll broadcasting." It also continued to speak of "radio telephony,"

---

* A possible exception was Colonel H. R. Green, an eccentric millionaire who in 1922 started WMAF, South Dartmouth, Mass., which broadcast from his estate. But it was operated as a hobby rather than a philanthropy.

probably for a strategic reason. Under the alliance agreements, telephony on a commercial basis was the exclusive province of AT&T. The new venture, AT&T was saying through its choice of words, was a form of commercial telephony and therefore reserved for AT&T and not open to GE, Westinghouse, or RCA. AT&T was laying the basis for such a claim, in case it was needed.

The AT&T plan envisioned a network of thirty-eight "toll" stations linked by the company's long lines. A New York station would be launched first.

The plan was made public in February 1922. "The American Telephone and Telegraph Company," the announcement said, "will provide no program of its own, but provide the channels through which anyone with whom it makes a contract can send out their own programs. . . . There have been many requests for such a service. . . ."

Reactions ranged from lukewarm to indignant. *Printers' Ink* predicted that many people would find the plan "positively offensive." At a Washington Radio Conference—the first of several, called to consider the cacophony in the ether as stations rushed to the air— there were unfriendly comments about the idea of "ether advertising." But there was no prolonged discussion; most people considered the idea impractical.

The following months seemed to confirm their view. Although AT&T had mentioned "many requests for such a service," more than a month went by before any customer applied for entry to the phone booth. By then it was clear that the plan had to be revised. AT&T had been determined *not* to produce programs. It wanted no more responsibility over content than it had in the case of phone calls. But sale of time to address the public was hardly feasible unless people were listening. Reluctantly, the company took up programming. First efforts involved intra-company talent recruitment. On the first evening program over WEAF, New York—which became the first "toll" station*—Helen Graves of the Long Lines

* WBAY, the original entry, had given technical trouble and was withdrawn. WEAF in later years was called WRCA and WNBC.

Plant Department sang "Just a Song at Twilight," and Edna Cunningham of the Long Lines Traffic Department recited James Whitcomb Riley's "An Old Sweetheart of Mine" and spoke of the value of effective speech. In following weeks the spotlight shifted to professional talent.

On August 28, 1922, at 5:00 p.m., WEAF finally broadcast its first income-producing program: a ten-minute message to the public from the Queensboro Corporation to promote the sale of apartments in Jackson Heights, on Long Island. An executive of the Queensboro Corporation spoke the message.

> . . . Let me enjoin you as you value your health and your hopes and your home happiness, get away from the solid masses of brick, where the meager opening admitting a slant of sunlight is mockingly called a light shaft, and where children grow up starved for a run over a patch of grass and the sight of a tree.

> Apartments in congested parts of the city have proven failures. The word neighbor is an expression of peculiar irony—a daily joke. . . .

> The fact is, however, that apartment homes on the tenant-ownership plan can be secured by . . .

During the following weeks the Queensboro Corporation broadcast four additional afternoon talks at $50 each and an evening talk at $100. Sales of apartments are said to have resulted.

The subject of the commercials had some significance. The 1920's saw an accelerated flight from the city. The rise of broadcasting, along with that of the automobile, was considered a factor in the trend. These had ended the sense of isolation once associated with life outside the city. According to *Country Life*—February 1922—radio had removed "the last objection to living in the country." In its first paid-for commercials, radio also helped to exploit the trend.

During August and September 1922 the total revenue from the radiotelephone booth was $550. Herculean selling efforts had brought slim results. Removal of the studio from the drab long-

Entertainment comes to the phone booth: Billy Jones and Ernie Hare—later known as the "Happiness Boys"—with WEAF hostess-accompanist Helen Hann, formerly of the AT&T Long Lines department.   NBC

lines building at 24 Walker Street to the more prestigious AT&T headquarters at 195 Broadway seemed to help. An interior decorator was enlisted. The approach of Christmas also helped. The Macy, Gimbel, and Hearn department stores rented the phone booth.

January 1923 brought an electrifying breakthrough. Through arrangements made by an advertising agency, the cosmetic Mineralava sponsored a talk by actress Marion Davies on "How I Make Up for the Movies." An autographed photo of her was offered free to listeners, and brought mail in the hundreds. The news suddenly brought other advertising agencies and their clients: Goodrich, Eveready, Lucky Strike, Happiness Candy. The tide was rising.

Although Secretary of Commerce Herbert Hoover had been among those deprecating "ether advertising," the Department of Commerce now gave the venture a crucial boost. At the urging of leading broadcasters, Hoover was beginning to take charge of the broadcast spectrum, to establish order. While assigning wave lengths, he also placed limits on power and operating hours. In doing so, he gave WEAF favored treatment—a clear channel, free of interference over a large area, and maximum power. He had apparently accepted the AT&T argument that other stations were all special-interest stations, whereas a toll station was for "everyone."

AT&T had meanwhile begun to make spectacular use of its telephone lines. In October 1922 it had broadcast a pickup of a football game between Princeton and the University of Chicago via long-distance lines from Stagg Field in Chicago to WEAF in New York. In November a Harvard-Yale game had likewise been broadcast via long-distance lines. Phone links were also used for an opera broadcast from an armory; a series of organ recitals from the College of the City of New York; and a series from the stage of the Capitol Theater—inaugurating the broadcasting career of S. L. Rothapfel or "Roxy."

Requests for similar use of telephone lines by other broadcasters were rejected—including those from RCA, GE, and Westinghouse. They were told that the alliance agreements ruled out their use of such pickups. The rebuffed allies tried to use Western Union and Postal Telegraph lines for the same purpose; but their lines, never intended for voice transmission, proved painfully inadequate. AT&T was clearly in a position to freeze its allies out of an important area of programming.

AT&T, developing special cables, also began to pioneer in the linking of stations into a network. WCAP, Washington, second of the projected toll stations, was inaugurated in 1923 and linked by cable to WEAF, New York. To hasten formation of a large network for the sale of advertising, AT&T now "licensed" selected other stations to become toll stations. For this they had to buy Western Electric transmitters ($8,500-$10,500) and pay AT&T a license fee of $500 to $3000. This was widely considered a form of extortion, but the rewards—in advertising revenue and network programming—were persuasive.

By 1924 the AT&T schedule represented the aristocracy of broadcasting: the Browning King Orchestra, the Cliquot Club Eskimos, the Gold Dust Twins, the Ipana Troubadours, the A&P Gypsies. The excitement was kept boiling by new achievements: drama experiments by the *Eveready Hour;* news comments by H. V. Kaltenborn, editor of the Brooklyn *Eagle**; the opening of Congress, broadcast for the first time in 1923; the sensational, acrimonious Democratic national convention of 1924, which required 103 ballots before choosing John W. Davis as its presidential nominee; and finally, an election-eve broadcast by President Calvin Coolidge over a nationwide AT&T chain of stations—preliminary to a smashing reelection.

Throughout 1922-24 the vision of broadcasting as a force in virtually all aspects of society—the new concert hall, theater, classroom, pulpit, newsroom, political arena—propelled experimenters forward. The vision already extended itself to television. All the RCA allies were pushing laboratory work in television. So were individual inventors—among them Charles Francis Jenkins, who in the 1890's had contributed to the evolution of the motion picture projector. During 1923-24 his television experiments began to

---

* These were soon dropped under pressure from the U.S. State Department after Kaltenborn criticized Secretary of State Charles Evans Hughes for his uncompromising attitude toward the Soviet Union. Hughes told AT&T that a public utility should not be used for such purposes.

achieve results, approximately paralleling those of John L. Baird in England. Both Baird and Jenkins—in that order—made public demonstrations in 1925. Following in the path of Nipkow, both used rotating disks with spiral perforations to accomplish a rapid scanning process—as did Ernst F. W. Alexanderson, chief television experimenter at General Electric. The camera at one end, the receiver at the other, had such disks. Some experimenters felt that this mechanical system should be replaced by some electronic scanning method. Vladimir Zworykin, at Westinghouse, was among those working to this end, but the solution was not yet in sight.

Meanwhile the research and the rapid expansion were expensive. AT&T had found a lucrative scheme to finance the enterprise. But it was warning its patent allies that the scheme was the sole property of AT&T.

As RCA, GE, and Westinghouse contemplated the emerging, flickering image of television, they found the AT&T stand especially worrisome. Would sponsored television, too, be declared a phone booth of the air—and an exclusive AT&T preserve?

RCA, GE, and Westinghouse began to experiment with a modified form of sponsorship. The 1923 WJZ schedule included such items as the Rheingold Quartet, Schrafft's Tearoom Orchestra, and the Wanamaker Organ Concert. The sponsor did not pay for the time; it merely contributed the program. Nevertheless, AT&T protested the arrangement as a violation of the patent agreements.

While tension was building over this issue, RCA, GE, and Westinghouse got wind of what they considered a new outrage. During 1923 they learned that AT&T planned to market receivers, to be made by Western Electric. GE and Westinghouse had thought this was their exclusive domain, with RCA serving as their merchandising arm. Not so, said AT&T: receivers were an integral part of the telephone toll service it was developing. A receiver, like a telephone receiver, was just a part of the system.

To the others—the "radio group"—the claim was ominous. Did AT&T, while claiming the exclusive right to sell broadcast advertising, now also intend to grab a share of their revenue from receivers—the only source of support for their own broadcasting activities? In the mounting antagonism between AT&T and its allies, this development was the last straw.

The patent agreements provided an arbitration machinery. All the allies considered it essential to arbitrate their differences in private, rather than air them in public. Early in 1924 the parties delivered preliminary statements to an agreed-on referee, Roland W. Boyden. Hearings began in utmost secrecy.

Meanwhile the disputants were startled by a bomb from Washington. The Federal Trade Commission, which had been studying monopoly complaints, issued a formal charge that the allies—AT&T, RCA, GE, Westinghouse, United Fruit, and subsidiaries—had "combined and conspired for the purpose of, and with the effect of, restraining competition and creating a monopoly in the manufacture, purchase, and sale in interstate commerce of radio devices . . . and in domestic and transoceanic communication and broadcasting." FTC hearings would look further into their agreements and competitive practices.

The FTC, like the public, seems to have been unaware of the behind-closed-doors arbitration in progress in New York, in which the division of empire was being reviewed. The behind-the-scenes drama remained secret until years later.

Much as the FTC action disturbed the allies, causing RCA to curtail its program of litigation, their own secret arbitration worried them even more. Here the status quo faced an imminent, decisive threat.

Both the FTC hearings and the arbitration were agonizingly deliberate. As the 1920's approached their mid-point, the broadcasting world was faced by converging crises—in courts, Congress, Federal Trade Commission, secret arbitration. From these crises a new structure in American broadcasting—for radio and television—began to emerge.

THE BIRTH OF NBC

Late in 1924 Referee Boyden sent a draft of his opinion to each of
the disputants. As the "radio group"—RCA, GE, Westinghouse—
read the draft, they could scarcely believe their eyes. Virtually all
their contentions, even on minor issues, had been upheld. AT&T
had been routed. Major General Harbord sent a jubilant radiogram
to Owen D. Young, who was in Europe:

DRAFT DECISION BOYDEN JUST RECEIVED STOP APPEARS SO FAR AS
STUDIED TO GIVE US EXCLUSIVE RIGHT SALE RECEIVING SETS . . . RIGHT
TO COLLECT TOLLS FOR BROADCASTING STOP

He followed with another:

FURTHER STUDY BOYDEN DECISION SHOWS TELEPHONE GROUP HAS NO
RIGHTS BROADCAST TRANSMISSION UNDER PATENTS RADIO GROUP STOP

Young, arriving back from Europe, saw it as a moment for diplomacy. Talks with AT&T could now produce a new and realistic
allocation of spheres. The victorious radio group could afford to
be generous, yielding a point or two.

But AT&T had a surprising, shattering weapon in its armory. It
presented to the radio group an advisory memorandum by no less a
person than John W. Davis, recent Democratic Party candidate for
President. It said simply that if the patent agreements of 1919-21
meant what Referee Boyden said they meant, they were illegal in
the first place—a conspiracy in restraint of trade, a violation of
United States antitrust laws. AT&T could not, of course, contem-
plate an illegal course.

Nothing could have altered more stunningly the situation confronting the radio group. Since John W. Davis had helped draft the
Clayton Act and was a former United States Solicitor-General, his
words could not be lightly dismissed. Each side of the arbitration
had bound itself to accept the referee's decision and not to take

"any proceedings intended either to modify it or set it aside," but how could AT&T be held to this?

AT&T had put its opponents (or allies) in a nerve-wracking predicament. If the quarrel were brought into open court, it would add fuel to FTC monopoly charges—enough to make a brilliant public bonfire. Moreover, AT&T would be aligned with government against RCA, GE, Westinghouse. AT&T had already put itself in position for such a move by selling its RCA stock and withdrawing from the RCA board. It could say—this was implicit in the John W. Davis memorandum—that it had not been aware of such illegality as the agreements proved "upon subsequent construction" to have.

There was an additional fascinating aspect to the memorandum. The patent agreements were still in effect, Davis advised—except for their illegal aspects. AT&T should continue to use the patents of the group. Only the illegal portions were not binding—those which allegedly forbade AT&T to enter available fields, such as the marketing of receivers, though its experience could "vastly benefit" the industry and the public.

In accordance with the plans of Owen D. Young, talks began—but under changed circumstances. There was now a quiet, dogged drive for solutions, amid utmost secrecy. Now came long, grueling explorations, digressions, deadlocks, confrontations, retreats, new beginnings. David Sarnoff, with his detailed knowledge of every phase of radio, moved gradually into a pivotal position.

AT&T's wish to market receivers and tubes had been a principal source of bitterness. Once it was conceded—with a royalty feature intended to limit production*—the talks began moving ahead. Curiously, the hard-fought-for right was to go almost unused by AT&T. Other prospects would take precedence.

During 1925 pieces began to fit together. Sarnoff, jotting down trading points, wrote:

* Sales over $5,000,000 in any one year would be subject to a 50 per cent royalty to the others of the patent group.

> Put all stations of all parties into a broadcasting company which
> can be made self-supporting and probably revenue-producing, the
> telephone company to furnish wires as needed.

Thus the future was seen in terms of "toll broadcasting" and a central broadcasting organization. Should this organization claim *exclusive* right to broadcast for tolls? Yes, thought Sarnoff at first.
By all means, wrote A. G. Davis of General Electric, "insofar as
the parties can give it that right."

In January 1926 the RCA board of directors approved the idea
of the new company. It would be owned by RCA (50%), GE
(30%), and Westinghouse (20%). Of course GE and Westinghouse would also have, indirectly, an ownership interest in the
RCA share.

The new company would lease, under long-term contract, the
AT&T web of wires. How much would their use be worth? It
became clear that a chain spanning fifteen cities should plan to pay
a telephone bill of at least $800,000 the first year, and that it would
rise into millions as the chain grew. A ten-year contract was discussed.

The new company would buy WEAF from AT&T. For how
much? AT&T suggested $2,500,000 but settled for $1,000,000—
$200,000 for "physical facilities" plus $800,000 for "good will."

AT&T would discontinue WCAP, Washington; RCA's WRC
would acquire its air time. Commerce Department policies presented no obstacle to this arrangement.

On July 7, 1926, twelve documents were signed. One was a
service contract for the web of wires. The others readjusted the
innumerable interrelationships between the allies. A new division
of empire had been made.

AT&T was stepping out of active broadcasting, but on terms that
would secure it a lucrative and steadily mounting revenue, with
freedom from editorial troubles. It had its toll as it had originally
wanted it—without content responsibility.

In September 1926 RCA in full-page advertisements proclaimed the formation of the new company—the National Broadcasting Company. A divide had been crossed. The toll venture had been formally transferred to the national scene. The mantle of toll had fallen on NBC.

RCA's full-page newspaper announcement did not say this. Perhaps Owen D. Young and Major James G. Harbord, who jointly signed it, were unsure how the toll aspect would be received. The term "toll" would now be dropped from the vocabulary of broadcasting.*

The emphasis of the announcement was on other matters. Through NBC, events of national importance would be broadcast throughout the United States. The public would be assured of the best programming.

It was estimated that five million homes already had radios; twenty-one million homes remained to be supplied. If assured of highest quality programming, all would buy. Therefore RCA, as the world's largest distributor of radios, handling all those made by General Electric and Westinghouse, had the greatest stake in program quality. To that end this "instrument of public service" had been created. Thus the birth of NBC was explained in somewhat the same terms as the birth of KDKA.

By January 1927, NBC had two national networks in operation —a "red" network fed by WEAF and a "blue" network fed by WJZ.† The aristocracy of American business flocked to its banners, and began by sponsoring an array of concerts—the *Ampico Hour*, the *Atwater Kent Hour*, the *Cities Service Orchestra*, the *General Motors Family Party*, the *Palmolive Hour*. Decorum ruled: announcers wore tuxedos, and the music was classical or semi-classical. The lighter *Ipana Troubadours, Cliquot Club Eski-*

---

* "Toll" would return in the television years with an opposite meaning, that of audience-supported broadcasting.
† The terms "red" and "blue" developed from use of these colors in early network charts. The "blue" network eventually became the American Broadcasting Company.

Announcing the

National Broadcasting Company, Inc.

National radio broadcasting with better programs permanently assured by this important action of the Radio Corporation of America in the interest of the listening public

THE RADIO CORPORATION OF AMERICA is the largest distributor of radio receiving sets in the world. It handles the entire output in this field of the Westinghouse and General Electric factories.

It does not say this boastfully. It does not say it with apology. It says it for the purpose of making clear the fact that it is more largely interested, more selfishly interested, if you please, in the best possible broadcasting in the United States than anyone else.

Radio for 26,000,000 Homes

The market for receiving sets in the future will be determined largely by the quantity and quality of the programs broadcast.

We say quantity because they must be diversified enough so that some of them will appeal to all possible listeners.

We say quality because each program must be the best of its kind. If that ideal were to be reached, no home in the United States could afford to be without a radio receiving set.

Today the best available statistics indicate that 5,000,000 homes are equipped, and 21,000,000 homes remain to be supplied.

Radio receiving sets of the best reproductive quality should be made available for all, and we hope to make them cheap enough so that all may buy.

The day has gone by when the radio receiving set is a plaything. It must now be an instrument of service.

WEAF Purchased for $1,000,000

The Radio Corporation of America, therefore, is interested, just as the public is, in having the most adequate programs broadcast. It is interested, as the public is, in having them comprehensive and free from discrimination.

Any use of radio transmission which causes the public to feel that the quality of the programs is not the highest, that the use of radio is not the broadest and best use in the public interest, that it is used for political advantage or selfish power, will be detrimental to the public interest in radio, and therefore to the Radio Corporation of America.

To insure, therefore, the development of this great service, the Radio Corporation of America, has purchased for one million dollars station WEAF from the American Telephone and Telegraph Company, that company having decided to retire from the broadcasting business.

The Radio Corporation of America will assume active control of that station on November 15.

National Broadcasting Company Organized

The Radio Corporation of America has decided to incorporate that station, which has achieved such a deservedly high reputation for the quality and character of its programs, under the name of the National Broadcasting Company, Inc.

The Purpose of the New Company

The purpose of that company will be to provide the best program available for broadcasting in the United States.

The National Broadcasting Company will not only broadcast these programs through station WEAF, but it will make them available to other broadcasting stations throughout the country so far as it may be practicable to do so, and they may desire to take them.

It is hoped that arrangements may be made so that every event of national importance may be broadcast widely throughout the United States.

No Monopoly of the Air

The Radio Corporation of America is not in any sense seeking a monopoly of the air. That would be a liability rather than an asset. It is seeking, however, to provide machinery which will insure a national distribution of national programs, and a wider distribution of programs of the highest quality.

If others will engage in this business the Radio Corporation of America will welcome their action, whether it be cooperative or competitive.

If other radio manufacturing companies, competitors of the Radio Corporation of America, wish to use the facilities of the National Broadcasting Company for the purpose of making known to the public their receiving sets, they may do so on the same terms as accorded to other clients.

The necessity of providing adequate broadcasting is apparent. The problem of finding the best means of doing it is yet experimental. The Radio Corporation of America is making this experiment in the interest of the art and the furtherance of the industry.

A Public Advisory Council

In order that the National Broadcasting Company may be advised as to the best type of program, that discrimination may be avoided, that the public may be assured that the broadcasting is being done in the fairest and best way, always allowing for human frailties and human performance, it has created an Advisory Council, composed of twelve members, to be chosen as representative of various shades of public opinion, which will from time to time give it the benefit of their judgment and suggestion. The members of this Council will be announced as soon as their acceptance shall have been obtained.

M. H. Aylesworth to be President

The President of the new National Broadcasting Company will be M. H. Aylesworth, for many years Managing Director of the National Electric Light Association. He will perform the executive and administrative duties of the corporation.

Mr. Aylesworth, while not hitherto identified with the radio industry or broadcasting, has had public experience as Chairman of the Colorado Public Utilities Commission, and, through his work with the association which represents the electrical industry, has a broad understanding of the technical problems which measure the pace of broadcasting.

One of his major responsibilities will be to see that the operations of the National Broadcasting Company reflect enlightened public opinion, which expresses itself so promptly the morning after any error of taste or judgment or departure from fair play.

We have no hesitation in recommending the National Broadcasting Company to the people of the United States.

It will need the help of all listeners. It will make mistakes. If the public will make known its views to the officials of the company from time to time, we are confident that the new broadcasting company will be an instrument of great public service.

RADIO CORPORATION OF AMERICA

OWEN D. YOUNG, *Chairman of the Board*   JAMES G. HARBORD, *President mos,* and *A&P Gypsies,* continuing from earlier days, were only slightly less decorous. Traditional culture also dominated drama offerings such as *Great Moments in History, Biblical Dramas,* and adaptations of classics on the *Eveready Hour.* During these early months, commercials on NBC were short and discreet. Mention of prices was forbidden, as too crass for network radio. This policy proved to be temporary, however.

NBC established an awesome Advisory Council of statesmen, churchmen, educators and others as guardians of the network's highest aspirations. A congressional committee was told that appeals could be made to this Council "over the heads of the operating executives." There is no evidence that this was ever done, but the Advisory Council added to the early aura of splendor surrounding the company.

During 1928-29 programming took a more earthy tone, especially in drama, which rose rapidly in prominence. A native hayseed vein was exploited in *Main Street Sketches, Real Folks,* and *Soconyland Sketches.* But the most sensational arrival, from the world of burnt-cork minstrel shows, was *Amos 'n' Andy,* written and performed by two white men, Freeman Fisher Gosden (Amos) and Charles J. Correll (Andy), and dealing with the "Fresh-Air Taxicab Company, Incorpulated." Word-distortion humor was a prominent element in the series. Sponsored by Pepsodent, the program became a legendary success—in later years, a racial issue. It also precipitated an avalanche of serials—*The Rise of the Goldbergs,** *Clara, Lu, and Em,* and scores of others. Beginning as evening programming, the serial soon became a daytime specialty.

The phenomenon of broadcasting, holding millions spellbound, was being compared to theater, film, and other entertainment. Yet its leading enterprise was something quite new in entertainment annals. Born of a military establishment, and still closely linked to it, it had now also acquired a special relationship to a wide spectrum of big business and its advertising agencies. No such constellation

---

* The title was later shortened to *The Goldbergs.*

had ever planned and controlled a nation's popular culture. Most
programs were being produced by advertising agencies, as an activity parallel to the planning and designing of billboards and magazine advertisements. The network, having "sold" a period, seemed
to regard it as sponsor property, to be used as he designated. Sponsors were, in effect, being encouraged to take charge of the air.

Whatever the ultimate implications of this might be, they were
not in the minds of audiences. The birth of NBC had stimulated a
flood of well-financed nationwide broadcasts, that were bringing
diverse and welcome delights into the home, all free of charge.
Most people were grateful, even excited. Amid general euphoria,
NBC and its corporate owners seemed to face a rich future in radio
and television—except for a few clouds that, momentarily, darkened
the road ahead.

BUT NOT THE OWNERSHIP THEREOF

In 1926, in *United States* v. *Zenith*, the U.S. District Court for the
Northern District of Illinois had decided that the Secretary of
Commerce, in his efforts to bring order to the ether—by detailed
stipulations and restrictions in station licenses—had exceeded his
authority. The law of 1912 had not conferred such authority. The
decision encouraged stations to move to more congenial wave
lengths, increase their power, and extend their schedules. The result was an ether free-for-all, a fantastic jumble—and pleas to Congress to restore order. For the first time, said Secretary of Commerce Herbert Hoover, an industry was begging to be regulated.
Within months Congress passed the Radio Act of 1927, and established a Federal Radio Commission to handle the licensing process.
For RCA and NBC, and their owners and sponsors, it brought the
peace they craved. Order was established—but at a price. Antimonopoly sentiment in Congress, the product of persistent agitation
by RCA's competitors—the defeated and the struggling—was able

Freeman Fisher Gosden and Charles J. Correll, playing Amos and Andy.

to make its mark on the bill. The Radio Act of 1927 provided for
the use of channels, *"but not the ownership thereof,"* by licensees
for limited periods; *"and no such license shall be construed to create
any right, beyond the terms, conditions, and periods of the license."*
In the granting of a license or transfer of a station, the guiding

Publicity photo—"the boys in character"—for *Amos 'n' Andy*.

standard was to be the *"public interest, convenience or necessity."* And every applicant for a license was to sign *"a waiver of any claim to the use of any particular frequency or wave length or of the ether as against the regulatory power of the United States."*

Hoover later spoke of pressures by broadcasters to support the assignment of wave lengths as permanent property. The 1927 law repudiated this idea.

In another crucial clause, the Federal Radio Commission was forbidden to license *"any person, firm, company, or corporation, or any subsidiary thereof, which has been finally adjudged guilty by a Federal Court of unlawfully monopolizing or attempting unlawfully to monopolize, after this Act takes effect, radio communication, directly or indirectly, through the control of the manufacture or sale of radio apparatus, through exclusive traffic arrangements, or by any other means or to have been using unfair methods of competition."*

Since the Federal Trade Commission was still pursuing its monopoly probe, this antitrust language put extreme pressure on the patent allies. The month in which the bill reached final form saw a loosening of RCA patent policy, with RCA agreeing to license a number of competitors, including recent "infringers," in return for a royalty based on sales. This seems to have brought a partial détente. In 1928 the FTC dropped its complaint.

While the law gave the Federal Radio Commission life-and-death power over licenses, it also put limits on the power. The commission was forbidden to act as censor. Its power was to be applied at license-renewal time, not in day-to-day decisions.

The industry had now arrived at a structure that would hold for years: a nationwide system based on advertising; a network linked by cables of the telephone system; stations on temporary licenses; a regulatory commission that was to base its decisions on the public interest, convenience, or necessity. This structure was to be the framework for the development of both radio and television.

Significantly, communication by *radio* was defined in the new Radio Act as *"any intelligence, message, signal, power, picture, or communication of any nature transferred by electrical energy from one point to another without the aid of any wire connecting the points. . . ."* Thus *radio* was intended to include television.

The stage was set for its first wavering steps.

FLICKERING SNAPSHOT

As peace came to the industry, television fever quickly spread. In 1927 Herbert Hoover, already considered a leading contender for the 1928 Republican presidential nomination, appeared in an experimental AT&T telecast. That same year the magazine *Television* appeared in New York, exerting a get-in-on-the-ground-floor appeal.* One of its advertisements said:

> I thought Radio was a Plaything
> But Now My Eyes Are Opened, And
> I'm Making Over $100 a Week.

In Schenectady, GE had moved from laboratory work under the inventor Ernst F. W. Alexanderson to program experiments. These were watched on experimental sets with a screen 4 inches wide, 3 inches high—the size of a file card or snapshot. On September 11, 1928, the tests included the first dramatic production, the melodrama *The Queen's Messenger*. The sound elements were broadcast by WGY, Schenectady; the picture by experimental television station W2XAD. Three cameras, all motionless, were in operation. Only close-ups were used.

Later the same group telecast a science-fiction drama, dramatizing a guided-missile attack on New York City. This imaginative production gave the viewer a missile-eye view of New York as the deadly weapon, electronically guided, approached its target. An aerial photo of New York, appearing on the television screen, came closer and closer and closer. Then an explosion, and the end of the drama.

The telecast was seen by a British visitor from the Royal Air Force, who considered the program one of the most interesting

* A magazine of the same title appeared at about the same time in Britain, where the Baird demonstrations were fomenting a similar fever.

TV audience, 1928: researcher E. F. W. Alexanderson and family watch experiments at home on 3″ x 4″ screen.   Smithsonian

GE PRESENTS

The Queen's Messenger, first drama venture, on W₂XAD, Schenectady—
1928.   Rosaline Greene collection

things he had seen in the United States "in its possibilities for future wars."

Following radio precedents, amateurs were assembling television
sets and watching these experiments. As far away as Pittsburgh a
veteran radio "ham," Edgar S. Love, picked up the Schenectady
experiments. The mechanical nature of the system made such amateur participation feasible. The images were hazy—little more than
silhouettes. But they seemed to augur a new epoch.

There were pressing reasons for intensified work on television.
The success of the partly talking film *The Jazz Singer*—premiered
by Warner Brothers October 6, 1927—made 1928 a year of upheaval in Hollywood. A vast changeover of theaters and studios
was under way. Dramatists were frantically imported from the
Broadway world. Stars with squeaky voices were set adrift. The
mood of revolutionary change communicated itself to the broadcasting world. As film moved to sound, broadcasters reached for the
image. The two industries had largely ignored each other, but now
saw a convergence—or a clash—of interests.

In 1927 a competitor for NBC made a shaky appearance, against
seemingly impossible odds—the Columbia Phonograph Broadcasting System, later Columbia Broadcasting System. Soon abandoned
by its first backer, the Columbia Phonograph Record Company,
the company had several hairbreadth escapes from bankruptcy, but
survived. One of its crises was eased in 1929 when a new owner,
the young cigar magnate William S. Paley, sold a 49 per cent interest to Paramount for $5,000,000 in Paramount stock. The deal at
once strengthened the credit standing of the young network. For
Paramount the dominant motive was the coming of television.

Meanwhile the tension between AT&T and RCA, so recently
eased in radio, reappeared in a new arena. As the film world re-
tooled for sound, AT&T's Western Electric, joining forces with
Fox, gained acceptance of its sound-on-film system by much of the
industry: Metro-Goldwyn-Mayer, Paramount, United Artists,
Universal, and First National (soon afterwards taken over by War-

JENKINS PRESENTS

Programming at
Jenkins experimental
station W2XCD.
        Smithsonian

Jenkins receiver
with round screen—
1929.   Smithsonian

ner Brothers). RCA and its principal owners, General Electric and Westinghouse, scrambled for pieces to pick up. Early in 1928 they formed RCA Photophone to exploit in film an old General Electric recording process, originally called Pallophotophone, developed during World War I and occasionally used in radio. To secure it a market they joined forces with the Keith-Albee-Orpheum theater chain and others to create—October 1928—Radio-Keith-Orpheum, or RKO. While equipping RKO theaters and studios, RCA Photophone also got its equipment accepted by Pathé (which was then taken over by RKO), Mack Sennett, and other lesser film companies. A vast interlocking was developing; in the struggle, many elements became valuable pawns. Music would rise in importance, so RCA bought two music-publishing companies, Leo Feist, Inc., and Carl Fischer, Inc. NBC's first president, Merlin Aylesworth, told a Senate committee: "It is necessary for us to be in the music business to protect ourselves . . . the movies have bought most of the music houses . . . we have got to control the music situation. It is a simple business proposition with a little touch of sentiment in it."

Amid these currents, the flickering image of television drew increasing attention. Within five years, said Sarnoff, television would be "as much a part of our life" as radio had become.

This time, his vision proved faulty. Surrounded by delirious optimism, Sarnoff could scarcely foresee the road-blocks and detours that lay ahead. In a way, they were a product of that very optimism. As every corporate maneuver seemed to promise boundless wealth, zooming stock prices reflected the expectations. Epitomizing the frenzy was the behavior of RCA stock.

Early in 1928 it stood at 85¼. Soon afterwards it began an astounding performance. On Saturday, March 3, RCA stood at 91½. On March 12 it *opened* at 107¾, closed at 120½. (Television rumors?) On March 12 it opened at 120½, closed at 138½. (Photophone news?) The next day it opened at 160—21½ points up. After a retreat, advance began again. By May it passed 200, then slipped

NEW NETWORK

Bing Crosby, factor
in the growth of
CBS.   CBS

William S. Paley at
ribbon-cutting cere-
mony for new CBS
home at 485 Madi-
son Avenue, New
York—1929.   CBS

early in June. By mid-June the skid stopped. (Hoover's nomination for President?) During the campaign the rise was resumed. ("We shall soon, with the help of God, be in sight of the day when poverty will be banished from this nation"—Hoover's broadcast acceptance.) In November RCA stock touched 400. (Electoral college vote: Herbert Hoover, 444; Alfred E. Smith, 87.) On December 7, a moment of panic: RCA slipped 72 points. But confidence rallied. After a period of ups and downs, RCA began another steep climb. (Dismissal of Federal Trade Commission complaint? RCA purchase of Victor? *Amos 'n' Andy?* Debut of Rudy Vallee?) In mid-summer 1929 RCA stock reached 500 and pushed beyond. The stock was split: each share became five shares, each of which, on September 3, stood at 101. It then edged up to 114¾. In eighteen months it had climbed about 600 per cent.

The feeling was that anybody who was anything would move to a suburban home with superheterodyne radio, television, air conditioning, and other things available on installments, with a place in Florida for later. Automobile and airplane had made this plausible. The stock market had made it seem inevitable. Radio had done its share in building the dream and inflating the credit bubble.

When it burst—"WALL STREET LAYS AN EGG," said *Variety*—RCA sagged to 20 within a month. Gradually paralysis took over the nation. During 1930 income and employment dropped catastrophically. Building almost stopped. The following year one in four factory workers was jobless. Breadlines stretched on and on. Innumerable projects were shelved. The flickering snapshot would not yet go to market.

For Sarnoff it was only a postponement. But his attention was also deflected to a new kind of crisis, one that threatened the very existence of RCA.

A BILL OF DIVORCEMENT

In 1930 David Sarnoff became president of RCA, while Major General Harbord moved up to chairman of the board. On the heels of these moves came jolting news.

In May 1930 the U.S. Department of Justice sued RCA, GE, Westinghouse, and AT&T. It demanded termination of the 1919-21 patent agreements and of interlocking ownerships and directorates. The renewed antitrust zeal was largely a product of the stock market crash, the Depression that had followed, and the business scandals they had brought to light.

To the broadcasting oligarchy, the move was beyond belief. The complex, closely knit setup had become an established way of life. But the Justice Department could not be dissuaded: to avoid trial, the companies would have to replace the patent agreements with an open patent pool, and untangle the corporate liaison.

A year went by. The problems seemed to defy solution. Owen D. Young wrote an eight-page letter to the Department of Justice calling attention to the "unprecedented economic and industrial crisis" of the nation. Much of this, he said, had been caused by "ruinous competition . . . destructive rivalry." He implied that the Justice Department demands would destroy what stability there was in the broadcasting field, and lead to further catastrophes.

The Justice Department stood firm. Late in 1931 AT&T, which no longer held RCA stock or board membership, made peace with the Justice Department by serving notice of withdrawal from the 1919-21 cross-licensing agreements. A number of the earliest patents, once so crucial, were in any case expiring.

For RCA, GE, and Westinghouse, with their symbiotic relationships, impending decisions were more perilous. And meanwhile business conditions worsened. In September 1931 Britain went off the gold standard, creating international shock-waves. In the United States, that same month, 305 banks closed; during the next month,

522 closed. Adding to the sense of international disintegration, Japan began overrunning Manchuria.

If the Justice Department antitrust suit were to go to trial and be lost by the defendants, the antimonopoly clauses of the Radio Act of 1927 would come into play. Broadcast licenses of incalculable value—KDKA, KGO, KOA, KYW, WBZ, WEAF, WGY, WJZ, WMAQ, WRC, WTAM, as well as experimental television licenses—would be imperiled. If the defendants had hopes of a more lenient political climate, the news of the moment dispelled them.

As 1932 began, most estimates of unemployment in the United States stood at ten million or more. People combed through city dumps. Bitterness increased. Farmers began to resist evictions with pitchforks and shotguns. In June the Republicans nominated Herbert Hoover for a second term as President. The Democrats nominated Franklin D. Roosevelt, Governor of New York. What was known of his views was not reassuring to executives of GE, Westinghouse, and RCA; many considered him to have socialistic tendencies. Against this background, representatives of the three companies pushed their divorce talks, to stave off trial. A date for trial was set: November 15, 1932, a week after election.

Among the negotiators was Owen D. Young, chairman of the board of GE, creator of RCA, member of innumerable boards and committees. He was world-famous as author of the Young Plan, an attempt to save Germany from economic collapse. Young was tired. A Westinghouse representative at the discussions, Walter C. Evans of KYW, Chicago, gives a vivid picture:

> I distinctly recall Mr. Young slouched down in an armchair in the RCA board room with the appearance of being more than half asleep. When the controversy reached a complete impasse his eyes would open only a slight amount and he would suggest the compromise which solved the question.

In this crisis David Sarnoff, with far-ranging grasp of detail and firmness for the RCA cause, emerged as a negotiator hardly less skillful than Young. RCA had throughout its life been a sales agent for others, and owned by others; it had been, in spite of its prominence, a puppet organization. Its ability to survive would depend on dispositions now made.

Sarnoff hammered at a favorite theme: "Unification." The radio manufacturing facilities of GE and Westinghouse should be "unified," he urged, under RCA—with GE and Westinghouse being reimbursed via RCA debentures. As additional reimbursement GE would get real estate—an RCA-owned building on Lexington Avenue, New York City, which at the moment was losing money.

By the end of October the divorce plans neared completion. GE and Westinghouse were to withdraw from the RCA and NBC boards. NBC would be a wholly owned subsidiary of RCA. GE and Westinghouse would retain their broadcasting stations, but NBC would manage them.

NBC would go ahead with a plan already widely discussed, of moving to a new complex of buildings being planned for mid-Manhattan. This vast Rockefeller project, for which blocks of brownstone buildings were being leveled, seemed to defy the Depression itself, and had caught the imagination of the public—which called it Radio City. To clinch the move, the Rockefeller interests made new concessions to RCA.

As election day approached, there were still unsolved questions concerning the extent of the RCA debt to GE and Westinghouse, and the value of debentures to be issued.

On November 8, Franklin Delano Roosevelt was elected President of the United States by an overwhelming popular majority, and an electoral vote of 472-59.

On November 10 there were day and night meetings of RCA, GE, and Westinghouse officials, committees, subcommittees, and teams of attorneys. On November 11 their proposals were delivered to the Department of Justice. A few changes were needed. On Sunday, November 13, came a final RCA-GE-Westinghouse meeting, all day and far into the night. The next day, a week's postpone-

Marconi (at right) and heir apparent, David Sarnoff: a tour of RCA facilities.

ment of the trial was granted. On November 21 a consent decree was signed. The trial was canceled.

Miraculously, RCA emerged as a strong and self-sufficient entity. No longer owned by other corporations, it had its destiny in hand. It had substantial new obligations in the form of debentures, but it owned two networks, broadcast stations, manufacturing facilities, international and ship-to-shore communication facilities, and experimental laboratories. It controlled a majority of the clear-channel stations in the United States. At its apex sat David Sarnoff.

In 1933 he moved his executive army and broadcasting personnel into Radio City. From a 53rd floor office he proceeded to keep watch over the radio world—and to prepare for television. It became his central concern.

FIFTY-THIRD FLOOR

In 1932 NBC had installed a television station in the newly built Empire State Building. Vladimir Zworykin was now experimenting for RCA instead of Westinghouse. The work went forward.

Prospects for television were strengthened by events in radio. The broadcasting industry, though momentarily jolted by the Depression, had in the long run been helped by it. As theater and film audiences shrank, home audiences grew. Broadcasting had won an almost irrational loyalty among listeners. According to social workers, destitute families that had to give up an icebox or furniture or bedding still clung to radio as to a last link with humanity.

Many factors contributed to this. Radio brought into homes President Roosevelt's "Fireside Chats"—an important cohesive force during darkest Depression days. At the same time, troubles overtaking theater and vaudeville were bringing a new surge of talents to radio audiences, including leading comedians like Ed Wynn, Eddie Cantor, Fred Allen, Burns and Allen, Jack Benny, Jack Pearl, and the Marx Brothers. Meanwhile daytime serials had developed an extraordinary hold over home audiences. Sociologists studying the phenomenon found that women looked to such serials as *Ma Perkins* and *Just Plain Bill* and *The Romance of Helen Trent* for guidance on personal problems. Many expressed a dire dependence on serials. Thanks to this devotion, many businesses were making a financial comeback through radio sponsorship.

If radio was increasingly successful, its tone was also increasingly —and aggressively—commercial. Many people found it shoddy. Radio offered advice to the lovelorn, fortune-telling, and diverse forms of quackery. The fortunes made by Dr. John R. Brinkley, who for years used his Kansas station to promote goat-gland rejuvenation transplants and drug sales, had brought an influx of patent medicine sponsors. Commercials, which had been brief and diffident in NBC's first days, were becoming long and unrelenting— but successful instruments of merchandising.

To Sarnoff the affluence was crucial: it would pay for the advent of television. Once again the formal, commercial debut of television seemed an early possibility. But once more a new problem intervened: this time, a crisis precipitated by events in the Senate.

Soon after taking office, the Roosevelt administration proposed replacing the Federal Radio Commission (FRC) with a new Federal Communications Commission (FCC), to regulate not only broadcasting but also the telephone—which had been under the jurisdiction of the Interstate Commerce Commission. The AT&T entanglement with broadcasting seemed to make the move logical.

But with change in the air, the congressional debate turned into an uprising against the status quo, fomented mainly by educators, churchmen, and labor leaders. They protested the growing commercialization of the air. They protested that channel assignments, both under the Commerce Department and the FRC, had delivered the field almost wholly to the advertising world, squeezing out competing interests and values. They now demanded cancellation of all licenses and their reassignment—with 25 per cent of all channels going to non-profit organizations.

Led by Senator Robert F. Wagner of New York and Senator

President Franklin D. Roosevelt in Fireside Chat.   CBS

Henry D. Hatfield of West Virginia, the insurrection seemed within reach of success. Its anger was epitomized by the writer James Rorty, who in 1934 published *Our Master's Voice*—a title adapted from an RCA trademark. Rorty wrote:

> The American apparatus of advertising is something unique in history. . . . It is like a grotesque, smirking gargoyle set at the very top of America's skyscraping adventure in acquisition *ad infinitum*. . . . The gargoyle's mouth is a loudspeaker, powered by the vested interest of a two-billion dollar industry, and back of that the vested interests of business as a whole, of industry, of finance. It is never silent, it drowns out all other voices, and it suffers no rebuke, for is it not the voice of America? That is its claim and to some extent it is a just claim. For at least two generations of Americans—the generations that grew up during the war and after—have listened to that voice as to an oracle. It has taught them how to live, what to

Comedians to radio: Ed Wynn as Fire Chief.   NBC

be afraid of, what to be proud of, how to be beautiful, how to be loved, how to be envied, how to be successful.

To Rorty, the earthly atmosphere was saturated with never-ending "jabberwocky" from hundreds of thousands of loudspeakers.

Is it any wonder that the American population tends increasingly to speak, think, feel in terms of this jabberwocky? That the stimuli of art, science, religion are progessively expelled to the periphery of American life to become marginal values, cultivated by marginal people on marginal time?

Powered by such rhetoric, the Wagner-Hatfield drive urged the redistribution of channels as an amendment to the pending Communications Act. It won wide support from educational, religious, and labor groups.

Most such groups had little prospect of financing broadcasting stations. Their amendment therefore proposed that non-profit stations be allowed to sell advertising to the extent of their expenditures. Advertising revenue would be permitted to defray costs, but not to yield a profit.

The idea opened them to scornful attack: these supposed haters of advertising were proposing *more* advertising. Apparently they just wanted to "muscle in" on advertising revenues. Besides, said commercial broadcasters, existing stations and networks had ample unsold time available for educators, churchmen, and others. To underscore this point, NBC-red gave a network berth to the *University of Chicago Round Table*, a program that had begun locally; NBC-blue inaugurated an *America's Town Meeting of the Air*, emanating from New York. Such ventures helped put down the insurrection. On the Senate floor, Wagner-Hatfield lost, 42-23. The Communications Act of 1934 thus became law without the troublesome amendment. At the same time, it had sparked an eruption of "public service" programs.

By 1935 a feeling of security had returned to the 53rd floor of the RCA Building. Sarnoff felt it was time for major moves on behalf of television.

Television could establish itself only if there were industry-wide standards, with telecasters and set users all committed to the same system. Sarnoff now wanted the new Federal Communications Commission to adopt standards—based, he hoped and expected, on the RCA system—and he asked the FCC to allocate the needed spectrum space.

In April 1935 Sarnoff made the dramatic announcement that RCA was appropriating a million dollars for television program demonstrations. The FCC, prodded by the RCA announcement, prepared for intensive study of the future of broadcasting, with special attention to television. Hearings would be held the following year; testimony was invited from all concerned.

In Radio City, NBC studio 3H—less than two years old—was

converted into a television studio, with light grills and catwalks for technicians. In his usual meticulous fashion, Sarnoff was coordinating all moves.

And yet, even now, the road ahead was not clear. Ironically, the veteran patent fighter was faced once again with patent problems —not from rival corporations, but from inventors in the mold of the boy Marconi—inventors who insisted on inventing on their own. Two such experimenters posed special—and eventually agonizing— problems.

OF ATTICS AND BACK ROOMS

Philo T. Farnsworth, child of a large Mormon farm family, did not encounter electricity until he was fourteen and his family got a Delco system. He at once knew how it worked and applied electricity to his mother's handcranked washing machine. He became an ardent reader of electrical journals. In 1922 at high school in Rigby, on the upper Snake River in Idaho, he staggered his science teacher by asking advice on an electronic television system he was contemplating. The boy said he had been reading about systems involving mechanical wheels and considered those doomed; covering several blackboards with diagrams to show how it might be done electronically, he asked, should he go ahead? The baffled science teacher encouraged him. Philo, thin and with an undernourished, pinched look, worked his way through college with a patchwork of jobs including radio repair work and, one year, work on a Salt Lake City community chest drive. He told George Everson, professional fund-raiser from California who was helping organize the campaign, about his television ideas, and Everson took the youth back to California and set him up with equipment in an apartment —first in Los Angeles, later in San Francisco—while Everson belabored financiers for funds. Philo worked with the blinds drawn, stirring suspicions that led to a raid by police. They found strange glass tubes but not the expected distillery. Philo had his first successes in 1927 when he transmitted various graphic designs including a dollar sign, which according to Everson "jumped out at us from the screen." Switching to bits of film, they used sequences of a Dempsey-Tunney fight and later of Mary Pickford combing her hair in *The Taming of the Shrew;* she combed it a thousand times for Farnsworth television. Applying for an electronic television patent, Farnsworth took RCA completely by surprise. Its attorneys contested the application, and in interference proceedings grilled Farnsworth for hours, but could not shake him. In August 1930 Philo Farnsworth, aged twenty-four, got his patent. Early in 1931 Vladimir Zworykin of RCA traveled to California to visit Philo's laboratory and have a look; he appeared impressed but was quoted as saying there wasn't anything RCA would need. Then Sarnoff came; RCA would not need anything young Farnsworth had done, said Sarnoff. But apparently RCA already felt it would have to negotiate with Philo Farnsworth.

Farnsworth was ready to license RCA on a royalty basis. But RCA had a policy: what it needed, it bought outright. It didn't pay royalties; it collected them. However, in due time it came to terms with Philo Farnsworth. The RCA attorney is said to have had tears in his eyes as he signed the contract.

The extraordinary victory may well have encouraged another embattled inventor, Edwin H. Armstrong. His dispute with Sarnoff, gradually growing into a complex feud, had fateful implications for both radio and television.

Armstrong and Sarnoff had known each other since 1914 when Armstrong, a Columbia University student—and a long-time amateur experimenter in his Yonkers attic—invented a new circuit that was said to do wonders; Sarnoff was delegated by American Marconi to evaluate it. In a drafty shack in Belmar, N.J., throughout a winter night, Armstrong and Sarnoff huddled together pulling in Ireland, Germany, Hawaii—taking down messages to be checked later with the originating stations. "Well do I remember that mem-

Edwin H. Armstrong, inventor—during World War I.   Smithsonian

orable night," Sarnoff was to write Armstrong years later. "Whatever chills the air produced were more than extinguished by the warmth of the thrill which came to me at hearing for the first time signals from across the Atlantic and across the Pacific." The encounter held the seeds of friendship—and of longer conflict. There was a gulf between them: Armstrong was a lone experimenter, Sarnoff a company man.

During and after World War I, Armstrong invented other sensational circuits and in 1922 sold a patent to RCA and was suddenly a millionaire. RCA also got first refusal on his next invention.

"I wish," said Sarnoff to Armstrong one day, "that someone would come up with a little black box to eliminate static." The implication of the phrase, an allusion to Marconi's black box, was not lost on Armstrong. He liked the challenge. And he himself had been thinking about static.

The world lay before him. He married Sarnoff's secretary. He accepted a Columbia University research appointment at $1 a year and began working ceaselessly at his own expense in the basement of Philosophy Hall, occasionally emerging to read brilliant papers at scientific gatherings—a tall, lanky figure with a drawling voice. When he argued with opponents, he was inclined to demolish them, and he won important enemies, including De Forest. But mostly he just worked.

Ten years passed. Late in 1933 Armstrong took out four patents and notified Sarnoff that the little black box was ready. Sarnoff and various RCA engineers made the trip to the Columbia University campus. What they found was not exactly a black box but two rooms full of equipment representing an entire new radio system —"frequency modulation," FM. Not just an invention, said Sarnoff at one point, but a revolution.

RCA decided on field tests. In March 1934 Armstrong was invited to install his transmitter equipment in the Empire State tower. The FM receiver was placed seventy miles away on Long Island. The log of the first day, June 16, 1934, included a prophetic notation by an engineer. A new era, he wrote, "is now upon us." Results exceeded Armstrong's claims. Defying thunder and lightning, FM transmitted a range of sound never before heard, and was virtually static-free.

The tests went on, reports were written and studied. Armstrong waited. Then, in April 1935, he was "politely" asked to remove his equipment from the Empire State Building. That same month RCA announced its allocation of $1,000,000 for television tests. A wave of publicity heralded the imminence of television, as the FCC prepared for crucial decisions on the spectrum.

Armstrong became fearful. He had worked more than a decade on FM. Since receiving his patents, he had maintained public silence on the subject for two years, partly because he felt he owed this to RCA, and partly because RCA seemed the one organization able to accomplish the revolution FM called for. Now the sudden flurry of RCA television moves, accompanied by total silence on FM, confirmed a feeling that the company hierarchy wanted no part of frequency modulation. Was RCA intent on sidetracking—even sabotaging—his invention? Armstrong became convinced it was.

He acted with resolution. He decided on a public demonstration, to be staged at the November 1935 meeting of the Institute of Radio Engineers. It was announced that Armstrong would read a paper on his latest work; the demonstration itself would be a surprise.

He prepared for months with the help of his friend Randolph Runyon, whose amateur station in Yonkers was adapted especially for the demonstration. Armstrong read his paper, then drawled: "Now suppose we have a little demonstration." As the receiver groped through space, the audience heard a sound that would become familiar to FM listeners. In the words of Lawrence Lessing, there was a

> roaring in the loudspeaker like surf on a desolate beach, until the new station was tuned in with a dead, unearthly silence, as if the whole apparatus had been abruptly turned off. Suddenly out of the silence came Runyon's supernaturally clear voice: "This is amateur station WZAG at Yonkers, New York, operating on frequency modulation at two and a half meters." A hush fell over the large audience.

The demonstration included music and other items. A glass of water was poured in Yonkers. In New York it sounded like a glass of water—not, as in AM, like a waterfall.

In the spring of 1936 Armstrong presented to the FCC the case for spectrum allocations for FM. RCA, pressing solely for television allocations, was represented not only by Sarnoff but by C. B. Jolliffe, who a few weeks earlier had been the FCC chief engineer but was now suddenly an RCA executive. The RCA witnesses hammered at one theme: the readiness of television and its needs in the spectrum. They did not mention FM. The battleground was the upper frequencies, where both inventions needed elbow room. The battle was joined.

The policies pursued by Sarnoff were in the interests of RCA as he saw them. He saw television as an invention "about ready" to

Armstrong builds transmitter tower.
Columbiana

Completed tower: W2XMN—1938.
Columbiana

take its place beside radio in every home. RCA had invested in television large sums from radio earnings, and counted on continued earnings to carry the work forward. FM was seen as an invention that could only disrupt the structure of radio and plunge it into years of readjustment and loss. FM posed a threat not only to the status of radio but to funds needed for television. RCA was therefore not inclined to promote FM. Because of RCA's position in the industry, its stand loomed as a fatal roadblock. To Armstrong it was "sabotage" of a major invention.

When Armstrong asked the FCC for a license for an experimen-

Philadelphia: Farnsworth experimenting at Philco—early 1930's. Philco

tal FM station, the request was at first denied. The FCC, influenced
by Sarnoff, had caught the television fever, and saw FM as an obstacle. With demonstration and argument, Armstrong persisted,
and finally got his license. He cashed a block of his RCA stock and
began to build a 50,000-watt FM station at Alpine, N.J., across the
river from Yonkers. He himself climbed around the huge antenna
tower, supervising each detail. It was the start of a long and bitter
war. He was tackling a giant.

TARGET DATE

RCA prepared for its million-dollar television program demonstrations. It was not alone in the field. Farnsworth had won backing
from Philco and moved to Philadelphia to continue his television

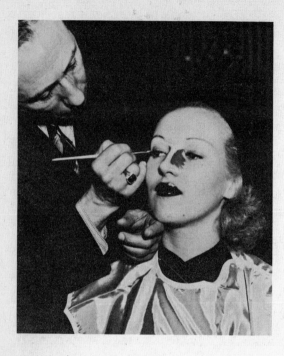

Make-up for Betty
Grable: green face,
purple lipstick—
1937.
National Archives

experiments there. Another young genius, Allen B. Dumont, who
had worked with Francis Jenkins, was making progress in New
Jersey. In Los Angeles there were tests by a regional West Coast
network, the Don Lee network. Various unresolved patent issues
would have to be resolved before commercial use was begun. Meanwhile experimenters pushed ahead.

To the Empire State transmitter elaborate productions, including
drama, began to travel by cable from rebuilt Studio 3H in Radio
City. The schedule began with two programs a week, Tuesdays and
Thursdays. Actors began to be seen in Radio City cafeterias with
green make-up and purple lipstick, and they were plied with questions. Before long the phenomenon no longer caused comment:
such things, it was understood, were somehow necessary in the new
medium.

Other kinds of programming were tested. In 1936 a "coaxial
cable" between New York and Philadelphia, developed by AT&T,

NBC mobile unit—into action 1937.   NBC

Fire telecast via mobile-unit relay—New York, 1938.   National Archives

was ready for use, setting the stage for remote pickups and net-
working tests. The following year a television mobile unit went into
action in New York City, to experiment in pictorial journalism.
It consisted of two huge busses; one was a studio crammed with
equipment for field use; the other housed the transmitter that relayed programs to the Empire State tower for rebroadcast by the
main transmitter. Television seemed indeed to be "about ready."
Sarnoff picked a target date for its commercial debut: the 1939
World's Fair, scheduled for New York City.

But news about the imminence of television began to be pushed
aside by other matters, relating to the international scene. In 1938
Adolf Hitler, in power in Germany since 1933, annexed Austria
and, under the infamous "Munich pact," a portion of Czechoslovakia. Japan intensified its attacks on China. Spain, in bloody conflict, was falling under the control of Francisco Franco, ally of
Hitler and Mussolini.

While Sarnoff and RCA and NBC were concentrating on the
emergence of television, these world upheavals were focusing increased attention on radio, and especially on CBS. Throughout the
1930's CBS had been trying to catch up with its formidable rival.
It had considerable unsold time in its schedule but, far more effectively than NBC, was making creative use of it. Substantial time
was given to experimental, unsponsored programming, including
news. As world turmoil increased, CBS was building—under Paul
White—a news service that soon made the voices of H. V. Kaltenborn, Edward R. Murrow, Eric Sevareid, William L. Shirer, Elmer
Davis, and others known in every home. In 1938 CBS introduced
the "world news roundup" format with short-wave pickups from
any and all continents. In drama CBS was winning a similar celebrity through the works of Norman Corwin, Archibald MacLeish,
Orson Welles, and others. These often touched on the world scene,
as in *They Fly Through the Air*, a scathing verse play on fascism
with which Corwin won a wide following; *The Fall of the City*, in
which MacLeish foreshadowed with startling accuracy the Nazi

BROOKLYN
QUEENS
LONG ISLAND

DAILY **NEWS**

NEW YORK'S PICTURE NEWSPAPER

Copyright 1938 by News Syndicate Co., Inc. Reg. U.S. Pat. Off.

Entered as 2nd class matter. Post Office. New York, N. Y.

FINAL

Vol. 20. No. 109   New York, Monday, October 31, 1938★   48 Main+12 Brooklyn Pages   2 Cents IN CITY LIMITS | 3 CENTS Elsewhere

FAKE RADIO 'WAR' STIRS TERROR THROUGH U.S.

RISE OF CBS

Orson Welles: "I had no idea . . ."
Wide World

Voice from London:
Edward R. Murrow
CBS

H. V. Kaltenborn
during Munich crisis
—with CBS news
chief Paul White.
CBS

take-over of Vienna; and the Welles production of the H. G. Wells *War of the Worlds*, with Martian landings placed in the New York area—with a realism that precipitated panic in many parts of the United States. The reaction to this drama apparently reflected the national edginess over the world situation; it also confirmed the rising competitive standing of CBS programming. NBC found itself trying to emulate CBS achievements in news and drama. At the moment when television was awaited, radio was strengthening its hold on the public. It was even winning admiration from intellectuals who had generally despised—or ignored—radio.

At the same time, the Roosevelt administration was turning from domestic concerns to rearmament. Once more executives of major corporations—this time including RCA delegations, led by a diligent David Sarnoff—were back and forth to Washington to discuss military production needs. When Germany invaded Poland in 1939, Roosevelt proclaimed a limited national emergency, diverting strategic materials from domestic manufacture to war requirements. In production was a navy item closely related in technology to television, but with a name not yet to be spoken, even in a whisper —radar. RCA, child of the military, was suddenly in the midst of war production.

Even at NBC, the atmosphere was militarized. In 1936 Sarnoff, to fill a vacancy in the NBC presidency, had selected a military man, Lenox Lohr. Sarnoff was following RCA tradition.

The sense of gathering crisis cast an atmosphere of doom around the anticipated coming of television. But this went forward on schedule, and generated some of the hoped-for excitement. On February 26, 1939, a test pickup from the unfinished fair grounds featured a telecast of *Amos 'n' Andy* in blackface make-up. On April 30 came the formal opening, in which Franklin D. Roosevelt became the first President to appear on television.* Sarnoff also spoke. RCA sets with 5-inch and 9-inch picture tubes went on display, later followed by sets with 12-inch tubes. In some, the tube was

---

* Herbert Hoover's 1927 appearance had been as Secretary of Commerce.

seen via a hinged mirror. Prices ranged from $199.50 to $600. Crowds came and stared at the programs. Every day brought new items. The NBC schedule now included one program a day from Studio 3H in Radio City, still the network's only television production studio; one program a day from the mobile unit; and assorted films, from a film-facilities room at Radio City.

The studio programs included plays, bits of opera, comedians, singers, jugglers, puppets, and kitchen demonstrations—usually salad-mixing, because it was really too hot for cooking. Three cameras were used. The ritual of live television was by now well developed. The control room had head-phone communication with studio technicians. A continual stream of cryptic jargon flowed over the intercom wires—abbreviated instructions for adjusting camera angles and distances. This was punctuated with: "Take one! . . . Ready two. . . . Take two!" Visitors from the theater found the continuous chatter bewildering and astounding; did no one ever listen to the performers? Visitors from the film world were equally amazed at the notion that shooting and editing could be done simultaneously. In the studio the performers, still in weird makeup, worked in heat that stung the skin. Actors took salt tablets. The big cameras swung slowly. "When I am on the television set," said Earle Larimore, who starred in *The Unexpected* on May 3, 1939, "I think of those cameras as three octopuses with little green eyes blinking on and off, their silvery forms moving ponderously." The actor always felt hemmed in. Everything had to be played "close." He had to cultivate microscopic gestures.

The mobile unit was somewhere every day. On May 17 it showed a Columbia-Princeton baseball game from Baker Field. Its single camera stood near the third-base line, sweeping back and forth across the diamond and conclusively proving its own inadequacy. By the time the unit went to Ebbets Field for a double-header between the Brooklyn Dodgers and the Cincinnati Reds, it had acquired a second camera. Sometimes the mobile unit went to Ridgewood Grove in Brooklyn for second-rate wrestlers or boxers,

April 20, 1939: Sarnoff opens
RCA exhibit.   NBC

May 17, 1939: first baseball telecast—Princeton *v.* Columbia,
Baker Field.   NBC

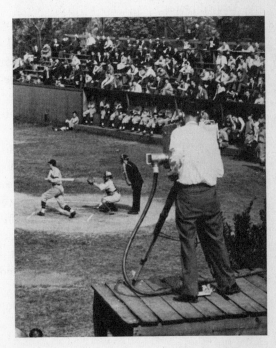

or merely picked up ice skating at Rockefeller Center or planes landing at La Guardia airport or interviews with visitors to the World's Fair. It was all equally amazing. High points of 1939 were a fashion show from the Waldorf-Astoria and pickups from the sidewalk and lobby at the Capitol Theater for the world premiere of *Gone With the Wind*.

The films included sponsored travelogues, old cartoons, government documentaries: *Jasper National Park, Washington—Shrine of Patriotism, Miracles of Modernization, Donald's Cousin Gus, Millions for Safety*. Films of major film companies were not available to television.

CBS, which had experimented in television for several years, was also telecasting in New York during 1939-40. So was the experimental station of inventor Allen B. Dumont, who had succeeded in putting the first all-electronic receivers on the market. In May 1940 twenty-three stations were reported to be telecasting in the United States.

But the atmosphere of doom clouded all this activity. The FCC had authorized only "limited" commercial operation, which meant that a station could invite sponsors to do program experiments and defray their cost, but it could not sell time. In May 1940 even this "limited" authorization was rescinded because of conflicts about technical standards; television went back to "experimental" status. The following year it finally went fully "commercial," but soon afterwards schedules were reduced from fifteen hours per week to four hours per week. Most television stations left the air. Six hung on with skeleton programming to serve the 10,000 sets—they would soon be museum pieces—that had already been sold. New sets disappeared from the market. A few went into police stations for the training of air raid wardens. In New York the NBC studio telecasts began to demonstrate the duties of the warden. Handfuls of volunteers at police stations watched and listened. Television was virtually forgotten.

Its first public steps had gone well enough, but the toddler was being hurried back into the nursery. Again its full emergence was postponed—this time, to postwar years.

But it was not merely a time of waiting. As with radio during World War I, the hiatus saw intense technical development. During this period Zworykin at RCA developed the image-orthicon, a camera tube of such improved sensitivity that performers would no longer be fried alive, and would no longer need strange, exaggerated makeup. And both RCA and CBS pushed color experimentation.

It was also a period of jockeying for position. Both Sarnoff of RCA and Paley of CBS plunged into war activity. For the Allied invasion of the Continent, both were on hand in uniform—Colonel William S. Paley with Psychological Warfare, and Colonel David Sarnoff with the Signal Corps. Sarnoff, accompanying the Allied forces into Paris, was among those who seized the French short-wave station CTSF, and promptly put it into service in the Allied cause. By the end of the war he was Brigadier General David Sarnoff. From then on, at RCA and NBC, he was "General Sarnoff" or "the General." It was appropriate to RCA tradition.

During the brief emergence of television, FM had gone through a similar cycle of ups and downs. The experimental FM station that Armstrong had built at Alpine, completed in 1939, performed so magically that a runaway boom seemed to start. CBS became an FM proponent. GE and other major companies prepared to make sets under Armstrong license. That year the FCC received 150 applications to build FM stations. This created a new crisis over spectrum space. This time, strongly backed, Armstrong won a victory. Channel 1 was removed from the television band and assigned to FM—over strong protests from television interests, especially RCA. In 1940 FM received a go-ahead, at about the same time as television. In addition, the FCC decided that television must have FM sound. Armstrong was jubilant. His struggles seemed to be heading for a triumphant climax. But suddenly it was all stopped—halted by war priorities. Armstrong, like Sarnoff and Paley,

An AFRS outlet. U.S. Department of Defense

FOR THE TROOPS

Sounds of home: Betty Hutton fries a steak—while Bob Hope provides commentary, beginning long career of entertaining troops.

U.S. Department of Defense

AFRS fan mail.

plunged into war work; he joined the Signal Corps. Soon FM became standard equipment on American tanks, jeeps, and command cars. But on the homefront it was in storage, and in a state of uncertainty.

While television and FM awaited a new day, AM seemed indestructible. In 1942 the armed forces, recognizing its powerful hold, built a worldwide Armed Forces Radio Service to bring American programs to troops overseas, wherever stationed. By 1945 AFRS had over 800 outlets. Some were mere 50-watt stations in Quonset huts, or wired systems on ships, but all received 42 hours of recorded programs per week, plus others by short-wave relay. Thus AM radio, on the eve of television, had a worldwide reach and great prestige, and looked forward to postwar splendor.

The industry was increasingly competitive. A 1941 FCC ruling had required RCA to divest itself of one of its networks; the purpose was to end its overwhelming dominance. RCA sued to block the order, but lost. Thus NBC-blue was sold in 1943 to Edward J. Noble, the Lifesaver king, for $8,000,000, and became ABC, the

American Broadcasting Company. Network competition became a three-way rivalry, on more nearly equal terms.* NBC, backed by RCA, was still the most formidable entity. But all were prosperous and potent. All eyed the postwar era.

The end of World War I had precipitated the radio-broadcasting boom. The end of World War II held similar promise for television.

* The Mutual Broadcasting System, a large group of stations exchanging programs, never achieved a truly competitive position.

PLASTIC YEARS 3

"My salad days,
When I was green in judgment."

SHAKESPEARE

In 1945, as peace came, it was possible to discern an explosive set of circumstances.

Electronic assembly lines, freed from production of electronic war matériel, were ready to turn out picture tubes and television sets. Consumers, long confronted by wartime shortages and rationing, had accumulated savings and were ready to buy. Manufacturers of many kinds, ready to switch from armaments back to consumer goods, were eager to advertise. The situation awaited a catalyst, a signal. It came with surprising suddenness.

In 1945 the FCC, once more reviewing spectrum allocations, made crucial decisions. It decided to resume television licensing. And it decided, after all, to move FM "upstairs" to another part of the spectrum. The move was desperately protested by Armstrong and the FM forces: they said it would make prewar sets obsolete, antagonize their owners, saddle the industry with huge conversion costs, and delay FM for years.

But the RCA-NBC forces rejoiced. The move tended to protect the status quo in radio while providing spectrum space for the expansion of television. RCA promised sets for mid-1946.

The pace of television activity quickened. By July 1946 the FCC had issued twenty-four new licenses. Returning servicemen with radar experience, whose knowledge was convertible to television, were snapped up by many stations. Advertising agencies were ready; many had already formed television departments and had experimented with television commercials and programming.

CBS was taken aback by the rush of events. It had expected television decisions to be held in abeyance because of unresolved issues relating to color. CBS had demonstrated a color system, which had been widely acclaimed, that offered brilliant, stable colors. But it involved a rotating wheel, and its pictures could not be seen on the existing black-and-white system, the prewar system. CBS therefore felt this system should be reconsidered; it had urged the FCC to hold off the freezing of standards. And it suggested to affiliates that they postpone television license applications, and give priority to FM.

RCA, however, was scornful of the CBS color method. In six months, Sarnoff promised the FCC, RCA engineers would demonstrate an electronic color system "compatible" with existing black-and-white sets. Asked how he knew they would have it ready, Sarnoff answered: "I told them to."

In the summer of 1946 RCA got its black-and-white sets on the market. That fall it demonstrated an electronic color system—crude and unstable but "compatible." In March 1947 the FCC shunted the CBS system aside. It postponed final color decisions, but reaffirmed a go-ahead under existing black-and-white standards. The RCA forces were exuberant. CBS, on the other hand, had suffered a major defeat.

In October of that year FCC chairman Charles Denny, who had presided over these pro-RCA decisions, resigned from the FCC to become NBC vice president and general counsel. The move brought a hue and cry: when had a network berth first been mentioned to the FCC chairman? Had the FCC decisions been made under circumstances involving a conflict of interest?

Amid such maneuvers, television fever spread again.

MOSAIC

During 1945-46, while the Washington struggles hung in the balance, programming moves were necessarily tentative, and some were curious. But wartime improvements in equipment were evident in the picture clarity. In June 1946 an NBC telecast of the Joe Louis-Billy Conn heavyweight championship prizefight caused the Washington *Post* to comment: "Television looks good for a 1000-year run."

In various branches of programming, preparatory moves were afoot. In 1945 NBC hired newsreel veteran Paul Alley, of the Hearst-MGM News of the Day, to lay the groundwork for a television news service. With little precedent to go on, the network gave him a radio-sized budget. Obtaining his first film free from the Signal Corps Pictorial Center on Long Island, Alley wrote narration himself, and hired another newsreel veteran, David Klein, at $10 a night for part-time editing. Later a small budget increase allowed Klein to become a full-time assistant. Another staff member came to them from the Office of War Information, bringing with him an $8,000 Mitchell camera which he was sure the government no longer needed. Throughout 1946—as the momentous maneuvers before the FCC moved to a climax—the "liberated" Mitchell camera was the mainstay of NBC-TV news operations.

By then it was clear that television news needed a more resolute attack, and NBC tried a strange experiment. It commissioned Jerry Fairbanks Productions, a producer of theatrical shorts and industrial films, to provide film for NBC newscasts. Later it switched to Fox Movietone, while CBS made a similar contract with Telenews, a newly formed unit related to the Hearst-MGM News of the Day. The rationale for these contracts was that the networks had news sources and voices and just needed help with pictures. The fact that the arrangements allowed the networks to postpone dealing with various film unions may also have played a part. In any case, both networks were trying to organize major newscast series.

As sets appeared on the market, taverns rushed to acquire them. They found sports events an especially powerful attraction. Wrestling was soon winning a new vogue. In every television city, groups clustered around tavern sets.

As program operations expanded, the tube was suddenly alive with activity. In January 1947 the opening of Congress was televised for the first time. In February a "blue baby" operation was televised by NBC at Johns Hopkins and witnessed on television sets by several hundred doctors and nurses. In May the *Kraft Television Theater* series, presenting a mixture of adapted classics and new plays, made its NBC debut. That summer the Zoomar lens got into action in a CBS telecast of a baseball game between the Brooklyn Dodgers and the Cincinnati Reds. Its ability to leap from a full-field long shot to a close-up of the pitcher working his wad of chewing tobacco caused a stir. Television entertainment for children was offered in New York by the *Howdy Doody* series, and in Chicago by *Kukla, Fran, and Ollie*, which also won adult admirers. *Meet the Press*, a long-time radio fixture, made a television debut.

For the 1947-48 season both NBC and CBS won sponsors for their main newscast series. The NBC early-evening news became the *Camel News Caravan*, featuring the breezy, boutonniered John Cameron Swayze and sponsored by Camel cigarettes. CBS launched *Television News With Douglas Edwards*, which acquired Oldsmobile as sponsor. Both were 15-minute programs. Both inevitably adopted newsreel patterns. Each was likely to include several filmed items. Film came from distant places by airplane, from newsreel crews maintained in principal news centers. NBC's *Camel News Caravan*, served by Fox Movietone, used 35mm film. The CBS series, served by Telenews, used 16mm film. This was less costly, and the equipment was more maneuverable, but it was considered not quite professional.

Camel News Caravan maintained a brisk tempo. Near the end of each telecast came a moment when John Cameron Swayze exclaimed with unbounded enthusiasm: "Now let's go hopscotching the world for headlines!" What followed was a grab-bag of items that had regrettably taken place without benefit of cameras. Each event had to be dispatched, it seemed, in one sentence. Then Swayze would say: "That's the story, folks. Glad we could get together!"

NBC and CBS were setting the pace in 1947-48 programming. ABC was, for the time being, badly outdistanced.

The continuing strategy at all networks was to try to make radio profits pay the television development bill. This affected decisions on corporate structure. An NBC research department memorandum of June 18, 1946, foresaw an $8,000,000 loss from television operations over a four-year period. It felt that radio could and should be made to finance it. The memo said:

> By deducting telecasting losses from sound broadcasting profits, it is estimated that during 1946-1949 some $3.5 million could be saved on federal income taxes . . . compared with what would have to be paid if the two activities were incorporated separately.

This meant that radio, provider of funds, had to be kept going at maximum profit and minimum expense. Many unsponsored radio features fell by the wayside. Even the world-famed NBC Symphony Orchestra under Arturo Toscanini, a creation of the late 1930's, was marked for oblivion.

Other economies came into play. NBC and CBS, ever since their formation, had generally banned recorded programming from network use. During and after the war the advent of the wire recorder and the tape recorder had somewhat modified this policy. By 1947 the ABC network was ready to welcome the disk-jockey, and the other networks followed suit.

Meanwhile CBS scored a competitive coup. During the war the leading radio comedians, most of whom were on NBC, had paid the very high income taxes associated with the upper brackets. CBS pointed out that if such entities as "the Jack Benny program" and "the Burns & Allen program" and "the *Amos 'n' Andy* program"— which were all owned by the comedians themselves—were sold as

Kukla, Ollie, Fran—of *Kukla, Fran and Ollie.*   NBC

properties, the deals would involve taxation at the low capital-gains rate. CBS was willing to make capital investments of this sort. The comedians would enjoy a bonanza at low tax rates and could also continue to receive salaries whenever broadcasting—on radio or television. CBS thus acquired control of a galaxy of leading entertainers for the television age. No one called it statesmanlike, but it was considered shrewd.

CBS and RCA became antagonists in another realm. In 1948 Columbia Records came out with the 33⅓ rpm long-playing microgroove phonograph record, RCA-Victor with the 45 rpm record. They battled hard for sovereignty in the disk-jockey world.

John Cameron Swayze.   NBC

Meanwhile television license applications poured in on the FCC, and precipitated another kind of struggle. Economic dog-fights began to have an element of international political tension.

OR AFFILIATED SYMPATHETICALLY

While considering license applications, the FCC began getting unsolicited memoranda from J. Edgar Hoover, director of the Federal Bureau of Investigation. Concerning a group applying for a California license, Hoover wrote:

I thought you would be interested in knowing that an examination of this list reflects that the majority of these individuals are members of the Communist Party or have affiliated themselves sympathetically with the activities of the communist movement.

The FCC asked Hoover for specific information. It pointed out that rejected applicants were by law entitled to a hearing. Could the FBI supply information that could be presented as evidence? Hoover said this would be impossible, because its sources must be kept confidential.

An FCC investigator, sent to California, reported that the people mentioned were, on the whole, well regarded. Their main political activity had been to work for the re-election of President Roosevelt. The FCC had no basis for a rejection that could be defended in court, but—nervous about the Hoover memoranda—postponed its decision for months while the applicants waited. One of the commissioners, Clifford Durr, felt that the commission's non-action—in effect, a rejection—violated the rights of the applicants. He described the circumstances in a speech to educational broadcasters. As a result, a Washington *Post* article brought the matter into the open.

FBI director Hoover was furious. He asked the FCC whether he should assume they were not interested in FBI data. The commissioners discussed his inquiry in a crisis atmosphere that reflected the awe surrounding Hoover. In these discussions Commissioner Durr argued that the FCC had no right to act on off-the-record allegations, especially of the sort submitted by the FBI—all stemming from unidentified sources—and that it should therefore not accept or consider them. But most commissioners wanted to placate Hoover, and their reply to him assured him that they valued his advice. The reply constituted a repudiation of Commissioner Durr.

The tide was running against Durr. The peace that had ended World War II, and with it the wartime alliance with the Soviet Union, had also ended the homefront truce between left and right. War had been replaced by "cold war"—at home, by a hunt for

Clifford Durr.

traitors, who might be anyone, including your neighbor—probably
your neighbor.

The cold-war atmosphere brought sharp divisions to government. In Congress a coalition of Southern Democrats and Northern
Republicans badgered President Harry S. Truman, blocked his proposals, and charged that his administration was deeply infiltrated by
communists. Truman, anxious to scotch the attacks, finally announced Executive Order No. 9835—a loyalty-security program
under which, at a cost of many millions of dollars, 2,500,000 federal
employees would be checked by loyalty review boards. Information from the FBI and other sources would be carefully, discreetly
weighed. As a guide, Attorney General Tom Clark prepared a list
of organizations he considered "subversive."

This loyalty-security survey applied only to government employees. But Clifford Durr, who at once criticized the program, asked:

. . . will the example of government stop with government itself? Once it has been established and accepted, can its influence be kept from spreading to industry, to the press, to our schools . . . ?

The questions were answered almost before he asked them. In October 1947 the House committee on un-American activities, chaired by Representative J. Parnell Thomas of New Jersey, opened public hearings on "communism" in the film industry. NBC, CBS, and ABC television cameras and microphones were on hand in a caucus room of the House office building in Washington as scores of celebrities assembled under banks of floodlights, hung among crystal chandeliers. Before them sat committee members John McDowell of Pennsylvania, Richard M. Nixon of California, J. Parnell Thomas of New Jersey (chairman), Richard B. Vail of Illinois, and John S. Wood of Georgia.

Chairman Thomas, in his opening, spoke of the propaganda power of film and the need to study infiltration by those "whose loyalty is pledged in word and deed to the interests of a foreign power."

After this opening with its implication of treason, the hearings seemed determined for a time to descend into farce. Jack L. Warner, setting the tone, described how communist propaganda was injected into films; writers did so by "poking fun at our political system" and picking on rich men. There was also, he said, "the routine of the Indians and the colored folks. That is always their setup." Producer Sam Wood likewise felt that communist writers worked by portraying bankers and senators as "heavies." Mrs. Lela Rogers, mother of Ginger Rogers, identified the film *None But the Lonely Heart* as communistic; to prove her point she quoted *Hollywood Reporter*, which had found the picture "pitched in a low key . . . moody and somber throughout, in the Russian manner."

But the comedy was merely preliminary. The climax of the show focused on ten writers—"unfriendly" witnesses who appeared under subpoena and were questioned before the cameras about membership in various organizations. All refused to discuss memberships of any sort, whether in the Communist Party or the Screen Writers Guild, and cited constitutional guarantees of free speech and assembly.

The first result seemed to be a closing of ranks in Hollywood. Speeches and resolutions supported the writers and criticized the House committee. But suddenly the show of courage collapsed. On November 24, 1947, a group of top film executives met at the Waldorf-Astoria in New York and decided that, for the safety of the industry, the "unfriendly" writers had to be cleaned out. Because of legal barriers to firing employees on political grounds, they were "suspended without pay." On the same day they were charged in Washington with contempt of Congress, because of their refusal to answer committee questions. All went to prison.* Hollywood entered a period of fear. Political discussion tended to vanish, but silence itself could seem suspicious. The patrioteering speech was much in evidence. A blacklist developed.

The broadcasting world was next. In the latter months of 1947, broadcasting executives and sponsors in the New York area began receiving copies of a publication called *Counterattack: The Newsletter of Facts on Communism*. It was published by three former FBI agents—Theodore C. Kirkpatrick, Kenneth M. Bierly, and John G. Keenan—who called themselves American Business Consultants. At an office on Madison Avenue they had assembled back files of the *Daily Worker*, *New Masses*, and other publications, along with programs of rallies, fund-raising appeals, organization letterheads, and other documents. The newsletter warned business-

---

* Two went to the same prison as chairman J. Parnell Thomas, who had meanwhile been convicted of conspiracy to defraud the government with mythical names on his payroll and other fraudulent practices, in which he was found to have engaged from 1940 to 1948.

men ceaselessly against infiltration by "commies," "subversives," "pinks," "dupes," "stooges," "fifth columnists," "quislings," "appeasers," "fronters"—terms used interchangeably. All "helped communism." They should be ostracized, eliminated from employment, treated as traitors. *Counterattack* provided lists of names. At first it dealt with various business fields, but the broadcasting industry soon became its main concern.

Its method was to list artists with "citations" of their "front" activities. A *Counterattack* citation might say that the *Daily Worker* had reported Actor X as attending a meeting of Organization Y, considered subversive. *Counterattack* did not check whether the artist *had* attended the meeting. If he hadn't, said Theodore Kirkpatrick in a radio interview, "that person has recourse to the *Daily Worker*."

Counterattack "citations" went far beyond the Attorney General's list of subversive organizations. The newsletter listed 192 organizations it considered "fronts"; the Attorney General had only seventy-three on his list.

American Business Consultants had been started on $15,000 provided by Alfred Kohlberg, an importer who was an ardent Chiang Kai-shek supporter and a backer of various anti-communist projects including newsletters. The broadcasting industry in 1948 was deriving $616,500,000 from the sale of time, in radio and television. That a $15,000 company could exert a lot of leverage on a $616,500,000 industry soon became clear.

FREEZE

Harry S. Truman at the start of 1948 seemed a lonely figure. The witchhunt clamor, which he had hoped to still with his loyalty-security program, had instead been fanned by it, and seemed about to engulf him. But Truman was a scrapper.

The Republican and Democratic parties both chose Philadelphia

1949: TV tubes roll from assembly lines.   National Archives

for their 1948 conventions, and for the same reason—television. It was on the AT&T co-axial cable that by now linked New York and Washington, and by mid-summer was expected to feed programs to fourteen eastern stations. According to Roger W. Clipp of WFIL-TV, Philadelphia, these would reach a television audience of millions.

That summer Harry S. Truman became the first President to sit in the White House and watch the nomination of his rival on television. Truman saw the Republicans nominate Thomas E. Dewey and Earl Warren. The Democrats nominated Truman and Alben Barkley. Two splinter parties also entered the field. The States' Rights Democrats, who repudiated Truman because of his interest in civil rights, nominated Strom Thurmond; the Progressives, who felt Truman had intensified the cold war, nominated Henry Wallace, a former Vice President under Franklin D. Roosevelt.

Truman made the surprising decision to de-emphasize broadcasting in his campaign. Broadcasters had "sold out to the special interests," he said. In his speeches he kept referring to the "kept press and paid radio." He decided instead on a herculean barn-storming drive in which he assailed the Republicans in salty terms. This was totally unlike the lofty addresses Dewey was delivering on radio and television; crowds swarmed to hear Truman. "Give 'em hell, Harry!" they shouted. The advertising agency for the Republicans, Batten, Barton, Durstine & Osborn, urged on Dewey a barrage of spot announcements, but he vetoed the idea and stuck to the speeches. As broadcast entertainment the 1948 campaign was an outstanding failure. But almost all polls agreed that Dewey would win.

On election night an exhausted Truman went to bed early. In the middle of the night he woke up, turned on the radio, and heard H. V. Kaltenborn saying, in his clipped tones, that Truman was ahead, but that it did not mean anything; he could not win.

Next day, after Dewey had conceded, Truman imitated H. V. Kaltenborn for the reporters. It was a smash hit. The vote ran: Truman, 24,105,812; Dewey, 21,970,065. In the electoral vote it was: Truman, 303; Dewey, 189; Thurmond, 39.

Thus Truman retained the White House. But an antagonistic Congress made it one of the most frustrating of presidencies. Throughout 1948-52 the witchhunt atmosphere continued, and increased in ferocity. The word *treason* was its keynote.

These were also the formative years for television. Its program patterns, business practices, and institutions were being shaped. Evolving from a radio industry born under military influence and reared by big business, it now entered an adolescence traumatized by phobias. It would learn caution, and cowardice.

It was, in another respect, a very special period for television. Late in 1948 the FCC, having issued approximately a hundred tele-

With Indoor Antenna
$149⁹⁵ Cash
$15.50 Down; $7 Mthly.

1949: television sets make first appearance in Sears, Roebuck catalogue.

vision licenses, called a sudden halt. Interference problems had to be studied. A television "freeze" was declared. The Korean War, breaking out in 1950, became a reason for keeping the freeze, which lasted three and a half years.

Thus 1948-52 was a strange television period—a laboratory period. New York and Los Angeles, each with seven stations, saw television in full operation. Some major cities—Austin, Texas; Little Rock, Arkansas; Portland, Maine; Portland, Oregon—had no television at all. Most other cities had only one station.

Because of this spotty distribution, advertisers who wanted national coverage were inclined to keep their radio network series.

At the same time, the "television cities" provided a priceless opportunity for testing and observing. Throughout the freeze, sponsors, advertising agencies, and leaders of other media closely watched the "television cities" for portents of the future.

Soon the portents were eloquent—or frightening—in their implications. Among stories of the hour was the experience of the lipstick maker Hazel Bishop. Doing a $50,000 annual business, the company took up television in 1950; solely through television, its sales zoomed to $4,500,000 in 1952 and continued upward.

Television cities saw signs of economic earthquake and drastic changes of habit. In 1951 almost all television cities reported a 20 to 40 per cent drop in movie attendance. In non-television cities, movie attendance continued unchanged, or grew.

Areas well provided with television reported movie theater closings in waves: 70 closings in eastern Pennsylvania, 134 in southern California, 61 in Massachusetts, 64 in the Chicago area, 55 in metropolitan New York. The rise of outdoor drive-in theaters was a factor, but television was considered the main cause.

A sharp decline at sports events was seen in most television cities, although wrestling, a prominent television feature, was doing well. Effective handling of television rights was clearly a life-or-death matter for professional sports.

Restaurants and night clubs felt the impact. A variety series starring Sid Caesar and Imogene Coca, launched in 1949—later titled *Your Show of Shows*—became a Saturday terror to restaurateurs. It made people rush home early. Television had briefly drawn people to taverns, but now home sets kept them home. Cities saw a drop in taxicab receipts. Jukebox receipts were down. Public libraries, including the New York Public Library, reported a drop in book circulation, and many book stores reported sales down. Radio listening was off in television cities; the Bob Hope rating dropped from 23.8 in 1949 to 12.7 in 1951 and continued downward. The freeze kept sponsors on hand but the omens were frightening.

For the film world they were equally so. And to the terrifying statistics, a new horror was now added.

Sid Caesar—on *Your Show of Shows*.   Max Liebman Productions

PANIC CITY

On the heels of the television statistics, a staggering blow descended on Hollywood: the 1948 U.S. Supreme Court decision in *United States* v. *Paramount et al.*

The defendants were the eight companies that had controlled the industry: Paramount, Loew's (including Metro-Goldwyn-Mayer), RKO, Twentieth Century-Fox, Warner Brothers, Columbia Pictures, Universal, United Artists. The Supreme Court—climaxing years of litigation—agreed with lower courts that the defendants had kept out foreign products and prevented domestic competition by control over theaters. The court now ordered an end to block booking and demanded "divorcement" of theater holdings from production and distribution; it left it to lower courts to work out details. This ushered in a series of consent decrees that—unbelievably—wrote *fade out* to the story of the Big Studios—those self-contained grand duchies that had been a way of life and had symbolized Hollywood. That old Hollywood was suddenly dead.

Convulsions shook the town. Fearing they could not unload 400 to 500 films per year on theaters no longer controlled, the major companies began to slash production schedules and cancel long-term contracts with actors, producers, directors, writers, technicians. A new reign of fear merged with the blacklist terror. No job seemed safe. Every day brought ominous television news and the rolling of heads.

The splitting of the big companies began almost at once. Loew-MGM delayed longest, whistling in the dark. Paramount split promptly into two companies—Paramount Pictures Corporation and United Paramount Theaters. By 1951 United Paramount Theaters was negotiating a merger with the ABC network. To the merger Paramount could bring substantial working capital—and a business of uncertain future. ABC could bring less working capital—and an apparently glowing future. The merger foreshadowed a more spirited competition among networks.

Hosts of artists, set adrift by Hollywood, began to eye the television tube. Some headed for New York. It had been, since the 1920's, the production capital for radio, and many assumed that it would have the same role in relation to television. Joining the migration were numerous fugitives from other media—newspapers, magazines, theater, nightclub, lecture hall. It was a struggle for footholds, a time for trial and error, success and failure. Amid a confusion of migrations and an atmosphere of upheaval, program experiments came and went.

Texaco Star Theater, 1949: Milton Berle is welcomed back for second season.   NBC

IT WILL BE A GREAT SHOW

Among variety hours launched in 1948 were two smash successes.

One was *Texaco Star Theater* with Milton Berle. He acquired the names "Uncle Miltie" and "Mr. Television." He was brash, uninhibited, and liked to cavort in funny clothes. He had never been successful in radio, but was soon regarded as the embodiment of television comedy. He was impertinent, but never politically risky.

Another variety entry was *Toast of the Town,* headed by Ed Sullivan as producer and master of ceremonies, and later known as the *Ed Sullivan Show.* Ed Sullivan occasionally took chances—at first.

The variety show formula, which had given Rudy Vallee a six-teen-year run on radio, was a promising one. Sullivan, a New York *Daily News* columnist, could give performers extra rewards with column items. He went after the biggest names and assembled impressive aggregations. Though he himself was kidded for his unsmiling face and awkwardly dangling arms, his program gathered momentum and soon reached the top in television ratings in several cities.* It acquired the Ford Motor Company as sponsor and began to look like big business. "Ed Sullivan will last," said Oscar Levant, "as long as other people have talent." As the series prospered, even Sullivan's performing deficiencies became assets. He became a man mimicked on amateur hours: in short, one of the great.

Late in 1949 Sullivan booked dancer Paul Draper for a *Toast of the Town* appearance in January 1950. This was, to an extent, a courageous act. An appearance by Draper and harmonica player Larry Adler in Greenwich, Connecticut, had recently called forth a campaign of letter-writing led by a Mrs. Hester McCullough of Greenwich, wife of a *Time* picture editor—abetted by Hearst columnist Igor Cassini, who wrote as "Cholly Knickerbocker." Mrs. McCullough, who had for some time been interested in the hunt for subversives—"I guess you might say I was always on the lookout for them"—demanded that the Greenwich appearance be canceled. She called Draper and Adler "pro-communist in sympathy" and said that any such person "should be treated as a traitor." Draper and Adler issued a statement, carried by the Associated Press, saying that they were not and never had been communists, members of the Communist Party, pro-communists or traitors, and that they owed and gave allegiance "solely to the United States under the Constitution." They filed suit against Mrs. McCullough. The Greenwich appearance proceeded without incident. Draper and Adler appeared to have weathered the storm. Under these circumstances Sullivan booked Draper for *Talk of the Town*. It appeared a further vindication.

* *Pulse* surveys, making local reports in a number of cities, showed Sullivan in first place in New York and Philadelphia by the end of 1948.

But "Cholly Knickerbocker," along with other Hearst columnists—George Sokolsky and Westbrook Pegler—and various newsletters, took up the battle again and demanded that the Ford Motor Company cancel the scheduled television appearance.

The Ford Motor Company and its advertising agency, Kenyon & Eckhardt, held nervous meetings and decided to go ahead with the Draper appearance. The possibility of a lawsuit was a factor in the decision.

The columnists and newsletters, continuing their protests, managed to call forth on the Ford Motor Company a barrage of 1294 angry letters and telegrams in response to the telecast. As in many such campaigns, there were duplicates. Clusters came from the same post office. Most letters echoed published attacks. Eight per cent said that "leftists" and "pinks" should be sent back to Stalin. Thirteen per cent said that communism threatened Western civilization. The mail caused enough anguish to produce further meetings between sponsor and agency, in which it was decided that Ed Sullivan should send a letter to William B. Lewis, president of Kenyon & Eckhardt—a letter which was drafted for the purpose by public relations counsel. It also served as a press release.

January 25, 1950

Dear Bill:

I am deeply distressed to find out that some people were offended by the appearance, on Sunday's *Toast of the Town* television show, of a performer whose political beliefs are a matter of controversy. That is most unfortunate. You know how bitterly opposed I am to communism and all it stands for. You also know how strongly I would oppose having the program used as a political forum, directly or indirectly.

After all, the whole point of the *Toast of the Town* is to entertain people, not offend them. . . . If anybody has taken offense, it is the last thing I wanted or anticipated, and I am sorry.

I just want *Toast of the Town* to be the best show on television. I know that's what you and the sponsor want, too. Tell everybody

SULLIVAN

Ed Sullivan brings the Beatles to American television.   CBS

Ed Sullivan, columnist—and television host 1948-71.   CBS

to tune in again next Sunday night, and if I can get in a plug, it will be a great show—better than ever.

> Sincerely,
> Ed Sullivan

Kenyon & Eckhardt, while assuring their sponsor that the incident had not damaged the Ford Motor Company, promised to do everything possible to prevent other such incidents.

Paul Draper found he could no longer earn a living in the United States and went to live in Europe.* Ed Sullivan began to turn to Theodore Kirkpatrick of *Counterattack* for guidance. Liaison between Sullivan and Kirkpatrick became "extremely close." In case of doubt about any artist, Sullivan now checked with Kirkpatrick. If the entertainer seemed to have "explaining to do," and Sullivan still wanted to use him, he would get Kirkpatrick and the artist together to see if things could be ironed out. Sullivan seemed anxious to proclaim this closeness. He told his column readers on June 21, 1950:

> Kirkpatrick has sat in my living room on several occasions and listened attentively to performers eager to secure a certification of loyalty. On some occasions, after interviewing them, he has given them the green light; on other occasions, he has told them: "Veterans' organizations will insist on further proof."

Sullivan asserted that *Counterattack* was doing "a magnificent American job." In this same column he gave readers some advance inside information: a "bombshell" was about to be dropped into the offices of networks, advertising agencies, and sponsors. It would be a book exposing a conspiracy.

It appeared the following day.

HANDY REFERENCE

On the paper cover of the 215-page *Red Channels: The Report of Communist Influence in Radio and Television* was a red hand clos-

---

* The lawsuit against Mrs. McCullough ended in a hung jury.

ing on a microphone. The title page reported the book to be the work of American Business Consultants, publishers of *Counterattack*.

The introduction said: ". . . the Cominform and the Communist Party USA now rely more on radio and TV than on the press and motion pictures as 'belts' to transmit pro-Sovietism to the American public." The book was offered as a portrait of the infiltration carried out for this purpose—by order, it was implied, from abroad.

Setting the stage with such words, *Red Channels* listed 151 people—alphabetically arranged for easy reference—with "citations."

The list was enough to bring gasps. Advance hints from *Counterattack* and columnists had made the industry expect revelations of insidious underground activity. What they received was a list of 151 of the most talented and admired people in the industry—mostly writers, directors, performers. They were people who had helped make radio an honored medium, and who were becoming active in television. Many had played a prominent role in wartime radio, and had been articulators of American war aims.

In short, it was a roll of honor.*

* The total list: Larry Adler, Luther Adler, Stella Adler, Edith Atwater, Howard Bay, Ralph Bell, Leonard Bernstein, Walter Bernstein, Michael Blankfort, Marc Blitzstein, True Boardman, Millen Brand, Oscar Brand, J. Edward Bromberg, Himan Brown, John Brown, Abe Burrows, Morris Carnovsky, Vera Caspary, Edward Chodorov, Jerome Chodorov, Mady Christians, Lee J. Cobb, Marc Connelly, Aaron Copland, Norman Corwin, Howard Da Silva, Roger De Koven, Dean Dixon, Olin Downes, Alfred Drake, Paul Draper, Howard Duff, Clifford J. Durr, Richard Dyer-Bennett, José Ferrer, Louise Fitch, Martin Gabel, Arthur Gaeth, William S. Gailmor, John Garfield, Will Geer, Jack Gilford, Tom Glazer, Ruth Gordon, Lloyd Gough, Morton Gould, Shirley Graham, Ben Grauer, Mitchell Grayson, Horace Grenell, Uta Hagen, Dashiell Hammett, E. Y. Harburg, Robert P. Heller, Lillian Hellman, Nat Hiken, Rose Hobart, Judy Holliday, Roderick B. Holmgren, Lena Horne, Langston Hughes, Marsha Hunt, Leo Hurwitz, Charles Irving, Burl Ives, Sam Jaffe, Leon Janney, Joe Julian, Garson Kanin, George Keane, Donna Keath, Pert Kelton, Alexander Kendrick, Adelaide Klein, Felix Knight, Howard Koch, Tony Kraber, Millard

Red Channels

The Report of
COMMUNIST INFLUENCE IN RADIO AND TELEVISION

Published By

COUNTERATTACK

THE NEWSLETTER OF FACTS TO COMBAT COMMUNISM
55 West 42 Street, New York 18, N. Y.

$1.00 per copy

To many observers the list seemed a preposterous hoax. The "citations" strengthened this impression. They gave a summary of what these men and women—with countless others—had been concerned with over the years. They had opposed Franco, Hitler, and Mussolini, tried to help war refugees, combated race discrimination, campaigned against poll taxes and other voting barriers, opposed censorship, criticized the House committee on un-American activities, hoped for peace, and favored efforts toward better U.S.-Soviet relations. Most had been New Deal supporters. The book could be seen as a move to pillory the liberal impulses of two decades as traitorous—and perhaps to control the course of television.

But it was scarcely an era given to calm appraisal. During the previous months a series of events had shocked Americans. The Soviet Union had detonated an atom bomb, the Chinese communists had won control of mainland China, eleven Communist Party leaders in the United States had been sentenced to jail, and former Assistant Secretary of State Alger Hiss had been convicted of perjury —after denying the passing of government documents to Whittaker Chambers. In addition, U.S. Senator Joseph R. McCarthy of Wisconsin had been seizing headlines with claims that he knew of scores of "card-carrying" communists in the State Department,

---

Lampell, John Latouche, Arthur Laurents, Gypsy Rose Lee, Madeline Lee, Ray Lev, Philip Loeb, Ella Logan, Alan Lomax, Avon Long, Joseph Losey, Peter Lyon, Aline MacMahon, Paul Mann, Margo, Myron McCormick, Paul McGrath, Burgess Meredith, Arthur Miller, Henry Morgan, Zero Mostel, Jean Muir, Meg Mundy, Lynn Murray, Ben Myers, Dorothy Parker, Arnold Perl, Minerva Pious, Samson Raphaelson, Bernard Reis, Anne Revere, Kenneth Roberts, Earl Robinson, Edward G. Robinson, William N. Robson, Harold Rome, Norman Rosten, Selena Royle, Coby Ruskin, Robert St. John, Hazel Scott, Pete Seeger, Lisa Sergio, Artie Shaw, Irwin Shaw, Robert Lewis Shayon, Ann Shepherd, William L. Shirer, Allan Sloane, Howard K. Smith, Gale Sondergaard, Hester Sondergaard, Lionel Stander, Johannes Steel, Paul Stewart, Elliot Sullivan, William Sweets, Helen Tamiris, Betty Todd, Louis Untermeyer, Hilda Vaughn, J. Raymond Walsh, Sam Wanamaker, Theodore Ward, Fredi Washington, Margaret Webster, Orson Welles, Josh White, Ireene Wicker, Betty Winkler, Martin Wolfson, Lesley Woods, Richard Yaffe.

members of a "spy ring," whose names were—he said—known to the Secretary of State but who were still "shaping the policy of the State Department." If such things were possible, was *Red Channels* strange?

Within days after *Red Channels* the Korean war broke out. Broadcasting executives were suddenly thumbing the pages of *Red Channels* against a background not of peace but of war.

The unbelievable nature of the *Red Channels* list multiplied its impact. Every *Counterattack* subscriber received a copy; a few others went on sale in stores at $1 a copy. Most copies disappeared quickly into the drawers of executive desks at networks, advertising agencies, and sponsors. Few people discussed its contents openly. If they spoke of it, they seldom mentioned who was listed. Artists, even those listed, seldom saw a copy. Many of those listed did not know about it for weeks. Some began to guess it from the changed behavior of friends, or from the fact that producers no longer accepted their phone calls. For many, results were more sudden and drastic.

The Aldrich Family after eleven seasons on radio was scheduled to start a television version on NBC in the summer of 1950. The Young & Rubicam advertising agency held auditions, chose screen star Jean Muir for the role of the mother, and announced it in a press release three days before the scheduled premiere—Sunday, August 27.

Then Jean Muir was suddenly notified that the opening telecast had been postponed a week. Later she was told her contract was being canceled: a cash settlement was offered. It was learned that General Foods executives had received a barrage of phone calls protesting the Muir casting. The firing had been decided at the highest echelons of the company. Her husband, an attorney, urged her to accept the settlement. The event was reported in newspapers throughout the country, with mention of the *Red Channels* listing.

Jean Muir flatly denied association with four of the nine organizations listed in her *Red Channels* entry. She dimly remembered

wartime appearances at two others. Three "citations" she admitted
and avowed. One was the signing of a cable of congratulations to
the Moscow Art Theater on its fiftieth anniversary. A student of
the Stanislavski acting method, she had rejoiced in the opportunity
to join in this message. But such matters were not an issue. General
Foods made no investigations, asked no explanations, claimed no
disloyalty on her part. It merely asserted the need to avoid "controversial" people on programs it sponsored.

Shortly after the Jean Muir episode a newly launched television
version of *The Goldbergs*, sponsored on CBS by Sanka, was subjected to protests over another *Red Channels* listee, Philip Loeb,
who played Jake. A stand by Mrs. Berg—author, star, and owner of
the series—for a time prevented a firing, but the sponsor dropped
the series "for economic reasons" a few months later. After an interval the series reappeared on NBC under another sponsor and
without Loeb. He was reported to have received a settlement. Mrs.
Berg told the New York *Times:* "Philip Loeb has stated categorically that he is not and has never been a communist. I believe him.
There is no dispute between Philip Loeb and myself." The Loeb
case was widely reported. His radio and television work ceased. His
theater appearances were harassed. He eventually took an overdose
of sleeping pills.

After the Muir and Loeb cases, dismissals were handled more
quietly, avoiding headlines. But the cases went on. Scores of artists
vanished from radio and television.

John G. Keenan, co-founder of American Business Consultants,
conceded that some listees should not have been listed. But he said
the "innocent" could always come forward and "clear" themselves.
Many artists seem to have visited the office of *Counterattack* for
such clearance. Most did not wish to plead for "clearance." One
said: "I don't want to have anything to do with pigmies playing
God." So *Red Channels* extended its sway, which soon received a
new form of support.

CRUSADE IN THE SUPERMARKETS

Mrs. Eleanor Johnson Buchanan of Syracuse, New York, whose father owned four supermarkets, read *Counterattack* and *Red Channels*, and became an anti-communist crusader. When her husband went to Korea with the marines, she busied herself with protest letters and speeches against "red sympathizers on radio and television." Her father, Laurence A. Johnson, the supermarket owner, helped her with mimeographing and mailing, and gradually took over leadership in the work.

Johnson, in addition to owning supermarkets, was elected to office in the National Association of Supermarkets, and this enabled him to give the impression—few wanted to test it—that he had influence over thousands of outlets throughout the country. An elderly man of imposing presence, he slipped easily into patriotic talk. Many people considered him naïve, but he devised a canny technique for bringing pressure on sponsors.

One of the most successful early television drama series was *Danger*, launched by CBS in 1950. It acquired as sponsor the Block Drug Company, maker of Amm-i-dent, a chlorophyll toothpaste. When Johnson learned that *Danger* used actors listed by *Counterattack*, he wrote a long letter to Mr. Block the sponsor, calling attention to the casting and making an offer.

He would display Amm-i-dent and its chlorophyll competitor Chlorodent side by side at his supermarkets. In front of each display would be a sign. The Chlorodent sign would say that its manufacturer, Lever Brothers, was using only pro-American artists and shunning "Stalin's little creatures." The Amm-i-dent sign, to be written by the Block Drug Company itself, would explain why its programs chose communist fronters. Johnson's letter asked: "Would not the results of such a test be of the utmost value to the thousands of supermarkets throughout America . . . ?"

As a final touch Johnson added: "This letter will be held awaiting your answer for a few days. Then copies will be sent to the following . . ." Here he added a list that included the United States Chamber of Commerce, the Sons of the American Revolution, the Catholic War Veterans, the Super Market Institute in Chicago, and other organizations—a list raising a specter of national obloquy.

The offers of such "polls" and the phrase "Stalin's little creatures" became trademarks of Johnson campaigns. His letters were reinforced by phone calls and frequent visits to sponsors and advertising agencies. That these made an impression is suggested by testimonial letters that Johnson was soon able to exhibit, all praising his patriotic achievements. The president of the General Ice Cream Corporation wrote him: "I think it is wonderful that you have taken this interest in ferreting communists out of the entertainment industry." A Kraft vice president wrote: "It is indeed heartening to know that you are continuing your crusade."

When he started on his zealous campaigns, Johnson felt he needed help from inside-information experts, and he eventually turned to a rising star in the blacklist field—Vincent Hartnett.

A former navy intelligence officer, Hartnett had later worked on the *Gangbusters* series, but digressed into work as a subversive-activities consultant, gathering his own files on the affiliations of artists. He wrote, on a freelance basis, the introduction to *Red Channels*. Offering his services to sponsors, agencies, and networks, he acquired the Borden Company, Lever Brothers, the Young & Rubicam agency, the Kudner agency, and the ABC network as clients. He began to advertise himself as "the nation's top authority on communism and communications." His collaboration with Laurence Johnson augmented the power of both. Johnson kept recommending Hartnett to food and drug companies to keep them out of difficulties. Hartnett watched casting announcements and fed Johnson up-to-date information on suitable targets.

In 1950, foods, drugs, cleaning products, and toiletries—items sold through supermarkets—accounted for over 60 per cent of the

revenue of the broadcasting industry. This was the force in the
Laurence Johnson whipsaw operation. To sponsors, agencies, networks, Laurence Johnson became a bane and a salvation. He was
their justification. They loathed and needed him. Executives who
felt foolish knuckling under to letters and phone calls found in
Johnson a certified demonstration in economic—i.e. respectable—
terms. He was *proof* that what they were doing was stark necessity
and that the alternative was ruin. The broadcasting world was itself
a sort of supermarket, where the voice from the supermarket was
readily understood.

Only one further step was needed to complete the blacklist structure. Networks and agencies grew weary of being attacked and decided to take charge of the whole business themselves. Blacklist administration became part of the built-in machinery of the industry.

CBS, which in 1950 established a sort of loyalty oath, followed
this in 1951 with the appointment of an executive specializing in security. At NBC the legal department assumed similar duties. Large
advertising agencies acquired special security officers under various
titles. Some agencies continued to employ Kirkpatrick, Hartnett,
and others, but during the early 1950's the kingpins of the structure
became the hush-hush officials at networks and large agencies.

Mysterious protocol was devised to veil their work. Producers
had to submit to superiors the names of writers, actors, and directors being considered. A copy was routed to the security chief. A
phone call later conveyed approvals or disapprovals. Memoranda
and face-to-face meetings were avoided. The voice at the other end
would go down the list of proposed names with "Yes," "No,"
"Yes," "Yes," "No." Questions were not to be asked. Rituals were
prescribed for staff producers and independent producers alike. David Susskind, who plunged into television early as a "packager"—
producing *Armstrong Circle Theater, Appointment for Adventure,
Justice,* and many other series—testified on one occasion about his
relations with Young & Rubicam. For one series he made "ten or
fifteen" phone calls daily to the agency to check names. About five

thousand name checks were made during a year. A third of the names, "perhaps a little higher," were rejected. He had to agree never to tell an actor why he could not be used. If a reason was needed, it must be "not tall enough," or "the leading man is too short." Each time an actor was used, he had to be checked again. Even children had to be checked. An eight-year-old daughter of a controversial father was banned; Susskind had to find "another child whose father was all right."

Among networks, CBS was especially zealous in institutionalizing blacklisting. There was an irony in this. CBS had been particularly noted for the vigor and range of its programming; the new development seemed, in fact, a by-product of the very policies that had won high regard for its work. The CBS rise of the 1930's had developed around news and the drama of ideas. At a time when NBC dominated the air with vaudeville comedians and singers, clung to established formulae, and avoided deviant ideas, CBS had welcomed the ferment of the Depression and thereby made its mark—and also made itself a happy hunting ground for blacklisters. CBS, reacting, had become purge headquarters—at precisely the time when it was taking over the NBC comedians. The networks appeared to be switching roles.

The blacklist gradually dropped out of the headlines but remained a felt presence. Drama plots were affected. In mystery stories bankers and businessmen were no longer useful characters because they could not be suspects. Numerous topics had become dangerous. But one subject was always safe: law and order.

CRIME AUTOMATED

Many of the early television drama programs were of the "episodic series" type—in which one or more characters ran through the series, but each episode was complete in itself. The formula, derived from radio, allowed many writers to contribute. Some episodic se-

ries were family series, like the *Aldrich Family*, but most were in
the law-and-order category: *Martin Kane, Private Eye; Mr. District Attorney; Man Against Crime*. Reliance on formula gave a
certain editorial security.

Man Against Crime, starring Ralph Bellamy, premiered in 1949
and soon achieved high ratings. It seemed set for a long run. In the
radio tradition, it was produced by an advertising agency, William
Esty; the program staff worked from the Esty office. Freelance
writers came and went; fifty different writers in due time contributed to the series.

In 1949 all such programs were produced *live*. Produced in this
way, *Man Against Crime* cost $10,000 to $15,000 per program; a
writer usually got $500 to $700. The live-production dominance
was expected to continue. Both Sarnoff of RCA and Paley of CBS
were said to be determined that it should.

The fact that *local* schedules were using a lot of film—mostly old
westerns and gangster films, not from the major Hollywood studios
—was not considered significant. In radio, local programming had
always had a similar dependence on recordings; yet network radio
in its heyday had remained live. This was expected to be the pattern in television.

While following a radio pattern, *Man Against Crime* faced television problems. In radio the length of a play could be gauged by
counting words—it usually ran 140 to 150 words a minute. Television timing, because of action intervals, was a trickier problem.
From one rehearsal to another, the length varied considerably.

On *Man Against Crime* the problem was solved by requiring
writers to include a "search scene" near the end of each program.
The hero-investigator would search a room for a special clue. A
signal would tell Ralph Bellamy how long to search. If time was
short, he could go straight to the desk where the clue was hidden;
if there was need to stall, he could first tour the room, look under
sofa cushions, and even take time to rip them open.

The CBS studio in the Grand Central Terminal building where

Man Against Crime was produced was under unceasing pressure. Here the cast had only one full rehearsal with cameras and lights. Earlier rehearsals were "dry runs" in offices or rented ballrooms. During the studio rehearsal, work might be in progress on sets for other programs.

Man Against Crime was sponsored by Camel cigarettes. This affected both writing and direction. Mimeographed instructions told writers:

> Do not have the heavy or any disreputable person smoking a cigarette. Do not associate the smoking of cigarettes with undesirable scenes or situations plot-wise.

Cigarettes had to be smoked gracefully, never puffed nervously. A cigarette was never given to a character to "calm his nerves," since this might suggest a narcotic effect. Writers received numerous plot instructions:

> It has been found that we retain audience interest best when our story is concerned with murder. Therefore, although other crimes may be introduced, somebody must be murdered, preferably early, with the threat of more violence to come.

The hero, said the instructions, "MUST be menaced early and often." Violence, if on-camera, was very briefly staged; one good blow or shot might suffice. Physical struggle was hardly feasible amid flimsy sets.

Although "other crimes" could be used as plot elements, arson was not one of them. Fires were not to be mentioned because they might remind a viewer of fires caused by cigarettes.

No one could cough on *Man Against Crime*. Romance, or the possibility of it, was as essential as violence. A plot had to include "at least one attractive woman." A passing romance for the hero was encouraged, "but don't let it stop the forward motion of the story." Doctors could be shown only in "the most commendable light." There were rumors of a coming report on health effects of smoking—a report of this sort had appeared in Britain—and this made the sponsor increasingly nervous about antagonizing doctors. Since doctors tended to take a dim view of fictional doctors, it seemed best to avoid doctors. On *Man Against Crime* it was usually someone other than a doctor who said, "He's dead." It took only a moment.

Before anyone was hired, his or her name had to be checked by phone with a designated agency division for a "yes" or "no."

The writer had to limit action to five sets, one of which had to be the "fashionable" Manhattan apartment from which the hero-investigator worked. Before the middle commercial, action had to "rise to a cliff-hanger." Costume changes were difficult and unwelcome. Between scenes Ralph Bellamy was always rushing from set to set. Transitions between scenes were sometimes eased by use of a film clip, as of traffic or a subway train.

With episodic series proliferating, groups rehearsing throughout the city, and artists and technicians converging for the briefest of studio run-throughs, the pressures on all were brutal. Possibilities for error were huge. By 1951 sponsor and producer began to doubt the sanity of the arrangements. That year a new phenomenon added to their doubts. Among Hollywood cast-offs who had decided on a television gamble were Lucille Ball and her husband Desi Arnaz. Their series *I Love Lucy,* filmed in a fringe Hollywood studio, began in 1951 and by the following year was a leader in the Nielsen ratings.* Within months its leadership was challenged by still another filmed entry, *Dragnet,* "based on" case histories of the Los Angeles police department. *Dragnet* had a highly mobile style, with many outdoor scenes for which the Hollywood area was made to order. That same year—1952—the *Man Against Crime* group decided to "go to film"; the production was moved to a studio in the Bronx built by Thomas Edison in 1904.

---

* Nielsen ratings were based on mechanisms—"audimeters"—inserted in a sampling of television sets, keeping a record of stations tuned. Their use in radio had dated from 1935, but they became especially prestigious in television.

Here actors came across relics of Mary Pickford, Richard Barthelmess, Thomas Meighan. In the Bronx, production costs jumped to $20,000 to $25,000 per program for three days of shooting—two in the studio, one on location.

But if film was called for, there were better places than the Bronx. The move really foreshadowed the doom of New York's episodic series. In Hollywood the *I Love Lucy* success was stirring a rash of similar projects. It did not yet involve the major studios; they were staying aloof. Most of the series featured actors set free by the studios, and many were produced by Desilu, the company formed by Lucille Ball and Desi Arnaz. Others emanated from Hal Roach productions, heir to a theatrical short-film tradition; Screen Gems, short-film offspring of Columbia Pictures; Ziv Television Productions, a radio syndicate branching into television; and most significantly, Revue Productions, subsidiary of the talent agency MCA.

It was not usual for a talent agent to make films on the side. Normally, talent guilds would have blocked the practice, because it involved a clear conflict of interest. MCA as agent was supposed to get the best possible terms for an artist; MCA as producer had an opposite incentive. But in a time of Hollywood panic, the readiness of MCA to finance production and provide employment was welcome, and soon mass-produced episodic series from MCA-Revue were pouring across the United States—and elsewhere. Some went into network schedules, while others were syndicated—sold on a station-by-station basis. Because AT&T's coaxial cables and relays did not yet reach all stations, syndication was a crucial source of programming.

A new element was further stimulating the film proliferation. Television, already established in Britain and Japan, was beginning in Mexico, Brazil, Argentina, and Cuba, and was about to begin in a dozen other countries. All of them might be program markets. All were suddenly a reason for producers to plunge into filmed programming, rather than the dead-end risks of live production. All of this added to the feeling of a coming boom.

IKE AND IKON

So did another event of 1952—the presidential election.

Although radio still commanded a larger audience, television for the first time received the main attention of campaigners. Television viewers, who were watching fifteen million sets, were assumed to be "influentials."

Each network found a sponsor for its broadcasts of the 1952 party conventions and of the election returns. NBC combined them into a $3.5 million package sponsored by Westinghouse, in which Betty Furness became famous demonstrating refrigerators in live commercials. She opened and closed refrigerator doors hundreds of times before the issues were settled.

Republican convention—1952.   NBC

The Republicans nominated General of the Army Dwight D. Eisenhower and, as his running mate, Richard M. Nixon, who had become prominent through hearings of the House committee on un-American activities. The Democrats nominated Adlai Stevenson, Governor of Illinois, and Senator John Sparkman of Alabama.

Stevenson was verbal. His speeches were eloquent, witty, polished. On television he never used a teleprompter because he always polished his speeches until the final moment, and there was never time to put them on a teleprompter. At the end of a program, the viewer's final glimpse was usually Stevenson still reading, turning a page, hurrying because he hadn't finished, but not hurrying enough. Again and again he ran over. It was the despair of his advisers.

While many responded to Stevenson's verbal brilliance, it also became a target for anti-intellectuals, who scorned his "teacup words." As the television campaign progressed, his brilliance tended to become a liability. He was waging a campaign of the radio age, but the radio age was waning. The word was battling the image, not knowing its strength.

Eisenhower was meanwhile conducting a very different television campaign. In charge—once again—was the agency Batten, Barton, Durstine & Osborn, and it decided from the start that an Eisenhower speech for a half-hour program must be twenty minutes long—no more. The broadcast was planned in three acts: (1) arrival of a hero; (2) speech; (3) departure of the hero. The middle part, the speech, was easy and could be left to speech writers. The other parts required experts, who would begin with study of the hall, and decisions on the use and placement of cameras. The drama was conceived in shots: Ike coming through the door at *back* of auditorium; Ike greeting crowd; people in gallery going wild, craning necks; Ike, escorted, making his way down the aisle; Mamie Eisenhower in box; Ike mounting platform; crowd going wild; Ike at rostrum, waving; Ike looking over toward Mamie; Mamie in box, smiling; on cue, Ike holding up arms as if to stop applause; crowd going wild. The final portion, the departure, was as carefully planned.

But BBD&O did not rely solely on pageantry. The kind of spot barrage proposed to Dewey in 1948, and rejected, was carried out for Eisenhower in 1952. The spots were all written by a volunteer from the Ted Bates advertising agency—Rosser Reeves. The basic formula called for a question and an answer in twenty seconds. All spots had the same four-word introduction.

> ANNOUNCER: Eisenhower answers the nation!
> CITIZEN: What about the cost of living, General?
> IKE: My wife, Mamie, worries about the same thing. I tell her it's our job to change that on November fourth!

The "citizens" were shot in various locales. Eisenhower filmed the answers for all fifty spots in one day in a mid-Manhattan film studio specializing in television commercials. Reading from huge prompt cards, he occasionally expressed amazement "that an old soldier should come to this," but he went along with his experts. The answers were subsequently spliced to the questions. The spots were scheduled for a saturation coverage during the last two weeks of the campaign at an expense of $1,500,000.

Stevenson and his close advisers—Senators J. William Fulbright of Arkansas and Russell B. Long of Louisiana, and others—heard about the spot plan, but felt that Stevenson should *not* emulate it. The candidate himself said he had no wish to be merchandised "like a breakfast food." The decision probably did not affect the outcome, for Eisenhower was the more merchandisable product.

A climactic feature of the campaign was the Nixon "Checkers" speech, so named after the family dog. There had been rumors about Nixon's finances—they related to a fund put together by California supporters after his election to Congress. At one point Thomas Dewey, polling various Republican leaders, found a majority of the opinion that Nixon should withdraw from the race because of the charges, but the Republican National Committee decided to invest in a half-hour period on a sixty-four-station television hookup—plus several hundred radio stations—for a reply by Nixon. Several advertisers offered to sponsor the broadcast, but it was considered unwise to accept. Nixon went into seclusion to work on his broadcast.

Eisenhower, who emphasized that the Republican crusade needed a candidate "as clean as a hound's tooth," arranged to watch the program on a television set in the manager's office of the Cleveland auditorium, where an Eisenhower speech was scheduled. Nixon spoke from a Los Angeles studio.

On television the program opened with a close-up of Nixon's calling card, then went to Nixon sitting at a desk. Mrs. Nixon—"Pat"—sat to one side, watching him. Occasionally during the program he turned to her; at these moments the camera would move to her. Nixon spoke about the fund:

> Not one cent of the $18,000 or any other money of that type ever went to me for my personal use. Every penny of it was used to pay for political expenses that I did not think should be charged to the taxpayers of the United States. . . .

Nixon did not explain what was meant by "other money of that type" or how much there was of it. But he added a "confession." It was inspired by a recollection of how successfully President Franklin D. Roosevelt had once used a dog story. Nixon said:

> One other thing I should probably tell you, because if I don't they'll probably be saying this about me too, we did get something—a gift—after the election. A man down in Texas heard Pat on the radio mention the fact that our two daughters would like to have a dog. And, believe it or not, the day before we left on this campaign trip we got a message from Union Station in Baltimore saying they had a package for us. We went down to get it. You know what it was? It was a little cocker spaniel dog in a crate that he sent all the way from Texas. Black and white spotted. And our little girl—Tricia, the six-year-old—named it Checkers. And you know the kids love that dog and I just want to say this right now, that regardless of what they say about it, we're going to keep it!

In conclusion he asked listeners to wire or write the Republican National Committee to help them decide whether he should stay on the ticket or "get off." He would leave it up to the committee. But whatever the outcome, he promised to campaign for the Republican ticket "up and down America until we drive the crooks and communists and those that defend them out of Washington. And remember, folks, Eisenhower is a great man, believe me. He is a great man. . . ."

Even before the deluge of supporting telephone calls and telegrams and letters began, it seemed clear that Nixon had survived his crisis. At the Cleveland auditorium office the group around Eisenhower had watched "seemingly without drawing breath." Mrs. Eisenhower and several of the men were seen to dab at their eyes with handkerchiefs. Immediately after the broadcast Eisenhower turned to Republican chairman Arthur Summerfield: "Well, Arthur, you surely got your $75,000 worth."

The 1952 campaign came after twenty years of Democratic party rule. They had involved world struggles, and a great expansion of American power. To Stevenson they had also been a time of humanitarian achievement. To another figure in the campaign, U.S. Senator Joseph R. McCarthy of Wisconsin, they had been "twenty years of treason." He blamed the Democrats for the "loss" of China. He continued to make charges about "communists and traitors" in high places—the State Department, its Voice of America, the Federal Communications Commission, the broadcasting field, and elsewhere. He made himself so effectively the spokesman of this theme that the whole blacklist mania had become "McCarthyism."

To some extent Nixon, promising to "drive the crooks and communists and those that defend them out of Washington," allied himself with McCarthyism. Eisenhower avoided doing so. He was said to despise McCarthy and his methods. Reports of this sort reassured many people; it was assumed that Eisenhower would, in due time, dissociate himself from McCarthyism.

Meanwhile the most resounding move of the Eisenhower campaign was his promise, if elected, to "go to Korea." The expectation that he would end the Korean conflict electrified the country.

To broadcasters it meant that the television boom, long confined to 108 scattered stations, would at last become nationwide.

As though in anticipation, restrictions on war materials were being lifted. Licensing was resumed. During the closing months of 1952 a number of new stations received a go-ahead. Among the first was KTBC-TV, Austin, Texas, licensed to Mrs. Lyndon B. Johnson, wife of the U.S. Senator from Texas; before it even reached the air, advertising sales were such that *Broadcasting* magazine reported: "AUSTIN'S BRINGING IN A GUSHER." Hundreds of additional applicants clamored for a go-ahead.

In November the vote ran: Eisenhower, 33,936,252; Stevenson, 27,314,992. The electoral vote was 442-89.

In December Eisenhower flew to Korea and back; the machinery for peace was in motion.

Now was a final chance to wheel and deal, to maneuver for position. Among the maneuverers were educators.

SIXTH REPORT AND ORDER

During the Truman years the Federal Communications Commission had acquired a woman commissioner. In 1948, a time when Truman could obtain from Congress almost nothing he requested, he played sly politics by nominating Frieda B. Hennock: he invited Senators to go on record as antifeminist or anti-Semitic. They risked neither and quickly confirmed her.

Commissioner Hennock soon launched a crusade to allocate a group of television channels to nonprofit, educational use. The licensing pause provided by the freeze was a chance to push this idea. In 1950 a Joint Committee (later renamed "Council") on Educational Television was formed; the attorney Telford Taylor became its counsel. Commissioner Hennock, with wide-ranging speeches and conferences, made herself its champion. Among the other commissioners, Commissioner Paul C. Walker showed some early interest. The others seemed lukewarm or cool.

1949: Francis Cardinal Spellman makes Christmas appearance on Dumont television.   National Archives

NON-PROFIT WORLD

NBC-TV covers United Nations session.   NBC

Industry spokesmen scoffed at the campaign. *Broadcasting*, which generally reflected the industry establishment, considered the idea "illogical, if not illegal." Most veteran broadcasters thought such ideas had been scotched with the defeat of the Wagner-Hatfield amendment of 1934. Some FM channels had been set aside by the FCC for education, but that seemed of little significance. Television channels were something else.

A device that helped educators dramatize their cause was a series of "monitoring studies," for which Ford Foundation funds were made available. In several cities, starting in January 1951, groups of viewers tabulated information about commercial television offerings. The finding that New York viewers could in one week witness 2,970 "acts or threats" of violence had an impact on many people.

With commercial television straining for a go-ahead, the campaign spearheaded by Commissioner Hennock began to have nuisance value. The FCC, encouraged by staff members, began to feel it had nothing to lose and much to gain from the reserved-channel idea. If educators failed to use the channels—as many industry leaders predicted—the FCC would at least have offered the chance. If educators seized the opportunity, the FCC would have led the way.

The 1952 Sixth Report and Order of the Federal Communications Commission was an omnibus package with items to please various groups. Channels 2 to 13 in the already established VHF (very high frequency) band were to be supplemented by seventy new channels in the UHF (ultra high frequency) band. Expansion for commercial television seemed to be assured. Meanwhile, both in VHF and UHF, a number of channels were reserved for education. Provision was made for a total of 242 educational stations; the number was later increased.

The educational channel reservations, snatching victory from old defeats, were occasion for oratory. Some hopefully predicted that the mounting problems of education—including teacher shortages and pockets of the disadvantaged—would be solved by this miraculous new resource. It was widely compared to the land grants that helped to create "land-grant colleges" after the Civil War.

There were also less sanguine views. It was pointed out that the new blueprint, unlike the long-ago Wagner-Hatfield proposal, involved no plan for financing the use of the channels. It was pointed out that boards of education faced desperate financial problems. Would educational television be one more demand on them, diverting funds from needed schoolrooms, equipment, salary increases? It seemed to some that educators had won special channels in which to go about with a tin cup in search of funds. But others said, one problem at a time. The channels first, financial problems later. Let the channels be saved. If not saved now, they would be gone forever.

So education, too, had a stake in the coming explosion.

HIGH LEVEL

Edwin Armstrong felt outmaneuvered. FM had been set back by its transfer to higher frequencies. It had received another blow when the FCC approved duplication of programming on AM-FM combination stations. The incentive to purchase FM sets had been lessened.

He had another problem. Although RCA was using FM in its TV as well as FM sets—as decreed by the FCC—RCA was not paying a cent of royalty. FM royalties were being paid to Armstrong by General Electric, Stromberg-Carlson, Westinghouse, Zenith, and others. RCA had paid nothing. A few lesser companies were following its example.

RCA had at times offered to negotiate a settlement—a million dollars had been mentioned. But this raised a question of fairness to those who had always paid royalties based on sales. Zenith had paid more than a million.

In 1948 Armstrong made his decision. He brought suit against the mammoth RCA. He had spent most of his royalty earnings on the battle for FM. This added to his determination to press the lawsuit.

RCA as defendant had the right to examine Armstrong in pretrial hearings. These began in February 1949 in the lower Manhattan law offices of Cravath, Swaine & Moore. RCA attorneys began questioning the inventor. They kept it going for a full year.

Q. You are the plaintiff in the present action?
A. Yes.
Q. What is your occupation?
A. I am an electrical engineer.
Q. Do you have any other occupation?
A. I am a professor of electrical engineering at Columbia University.
Q. Do you have any other occupation?
A. I occasionally make inventions.

Armstrong, normally patient, became a man possessed. All his energies came to be centered on the suit. Three o'clock in the morning would find him poring over transcripts. At all hours he called attorneys to discuss tactics.

The RCA position gradually emerged. RCA, Sarnoff said, had done more than anyone to develop FM. Early discussions with Armstrong were even cited in support of this. The claim stirred Armstrong to fury.

His expenses mounted. His wife and friends pleaded with him to accept a settlement. But now victory had become a terrible need. The meaning of his life was at stake. In 1953 he fell ill; it was thought he had had a stroke. A broken man, at odds with family and friends, he finally authorized a settlement.

He had always had an obsession about high places. As a boy he had frightened Yonkers neighbors, swaying in the wind on a huge antenna pole. Later he had climbed around his fantastic Alpine FM tower to supervise every detail of construction.

One day, neatly dressed, he stepped out of a window of his thirteenth-floor East Side apartment. He was found on a third-floor extension. Shortly afterwards RCA made a million-dollar settlement with the estate.*

MAELSTROM

As 1952 drew to a close, the world of broadcasting was a maelstrom of probes, experiments, deals, adjustments. Everything was in flux. All was expectancy.

Radio, sensing disaster, looked for new functions. Some stations became "Negro stations"; most of these were owned by whites but aimed at a Negro "market" with various kinds of "Negro" music. Some people thought radio should become the medium of intellectuals. One-time radio greats like Eddie Cantor and Paul Whiteman were disk-jockeys. Taboos had vanished; now almost anything could be discussed on radio. But ratings still plunged, and major sponsors were ready and eager for the switch. As the comedian Fred Allen put it, they were ready to abandon radio like the bones at a barbecue.

Droves were pushing into television. Bishop Fulton J. Sheen was pitted in a weekly series against Milton Berle and his Texaco program. (Berle quipped: "We both work for the same boss, Sky Chief.") Violent roller-skating derbies were winning a vogue. The wrestler Gorgeous George, with marcelled hair, made periodic appearances. *Information Please*, transplanted from radio, provided an erudite touch. Another radio veteran, Walter Winchell, wearing his hat like a 1930's movie reporter, shouted out scoops with gravelly voice. Edward R. Murrow and a young collaborator, Fred W. Friendly, had transformed their documentary radio series *Hear It Now* into *See It Now*. Jackie Gleason had become a bus driver in *The Honeymooners*. Dr. Frances Horwich talked to pre-school

* Litigation with other companies continued for thirteen years. All suits were won by the Armstrong estate.

NEGRO DJ'S
EARN MORE MONEY

HOW WOULD YOU LIKE TO JOIN A SUCCESSFUL
ORGANIZATION WITH A LONG RECORD OF
HIGH PAY AND FAIR TREATMENT TO ITS NA-
TIONALLY FAMOUS NEGRO DISC JOCKEYS. WE
ARE EXPANDING OUR ORGANIZATION AND
REQUIRE THE FOLLOWING:

1. Negro frantic type, blues and jive.

2. Negro spiritual and gospel smooth type.

3. Negro blues singer, guitar player, show-
   man.

4. Negro woman for spiritual gospel and
   homemaker show. Good personality.

IF YOU ARE THE RIGHT PERSON YOU WILL BE
HEAVILY PROMOTED ON A NATIONAL LEVEL.
GOOD BASE PAY, TALENT, COMMISSIONS, AND
YEARLY BONUS. WRITE FULL DETAILS, EDU-
CATION, EXPERIENCE, AND SEND DISC AND
PHOTO.

APPLY BOX 107C, B•T

A radio station announces its needs—January 1954.   *Broadcasting*

children on *Ding Dong Schoolhouse*. Arthur Murray and his wife taught dancing. World War II battle footage was impressively assembled into the film series *Victory At Sea*, with music by Richard Rodgers. Children sat spellbound by ancient cartoons and westerns. Politicians came when they could: televised crime hearings had made a national figure out of U.S. Senator Estes Kefauver of Tennessee. The *Today* series began, partly newscast and partly variety show; its purpose at first baffled reviewers, and it won neither audience nor sponsor until the arrival of J. Fred Muggs, a baby chimpanzee owned by two former NBC pages. A *Today* staff member saw him waiting for an elevator while sucking formula from a plas-

David Garroway, J. Fred Muggs, and friend, on *Today*.   NBC

TODAY

Crowd on 48th Street, New York, watches *Today* telecast—and occasionally sees itself on the monitors.   NBC

tic bottle. Everybody said television should be visual, and Muggs seemed to be that; he was not verbal. Producer Gerald Green has described what happened after Muggs became a *Today* regular.

> Women proposed to him; advertisers fought for the right to use his photo in their supermarket flyers; Chambers of Commerce sought his good offices; actresses posed with him; officers of newly commissioned naval vessels demanded that he christen them.

In Florida he got a room in a restricted hotel. He appeared as guest of honor in Central Park in New York at an I Am an American Day rally, although really a native of Cameroon.

But the television crown was firmly on the head of Lucille Ball of *I Love Lucy*. She was pregnant. Throughout the final months of 1952 this provided the comedy plotting as the nation watched Lucille—or Lucy—grow larger. A program about the big day was filmed when the event became imminent. Then on January 19, 1953, Desiderio Alberto Arnaz IV, 8½ pounds, was born on the exact day of the Lucy-has-her-baby telecast. The event found 68.8 per cent of television sets tuned to *I Love Lucy** and was headline news even in competition with the Eisenhower inaugural, which came the following morning. The two events symbolized the moment. Amid the delirium, telecasters awaited the greatest of all booms.

* According to Trendex, a rating system based on telephone calls.

PRIME

4

"In prosperity there is never any dearth of friends."

EURIPIDES

Throughout 1953 stations made their debuts and were joined by co-axial cable and radio relay. National networks took shape. Sponsors made their moves. Schedules expanded. Important stars made the plunge. Sets sold rapidly. Euphoria ruled in executive offices.

The mass acceptance that David Sarnoff had so long predicted—and which had been delayed by financial debacles, wars, technical problems, spectrum disputes—was finally taking place. The stop-and-start period was finally over.

From studios came impressive, sometimes dazzling experiments in drama, documentary, dance, opera, and other genres. To be sure, competition between the migrations from various media was still in process. Many programming issues were unresolved. And certain disputes still rumbled in the background.

Before the Eisenhower inauguration *Broadcasting* magazine speculated that there would be a cleanout at the FCC and that Senator Joseph R. McCarthy might well conduct a probe of its affairs. He was widely regarded as leader of a coming purge. A "loyal underground" of McCarthy followers in government agencies was said

Station identifications.

to be feeding his dossiers with tidbits on anyone who might be one of "them." Dog-eared lists of such people were in circulation. McCarthy had become the center of a confident, active coterie that included two broadcasters: Fulton Lewis, Jr., a radio commentator; and George Sokolsky, a commentator who was also a Hearst columnist. The importer Alfred Kohlberg, financier of *Counterattack*, was a leading McCarthy backer.

Eisenhower, taking office, had an immediate chance to appoint an FCC commissioner, to fill a vacancy. He appointed a McCarthy protégé, John C. Doerfer—apparently hoping to placate McCarthy. Doerfer promptly made McCarthyist moves. Some stations had nettled McCarthy by not carrying his campaign speeches, and the Senator had hinted that this was a communist symptom. As commissioner, Doerfer set out to substantiate this—an effort that occupied him and the commission for several years.

Late in 1953 another FCC vacancy occurred. Again Eisenhower appointed a McCarthy friend—this time Robert E. Lee, regarded as a member of the McCarthy inner circle. A former FBI agent, he was said to have provided information on which McCarthy based his charges of subversives in the State Department. Lee acknowledged admiration of McCarthy, though saying he was not "beholden" to him.

At the State Department, which included the Voice of America, the McCarthy drive was bringing similar developments. John Foster Dulles, the new Secretary of State, at once appointed as his director of "personnel and security" Scott McLeod, another FBI man and McCarthy adherent. Two young McCarthy aides, Roy M. Cohn and G. David Schine, began badgering State Department division heads with lists of "undesirables" who had to be fired right away to avoid trouble with "Joe."

At the FCC the drive meanwhile brought strange events. A station owner particularly objectionable to McCarthy because of failure to carry his speeches was Edward Lamb, who had stations in the Midwest and South. Lamb was a lawyer with various other business interests including television and radio—which had made him rich. A former Republican turned Democrat under the spell of Franklin D. Roosevelt, Lamb had become an important Democratic Party contributor, and was often mentioned as a possible treasurer of the Democratic National Committee. His standing made him an attractive McCarthy target. The trade press began to carry reports that Senator Joseph McCarthy and associates were "gunning" for Lamb. Commissioner Doerfer was said to be in charge of "the Lamb case."

As a lawyer, Lamb had represented labor leaders and handled civil liberties cases. He had also visited the Soviet Union and published an analysis of what he considered the successes and failures of its economic system. He probably seemed an easy target.

As a licensee Edward Lamb had signed affidavits that he was not and never had been a communist. Early in 1954, while awaiting FCC action on pending licenses and renewals, he received instead an FCC notice charging that he had been a Communist Party member. The implication was that he had committed perjury and that his licenses would be voided. The FCC released the accusing letter to the press—apparently before mailing it.

Lamb reacted with a vigor that was perhaps unexpected. He placed advertisements in the New York *Times* and many other publications, offering $10,000 reward to anyone who could disprove a single one of his noncommunist affidavits. Meanwhile he demanded a public hearing by the full FCC and asked for a bill of particulars on its charges.

The FCC declined, saying this would be premature. Meanwhile its investigators apparently began an intense hunt for particulars—of various kinds. A former secretary of Edward Lamb was asked if she could tell of any "girl trouble" he had had. Finally the FCC brought to Washington, and placed on the witness stand, a lady who said she had known Lamb as a communist in Columbus, at meetings where gin was drunk and caviar eaten. But then she took it all back, said she had never known Lamb, had never been a communist, and had only been trying to be helpful to the government. She testified:

> The FCC lawyers told me it was my duty to testify because Lamb's radio station could beam atom bombs from foreign countries and also beam in enemy broadcasts.

The case against Lamb collapsed in confusion and his licenses were eventually renewed. But the case stirred questions. What was going on at the FCC?

The search for subversives had its lighter moments. It was revealed that Lucille Ball of *I Love Lucy*—No. 1 in all ratings—had registered as a Communist Party member in 1936. CBS and the sponsor, Philip Morris, were dismayed; they feared "trouble." The House committee on un-American activities began an inquiry. But a few days later Representative Donald Jackson of California, a member of the committee, announced that he had "cleared" her. *Broadcasting* reported: "LUCILLE BALL CLEARED OF COMMUNIST ASSOCIATION." It was explained that she *had* registered with the Communist Party, but only to please her grandfather. The case was quickly forgotten.

TELEVISION THEATER

While wars of McCarthyism rumbled on various levels, studio struggles between the migrations continued. Though episodic series had come to television from the radio world (and were being taken over by film makers) another kind of drama was largely the creation of theater people. During 1953 it was gathering strength and even brilliance. This was the anthology series.

Unlike the formula-bound episodic series, the anthology series emphasized diversity. The play was the thing. Actors were chosen to fit the play, not vice versa. The anthology series said to the writer: "Write us a play." There were no specifications as to mood, characters, plot, style, or locale—at least, not at first.

Lucille Ball and Desiderio Alberto Arnaz IV. UPI

Length was specified. And the play had to be producible as a live program in a gymnasium-sized studio. Except for such technical requirements, *Philco Television Playhouse*, *Goodyear Television Playhouse*, *Kraft Television Theater*, and other anthology series began as carte-blanche invitations to writers—and writers responded.

High fees were not the lure. During the most fertile period of the television anthologies—1953-55—writers generally received $1200 to $2500 for a one-hour script.

From the start, artists from the theater were active in the anthology series. The New York theater world, struggling to survive, comprised not only Broadway but also various peripheral theaters and workshops—notably Actors Studio—where actors and directors found challenges the Broadway theater seldom offered. At the workshops even established stars gathered to exercise and stretch their talents, and young actors received intensive training. From this dedicated environment the anthology programs drew such rising performers as Paul Newman, Sidney Poitier, Kim Stanley, Rod Steiger, Joanne Woodward, and such directors as Delbert Mann, Arthur Penn, Sidney Lumet.

The Philco and Goodyear series were broadcast Sunday evenings, not conflicting with theater performances—which at that time were forbidden on Sundays. Each program got seven or eight days of concentrated rehearsal—which Joanne Woodward would remember as "marvelous days." One reason they were marvelous was that a producer, not a committee, was in control. Fred Coe, producer of the Philco and Goodyear series, had established himself in television with experimental productions at the NBC studios during 1946-47. When Philco and Goodyear became alternate-week sponsors, he already commanded so much respect that neither sponsor nor advertising agency were inclined to interfere with him. For the moment, Coe was given his head. He chose directors, dealt with writers. Under his encouragement the talents of scores of writers and directors struck fire.

During 1953 programs of this sort included, in addition to the

Philco and Goodyear series, *Kraft Television Theater, Studio One, Robert Montgomery Presents, U.S. Steel Hour, Revlon Theater, Medallion Theater*. There was also *Omnibus*, set up by a Ford Foundation grant but carried on under commercial sponsorship—a 90-minute series of diverse elements, using scripts of various lengths. These series were later joined by *Motorola Playhouse, The Elgin Hour, Matinee Theater*, and *Playhouse 90*. Thus a sizable "open market" attracted the writer. What had been a trickle of scripts in 1952 became a deluge a year later. The various series were flooded with submissions—synopses and completed scripts. Writers came and went. Brilliant scripts arrived from surprising sources.

An advertising writer for women's garments, Reginald Rose, came to script editor Florence Britton at *Studio One* with a script titled *The Remarkable Incident at Carson Corners*, followed soon afterwards by *Thunder on Sycamore Street*, and suddenly found he had launched a new career. A thin-faced ex-paratrooper, Rod Serling, working at a Cincinnati radio station, sent a script to *Kraft Television Theater;* flying to New York for a script conference he nervously dropped his suitcase in the J. Walter Thompson office and scattered socks and underwear but sold *You Be the Bad Guy* and, soon afterwards, other scripts, including *Patterns*. An ex-novelist, David Davidson, gave *U.S. Steel Hour* its premiere script, *P.O.W.*

A landmark in the history of anthology series, and an inspiration to many writers, was Paddy Chayefsky's *Marty*, broadcast on *Goodyear Television Playhouse* on May 24, 1953. The role of Marty, a young butcher in the Bronx, was played by the unknown Rod Steiger, and the direction was by Delbert Mann.

Marty had a deceptive simplicity. "I tried to write the dialogue as if it had been wire-tapped," said Chayefsky. The talk had an infectiously natural rhythm. Marty says, "You want to go you should go." At the same time the play provided a crowded tapestry of metropolitan life: the Waverly Ballroom, the RKO Chester, an all-night beanery. The play opened in a butcher shop.

YOUNG MOTHER: Marty, I want a nice fat pullet, about four pounds. I hear your kid brother got married last Sunday.
MARTY: Yeah, it was a very nice affair, Missus Canduso.
YOUNG MOTHER: Marty, you ought to be ashamed. All your kid brothers and sisters, married and have children. When you gonna get married?

Pressures of this sort are also a factor in the talk on Saturdays, when the unattached young men gather with much male camaraderie—ritualistic, self-protective.

ANGIE: Well, what do you feel like doing tonight?
MARTY: I don't know, Angie. What do you feel like doing?

Marty is short and stocky. He calls himself "a fat little man." Girls have brushed him off often enough at the RKO Chester and elsewhere to make him cautious. He thinks he will stay home and watch Sid Caesar on television. How he finally puts on his blue suit and goes to the Waverly Ballroom, picks up a skinny schoolteacher whom his friends consider a "dog" and who doesn't impress his mother either; how their opinions halt his romance temporarily but how he finally pursues it—this is the story of *Marty*. When he does pursue it, we are not sure whether he is drawn mainly by his liking for the girl, or a feeling of identification with her (she too has been hurt), or whether he is escaping from the ritual of:

MARTY: I don't know, Angie. What do you feel like doing?

The choice of heroes and heroines defying Hollywood standards of beauty was a central aspect of Chayefsky's work, and important to its success. He sensed that television, with its potential for intimacy, offered opportunities for such a revolt, and the response bore him out. Rod Steiger could scarcely believe the impact of his own performance. "People from all over the country and all different walks of life, from different races and religions and creeds, sent me letters. The immense power of that medium!"

Chayefsky's work had wide influence on anthology drama—its successes and failures. During 1953-55 the riches came in profusion:

Marty, with Rod Steiger and Nancy Marchant—on *Goodyear Television Playhouse*.   State Historical Society of Wisconsin

The Philco-Goodyear series offered Chayefsky's *Holiday Song* (1953), *The Mother* (1954), *Bachelor's Party* (1955), and *A Catered Affair* (1955); Robert Alan Aurthur's *Man on a Mountaintop* (1954) and *A Man Is Ten Feet Tall* (1955); Horton Foote's *A Young Lady of Property* (1953); Gore Vidal's *Visit to a Small Planet* (1955). The *Studio One* series came up with Reginald Rose's *Thunder on Sycamore Street* (1954) and *Twelve Angry Men* (1954). The Kraft series had Serling's *Patterns* (1955). All these had a subsequent history.*

* All appeared in print: see Chayefsky, *Television Plays*; Rose, *Six Television Plays*; Serling, *Patterns*; Vidal (ed.), *Best Television Plays*. Feature

The structure of these plays related to circumstances under which they were produced. Such problems as costume changes and aging were unwelcome. This encouraged plays of tight structure, attacking a story close to its climax—very different from the loose, multiscene structure of films.

Ingenuity could ease the limitations. An actress could start a play wearing three dresses and peel them off en route between scenes. Color lighting could make painted wrinkles invisible in one scene, emphasize them in the next. A studio was sometimes crammed with small sets and fragments—telephone booths, park benches, street corners. Some producers—especially on *Studio One*—felt compelled to prove they could stage whole floods, as in Robert Anderson's *The Flood,* or sink an ocean liner, as in *A Night To Remember*, adapted by George Roy Hill and John Whedon from the book by Walter Lord. But amid such technical wizardry an actor was likely to become a zombie, and in the end it emphasized what others could do better. The Philco-Goodyear directors were not inclined to think of live production as a limiting factor; it merely influenced the kind of drama to be explored. They found its niche in compact rather than panoramic stories, in psychological rather than physical confrontations.

Close-ups became all-important. A Marty-Clare scene in an all-night cafeteria was played almost wholly in close-up. The human face became the stage on which drama was played.

To this close-up drama, live television brought an element that had almost vanished from film—one which few viewers noticed consciously but which undoubtedly exercised a hypnotic influence.

Film had long been dominated by its own kinds of time, made by splices in the editing room. The final tempo and rhythm were gen-

---

films of like title were made from *Marty, Bachelor's Party, A Catered Affair, Twelve Angry Men, Patterns; A Man Is Ten Feet Tall* became the film *Edge of the City.* Broadway plays were derived from *Twelve Angry Men, Visit to a Small Planet;* elements of *Holiday Song* turned up in *The Tenth Man.*

erally created not by an actor, nor by actors interacting, but by an editor and the director working with him. The possibilities of this kind of control had led to production methods in which films were shot in fragments—often as short as two or three seconds. A feature film might consist of seven or eight hundred shots. The manipulation of "film time" offered creative pleasures so beguiling to film makers that they had virtually abolished "real time" from the screen. Its appearance in long stretches of television drama gave a sense of the rediscovery of reality—especially for people whose only drama had been film.

When a play involved a number of sets, these were generally arranged around the periphery of the studio. In the middle the cameras—three or more—wheeled noiselessly from set to set, each tended by its cameraman, and each trailing behind it the long, black umbilical cord leading to the control room. Each camera had a turret of several lenses, so that its cameraman could, in a second or two, switch from close-up to medium or long shot. Each cameraman had in front of him, mounted on the camera, a list of the shots he would do during the play. Over earphones he got supplementary instructions from the control room. "A little tighter, Joe." A light on his camera told him—and others—when he was on the air. When it went off, he changed position and lens for his next shot. One camera was likely to be on a boom, which could take camera and cameraman sailing to a position above the action; this required an extra operator.

If a play had only one set, it might be in the middle of the studio so that cameras could roam on all sides. Some directors favored shots through specially planned apertures. A hinged picture might swing open to permit a through-the-wall camera angle, then close quickly for shots from the other side. Timing mishaps were part of the lore of live production.

Live television, like Ibsen theater, drove drama indoors. "Outdoor" sets looked artificial and tended to be avoided. In contrast, film was irresistibly drawn to outdoor drama and physical action.

Of Human Bondage, with Charlton Heston and Felicia Montealegre—on *Studio One.*
State Historical Society of Wisconsin

Paddy Chayefsky's own prefaces to his plays superbly articulated the feelings of many anthology writers. He wrote: "There is far more exciting drama in the reasons why a man gets married than in why he murders someone." He was just becoming aware, he wrote, of the "marvelous world of the ordinary."

That this "marvelous world" fascinated millions is abundantly clear from statistics. These plays—akin to genre paintings—held consistently high ratings. But one group hated them: the advertising profession. The reasons are not mysterious.

Most advertisers were selling magic. Their commercials posed the same problems that Chayefsky drama dealt with: people who feared failure in love and in business. But in the commercials there was always a solution as clear-cut as the snap of a finger: the problem could be solved by a new pill, deodorant, toothpaste, shampoo, shaving lotion, hair tonic, car, girdle, coffee, muffin recipe, or floor wax. The solution always had finality.

Chayefsky and other anthology writers took these same problems and made them complicated. They were forever suggesting that a problem might stem from childhood and be involved with feelings toward a mother or father. All this was often convincing—that was the trouble. It made the commercial seem fraudulent.

And then these non-beautiful heroes and heroines—they seemed a form of sabotage, as did the locales. Every manufacturer was trying to "upgrade" American consumers and their buying habits. People were being urged to "move up to Chrysler." Commercials showed cars and muffins and women to make the mouth water. A dazzling decor—in drama or commercial—could show what it meant to rise in the world. But the "marvelous world of the ordinary" seemed to challenge everything that advertising stood for.

Quite aside from the revulsion against lower-level settings and people, advertisers often felt uneasy about political implications. Such settings had a way of bringing economic problems to mind. And some writers kept edging into dangerous areas. In 1954, and increasingly in 1955, sponsors and their agencies began to demand

	% TV Homes	
Dragnet (NBC)	43.0	For December 1-7, 1954, Video-
I Love Lucy (CBS)	38.1	dex showed *Dragnet* leading *I*
You Bet Your Life (NBC)	34.9	*Love Lucy.* Comedy-variety re- mained strong. Leaders included
Jackie Gleason (CBS)	32.8	four anthology drama series, of
Ed Sullivan (CBS)	31.5	which three were live produc-
Studio One (CBS)	31.4	tions—*Studio One*, the Philco-
Bob Hope (NBC)	30.3	Goodyear *Television Playhouse*,
TV Playhouse (NBC)	29.0	and *Kraft Television Theater.*
Kraft Theater (NBC)	28.8	NBC was dominant network.
Ford Theater (NBC)	28.3	

drastic revisions and to take control of script problems. The result was a fascinating series of disputes and explosions.

Most were settled behind closed doors. A writer who brought a script quarrel to public attention risked his livelihood. But a few cases leaked out. They throw indirect light on pressures at work in the nation and the industry.

Reginald Rose's *Thunder on Sycamore Street*, broadcast on the Westinghouse *Studio One* series over CBS-TV, directed by Franklin Schaffner, was derived from an incident that took place in suburban Cicero, Illinois. A group of residents, disturbed to find a Negro family moving into their neighborhood, organized to get the family out. The resulting events received newsreel coverage.

Rose presented to *Studio One* a meticulous outline of a drama based on these events. He proposed that three small suburban houses be built side by side in the studio—virtually identical, with a neat patch of lawn for each. Action would move from one to another, showing the evolution of vigilante activity against the new family in the third house—the Negro family. In the end, a mild-mannered man in the second house would turn against his neighbors and take his stand with the new family.

As usual, Rose's plan was shrewdly organized, and enthusiastically received by the staff. It was approved with one proviso. Network, agency, and sponsor were all firm about it. The black family would have to be changed to "something else." A Negro as beleaguered protagonist of a television drama was declared unthinkable. It would, they said, appall southern viewers.

Rose first considered the demand a mortal blow, but persuaded himself otherwise. Wasn't *vigilantism*, after all, the essential theme? He agreed to make the neighbor an "ex-convict." The problem seemed to have been settled smoothly.

But Rose, to minimize the setback, adopted an ingenious strategy. The audience would not be allowed to know, throughout most of the play, why the new neighbor was unwanted. It would only be aware of the determination to get rid of him.

This evasive strategy turned the play into an extraordinary social Rorschach test. Comments indicated that viewers filled in the missing information according to their own predilections. Some at once assumed he was a communist; others, that he was a Puerto Rican, atheist, Jew, Catholic, Russian, or Oriental. The information that he was an ex-convict, mentioned with utmost brevity in the final act, was accepted as a logical supplementary detail. The sponsors found, with some uneasiness, that they had presented precisely the kind of controversial drama they had tried to avoid.

During 1954-55 anthology writers and directors found sponsors and their agencies increasingly intent on interfering with script matters, dictating changes, vetoing plot details. The series began a rapid decline. There were a few further moments of impressiveness, as in Serling's *Requiem for a Heavyweight*, a 1956 *Playhouse 90* offering, but most leading anthology talents were turning elsewhere—some to Broadway, but many in other directions. The year 1955 saw the appearance of the motion picture version of *Marty*, again directed by Delbert Mann. It won four Oscars, including the Best Picture of the Year award, and got the Grand Prix at the Cannes film festival. A worldwide success, it had been produced independently on a low budget. The deflation in big-studio production during the Hollywood panic and the resulting shortage of features encouraged such projects. The triumph of *Marty* drew a parade of anthology talent into similar ventures, for which backing was suddenly available. Besides Delbert Mann, such directors as Arthur Penn, Sidney Lumet, and John Frankenheimer moved into a new arena.

Ironically, while sponsors were beginning to exert a choke-hold on anthology drama, feature films were winning new freedom. In 1952 the U.S. Supreme Court had reached the belated conclusion that film was a part of the press and, as such, endowed with a constitutionally guaranteed freedom. This threw doubt on the legality of the long-established state and local censor boards. During the 1950's a number of these boards disappeared—with mixed results. Films of the sort once reserved for stag parties took over many theaters, and flourished. At the same time, independent production became the magnet for any director who wanted to deal with a subject without compromise. Film, when at its best, gained strength even as television was losing it.

If artists were deserting the live anthology series, so were sponsors. In 1955 Philco switched to a Hollywood-produced series, and others followed. A few New York anthology series hung on, but with a sense of doom. The *U.S. Steel Hour*, a survivor for a few years, relied increasingly on commissioned adaptations—a policy that tended to shut out new talent. Unsolicited work ceased to be a major source of material.

The death of the live anthology was Hollywood's gain; the trend was to film. The anthology form survived to some extent on film, but was eclipsed by filmed episodic series of upbeat decor, preferred by most sponsors. Identification with a continuing, attractive actor had merchandising advantages, and some actors were willing to do commercials. Above all, the series *formula* offered security: each program was a variation of an approved ritual. Solutions, as in commercials, could be clearcut.

The years 1954-55, which saw the fall of the anthology, also marked an increase in blacklist pressures. A new group calling itself Aware, Inc., formed late in 1953, had joined the war on the "communist conspiracy in the entertainment world." One of its leaders was Vincent W. Hartnett, the one-time *Gangbusters* assistant who had allied himself with Laurence Johnson of the Syracuse supermarkets. Hartnett carried on a constant search for additions to his lists, and managed to generate considerable uneasiness and indignation. But criticism of "anti-communist" warfare was no longer considered safe—it "helped the communists." Dan Petrie, a director for *Studio One, U.S. Steel Hour*, and other anthology series, received a phone call at two o'clock one morning. He and his wife were awakened from sound sleep.

"Hello?"

"Hello. This is Dan Petrie?"

"Yes."

"You the director?"

"Yes. Who is this?"

"Never mind who I am. Do you have a wife who's tall and blonde?"

"Yes, I do. Now who's calling? What are you calling at this hour for?"

"I just want to give you a little piece of advice, Mr. Petrie. You better tell your wife to be careful about how she talks about the blacklist at cocktail parties."

(CLICK)

Amid such maneuvers, the dying New York anthology series was not likely to become a rallying point against blacklists, vigilantism, McCarthyism—especially in the absence of any sign of support from the executive level.

If there was to be resistance, it would have to come from another sector of the program world. And it did.

HOPSCOTCHING

Television news, at the start of 1953, was an unpromising phenomenon. Its main showpiece on NBC was still the 15-minute, early-
evening *Camel News Caravan* with John Cameron Swayze—whom
Broadcasting eulogized that year as "the best dressed TV news
commentator . . . whose suave handling of the news matches perfectly his handsome face and impeccable garb"—and the early-
morning *Today* series, in which David Garroway was still abetted
by the charismatic chimpanzee, J. Fred Muggs. The main CBS-TV
news offering was still the 15-minute, early-evening *Television
News with Douglas Edwards*. Like *Camel News Caravan*, it tended
to be thin, but suavely produced.

The two evening series had changed somewhat since their 1948
beginnings. Switches to correspondents in other cities—an inheritance from radio rather than from newsreels—had assumed increasing importance. But the main substance of the programs continued
to be newsfilm items threaded by an anchorman.

The series no longer depended on Fox and Telenews film crews.
The networks had gradually come to terms with film unions and
built their own newsfilm staffs—first NBC, then CBS, then ABC.
The staffs came largely from the theatrical newsreels, which shrank
as their moment in history passed.

Like the newsreels in their heyday, the networks now tried to
maintain one or more film crews in such principal centers as New
York, Washington, Chicago, Los Angeles, London, Paris, Rome.
A newsfilm crew consisted of two or three men. Many other places
were covered by "stringers"—often cameramen attached to foreign
film units, who could do some shooting on the side, or retired cameramen who liked to keep busy. The stringer, in accord with newsreel tradition, was paid for footage used; in important spots he
might also get a retainer. He received new film to replace film sent

in, whether used or not. When sending a fragment of a reel, he received a full reel to replace it; this alone was enough to encourage submissions.

Each of these series managed to fill its time with interesting and diverting material, and viewers were not particularly aware of shortcomings. But for presenting "the" news, crews and stringers in a few dozen cities were ludicrously inadequate in number, while the tools of their trade were often irrelevant. Except for catastrophes of some duration—fires, floods, wars—the crews were usually "covering" predictable events, many of which had been staged for the purpose—press conferences, submarine christenings, cornerstone layings, beauty contests, campaign speeches, ribbon cuttings, dam dedications, air force demonstrations, high society events, award banquets. Many matters of greater importance were handled by— as Swayze put it—"hopscotching the world for headlines."

A favorite pronouncement of the day was that television had added a "new dimension" to newscasting. The truth of this concealed a more serious fact: the camera, as arbiter of news value, had introduced a drastic curtailment of the scope of news. The notion that a picture was worth a thousand words meant, in practice, that footage of Atlantic City beauty winners, shot at some expense, was considered more valuable than a thousand words from Eric Sevareid on the mounting tensions of Southeast Asia. Analysis, a staple of radio news in its finest days, was being shunted aside as non-visual.

While all this introduced a distortion of values, a more serious problem was the news management involved in staged events. Behind every planned event was a planner—and a government or business purpose. Television dependence on such events gave the planner considerable leverage on news content. This might be especially serious in the case of foreign news, often based on scant information. A crisis in Iran, for example, might be explained—with apparent objectivity—in a 40-second filmed statement made at a State Department press conference. The extent to which reliance on such items might color—and limit—American conceptions of distant events was hardly guessed at this time.

Aside from such problems, *Camel News Caravan* had a few special distortions of its own. Introduced at the request of the sponsor, they were considered minor aspects of good manners rather than of news corruption. No news personage could be shown smoking a cigar—except Winston Churchill, whose world role gave him special dispensation from Winston-Salem. Shots of "no smoking" signs were forbidden.

What was missing from the newsfilm pictures? So much, obviously, that the problem defied consideration. Happenings in places away from crews or stringers tended to become non-events. This was true of almost anything in Africa, which was generally considered to be "covered" from Rome, with help from a few scattered stringers.

The old newsreel addiction to imperial and ecclesiastical panoply persisted strongly in the television news stories. This was illustrated by a bizarre inter-network contest of 1953, with results that were considered a triumph at the time. The date for the coronation of Elizabeth II of England was set months ahead, and NBC-TV at once decided to make it a breakthrough television event. The aim was to get footage on the air within hours of the ceremony—particularly, ahead of CBS. NBC began working with experimenters at the Massachusetts Institute of Technology—the people at the Eastman Company said the plan was not feasible—to build a portable film developer for rapid use on location. The result was a box —about four feet square, two feet high—that could develop 100 feet of film in 25 minutes. Its secret chemical formula had to be mixed on the spot and used fresh; David Klein carried the formula in his wallet. Four such developers were shipped to England by boat and set up in a Quonset hut near an airfield outside London. Here NBC technicians also placed a television set, which they tuned to the BBC coverage of the events in Westminster Abbey. This BBC coverage was photographed from the television tube, and within an hour the developed film was on a chartered DC-6 from which the seats had been removed—replaced by bolted-down editing equipment. Editing went on as the plane sped westward via the great circle route, skirted Greenland, refueled at Gander, landed at Boston. From there the film was put on the NBC-TV network, beating CBS-TV. It was hailed as a coup, even though it was actually BBC coverage, reprocessed. Ironically ABC-TV, which had not entered the race, won it. BBC pictures reached Canada before the NBC plane arrived in Boston. ABC-TV, taking a Canadian Broadcasting Corporation telecast via cable, scooped its rivals by minutes.

There was some British indignation over American television commercials exploiting the event. An automobile had been praised for its "royal carriage"; another was called "queen of the road." Juxtaposition of coronation footage with *Today*'s J. Fred Muggs also brought expressions of outrage. There was a special reason for this hubbub: it was, in part, an attempt to block the imminent introduction of American-style commercial television in Britain, which some resisted on grounds of vulgarity and triviality.

Dissatisfaction with newsreel superficialities, and their addiction to pseudo-events, existed among both film and broadcasting people. In theaters *The March of Time* films, which appeared from 1935 to 1951, had aimed at something more significant. Avoiding spot news, they had tried to expose underlying issues. Differing sharply from most newsreels, they were regarded as belonging to the documentary rather than the newsreel tradition. The television series *See It Now*, which Edward R. Murrow and Fred W. Friendly had launched in November 1951—as *The March of Time* was dying—had a somewhat similar purpose. They had, however, begun cautiously in their choice of subject matter. The first telecast, for which they spent $3000 on a video line to San Francisco to show the Golden Gate Bridge and Brooklyn Bridge simultaneously on a split screen, was symptomatic. They felt awed by their new medium and needed to spend time exclaiming over the wonder of it.

And they had to find out, by trial and error, what could be done with it.

During their first year they were babes in the wood. Knowing nothing about film, they did as the newscast producers had done, and turned to newsreel personnel. Palmer Williams, a veteran of the Signal Corps Pictorial Center who had worked on the *Army-Navy Screen Magazine* during World War II, joined them and became an indispensable member of the operation. They also contracted with the Hearst-MGM News of the Day for camera work and other technical services on a cost-plus basis, and library footage as needed.

During its first two years *See It Now* examined a number of issues, but not that of rampant McCarthyism. That Murrow, a symbol of courage during World War II, should ignore such a subject troubled many people. Some accused him of having settled into comfortable affluence, to which he answered, "You may be right." He used the same words to those who said he should get behind Senator McCarthy, as some newsmen and executives were doing. It seemed to Friendly that Murrow was husbanding his energies for some decisive action, on a battlefield to be chosen with care.

Late in 1953 the action began.

THE MURROW MOMENT

One October day, at lunch time, Murrow handed Friendly a wrinkled clipping. "Here, read this." It concerned Lieutenant Milo Radulovich, aged twenty-six, a University of Michigan student who was in the Air Force Reserve as a meteorologist, and who had been asked to resign his commission because his sister and father had been accused—by unidentified accusers—of radical leanings. When Radulovich refused to resign, an Air Force board at Selfridge Field had ordered his separation on security grounds.

A *See It Now* staff member, Joe Wershba, was sent to Detroit to gather further information. He read the transcript of the Air Force hearing and talked to Radulovich, his family, and their neighbors. At Wershba's urging, Murrow then dispatched a News of the Day camera crew to film their statements. A day later Murrow and Friendly began to look at shipments of film. Lieutenant Radulovich in a filmed statement said that the Air Force had in no way questioned his loyalty but had told him that his father and sister had allegedly read "subversive newspapers" and engaged in activities that were "questionable." These activities had not been specified.

RADULOVICH: The actual charge against me is that I had maintained a close and continuing relationship with my dad and my sister over the years.

In another film sequence the lieutenant's father, a Serbian immigrant, read a letter he said he had written to President Eisenhower. "Mr. President . . . they are doing a bad thing to Milo. . . . He has given all his growing years to his country. . . . I am an old man. I have spent my life in this coal mine and auto furnaces. I ask nothing for myself." He asked only "justice for my boy."

It became clear that the family and acquaintances of Lieutenant Radulovich were ready and willing to talk, but that no Air Force spokesman, in Detroit or Washington, would say a word. It became a question of whether *See It Now*, being unable to present "both" sides, should drop the case. Discussion programs regularly dropped issues unless "both" sides could be presented. But Murrow regarded this as a dubious policy since it allowed one side, by silence, to veto a broadcast discussion.

Murrow decided to proceed and notified CBS management that the title of the next *See It Now* broadcast would be "The Case Against Milo Radulovich, A0589839." He also notified the Air Force at the Pentagon and continued to urge its participation. *See It Now* wanted to do a balanced job of reporting, the Air Force was told. This could be difficult if the Air Force refused to comment, but *See It Now* would in any case do its best. All this brought a visit by an Air Force general and a lieutenant colonel to the office of Edward R. Murrow—who asked Friendly to join them.

The dialogue was cordial and restrained. The general seemed to consider it unlikely that the broadcast would ever get on the air. The fact that Murrow had once won the Distinguished Service to Airpower award was mentioned. The visitors considered Murrow an Air Force friend, and wanted him to know that. The general concluded: "You have always gotten complete cooperation from us, and we know you won't do anything to alter that." Murrow stared quietly at the general.

Because of the importance they attached to the case, the *See It Now* producers asked CBS to provide newspaper advertising for the telecast, but the management declined. Murrow and Friendly made an unusual decision: they withdrew $1500 from their own bank accounts for an advertisement in the New York *Times*. It did not carry the CBS symbol—the eye. It was signed, "Ed Murrow and Fred Friendly."

The relation of Murrow to CBS management was a very special one. His World War II broadcasts from London and his role in building a European news staff had been key factors in establishing CBS leadership in the radio news field. During this period William Paley, while working in London in Psychological Warfare, had come to know Murrow personally and to admire him. Murrow, returning from Europe, became a member of the CBS board of directors. In 1953, in addition to co-producing *See It Now*, he was on the air each evening, Monday to Friday, as a radio newscaster.

As co-producer of *See It Now* he was technically responsible to Sig Mickelson, who headed all CBS television news operations. But the relationship was a pro forma one, involving some discomfort for both Murrow and Mickelson. In practice, Murrow had almost total autonomy. Even CBS president Frank Stanton was not likely to attempt to limit it. But it was a position of power that Murrow had scarcely tested. In "The Case Against Milo Radulovich, A0589839" he was doing so and was aware of it. Before air time, after a prebroadcast gulp of scotch, he told Friendly: "I don't know whether we'll get away with this one or not . . . things will never be the same around here after tonight. . . ."

The circumstances under which *See It Now* was assembled and telecast in 1953 were primitive. As with drama, studios planned for radio were proving disastrously inadequate for television needs, and program operations were spilling out of headquarters into makeshift facilities in every corner of town. The "Radulovich" material, shot in Michigan and developed in a laboratory on Ninth Avenue in New York, was assembled in a special *See It Now* cutting room in a loft at 550 Fifth Avenue. The Murrow off-camera narration—but not his final comment, or "tail piece"—was recorded in a radio studio near his office at CBS headquarters at 485 Madison Avenue. This was then mixed via telephone wire with the other sound elements at the Fifth Avenue facility. For the telecast all the material was then taken to the CBS Grand Central studios where many other CBS programs also went on the air. Here there was always anxiety over whether the film and the composite sound track would synchronize properly; sometimes the film slipped "out of sync." The final tail piece by Murrow—on camera—was done live from Grand Central, after the film.

The insane pressure involved in this process always put Murrow on the air in high tension, which communicated itself to all concerned. In "The Case Against Milo Radulovich A0589839," the tension was especially felt. All were aware that Murrow was not merely probing the judicial processes of the Air Force and Pentagon—a quixotic venture few broadcasters would have undertaken at this time—but was examining the whole syndrome of McCarthyism with its secret denunciations and guilt by association. They were also aware that the disease was not peculiar to government but had virulently infected the broadcasting industry—including CBS.

Lieutenant Milo Radulovich, in his quiet way, suggested the meaning of the case.

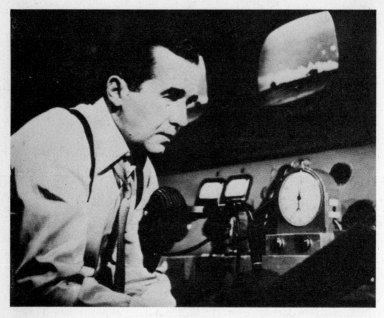

Edward R. Murrow on *See It Now*—telecast from Grand Central Studio.
Wide World

RADULOVICH: If I am going to be judged by my relatives, are my children going to be asked to denounce me? . . . Are they going to have to explain to their friends why their father's a security risk? . . . This is a chain reaction if the thing is let stand . . . I see a chain reaction that has no end.

In his tail piece Murrow offered the Air Force facilities for any comments, criticism, or correction it might care to make in regard to the case. He then suggested that the armed forces should be more frank concerning their procedures. He added:

MURROW: Whatever happens in this whole area of the relationship between the individual and the state, we will do ourselves; it cannot be blamed upon Malenkov, Mao Tse-tung or even our allies.

It seems to us—that is, to Fred Friendly and myself—that it is a subject that should be argued about endlessly. . . .

Friendly has described Murrow as "bathed in sweat and smoke" as *See It Now* staff members and engineers crowded to shake his hands. Some had tears in their eyes. The phones began ringing. For days congratulatory telegrams and letters poured in. A few newspaper columnists denounced the program, but there were many paeans of praise. Not a word of comment came from CBS management.

The program had given Murrow a momentum that now would not let him go. In Indianapolis a group of citizens had rented a civic auditorium for a meeting to organize a local chapter of the American Civil Liberties Union. The noted civil liberties lawyer Arthur Garfield Hays was to speak. But local units of the American Legion and other groups became indignant and managed to work up enough pressure to force cancellation of the hall, and to block use of several other halls. A Roman Catholic priest, Father Victor Goosens, finally offered his church for the Civil Liberties meeting.

See It Now dispatched camera crews to Indianapolis to film both the Civil Liberties meeting and an American Legion meeting denouncing the Civil Liberties meeting. The November 24, 1953, program on *See It Now*, "Argument at Indianapolis," was a brilliant intercutting of the two meetings. It was also memorable for another—and totally unexpected—reason. The day of the broadcast brought much telephoning between New York and Washington. That night the opening of the *See It Now* program was postponed for an announcement. Murrow introduced Secretary of the Air Force Harold E. Talbott in a statement filmed that day. Talbott said he had reviewed the case of Lieutenant Radulovich and decided he was not a security risk. "I have, therefore, directed that Radulovich be retained in his present status in the United States Air Force."

Although it left the loyalty-security apparatus untouched, the decision was an extraordinary triumph for *See It Now*, of which

CBS had reason to be proud. But CBS management seemed more aware of rising friction. There were increasing anti-Murrow pressures on the *See It Now* sponsor, Alcoa. Attacks on CBS were a regular feature of the Hearst newspapers, and particularly a specialty of television columnist Jack O'Brian, who delighted in attacking "Murrow and his partner in port-sided reporting, Mr. Friendly." Some CBS affiliates were also becoming restive. But Murrow was not drawing back. Many looked to him for sanity amid hysteria.

In October 1953 Murrow launched a second television series, *Person to Person*—in a sense, a spin-off of *See It Now*. On two *See It Now* programs Murrow had paid a "television visit" to a celebrity. The celebrity, allowing television cameras to prowl his home, would lead the way, show treasured possessions, and answer questions asked by Murrow from a CBS studio. This became the *Person to Person* formula, and it brought out a different aspect of the Murrow personality. Here he was the urbane man of the world, intimate of the great. For celebrities the *Person to Person* visits had a public-relations aspect, which seemed to control the kinds of questions used. The series was seldom controversial; it had a *Vogue* and *House Beautiful* appeal, along with a voyeuristic element. It immediately developed a large audience rating—larger than *See It Now*. Some Murrow admirers deplored its superficial, chic quality, but its commercial success clearly strengthened his position at CBS. Asked by the actor John Cassavetes—who, with his wife, had been booked for a *Person to Person* visit—why he did "this kind of show," Murrow answered: "To do the show I want to do, I have to do the show that I don't want to do." Although Murrow probably enjoyed *Person to Person* more than this remark would seem to indicate, it was clearly *See It Now* that dominated his thinking and his life.

It was perhaps inevitable that *See It Now* should eventually take up the subject of Senator McCarthy himself. During 1953 Murrow suggested that the staff gather all available McCarthy footage, and from time to time he and Friendly studied the growing accumulation. McCarthy had long kept opponents off-balance by bewildering tactics. He often waved sheafs of paper which he called "documentation," but no one ever learned what the papers contained. In subsequent appearances he would shift to new charges, and again seize headlines. The *See It Now* producers decided on a simple compilation that would speak for itself. Murrow would add only brief comments.

When the Murrow-Friendly team informed CBS that the March 9, 1954, broadcast would concern Senator Joseph McCarthy and again asked for advertising support, the management again declined. Once more Murrow and Friendly personally paid for an advertisement in the New York *Times*. It said: "Tonight at 10:30 on *See It Now*, a report on Senator Joseph R. McCarthy over Channel 2. Fred W. Friendly and Edward R. Murrow, co-producers."

At the start of the program, in the control room, Friendly found his hand was shaking so hard that when he tried to start his stopwatch, he missed the button completely on the first try. The program ended with words by Murrow.

MURROW: As a nation we have come into our full inheritance at a tender age. We proclaim ourselves—as indeed we are—the defenders of freedom, what's left of it, but we cannot defend freedom abroad by deserting it at home. The actions of the junior Senator from Wisconsin have caused alarm and dismay amongst our allies abroad and given considerable comfort to our enemies, and whose fault is that? Not really his. He didn't create this situation of fear; he merely exploited it, and rather successfully. Cassius was right: "The fault, dear Brutus, is not in our stars but in ourselves . . ." Good night, and good luck.

If the program was damaging to McCarthy, it was partly because Murrow himself had said so little. Senator McCarthy had done most of the talking. He was offered time to reply, but would seem to be replying to himself. Yet he decided to do so. A script was prepared with the help of McCarthy advisers, including commentator

George Sokolsky, and filmed at Fox Movietone studios at a cost
of $6,336.99—which CBS paid. It was telecast April 6 at the regular
See It Now time, and made a strong attack on Murrow.

MC CARTHY: Now, ordinarily I would not take time out from the
important work at hand to answer Murrow. However, in this case
I feel justified in doing so because Murrow is a symbol, the leader
and the cleverest of the jackal pack which is always found at the
throat of anyone who dares to expose individual communists and
traitors.

The *See It Now* McCarthy programs inevitably polarized opinion. Some felt that the Senator's reply had been totally ineffectual.
Others felt quite otherwise.

Friendly was surprised when CBS president Frank Stanton, a
few days afterwards, invited him into his office. He showed
Friendly a survey which CBS had commissioned the Elmo Roper
organization to make. It sampled opinion on the Friday and Saturday after the McCarthy rebuttal. Stanton seemed disturbed about
the results, to which he evidently attached great importance. They
showed that 59 per cent of those questioned had seen the program
or heard about it; of these, 33 per cent believed that McCarthy had
raised doubts about Murrow, or proved him pro-communist.

To Friendly, the findings had a different meaning than to Stanton. Friendly suggested that if the figures had been even more
favorable to McCarthy, they would have demonstrated even more
compellingly the need for the original program. It was not a reaction that Stanton was likely to appreciate.

See It Now offered still other programs touching on McCarthyism—including one of particular significance. In his reply to
Murrow, McCarthy had, as usual, shifted to new, sensational
charges. He hinted that the hydrogen bomb, recently added to the
United States arsenal of weapons, had been delayed eighteen
months by "traitors in our government." Soon afterwards J. Robert
Oppenheimer, who had been one of the creators of the atom bomb
but had opposed a crash program to perfect the even more destruc-

tive hydrogen bomb, was suddenly stripped of his security clearance by the Atomic Energy Commission. He was, in a sense, forbidden access to scientific secrets he himself had unlocked and made meaningful. The board of inquiry went through the usual, perplexing ritual of stating that Oppenheimer's loyalty was beyond question; it was a matter of "security."

On January 4, 1955, *See It Now* offered "A Conversation With Dr. J. Robert Oppenheimer"—a long filmed interview made at the Institute for Advanced Study in Princeton. Oppenheimer did not refer to the security ruling but discussed on a philosophic plane the implications of increasing government control over research and its bearing on the freedom of the human mind and the future of man on earth.

Murrow took the unusual step of inviting board chairman William Paley to look at the film in workprint stage. Paley was moved, impressed, enthusiastic. Nevertheless the co-producers had to dig into their own pockets again to advertise the program. And once more *See It Now* precipitated furious attacks, including a denunciation from George Sokolsky in his Hearst newspaper column, and pressures on CBS and Alcoa. But to many it was one of the mightiest hours ever seen on television. There was no hint of the arrogance some scientists ascribed to Oppenheimer; instead there was fragility, dedication, tension, and an unsparing urge to dig to the heart of issues. There were no easy slogans. The reaction among educators was overwhelming; praises showered on the producers and on CBS. Prints of the film remained in demand for years.

The sequence of *See It Now* programs on McCarthyism—1953-55—had extraordinary impact. They placed Murrow in the forefront of the documentary film movement; he was hailed as its television pioneer. There were, of course, others: impressive documentaries came occasionally from the NBC *Project Twenty* unit that had produced *Victory at Sea;* from the *Omnibus* series; and at CBS from a documentary unit in the news division, led by Irving Gitlin. But their work was, for the moment, overshadowed by the triumphs of *See It Now*. Coming at the same time as the finest of the anthology programs, the Murrow documentaries helped to make television an indispensable medium. Few people now dared to be without a television set, and few major advertisers dared to be unrepresented on the home screen.

The McCarthy programs had many effects—the first, on McCarthy himself. They set the stage for televised hearings on his dispute with the Army. These began April 22, on the heels of the Murrow-McCarthy exchange, and proved the decisive blow to the Senator's career. A whole nation watched him in murderous close-up—and recoiled.

The hearings opened murky vistas of the great in action. David Schine, Roy Cohn's companion in harassments on behalf of McCarthy, and also heir to a hotel fortune, had been drafted, and Cohn had importuned the Secretary of the Army and his aides for special favors for Schine.

The Secretary was not entirely averse. He even, at David's invitation, paid a visit to the Schine suite at the Waldorf Towers in New York to discuss a possible assignment for the young man as "special assistant" to the Secretary. But the Army, while negotiating on these matters, was dilatory and coy, with the result that McCarthy began to berate it for using Schine as a "hostage" to obtain favors from McCarthy—such as calling off his inquiry into subversion at Fort Monmouth. The hearings became a Roman candle shooting out sparks of charge and innuendo; in the end, the close-up exposure left a feeling of distaste for many of the participants, but especially for McCarthy. By the end of the year the Senate passed a vote condemning McCarthy, 67 to 22.

The second effect was on the American Broadcasting Company. Its merger with the Paramount theater chain, completed in 1953, had strengthened the network, but ABC-TV was still a weak third, and was not yet giving its affiliates a daytime schedule. It would have to do so to become competitive.

The Murrow-McCarthy conflict prepared the moment. In April

Senator Joseph R. McCarthy and aide Roy Cohn—during Army-McCarthy
hearings.   Wide World

1954 it was the ABC-TV network that carried the hearings in full.
CBS-TV and NBC-TV, already well provided with daytime programs and sponsors, carried only excerpts. ABC-TV, carrying the
full hearings, riveted national attention. Winning impressive ratings,
it began to make daytime sales and to challenge its rivals.

Another effect was on News of the Day, the newsreel owned
jointly by Hearst and MGM. Throughout the Murrow-McCarthy
struggle the camera work, editing and sound-recording for *See It
Now* were done by Hearst-MGM personnel. Meanwhile Hearst
newspapers, unaware of the irony, were especially virulent in their
attacks on the series, as well as on other CBS news programs. Along
with Murrow, a constant and favorite target was Don Hollenbeck,
who broadcast a weekly analysis of the press, *CBS Views the Press,*

which Murrow had helped launch and admired. Hollenbeck, ill and harried by the ceaseless attacks, committed suicide. Hearst columnist Jack O'Brian wrote that his suicide "does not remove from the record the peculiar history of leftist slanting of news . . . he was a special protégé of Edward R. Murrow, and as such, apparently beyond criticism or reasonable discipline. He drew assignments which paid him lush fees, pink-painting his news items and analysis and always with a steady left hand." Murrow, a pallbearer at Hollenbeck's funeral, decided to end the Hearst relationship. All the technicians resigned from News of the Day to join *See It Now*.

A final effect was on Murrow himself and all he represented. The television excitements of 1953-55 and rising audience statistics were bringing many new sponsors into television. They wanted television time and programs, but generally not of the *See It Now* type. News and documentary were being pushed toward the edges of the schedule. Murrow himself, though at the height of his fame, and winner of more awards than any other broadcaster, felt a stab of ill omen on the night of June 7, 1955. Awaiting the start of a *See It Now* broadcast—on cigarettes and cancer—he watched the preceding program, the premiere of a new series. Horrified by what he saw, he predicted its overwhelming success. He said to Friendly: "Any bets on how long we'll keep this time period now?" The program was *The $64,000 Question*.

BIGGEST MONEY

For months Charles Revson, president of Revlon, had looked for a vehicle for a big, resounding television plunge, because Hazel Bishop lipsticks, on the strength of early television success, were "murdering" Revlon.

In 1955 Walter Craig, ex-vaudeville hoofer and writer turned television producer, became partner in a new advertising agency,

Norman, Craig & Kummel. The moment he heard the idea for *The $64,000 Question*, brought to him by Steve Carlin of Louis G. Cowan, Inc.—an independent producer—Craig could not contain his excitement. He managed to communicate some of his fever to Charles Revson, whose account he hoped to capture, and next morning got representatives of Revlon, of Louis G. Cowan, Inc., and of the CBS network into one office.

> I locked the door . . . and I said, very dramatically, "Nobody leaves this room till we have a signed contract." Well, I had the lawyers for everybody concerned in the room at that time—there must have been twenty of us. And about one o'clock a knock came on the door, and it was Norman, and he said, "How are you doing?" And I said, "You'd better have some lunch sent in, because we're going to stay till we get a contract." And we did have lunch sent in, and we signed the contract at four o'clock the next morning. . . .

The basic idea of the series was to hold contestants over several weeks to make possible an unprecedented cash award. For years quiz programs had given small cash prizes—such as $64—or merchandise prizes, donated by manufacturers in return for mention of the brand names. Now it was proposed to make a quantum jump in prize-giving. Before four o'clock in the morning, other details had been resolved. On *The $64,000 Question* a losing contestant, as "consolation prize," would get a Cadillac. Contestants would be entombed in a glass "isolation booth" as a security measure. A "trust officer" from a prominent bank would certify to the inviolability of the proceedings—in exchange for a program credit.

When *The $64,000 Question*, "biggest jackpot program in radio-TV history," opened, the results were sensational. The reviewer of the magazine *Broadcasting* described himself as in a dazed state. Ratings began high and climbed higher. On each program actress Wendy Barrie did stylish commercials for a new Revlon product, Living Lipstick, but in September the Living Lipstick message was suddenly omitted and a commercial for Touch and Glow Liquid

Make-up Foundation substituted because, it was explained, Living Lipstick was sold out everywhere. Stores were phoning the factory with desperate pleas for additional shipments. Hal March, master of ceremonies, pleaded with the public to be patient. The program was drawing a 49.6 Trendex rating, with an 84.8 per cent share of audience. A Marine captain, Richard S. McCutchen, having survived several appearances as a contestant, seemed to have the whole nation rooting for him. Bookmakers were said to be quoting odds on whether he would answer the climactic $64,000 question. It was said that Las Vegas casinos emptied during the Tuesday evening programs. A convention of wholesale druggists in White Sulphur Springs, West Virginia, was halted for the announcement: "The Marine has answered the question!" The druggists cheered wildly before going on with their business. Louis Cowan, packager of the series, was asked to join CBS and became its vice president in charge of "creative services."

In January 1956 board chairman Raymond Spector of Hazel Bishop, Inc., explained ruefully to stockholders that the surprising 1955 loss was "due to circumstances beyond our control." He said that during the preceding six months "a new television program sponsored by your company's principal competitor captured the imagination of the public."

Within months the series had imitators—*The Big Surprise* arrived late in 1955, followed soon by *The $64,000 Challenge*—under the same auspices as *The $64,000 Question*—and *High Finance, Treasure Hunt, Twenty-One, The Most Beautiful Girl in the World, Giant Step, Can Do, Nothing But the Truth*. At one point *The $64,000 Question* and *The $64,000 Challenge* held first and second places in rating lists. When Charles Van Doren, a Columbia University English instructor, began appearing on *Twenty-One*, the series climbed among the leaders. Winnings kept getting larger: Charles Van Doren's $129,000 on *Twenty-One* was quickly topped by Teddy Nadler's $152,000 on *The $64,000 Challenge* and Robert Strom's $160,000 on *The $64,000 Question*.

	Rating
$64,000 Question (CBS)	35.2
Gunsmoke (CBS)	34.0
I've Got a Secret (CBS)	31.9
Twenty-One (NBC)	31.5
Ed Sullivan (CBS)	31.4
What's My Line (CBS)	31.2
Lawrence Welk (ABC)	30.2
$64,000 Challenge (CBS)	27.7
Alfred Hitchcock (CBS)	27.1
Studio One (CBS)	26.0

In July 1957 the ARB ratings of the American Research Bureau reflected rampant quiz fever. Five of top ten were quizzes. CBS, with several leading quizzes, dominated ratings. ABC had foothold with Lawrence Welk.

The atmosphere of television was changing. In 1955 Alcoa decided to drop *See It Now* for something different—perhaps fictional or "like the Ed Sullivan program." This was ascribed to an increasingly competitive consumer-goods market.

That summer William Paley had a suggestion for Murrow. Would it not be a fine idea, instead of having *See It Now* each week, to do it now and then? It might be a 60-minute program or even, occasionally, a 90-minute program. Wasn't thirty minutes, after all, too confining? Would it not be more satisfying to do fewer programs, in greater depth?

It was a shrewd approach. Murrow and Friendly were exhausted, and the notion of longer, fewer programs held attractions. Yet the move was the first step toward edging *See It Now* out of the picture. The period long held by *See It Now* was sold to Liggett & Myers for a quiz program.

The Paley move had another element of shrewdness. The occasional program—the "spectacular"—was finding favor in television. In some quarters it was considered the wave of the future, thanks to the virtuoso salesmanship of an executive at another network—Pat Weaver of NBC.

EXECUTIVE SUITES

Early in 1953 Sarnoff—General Sarnoff—became troubled about NBC, which seemed in organizational confusion. Several NBC presidents had proved unsatisfactory, and the network apparently had morale problems.

These stemmed partly from its status as a fragment of a large organization with diverse interests, and also from Sarnoff's own style of leadership. He had become a remote executive. Lesser executives, including the NBC president, hesitated to phone him about a problem. They addressed him in formal memoranda on which he might pencil brief answers—"Yes!"—"No!"—or "PSM," meaning "please see me." An appointment was a sort of audience. When angry, Sarnoff could show an icy reserve more frightening than an explosion of anger. The back of his neck would grow red. When he spoke, it was in well-constructed prose, without the slightest hesitation.

His neat desk reflected a well-organized mind. But the fifty-third floor neatness did not penetrate to lower floors. Sarnoff seemed to avoid defining lines of authority. It was as though he wanted to see who would scrap his way to the top, as he had done in his remarkable career.

While his office was physically close to NBC, which inhabited lower floors of the same Radio City building, Sarnoff had a more obsessive interest in the research and manufacturing role of RCA. This had long focused on the creation of a television industry, but World War II and the cold war had brought RCA back to its original concerns. Its income, which had stood at a million in 1920, would reach a billion by 1955, when Senator Lyndon B. Johnson would refer to the company as "a key element in our defense structure." Sarnoff kept in touch with government leaders, and wrote long memoranda on possible weaponry: use of electronics to detect and intercept incoming missiles; use of television, the new "eyes of the top command," to coordinate military action on land, sea, or in the air; and the potentialities of weapons-carrying satellites, applicable to atomic or germ warfare. He wrote constantly on the communist threat to world peace. He aided government anti-communist broadcasting projects, both overt and covert. Staff members of Radio Liberation, a CIA operation aimed at Russian audiences, had a training course at NBC. Sarnoff urged that miniature radios be dropped in communist areas, capable of receiving only American transmissions; the plan was eventually tried in South Asia.

But in 1953, as television moved into high gear, he was concerned about NBC. His worries led him to seat himself temporarily in the NBC presidential office—he was already chairman of the board—to end the chaos. Searching for qualities of leadership among NBC executives, he felt he saw them in Sylvester L. ("Pat") Weaver, who in 1949 had left a vice presidency at the Young & Rubicam advertising agency to head television activities at NBC. In December 1953 Weaver became NBC president.

Sarnoff was frank about his plans. He had thoughts about his son, Robert W. Sarnoff, moving up to take over, but Robert first needed more grooming; he had, over a period of years, headed several NBC divisions. "I knew," Weaver told associates later, "that I was just warming up the seat for Bobby."

Nepotism was a word often heard in NBC corridors, and often spoken with resentment—but not by Weaver. His attitude, always free-swinging and jovial, was that nepotism was as useful to him as to the General. When major plans needed approval, he took them first to Bobby, who became the spokesman when they went to his father.

There was protocol for such matters. Talking to Robert Sarnoff, no one at NBC ever said, "Your father . . ." It was always, "The General . . . ," as though no connection existed.

Bobby Sarnoff, as everyone persisted in calling him—it was a mild kind of retaliation—was a pleasant fellow who quickly benefited from tutelage. Accustomed to dwelling at high levels, he was a relaxed executive. He was never pretentious. Appearing before government committees, he learned to handle himself well, even though his knowledge of the industry and its history was limited. Asked what had happened to the NBC Advisory Council, the highly touted body to which, according to early NBC statements to a Senate committee, a citizen could appeal "over the heads of the operating executives," Bobby Sarnoff looked nonplussed. He simply explained: "I have not boned up on that part of the history of NBC."

Weaver made good his promise of leadership. In his days at Young & Rubicam, programming was controlled by advertising agencies and sponsors. Now Weaver was determined that the control should shift to the networks. He pushed hard for the "magazine concept," under which advertisers bought insertions in programs produced and controlled by the network. *Today* was set up on this basis, and so was *Tonight*, another Weaver creation, which began under Steve Allen and soon afterwards became a smash-hit under Jack Paar.

Equally important was his espousal of the "spectacular." Contracts with sponsors for television time were revised by Weaver to allow the network to "withhold" occasional periods for special programs. Such preemptions had always been possible but had involved reimbursement of talent costs to the sponsor and of commissions to advertising agencies—all of which had discouraged special programs. Weaver institutionalized the special.

He devised names and banner phrases for every purpose. The radically revised relation to sponsors was called "the new orthodoxy." A special program—or "spectacular"—was designed to create "excitement and controversy and washday gossip," and to "challenge the robotry of habit viewing." If it was of a documentary nature, like the series *Wide, Wide World*, it belonged to "operation frontal lobes." Weaver dictated fantastically long memoranda to NBC executives, which soon filled forty bound volumes in his office. He said, "Let us dare to think and let us think with daring."

He radiated enthusiasm and communicated a lot of it to his subordinates.

The magazine concept and the new sales orthodoxy were resisted by some agencies. NBC's own sales people, who received the brunt of their protests, also gave him determined battle. Weaver welcomed this cheerfully. "There is some advantage," he said, "in having your enemy on your own payroll."

Some of Weaver's specials were spectacular successes. Some were largely booking triumphs. *Peter Pan* with Mary Martin, telecast immediately after its Broadway run, was apparently watched by 65,000,000 viewers. At first most specials were live, but film made an early appearance. *Richard III*, a Laurence Olivier film, became a television spectacular by virtue of making its first United States appearance on television, rather than in theaters. The event suggested the precariousness of the live spectacular.

Weaver effected an impressive change of atmosphere at NBC. He created talk and riveted press attention on the network. He was one of the forces that made television an indispensable adjunct to the home.

When in 1955 David Sarnoff reverted to the subject of Robert Sarnoff becoming president, Weaver said, "Of course, but let's not do it yet." But the General felt the precise moment had come. In December Pat Weaver became chairman of the NBC board, and Bobby moved into the presidency. The NBC news release quoted General David Sarnoff. Because things had been going so well the past two years, it "seemed to me a fitting time to recommend that Pat Weaver succeed me as chairman of the board of NBC. He, in turn, recommended that Bob Sarnoff succeed him as president of the company."

When Weaver came to his first meeting as chairman he is said to have noted—smiling—that General David Sarnoff had seated himself at the head of the table. "Why, General, that's my seat!" The General vacated the chair. Some months later Weaver, well provided for, left the chairmanship, seeking other fields for spectacular

Peter Pan, with Mary Martin—1955.   NBC

achievement. Again Robert W. Sarnoff was promoted, becoming chairman of the board. Into the NBC presidency moved Robert Kintner, who had been president of ABC. In place of "Pat and Bob" the trade press now referred to "Bob and Bob."

Behind the musical chairs were powerful economic changes. Weaver was a supershowman of the New York entertainment world, and had given valued leadership to a live-production era. If he suddenly seemed expendable, it was because the whole structure he represented showed signs of crumbling. Among the signs were

events at ABC-TV, the upstart network—events that had been set
in motion by Leonard Goldenson and Robert Kintner, and were
centered in Hollywood.

GO WESTERN

In 1954 the major film companies were still aloof. At Warner
Brothers, Jack Warner frowned on any appearance of a television
set in a home scene in a Warner feature. The assumption seemed to
be that if television could be banned from feature films, it could not
survive.

But signs to the contrary were highly visible, even to Warner.
His son-in-law, William Orr, back from an eastern trip, described
miles of Chicago slums sprouting forests of antennas. History,
thought Orr, might be passing them by.

Warner got similar warnings from Leonard Goldenson, the ex-
Paramount executive who, at the time of the split, had gone with
the theater chain—and on into the ABC merger. As soon as the
merger was complete, he and Kintner began wooing the film companies, where Goldenson as a film veteran had ready entree.

In April 1954 ABC won a foothold via a deal with Walt Disney
for a *Disneyland* series. The terms looked so good to Jack Warner
that they became the basis for a similar deal under which Warner
undertook to produce films for ABC-TV for the 1955-56 season.
It was considered far more momentous than the Disney contract
because Warner Brothers was one of the "majors"—the aristocracy.

The detail that clinched the deal for Jack Warner was that Warner could include in each one-hour film a 10-minute segment to be
called *Behind the Cameras*, which would show Warner movie stars
and crews at work on feature films soon to be shown in theaters.
Behind the Cameras would be a glorified 10-minute commercial for
Warner features. It was felt that this would ease theater exhibitors'
anger over Warner dealing with the enemy.

Warner agreed to produce forty one-hour programs at $75,000

per program, all for use in the 1955-56 season. Twelve of the programs would be repeated during the summer, and Warner would get an additional $37,500 for each of these re-uses. Thus ABC-TV was assured of fifty-two programs, while Warner was assured of more than $86,000 for each film it made. They agreed on the overall title *Warner Brothers Presents*, but this was really an umbrella for three series to be used in rotation, each based on a Warner "property"—a *Casablanca* series, a *King's Row* series, a *Cheyenne* series. The first two, based on outstanding Warner successes, were regarded as surefire prospects. But the *Cheyenne* series, derived from a comparatively unknown feature, was at once so successful that ABC-TV pressed Warner to increase the number of *Cheyenne* programs and reduce the others. *Casablanca* and *King's Row* were eventually dropped, and the series became *Cheyenne*—a network staple for seven years. It propelled into stardom Clint Walker, a spear-carrier before *Cheyenne*. It had seemed unthinkable to use a well-known actor.

The *Behind the Cameras* item was short-lived. The network showed Warner some survey statistics indicating that the audience disappeared during these sequences, which might therefore threaten the whole venture. The item was abbreviated and finally dropped.

Most *Cheyenne* films were shot in five days, with many economy measures. A "low-budget" theatrical feature of the time generally cost between $300,000 and $600,000, so the television venture was felt to call for drastic economies. For herds on the move, cattle stampedes, Indian battles, crowds, and even barroom scenes, the producers drew on leftover footage of old features. Hollywood quipped, "when you see more than two characters, it's stock footage."

Because the entrance of a major studio into television production was considered an historic event, sponsor and agency were at first very deferential, and were kept at arm's length. When an advertising agency expressed interest in being consulted as the work progressed, Jack Warner was incredulous. "They're going to tell *us* how to make pictures?" Protocol meetings were arranged, but there was no script review—not at first.

Another rebuff came. An agency wanted Clint Walker to do cigarette commercials but was told, "Cheyenne doesn't smoke." Warner would not let the actor be involved in commercials in any way, even to introduce them. This rule, too, held—for a time.

By 1956 *Cheyenne* was so successful that carbon copies became highly marketable, and Warner Brothers, with William Orr supervising television production—Warner, like Sarnoff, was a family man—began grinding out *Maverick*, followed by *Sugarfoot, Colt 45, Lawman*—all quickly acquiring sponsors.

Although Jack Warner, in negotiating, groaned over the financial arrangements and said that films could not be made on such a cut-rate basis, the early *Cheyenne* films were made within the allotted sums and even contributed to studio "overhead." Receipts from residual uses were pure profit. Since residual profits were not yet shared with artists, the early films were a bonanza for Warner Brothers. The signs were noted elsewhere. Down the canyon, racing for buried gold, came others. The years 1955-56 brought *Wyatt Earp, Gunsmoke, Tales of the Texas Rangers, Death Valley Days, Frontier, Broken Arrow, Adventures of Jim Bowie,* and more.

The stampede to westerns was also a stampede to the West. On the heels of *Warner Brothers Presents* came *MGM Parade* and *Twentieth Century-Fox Hour*—both exploiting studio properties, and both starting points for other series. It meant that the majors, though still with an air of condescension (television series could not have the best sound stages, nor the really big stars), were joining up. Paramount also announced television production plans.

Others were stepping up action. Columbia Pictures, through Screen Gems, was in high gear with *Ford Theater, Rin Tin Tin, Captain Midnight, Father Knows Best.* United Artists was negotiating for purchase of Ziv, the radio-television syndicate. MCA, acting as agent for many of the Hollywood great and less great while bursting at the seams with Revue Productions projects, was pre-

Perry Mason, starring Raymond Burr.   CBS

Gunsmoke, with James Arness. At left, Dennis Weaver.   CBS

paring to buy the Universal lot—eventually, Universal Pictures it-self. MCA was growing into a Hollywood colossus.

While Warner and Disney were programming blocks of time on ABC-TV, a similar alliance was developing between MCA and NBC-TV. Reports told of an NBC meeting early in 1957 at which the following season was being charted. In the presence of president Sarnoff an executive turned to MCA vice president David A. ("Sonny") Werblin: "Sonny . . . here are the empty spots, you fill them." He filled them—with *Tales of Wells Fargo*, *Wagon Train*, *M Squad*, and others. CBS-TV was drawing on diverse sources, getting *I Love Lucy* and *December Bride* from Desilu, *Schlitz Playhouse* from MCA, and starting a *Perry Mason* series at Twentieth Century-Fox.

But film production was only one part of the stampede at the majors. In 1955 RKO—the only one of the big five not actively producing—decided to unload its feature-film backlog and studio. One $25,000,000 check from General Teleradio, offspring of the General Tire and Rubber Company, did it. By the end of the year, through various distributors, 740 RKO features were being offered to television stations, while the RKO studios were taken over by Desilu. Again the action broke a logjam. March 1956 brought an-nouncement of a $21,000,000 deal covering distribution of Warner Brothers features. November brought word of a $30,000,000 deal covering Twentieth Century-Fox features. A few months later came a $50,000,000 deal for Paramount features. Meanwhile Screen Gems began distributing Columbia Pictures features, and later a block of Universal features. All these films were pre-1948 features, owned outright by the studios, and requiring no residual payments. Most of the deals involved cash payments by distributors, toward guarantees. The distributors taking these gambles recouped their investments with astonishing speed as countless stations reduced staffs, closed expensive studios, and took up round-the-clock film projection, alternating with occasional sports events. WOR-TV, New York, which in 1954 had had live drama every night, had none two years later. In the fall of 1956 its schedule was 88 per cent film, and almost all of it consisted of feature films, organized in series under such titles as *Million Dollar Movie*. The trend was followed at countless stations.

For many artists it was disaster; for others, upheaval. Some trekked to Hollywood, where the important action now seemed centered. New York was for news and documentaries, a few variety hours, and quizzes. As a television drama center it was dying. Hollywood was now the mecca.

For stations and networks, the road was clear. Film salesmen were lining up. Much had been settled.

BOOM LAND

The boom that in 1956-57 was taking shape and direction touched every corner of American life. The 108 television stations of the freeze period had grown to over 500 stations, which forty million television homes—85 per cent of all homes—were watching some five hours a day. The programs were supported by tens of thousands of sponsors, to the tune of almost a billion dollars a year.

The range of sponsors plunging into the boom had exceeded all expectations. Films of the pianist Liberace, who wore a velvet jacket with sequins, were at first sponsored on various stations by Breast o' Chicken Tuna, Maybelline, Serta Mattresses, Yes Tissues, and other consumer products. But when a Cleveland bank tried the program, offering a Liberace recording to new depositors, and gained $15 million in deposits in 1954, other bank sponsors flocked to him and apparently won a host of women depositors. Other phenomena included evangelist Oral Roberts, both sponsor and performer. He bought time on 125 stations and recouped the cost many times over via donations resulting from his on-camera faith-healing. There were complaints to the Federal Communications Commission about "undocumented" miracles, but Roberts declared that if the FCC took to evaluating miracles, it would violate the First Amendment.

Products backed by the largest sums were headache tablets (Anacin *et al.*), stomach settlers (Alka-Seltzer *et al.*), cigarettes (Winston *et al.*). Cigarette companies were stressing their long, filter, and menthol cigarettes, in an effort to counteract an American Cancer Society report about effects of smoking. Interest in backing westerns, with their aura of fresh air, health, and vigor, received extra impetus from the cancer scare.

The boom was sprouting beguiling new advertising theories. Advertising agencies employed consultants like the high-priced Dr. Ernest Dichter, who fascinated them with analyses of latent psychosexual factors involved in a buyer's choice of a car, cigar, or brand of prunes. Advertising themes and program purchases were increasingly influenced by theories about subliminal associations. Dr. Dichter also gave advertising men a sense of destiny about their own role. In our culture, said *Motivations*, a Dichter periodical, "psychological demands are being made upon the family today which it cannot fulfill. There is a gap between human need and the capacity of the family institution to fill that need." This gap, according to *Motivations*, was being filled in part by the acquisition of consumer goods.

The television boom inevitably entwined it with politics. The Lyndon Johnson family was a notable example. It was not clear whether the scores of sponsors who bought time on KTBC-TV, Austin, soon giving the family multimillionaire status, needed the advertising, or whether they liked to do business with a Senator who had become Minority Leader—after 1955, Majority Leader—of the Senate. Such lines of interest inevitably converged.

The fight for channels—gold-mining claims—was bitter. Rumors of sharp practice and political pressure were rife. There were even rumors about bribery. Such reports only seldom broke into print and were never heard on the air, but because of their persistence a New York University professor, Bernard Schwartz, was brought to Washington in 1957 by the House subcommittee on legislative oversight to conduct a probe of the regulatory agencies, including the FCC.

Among his first findings was that Representative Oren Harris, chairman of the commerce committee—which had jurisdiction over the subcommittee and the probe—had acquired a 25 per cent interest in television station KRBB, El Dorado, Arkansas, for $500 plus a $4500 promissory note, which was never paid. Shortly afterwards the station applied for an increase in power—previously denied—and got it. Harris apparently saw no impropriety in this sequence of events. Professor Schwartz hardly knew how to proceed. He encouraged reporters to ask Representative Harris questions about his television coup; the press interest embarrassed Harris into selling his share, but he continued to have jurisdiction over the oversight probe. Schwartz wondered whether its task was to oversee or to overlook.

The boom atmosphere also gripped the programming world and gave rise to varied corruptions that seemed to be taken for granted as suitable to an era of enterprise. Writers, directors, and actors could get cash pay-offs for injecting various products or brand-names into their programs; the use of potato chips in a party scene was worth $100 to a director. Awareness of this kept network checkers busy with questions. Why did Bob Crosby on a CBS-TV variety show suddenly find it necessary to eat a Lifesaver? Did that dinner scene in the drama have to end with use of a Diners Club credit card? In that contract-signing scene, did the camera seem to linger on the Papermate pen?

Rumors of "fixed" quiz programs were frequent. In radio, "payola"—cash payments and gifts to disk-jockeys from record companies, to favor their records—was considered a normal fringe benefit.

At the FCC things were hardly different. Professor Schwartz, browsing through files and expense vouchers, found that some commissioners made speeches for broadcasting groups, collected fees covering travel and other expenses from these groups, and then charged the same travel and expenses to the government. Commissioner Doerfer made a trip during which he addressed two groups and was reimbursed for travel three times—twice by the groups, once by the government. He also accepted transportation on company planes, and took a week-long yacht trip to Bimini at the expense of station owner George B. Storer at a time when Storer had at least one case before the commission. Doerfer later described all this as "the usual amenities."

Doerfer, who recommended that licenses be made permanent, was very popular with licensees. They constantly urged his promotion to the chairmanship, and in July 1957 President Eisenhower made him chairman of the FCC.

The figure of Eisenhower, hovering remotely and benignly above this turmoil, seemed to assure that nothing much could be wrong. A television glimpse of Ike heading for the golf course was a comforting symbol of the time. He presided over a laissez-faire era that had let loose a flood of enterprise. Television had helped set it in motion, and was also its most spectacular expression. It was an upbeat era, and television was its upbeat voice.

It was not boom time for all of television. Theoretically the United States now had a dual television system, with noncommercial channels reserved for most cities. But little could be done with such a channel without substantial funds. The fact that the system had survived to 1956-57 was mainly due to the Ford Foundation.

In 1952 the Ford Foundation had launched two major investments in television—one in commercial, the other in non-commercial television.

It had set up a Ford Television Workshop under Robert Saudek, former ABC vice president for public affairs, to produce a network series of quality and challenging content, to be available for commercial sponsorship. The idea was to test—and perhaps demonstrate —the compatibility of such material with commercial television. This had led to the *Omnibus* series, hosted by Alistair Cooke and offering diverse cultural items. In five seasons of Sunday afternoon programs it won innumerable awards, a devoted following—and sponsors. Yet it had no noticeable impact on network programming. The Foundation decided to end its support and to concentrate on noncommercial television. *Omnibus* was carried on by Saudek as a private venture; it eventually—like *See It Now*—became an occasional special.

In noncommercial television, Ford Foundation aid had taken several forms. While helping early stations with construction grants, it had also—in 1952—made a grant to establish a program production center, which came to be known as NET, National Educational Television. Its task would be to provide the stations with a basic program service. The Foundation hoped this would soon become self-supporting. But without repeated Ford Foundation transfusions, NET and the whole system would soon have collapsed.*

There were several reasons for this. The system was invisible to most Americans. In such major cities as New York, Washington, Los Angeles, the channels in the standard VHF waveband (channels 2 through 13) had been assigned before the birth of educational television. The available channels in the UHF band could not be seen on sets already sold in these markets (except by adding a converter), so the chance of developing an audience was minimal.

The New York State Regents nevertheless proposed state-supported stations in New York City and other locations, but Governor Thomas Dewey, who was frequently at odds with the Regents, sidetracked and buried the proposal. In Washington, efforts to find support for a noncommercial station likewise failed.

In Los Angeles a start was made—disastrously. A member of the board of trustees of the University of Southern California, Captain Allan Hancock, provided a grant to build a station on the campus of

---

* The NET organizing grant was for $1,350,000. This was followed by many annual grants, beginning at $3 million in 1953 and reaching approximately double that amount a decade later. The Ford Foundation investment in *Omnibus* had totaled approximately $8.5 million, of which $5.5 million was offset by sponsor payments—for a net expenditure of $3 million.

the University—KTHE, Los Angeles, channel 28. Launched in 1953, it was shaky from the start; few sets were equipped to view it. Its almost complete dependence on Captain Hancock made its existence all the more precarious. One of the station's features was the Hancock string quartet, in which Captain Hancock played the violin. The station lasted only a few months. Captain Hancock disagreed with decisions of the University trustees on other matters and decided to discontinue his support. Station and string quartet vanished and noncommercial television had had a serious setback.

In San Francisco a noncommercial station was started in June 1954 on channel 9, in the standard waveband—a circumstance that offered more hope. Yet even here, in spite of a limited schedule— two days a week, KQED broadcast only one hour per day—the financial pressure seemed lethal. Early in 1955 the KQED board of trustees decided to dissolve the station. The action was stayed by pleas from the program staff, which asked for a chance to tackle the KQED financial crisis. In desperation it arranged an on-the-air auction in which celebrities turned with gusto to the business of auctioning donated items. As hundreds phoned in bids, noncommercial television turned the corner in San Francisco. The receipts alone did not save the station, but the community involvement that had been set in motion began to bring in new support. The auction became an annual event and was emulated by other noncommercial stations—with particular success in Boston and Chicago.

Other stations survived; but some of the most stable were among the least promising. The University of Houston, a young institution, had expensive building plans on the drawing boards when the noncommercial reservations were proclaimed. The University promptly cut its building plans and, instead, built KUHT, launched in 1953. *Broadcasting* reported: "HOUSTON U SEES TV EDUCATIONAL STATION SAVING $10,000,000 IN BUILDINGS." The rationale was that large lecture halls were now obsolete. A student could watch two lectures a week via television, then attend a seminar to discuss the implications. Television viewing

KQED

On-the-air auction of donated items pulls KQED through financial crisis.

could be done at home, in a dormitory room, or in special viewing rooms.

Lectures-by-television were probably no worse than lectures in large halls—in some cases, undoubtedly better. But KUHT's succession of lectures was scarcely a beacon light for noncommercial television.

In 1956 only two dozen noncommercial stations maintained a struggling existence. Some showed promise and vigor—WGBH-TV, Boston; KQED, San Francisco; WQED, Pittsburgh. At most stations, survival depended on arrangements with schools or boards of education, whereby selected courses were taught by television.

NET, kept alive by its Ford Foundation grants to provide stations with a skeletal program service, was also hard-pressed. Its average budget of $4500 per half-hour program forced it to rely to some extent on kinescope films of local productions.* The stations, having no cable connections, had to be served through a cumbersome procedure of shipping films from station to station. It was called "bicycling."

Many reserved channels were still unused. There was constant demand that the FCC release them for commercial use. Typical was the pressure from *Broadcasting*, which editorialized: "One day the FCC must take another look at the Communications Act in relation to these socialistic reservations. . . ."

Some commercial broadcasters, while holding a similarly low opinion of noncommercial television, favored the reservations on the ground that they kept channels out of the hands of possible competitors. They also saw the stations serving a useful function comparable to that of London's Hyde Park. A lot of talk could go on there without doing much harm. To some extent fringe periods on commercial stations served a similar purpose.

By 1956 a hierarchy of restraints had evolved. Peak network hours, being virtually sold out, were most hostile to material dealing

---

* A kinescope film was a film photographed from a television tube, usually during a live telecast.

specifically with any current issue. If such material did enter these hours, it was likely to be opposite a leading success on another net-work—that is, in a temporarily unsalable period.

More often, "controversial" material went into fringe periods like Sunday afternoon. Here *See It Now* came to rest, offering some of its most telling work in semi-banishment. This included "Clinton and the Law," which provided a brilliant vignette of a racist provocateur at work in a Tennessee town. But most programs in the Sunday "cultural ghetto"—as it came to be called—took the form of round-table, panel, or interview. These had the virtue of economy. They also automatically eliminated many viewers, especially the young, who tended to shift at once to drama, which invited emotional identification. The limited audience of the talk program gave it a special permissiveness.

This too had limits. In 1957 Tex McCrary, leading a discussion program over NBC's channel 4 in New York, invited Dr. David M. Spain, who had done research indicating a link between cigarettes and lung cancer, to appear on the series. Soon afterwards the invitation was canceled with the explanation that no one could be found to present "the other side." The tobacco industry had apparently succeeded in vetoing the discussion, simply by declining to appear.

A remoter fringe area, with even greater permissiveness, was radio, particularly in very late hours. Thus Tex McCrary in his radio series could talk at length with Helen Gurley Brown about sex life on campuses, and her observation that the diaphragm had become the new status symbol among co-eds. Such discussion would have been unthinkable on radio when its audiences were larger, but now caused little tremor.

The hierarchy of restraints made it always easy for industry leaders to cite their liberality, while at the same time keeping the peak hours as a world of refuge. Those who dwelt in that world, either as programmers or audience, could be—and apparently were —almost oblivious to problems of the fringe worlds. They could even be unaware of their unawareness.

In 1954 a black student at the University of California, Estelle Edmerson, completed a graduate study of the Negro in broadcasting. A lady in the CBS personnel department in Los Angeles, freely answering her questions, told her there was no racial discrimination at CBS; all jobs were open to qualified workers. Of course, she said, there were special circumstances to be considered. "There are certain positions where you feel it might not be advisable to use Negroes: one, receptionists; two, script girls who sit in on shows with the client. . . ." However, she concluded, "except where a company must be diplomatic in hiring, all jobs are open to Negroes." This diplomatic lady was certain she was racially enlightened.

That same year the U.S. Supreme Court declared separate education to be "inherently unequal," and the following year—May 21, 1955—it called for integration of public schools "with all deliberate speed." The decisions set the stage for unrelenting pressure to end racial inequalities. That December a twenty-seven-year-old black minister, Martin Luther King, began to rally Negroes in massive nonviolent struggle against the might of the South. Beginning with a battle over bus seating in Montgomery, the struggle shifted to drugstore counters, restaurants, and other fields. By the end of 1956, when Montgomery blacks began riding unsegregated buses, the Reverend Martin Luther King was world famous—less for his fantastic first successes than for the style of his leadership. He was arrested, spat on, imprisoned, fined, and reviled, but he told his followers:

> We must have compassion and understanding for those who hate us. We must realize so many people are taught to hate us that they are not totally responsible for their hate. But we stand in life at midnight, we are always on the threshold of a new dawn.

At first television and radio paid little attention to King. But soon his Gandhi-inspired crusade, which always ran the risk of bloodshed, began to draw cameramen and tape recorders, sometimes resulting in 2-minute items on newscasts. The issues were also discussed on Sunday-ghetto talk programs, but seldom penetrated to the citadel of the peak hours. The commercials remained purest white, and the surrounding dramas were kept in harmony.

The roster of the great and famous visited in 1956 on *Person to Person*, even by so enlightened a man as Edward R. Murrow, gives some indication of prime-time criteria. In his alter ego as establishment figure he found occasion for visits to Liberace, Pat Weaver, Eddie Fisher and Debbie Reynolds, Jane Russell, Billy Graham, Hal March, Dr. George Gallup, Jayne Mansfield, Rocky Marciano, the Duke and Duchess of Windsor, Admiral Richard Byrd, Lawrence Welk, Anita Ekberg, and others—but not Martin Luther King. The 93 guests during 1956 included two show-business Negroes—"Dizzy" Gillespie and Cab Calloway.

The obliviousness of the peak hours applied especially to issues affecting broadcasting itself, including blacklists. The subject was almost never mentioned on the air and therefore, for the larger public, scarcely existed. The death of Senator Joseph R. McCarthy in May 1957 led even people in the industry to think that McCarthyism might be dead. That it was not became clear from the Faulk case.

In January 1956 CBS newsman Charles Collingwood and WCBS disk-jockey John Henry Faulk, a frequent participant in television panel shows, took office as president and vice president of the American Federation of Television and Radio Artists, New York chapter. They had been elected as a "middle of the road" slate, declaring themselves non-communist but also repudiating the tactics of Aware, Inc. Their election aroused the anger of Aware. Although Faulk had never appeared on any blacklists, not even those of Aware, it now issued a bulletin denouncing Faulk with "citations" of various "communist" activities. The bulletin had the usual result. Prodded by Syracuse supermarket executive Laurence Johnson, sponsors quickly deserted Faulk. In June 1956 Faulk brought suit against Aware, Inc., its leader Vincent Hartnett, and its patron Laurence Johnson. At this point Faulk still had his WCBS disk-jockey stint, but CBS, perhaps under sponsor and supermarket pressure, fired him.

Edward R. Murrow was outraged. Along with Collingwood, he had sought to stay the action. He had argued that CBS should finance the Faulk suit; having lost this argument, he had himself sent Faulk a check for $7500 so that he could retain the famed attorney Louis Nizer. To Murrow, the case seemed a chance to open and expose a festering sore that had long afflicted the industry.

Some of the "citations" against Faulk were false and easily disproved. Others, in their use of half-truths, showed even more tellingly the towering malice of the "anti-communist" crusade as conducted by Aware—and abetted by networks, agencies, sponsors. One item charged:

> A program dated April 25, 1946, named "John Faulk" as a scheduled entertainer (with identified communist Earl Robinson and two non-communists) under the auspices of the Independent Citizens Committee of the Arts, Sciences and Professions (officially designated a communist front, and predecessor of the Progressive Citizens of America).

Aware did not mention the following facts, which it knew. The event was a first-anniversary salute to the United Nations, and was sponsored by numerous organizations, including the American Association for the United Nations, the American Bar Association, the American Association of University Women, the American Jewish Committee, the Young Men's Christian Association, and others. Speakers included U.S. Secretary of State Edward S. Stettinius. Presiding over a portion of the program was United Nations Secretary General Trygve Lie. Ambassadors of many countries were present. CBS broadcast the event, and had asked Faulk to take part.

Louis Nizer took the Faulk case, but Faulk remained unemployable. Most listeners knew only that he had vanished from his CBS spot. The lawsuit, with little public attention, dragged on for years.

The year 1956 brought a presidential election. Re-election of

Dwight D. Eisenhower, on a wave of prosperity, seemed certain. The campaign as conducted on television was an almost perfect reflection of the boom environment.

The Republican National Committee, as in 1948 and 1952, enlisted the Batten, Barton, Durstine & Osborn advertising agency, which also handled United States Steel, Du Pont, General Electric, American Tobacco, Armstrong.

They developed a new strategy. In previous campaigns, commercially sponsored programs had been canceled for political speeches, but this had sometimes caused resentment. In 1952 Adlai Stevenson, having displaced an *I Love Lucy* episode, got letters saying: "I Love Lucy, I like Ike, drop dead." The Republicans felt the tides were running with them, and that all would be well if they could avoid stirring up trouble. Leading sponsors were persuaded to surrender the last five minutes of their programs for political appeals. The sponsor paid for 25 minutes, the party for 5 minutes. The most popular programs became lead-ins for political appeals, although technically there was no relationship. For the viewer, the temptation to switch elsewhere was minimal. For the party, costs were reduced. For the network, disruption and loss were eliminated. Thanks to the use of these 5-minute "hitch-hike" programs, supplemented by station-break spots, the 1956 campaign hardly disturbed the television boom.

The mood of the day also affected Democrats. The Democratic National Committee could hardly find an advertising agency willing to take its account. A number of major agencies, apparently feeling their clients would look with suspicion on them if they dealt with Democrats, rejected overtures.

The eventual solution carried irony. Norman, Craig & Kummel was the young agency that had secured for Revlon the spectacularly successful *The $64,000 Question*. In spite of this, Revlon decided shortly afterwards to switch its business to Batten, Barton, Durstine & Osborn. Norman, Craig & Kummel, stung by the loss and facing uncertainties, decided to risk the Democratic Party account. The agency also handled Schenley, Consolidated Cigar, Chanel Perfumes, Cook's Imperial Champagne, Bon Ami, and Maidenform Brassieres.

Although Adlai Stevenson, the Democratic nominee, considered the merchandising of candidates "the ultimate indignity to the democratic process"—as he said in his televised acceptance speech—he was persuaded to emulate the Republicans with some 5-minute spots titled *The Man from Libertyville*.

The Democratic National Convention produced a television dispute. The Democrats decided that the keynote address as an institution could be modernized by presenting a portion of it on film. The networks were told of this, and, according to party chairman Paul Butler, raised no objection; all were planning convention coverage. Young Massachusetts Senator John F. Kennedy—rising rapidly in party favor—narrated the film, which was produced by Dore Schary. But when it came time for the keynote presentation, CBS-TV decided not to take the film portion, and cut away to a round-up of news analysts. Paul Butler denounced the action as "sabotage." NBC-TV and ABC-TV, however, carried the film, and its impact may have helped spur a sudden surge of support for Kennedy for the vice presidential nomination, for which he was narrowly edged out by Senator Estes Kefauver.

Both conventions were tangled in masses of television cables. In the hotels they slithered into the rooms of the great; at the convention hall they writhed down the aisles, which were also crawling with walkie-talkies and creepie-peepies. To reporter Marya Mannes the newsmen with battery backloads and weird antennae looked like "displaced frogmen." Equipment statistics were dizzying. CBS had a hundred television cameras; NBC had ten thousand pounds of equipment.

NBC-TV, which had been bested by CBS-TV in the 1952 coverage, seemed to win the competition this time, largely because of the work of NBC newsmen Chet Huntley and David Brinkley. This later led to their installation as a team of anchormen on the

NBC-TV early evening news program, replacing the breezy John Cameron Swayze. This did not at once affect the flimsiness of the 15-minute newscasts, but it did set the stage for changes.

The Republicans spent $2,739,105 on the presidential race; the Democrats $1,949,865. The Eisenhower-Nixon team won a resounding victory—35,581,003 to 26,031,322 in popular vote, 457 to 73 in electoral vote.

The inauguration, for the first time, was recorded by a new process—*videotape*, which could record both picture and sound magnetically. At once superior to kinescope film, it doomed the kinescope. Ampex videotape recorders were expected on the market late in 1957 at a price of about $45,000.

The second-term inauguration of Dwight D. Eisenhower was probably the high-water mark of Republican confidence. Not since Coolidge had business and government been so closely meshed. In the Coolidge days the press, overwhelmingly Republican, had been almost an arm of government. During the Eisenhower period the broadcasting industry was edging into a similar position.

Prime-time programming, in particular, reflected the alliance—not only in its restraints and taboos, but also in ideas it furthered. And "entertainment," rather than news programs, seemed to play the dominant role in this respect.

Accepted doctrine had it otherwise. The word "entertainment" was used to imply relaxation for an idle hour, apart from the world's business. And of course, entertainment had been that. For the young, once upon a time, movies were a weekly gap in a learning schedule. But telefilms had become the learning schedule. Hours each day, they told of a larger world, and defined the good and great.

Networks played down the influence. They made a point of proclaiming that news programs were done under their "supervision and control," suggesting that only those were crucial. The others were something else—"entertainment."

But if television was playing a formative role, it was scarcely through news, which operated on the fringes, seldom watched by the young, but through a rival form of journalism—telefilms. Their role might be suggested by a paraphrase of Jefferson. "Let him who will write the nation's laws, so long as I can produce its telefilms."

TELEFILM

By the end of 1957 more than a hundred series of television films—*telefilms*—were on the air or in production. Almost all were Hollywood products, and most were of the episodic-series type. They came from majors and independents alike. The films processed by film laboratories were now mainly for television.*

In 1957 the various family-comedy series that had followed *I Love Lucy* were being submerged by tidal waves of action films. These came in several surges but were essentially the same phenomenon, in varying guise. Their business was victory over evil people.

A crime-mystery surge, on the *Dragnet* model, already included *Big Town, The Falcon, Highway Patrol, The Lineup, Official Detective, Racket Squad, The Vise,* which were joined in 1957 by *M Squad, Meet McGraw, Perry Mason, Richard Diamond, Suspicion,* and others.

An international-intrigue surge, exploiting unusual backgrounds, included *Biff Baker USA, Captain Gallant, Captain Midnight, Dangerous Assignment, The Files of Jeffrey Jones, I Led Three Lives, A Man Called X,* as well as the more fanciful *Superman* and *Sheena, Queen of the Jungle;* which were followed in 1957 by *Assignment Foreign Legion, Border Patrol, OSS, Harbor Command, Harbor Master, Passport to Danger, The Silent Service,* and others.

And a mighty western surge, on a trail blazed by Hopalong

---

* Signs appeared in laboratories: "Unless otherwise specified, all film will be processed for TV." This meant that contrasts between light and shade were to be reduced, to compensate for the fact that television accentuated the contrasts.

Cassidy, Lash Larue, Gene Autry, Roy Rogers, and Tex Ritter, included *Adventures of Jim Bowie, Annie Oakley, Brave Eagle,
Broken Arrow, Cheyenne, Cisco Kid, Davy Crockett, Death Valley Days, Frontier, Gunsmoke, The Lone Ranger, Tales of the
Texas Rangers, Wild Bill Hickok, Wyatt Earp, Zane Grey Theater*—joined in 1957 by *The Californians, Colt 45, Have Gun—Will
Travel, Restless Gun, Sugarfoot, Tales of Wells Fargo, Tombstone
Territory, Trackdown*, and others. Somewhat related were series
in which animals were heroes but evil men supplied the occasion for
drama—*Fury, Lassie, My Friend Flicka, Rin Tin Tin*, and others.
By 1958 thirty western series were in prime-time television, dominating every network.*

Although many fine films throughout film history have dealt
with internal character conflicts, such conflicts were seldom important in telefilms. Telefilms rarely invited the viewer to look for
problems within himself. Problems came from the evil of other
people, and were solved—the telefilm seemed to imply—by confining or killing them.

Simplistic drama was probably fostered by the shortness of playing time—usually 24 or 48 minutes—and by the function of providing a setting for a commercial. Dr. Ernest Dichter, who gave
advertisers socio-psychological rationales to go with his recommendations, had additional observations. In the western series he saw a
defense against frustrations of modern society. Most people felt a
great hopelessness, he wrote, about the world's problems. But in
westerns "the good people are rewarded and the bad people are
punished. There are no loose ends left. . . . The orderly completion of a western gives the viewer a feeling of security that life
itself cannot offer." In Dichter's view, the western seemed to serve
the same emotional needs as consumer goods, and their alliance was
presumably logical.

---

* The western vogue seemed to have high-level approval. In 1953 President
Eisenhower, in a three-network telecast, spoke nostalgically about Wild Bill
Hickok. "If you don't know about him, read your westerns more."

But his explanation also indicated a political dimension. It seemed to say that the American people, exasperated with their multiplying, unsolved problems, were looking for scapegoats, and that telefilms provided these in quantity; also, that frustrations were making Americans ready for hero solutions—a Hickok, an Eisenhower.

Telefilm writers thought little about such matters. The "market lists" issued regularly by WGA-w—Writers Guild of America, west*—tabulated the announced needs of producers and made it clear that hero-villain drama was about all that was wanted. Producers, in turn, saw little network or sponsor interest in other kinds of drama.

Along with hero-villain conflicts, another ingredient had become standard. At the end, the evil man was not merely arrested—as in radio or theater. He almost always resisted or "made a break," precipitating a final explosion of action in which he was subdued by fistfight, gunplay, knife battle, lariat strike, karate action, or secret weapon. A few series, like the Perry Mason courtroom dramas, did not go in for climactic combat; in most, it was a formula requirement. There seemed to be an unspoken premise that evil men must always, in the end, be forcefully subdued by a hero; that the normal processes of justice were inadequate, needing supplementary individual heroism.

No such implication was consciously intended. Films used the violent climax because they, and only they, could do so. Physical combat was always impractical in theater, seldom going beyond a ritual ballet. Radio could offer only a few seconds of sound-effects clatter and grunts. Only film could make use of what has been called the "pornography of violence."

A few voices of concern were heard. Senator Estes Kefauver,

---

* Writers Guild of America was formed in 1954 to represent film, television, and radio writers, who had previously been in various Authors League of America units. WGA was organized in two regional divisions, WGA-e and WGA-w. In separating from the Authors League, they moved in a labor-union direction, with emphasis on collective bargaining.

holding hearings on the rising juvenile crime rate, wondered whether television violence was contributing to it. *Reader's Digest*, quoting Kefauver, published an article titled "Let's Get Rid of Tele-Violence." An officer of the National Association of Broadcasters, Thad H. Brown, promptly called the article "vicious."

Telefilm artists saw little cause for concern—for obvious reasons. The ingredients of the telefilm were not new. The only revolutionary element—one which did not involve them or their work—was its constant presence in the home, as the center of the home environment. They were conscious of this, but it seemed a vote of confidence. A writer was concerned with one script at a time—not with possible effects of a ceaseless barrage, and its displacement of other influences.

Telefilms were showing increasing interest in foreign settings, real or imaginary. The trend took advantage of increasing American interest in the world scene. The series *The Man Called X*, produced by Ziv, tried to give the impression that it was based on exploits of the Central Intelligence Agency. Its stories were "from the files of the man who penetrated the intelligence services of the world's Great Powers." Advertisements for the series included numerous references to the CIA. A CIA trainee, said one advertisement, must learn to kill silently when necessary "to protect a vital mission." *The Man Called X* was full of vital missions and silent killings. "Secret agents," said the same advertisement, "have molded our destiny." Ziv's *I Led Three Lives*, a widely distributed success, was derived from *I Was a Communist for the FBI*, which the company had also distributed in a radio version. Its local sponsor received promotion material proclaiming him a member of "the businessman's crusade" against the communist conspiracy. An early MCA series, *Biff Baker USA*, combined similar material with family drama. It offered "an American husband and wife behind and in front of the iron curtain." Described as "full of overseas intrigue and color," it was also "safe and satisfying for the kids."

If this was livelier journalism than the *Camel News Caravan*, it

Richard Carlson in *I Led Three Lives*.

must also have had greater political impact, especially "for the kids." By 1956-57 the significance of this was growing. For American words and images were addressing audiences not only in the United States, but worldwide. They were part of a growing United States involvement—of imperial scope—in the affairs of other nations.

DYNAMIC DUO

If the United States was a felt presence throughout the world, its broadcasts had something to do with it. People of all nations, including Russians and Chinese, were aware of them.

At the Voice of America, which in 1953 had been placed in a newly formed U.S. Information Agency, the McCarthy purge had put anti-communist crusaders in the saddle and stepped up the cold war. Its radio transmissions took a more aggressive form than Soviet transmissions, even injecting themselves into domestic Soviet wavebands, "cuddling up" to Russian stations, including the Moscow station operating at 173 kc. The United States used relay transmitters ringing the Soviet Union, carrying out a USIA "Ring Plan." Russians combated these intrusions with local "jammers." The United States protested the jamming in the name of "freedom to listen," and also cited the jamming to justify further intrusions.

As television began in countries that were friendly or nonaligned, the USIA began supplying them with free films, often "informational" or "cultural" but designed, overall, "to fight international communism." By 1954 USIA was supplying nineteen countries. By presidential order, policy matters were controlled by the Secretary of State, John Foster Dulles.

Another worldwide presence was the Armed Forces Radio Service, which in 1954 became the Armed Forces Radio and Television Service. By 1956 AFRTS had twenty television stations, each receiving seventy hours of filmed network programming per week from the United States, and it also had two hundred radio outlets. Virtually all United States military installations abroad had AFRTS outlets.* Unlike the 50-watt Quonset hut stations of World War II, some were extremely powerful—using, in a few cases, more power than the most powerful domestic stations in the United States, and commanding large foreign audiences. AFRTS stations were forbidden to carry news analyses other than policy statements provided by the U.S. State Department, such as those of Secretary of State John Foster Dulles.

Another worldwide presence was the group of radio stations of the Central Intelligence Agency, all purporting to be "private, non-governmental" services supported by citizen donations. Using scores of powerful transmitters in Germany, Spain, Portugal, Philippines, Taiwan, Thailand, they included Radio Free Europe, Radio Free Asia, Radio Liberation (later Radio Liberty), and subsequently others. CIA responsibility for these stations was long and firmly denied by government spokesmen. All had "front" organizations. In 1953 all came under the jurisdiction of the newly appointed CIA director, Allen Welsh Dulles, brother of John Foster Dulles.

Thus the Dulles brothers had an extraordinary battery of world voices and images at their disposal. The two men worked closely together, but differed sharply in personality. Allen Dulles, the younger, was socially adaptable and gave a country-squire impression. John Foster Dulles was religiously inclined, and liked to refer to "atheistic communism." President Eisenhower praised his moral fervor and compared him to an Old Testament prophet. He was the leader; Allen Dulles deferred to him on important issues.

As Secretary of State, John Foster Dulles devised apocalyptic

---

* In 1956 the United States had military installations in Japan, Marshall Islands, Okinawa, Philippines, Saudi-Arabia, South Korea, Taiwan, Turkey, Eritrea, Libya, Morocco, Azores, France, Greece, Greenland, Iceland, Italy, Spain, United Kingdom, West Germany, Bermuda, Canada, Cuba, and the Panama Canal Zone.

phrases that seized headlines. The Republicans would "roll back" the iron curtain. People of "the captive nations" would no longer be abandoned to "godless terrorism." In the Far East Dulles hoped to "unleash" Chiang Kai-shek. Aggressive moves by communists could expect "massive retaliation." Unrelenting pressure would make communist rulers "impotent to continue in their monstrous ways."

The Dulles team, while controlling an array of international media, also began to influence television and radio in the United States. The Secretary of State became a skillful manipulator of news and a constant broadcaster.

As broadcaster he acquired an effective, devoted assistant. Appearing on a Chicago television program in 1954, Dulles was impressed by the businesslike young man running the program. Before the broadcast David Waters suggested that Dulles, instead of remaining at a desk, walk to a large globe and point to world trouble spots as he discussed them. In preparation, Waters had had a magnificent globe brought from the prop room, which impressed Dulles, who said, "You know your business." The young man was invited to visit Dulles in Washington, if he cared for a job in the State Department. Waters for his part was awed by the formidable, crusty man in the black Homburg hat, and a few days later turned up in Washington and was made television and radio aide to the Secretary of State. Overnight he became a leading arranger of news events. In the next few years John Foster Dulles traveled over half a million miles, and every trip became an occasion for "departure statements" and "arrival statements" and, in between, press conferences and speeches. Waters was constantly on the phone with NBC and CBS and ABC to make sure there would be cameras at the airstrip. Waters regularly predicted policy statements on which the free world might depend. Waters went along on trips, carrying a collapsible lectern that could be set up instantly anywhere. En route, in plane or hotel room, he got Dulles to rehearse statements. The Secretary made extraneous lip movements that sometimes made him seem "out of sync" on film. Under the young man's tutelage, Dulles worked hard to sharpen his delivery, and acquired a very decisive manner. Waters often urged cameramen to shoot from a low angle, which he felt gave Dulles an "American eagle look." Although an upstate New Yorker, Dulles pronounced *communism* as a southerner would—*commonism*. Waters did not try to change this.

In 1955 Eisenhower began admitting newsfilm cameramen to his regular press conferences, and Dulles followed suit. Sensitive film that reduced the need for oppressive light made all this possible—to the annoyance of pad-and-pencil reporters, who tended to become extras in a television show. Dulles developed into a bravura camera performer. No film was permitted to be used until he had had a chance to examine transcripts and order cuts. This gave him firm control, and he came to relish the sessions. Beforehand he would say to Waters, "Well, let's go down and see the lions." En route Waters would find the elder man's steps quickening. "He'd get a pace and excitement about it . . . he loved the exchange." NBC, CBS, ABC, Fox Movietone, Hearst-MGM News of the Day, and Voice of America covered the sessions.

Some correspondents, including David Schoenbrun of CBS, distrusted Dulles. Dulles, aware of their skepticism, seemed to enjoy baiting them. To a reporter who intervened with a new question, Dulles said: "Schoenbrun hasn't finished working me over. You've interrupted his train of thought."

Dulles also made skillful use of off-the-record "background" sessions for favored reporters. There were several groups of these; one met with Dulles periodically at the home of Richard Harkness of NBC. Harkness would be the host; there would be drinks. Dulles fascinated reporters with his habit of stirring his highball with a forefinger. With apparent frankness he would discuss faraway crises—not for quotation. Foreign newscast items attributed to a "high government source" often stemmed from Dulles himself. The sessions seemed to give reporters a pipeline to inside information but made them to some extent tools of the Secretary.

For Dulles and the public, the importance of all this was that

President Dwight D. Eisenhower—press conference.   Wide World

CAMERA . . . ACTION!

Secretary John Foster Dulles—arrival statement.

U.S. Department of Defense

world events were seen to a large extent through the eyes of Dulles. Crises erupted during these years over Guatemala, Vietnam, mainland China, and other places without network bureaus. The troubles were, in any case, not of a sort that could yield their essence to newsreel cameras, even if available. This meant that a filmed press conference excerpt, or a newsman's report "from a reliable source," or a filmed statement by Dulles from a lectern at the edge of an airstrip, *became* the news. For networks he often seemed a welcome *deus ex machina*. In a 15-minute newscast, a 90-second report on Southeast Asia by the Secretary of State himself seemed grand and took care of Southeast Asia nicely. That television was beginning to pay a high price for its dependence on pseudo-events was guessed by few.

The façade held firm. Events all fitted into a world drama of good against evil—or, as Schoenbrun put it, of "Christ against anti-Christ."

What went on behind the façade was still largely a mystery. A handful of congressmen—apparently selected for their acceptable attitude toward military ventures—received fragmentary briefings on CIA activities. Among them was Senator Richard Russell of Georgia, who in 1956 learned things—as he reported with admiration—"which it almost chills the marrow of a man to hear about." There were hints of this sort but—as yet—few public facts.

When information later began to emerge, it was partly because of leaks and partly because Allen Dulles decided that it should. Several CIA interventions abroad had been so masterfully conducted that he felt that they should become known. The effectiveness of the CIA would be further heightened, he felt, by making it an "advertised fact." The information thus revealed—mostly during the 1960's—gave hindsight glimpses of how news conference façades differed from hidden events.

Allen Dulles began to take bows for the overthrow of Premier Mohammed Mossadegh of Iran in 1953 and of President Jacobo Arbenz Guzman of Guatemala in 1954. Both had come to power,

Allen Dulles conceded, "through the usual processes of government and not by any Communist coup." But did that absolve the United States, he asked, of the responsibility "to right the situation"? He was sure it did not.

The Guatemala intervention proved to be especially important. As the Eisenhower administration took office, President Arbenz of Guatemala, who had been elected on a reform platform, was preparing to expropriate United Fruit Company lands—not lands planted in bananas, but reserve areas. In a country where 90 per cent of the land was held by a few dozen owners and most people were indescribably poor, the move was expected and widely supported. The right of expropriation was recognized by the United States, provided payment was prompt and adequate. The Arbenz government offered prompt payment—in 3 per cent government bonds—but the United States said it was not adequate, and negotiations began.

Then Secretary of State Dulles began telling reporters that a conspiracy directed from Moscow was taking over Guatemala and that a "reign of terror" was in progress. At a press conference he mentioned intelligence reports that a "beheading of all anticommunist elements in Guatemala" was imminent. As Dulles reported subsequent events, this grisly development was averted by a spontaneous patriotic uprising and the overthrow of Arbenz. Dulles hailed it as a victory of free men over "red colonialism." He ordered the theme trumpeted throughout the world.

Later, in retrospect, events acquired a different look. During diplomatic negotiations on the expropriation, the CIA had assembled and armed a military force in neighboring Honduras and Nicaragua, both ruled by dictators amenable to such activities. The CIA also arranged an "air cover" of United States planes, to be flown by United States pilots. To head the ground forces the CIA selected a right-wing Guatemalan colonel, Carlos Castillo-Armas, trained at the Fort Leavenworth army command school. President Arbenz, unable to buy arms from his usual source, the United

States—which had halted all trade—ordered arms from Czechoslovakia; this was later cited as proof he was under Moscow orders. In mid-June 1954 the CIA-Armas force entered Guatemala. It did not have to fight, however. The unmarked American planes, flown by Americans, attacked Guatemala City to prepare the way; some planes were lost but they were promptly replaced by order of President Eisenhower. President Arbenz, startled at the power arrayed against him, fled, and Armas was installed. He was promptly promised $6,500,000 in United States aid, and the United Fruit expropriation was halted.*

At the United Nations, Ambassador Henry Cabot Lodge, in answer to protests, categorically denied any United States connection with the invasion. USIA executive Thomas C. Sorensen later confirmed that the Voice of America "made much" of the Arbenz downfall and "of course" did not mention "the behind-the-scenes role of the CIA."

The operation had been so smooth that it inevitably led to other such adventures. They seemed to promise cheap and easy victories for the "free world."

Vietnam offered such a possibility—though the details were perhaps more marrow-chilling. When in 1954 the French at Dienbienphu faced defeat by Vietnamese forces under Ho Chi Minh fighting for independence, Dulles told the U.S. Joint Chiefs of Staff that the French position must be saved at any cost. He was advised that three "small atom bombs" would do the job and let the French march out, as one chief put it, with the band playing "The Marseillaise." According to French Foreign Minister Georges Bidault, Dulles twice offered him atom bombs, but he declined. However, when the war was halted by a Geneva peace agreement, calling for internationally supervised elections, with interim ad-

---

* The sequence of events involved intriguing relationships. The United Fruit vice president for public relations was Edmund S. Whitman, whose wife was confidential secretary to President Eisenhower throughout his presidency. Allen Dulles was for a time a director of United Fruit.

ministration in two regions, the Dulles team embarked on a program of its own. With the CIA going into action, the southern region was to be turned into a bastion of the free world under Ngo Dinh Diem, who had recently been living at the Maryknoll Seminary in Lakewood, New Jersey. The United States began a determined effort to bolster Diem as a rival to Ho Chi Minh; Diem was offered millions—it became billions—in United States aid. Meanwhile the proposed elections were blocked by Diem, with American approval. Later, in his memoirs, Eisenhower told why this was considered essential: his advisers said that "possibly 80 per cent of the population" would have voted for Ho Chi Minh.

Again all this was cloaked in free-world rhetoric. In May 1954 Secretary Dulles told a news conference that "the United States should not stand passively by and see the extension of communism by any means into Southeast Asia." The words *by any means* sounded sinister and suggested that Dulles would not permit a communist coup, but they really meant that he would not permit a Ho Chi Minh victory at the polls, even though 80 per cent of the population might want him.

If Secretary Dulles dominated reporting on many remote events, it was partly because of a thinness—sometimes a vacuum—in available information. Dulles often seemed determined to keep it that way—especially with respect to mainland China.

The Chinese civil war had halted organized reporting from China. But when, in August 1956, the communist regime of Mao Tse-tung announced a willingness to admit American newsmen, in return for United States willingness to admit an equal number of Chinese newsmen, Secretary Dulles flatly refused. Severely criticized, he shifted his position: he would permit the arrangement, but the United States would have to approve each Chinese reporter individually. He intimated, at the same time, that it could not admit communist reporters. This ended the negotiation. In the United States, news and opinion about China continued to rest heavily on items fed by the State Department plus reports from such tenuous sources as Hong Kong "China watchers."

Three reporters, in defiance of the State Department ban, nevertheless went to China. One was William Worthy of the Baltimore *Afro-American*, and CBS took advantage of his presence in China by broadcasting short-wave bulletins by Worthy from Peking and Shanghai. According to Worthy, Under Secretary of State Robert Murphy telephoned William Paley of CBS to urge him to discontinue such broadcasts. CBS did so, and also killed a 5-minute discussion on the subject by Eric Sevareid, criticizing the State Department policy—the first time in seventeen years that a Sevareid program had been vetoed in entirety. The episode angered Edward R. Murrow, who spoke on the subject on his own radio news series—and was rebuked by CBS. The industry, except for newsmen, seemed to take the issue calmly. *Broadcasting* considered it purely a CBS matter, to be settled "within the family."

Murrow thought otherwise. When Worthy's passport was revoked on his return and he took the matter to court, Murrow drafted a brief in support of Worthy, stressing his rights as a citizen, but also stressing the public's right to be informed. Again he felt that CBS, which had carried the China broadcasts, should itself be fighting the case.

Only in later years would the extraordinary reach of the Dulles team into channels of communication begin to be revealed. When the two surviving newsreels, Fox Movietone and the Hearst-MGM reel, faced extinction, a secret government subsidy was arranged—under the code name "Kingfish"—which provided that propaganda items prepared under USIA direction would be inserted in foreign editions of the reels. The secret subsidy helped the newsreels remain alive. Secret CIA subsidies were also used to infiltrate and control feature-film units, magazines, newspapers, book publishers, labor unions, youth groups. Apparently no medium was immune.

The Dulles team felt no noticeable qualms over activities of this sort. The United States was not "really" at peace, wrote Allen Dulles later, since "Communism declared its own war on our system of government and life." Thus he felt we should apply wartime rules and "mobilize our assets." He spoke of a Moscow "orchestra of subversion" which included secret subsidies to communication media. It seemed to him axiomatic that this and other threats must be met by an American orchestra of subversion.

John Foster Dulles added the sanctifying note. It was a "basic fact," he told one of his first press conferences as Secretary of State, that Soviet leaders "do not admit the existence of such a thing as moral law." Most Americans—especially those relying on television and radio for news—had little reason to doubt that American foreign policy was rooted in moral and religious principle. The Dulles rhetoric won wide response. "I am grateful," said a 1954 fan letter from Vermont, "that our country has a true Christian in a top government post." A 1955 letter from Indiana told him, "God is trusting you to help redeem the world." Hundreds of letters struck this note.

Dulles even precipitated a song sung by Carol Burnett on a Jack Paar program over NBC-TV, "I Made a Fool of Myself over John Foster Dulles." NBC officials were afraid it might be considered in bad taste but were relieved to learn that the Secretary of State had found it "marvelous" and hoped for a repeat.

But where was the crusade heading? While arguing for massive propaganda, Dulles also urged large military appropriations to add to the "stresses and strains." When in cabinet meetings Secretary of the Treasury George Humphrey called for cuts in military budgets, Dulles would protest—as he did during reports of turmoil in Moscow after the death of Stalin—that "we ought to be doubling our bets, not reducing them. . . . This is the time to *crowd* the enemy—and maybe *finish* him, once and for all." Did this mean that Dulles looked to a military climax? His television aide David Waters, a total believer, thought not. He was convinced that Dulles expected an early collapse of "communism" mainly through propaganda pressures.

The American public was scarcely aware of these pressures. And no one, in the United States or abroad, could accurately assess their impact. But in the mid-1950's the government-produced images and words were beginning to be overshadowed by something else—of seemingly larger propaganda significance, although not so planned.

BONANZA GLOBE

The start of commercial television in Britain late in 1955 opened a crucial market for American advertisers and their agents. That they were ready to leap in was not surprising, for they had worked hard to bring this transition about.

Before television many American advertisers had promoted British sales via powerful Radio Luxembourg, which provided efficient coverage of the United Kingdom. The shrinking of radio audiences threatened these advertisers with shrinking British sales—unless alternative television facilities became available. Television coverage from locations like Luxembourg was not feasible, because television, unlike radio, was limited to a line-of-sight range. The strategy for achieving commercialization of British television is said to have been master-minded by the London branch of the J. Walter Thompson advertising agency, working with a group in Parliament. Their well-financed campaign did not emphasize commercial advantages but shrewdly attacked the British Broadcasting Corporation at its most objectionable point—its monopoly status.

Commercial television brought to Britain the same sort of explosion that had taken place in the United States. A television license, said the enthusiastic Roy Thomson, the Canadian who in 1956 won the television franchise for Scotland, is "like having a license to print your own money!" His franchise soon won him a fortune which he parlayed into worldwide holdings in communication media, including television stations in such places as Aden, Australia, Ethiopia, Mauritius, Sierra Leone, and Trinidad.

British commercial television, shaking up economics and customs at home, also had reverberating effects elsewhere, as other nations followed the British example. All instantly became purchasers of

American telefilms. They also became outlets for the advertising of many American companies and their subsidiaries.

The advertising agency Foote, Cone & Belding, studying foreign markets for its clients early in 1958, reported that commercial television was already in operation in twenty-six countries and in the planning stage in others. Television systems accepting advertising included both government and private systems. At all these systems, salesmen of telefilms were converging. They were reporting sales in clusters—seven series here, five series there. Some countries with noncommercial systems, such as Denmark, the Netherlands, and Sweden, also began buying American telefilms.

To translate telefilms, dubbing operations were springing up far and wide. Practices evolved through trial and error. Screen Gems found that films dubbed into Spanish in Madrid were considered unusable in Latin America, the chief Spanish-language market. Thus Mexico and Cuba became the main centers for dubbing into Spanish. Similarly, Brazil became headquarters for dubbing into Portuguese. On the other hand, dubbing into French was done in France; powerful French unions made this necessary, and the films so dubbed proved usable in French Canada and other French-speaking areas. Egypt and Lebanon became preferred sites for Arab dubbing, Hong Kong for Chinese dubbing. Japanese versions were prepared in Japan, Italian versions in Italy—where dubbing had long been a skilled specialty in the feature-film field. A number of smaller countries used English-language versions, in some cases with subtitles.

For the dubbing procedure a film was cut into innumerable short sequences. A 10-second sequence, spliced to form a loop, would be projected so that an actor would see it over and over and over without pause. After memorizing the rhythm of the lip movements he would record the translation, written to fit the original. In the late 1950's this time-consuming operation—which employed many former radio actors—cost $1200 to $1400 per half-hour program in most parts of Europe, much less in Asian or Latin American countries. But costs soon began to rise.

While some comedy series, like *I Love Lucy* and *Father Knows Best*, were international successes, series emphasizing action rather than dialogue were far more translatable. Climactic gun battles or fist fights, following a chase up a fire escape or down a canyon, needed no "looping" and conveyed their meaning readily in any city or hamlet on the globe. The networks and major film companies, who soon dominated the foreign distribution, acquired an extra incentive toward production of action series—which in any case stood high in United States ratings. By 1958-59 a television writer could scarcely find a market for any other kind of material. That winter's *Television Market List*, issued for its members by WGA-w, listed 103 series, of which 69 were in the action-crime-mystery category. They were peopled by cowboys, policemen, and detectives whose terse words would issue in many languages from the screens of the world.

The worldwide explosion seemed to Hollywood a show-business phenomenon, but it was more. To every nation, along with tele-films and their salesmen, came advertising agencies—often branches of American agencies. (By 1958 J. Walter Thompson had 34 branches abroad, including 8 in South America, 8 in Asia, 5 in Africa.) And along with them came new advertisers—often companies affiliated with or owned by American companies. Television was merely the highly visible crest of a huge economic surge.

There were reasons why American companies, at this moment of history, turned by thousands to investments abroad. In the period after World War II they had made substantial foreign sales—by-products, to some extent, of the Marshall Plan and other aid programs. Some of the earnings were in "blocked" funds and could not be transferred to the United States. Even when they could, there were tax advantages in investing them abroad. Labor costs, low compared with pay scales in the highly unionized United States, were an additional incentive. Another was the attraction of markets with huge growth possibilities; the United States was, in comparison, product-saturated.

Beyond these incentives was another factor. The foreign policy of Secretary of State Dulles seemed to promise the American investor protection abroad, by force if necessary. The risks of foreign investment seemed to decline.

The investment trend, once launched, created earnings which led to further investments, in a growing tangle of relationships. In the television and film fields, the ramifications were endless. Some of the companies marketing telefilms also sold receivers and transmitters; some sold consultant services; some invested in foreign stations, production companies, dubbing services, animation studios, theaters.

To lobby for their interests throughout the world, the major motion picture companies in 1959 formed a television division in the Motion Picture Export Association. The following year the networks formed the Television Program Export Association to serve similar purposes. The moves reflected rising expectations. These moves by media men were possible only because manufacturers in many fields were making similar moves. The launching of commercial television in a new market was often done by a consortium of interests—a group of set manufacturers, advertisers, and program distributors could virtually guarantee success.

If newly developing nations yielded generous franchises to such groups, they were moved by enticing vistas. Entrance into the television age had symbolic values. In addition, studies from UNESCO and others offered heady visions of what television might do for a developing nation. From one television studio, it was said, classrooms of a whole nation could learn physics or chemistry. No longer would a school have to rely on its own pitiful supply of laboratory gadgets. In similar fashion, adults could have instruction in scientific farming, soil conservation, family planning. There was also talk about cultural exchange. And all of this would cost almost nothing; advertising would pay for it, as in the United States.

Using such arguments as these, Robert E. Button, deputy director of the Voice of America, made a television-promotion tour in 1956 that took him to Indonesia, Iran, Lebanon, Pakistan, Taiwan, and other countries. He came back in a state of heady optimism. "If I ever saw anything that would lick the communists on their own front, this is it," he said. "Talk about jumping from camel to jet plane, this is jumping from papyrus scroll to television." Aside from the explosion of private enterprise involved in the process, he saw the stations providing added exposure for USIA films.

American aid programs gave impetus to television in a number of developing countries. Under the Marshall Plan as launched by Truman, aid was without strings. Under Eisenhower all aid came to have strings. Some aid was in the form of loans; in other cases, aid funds had to be used for equipment or materials or services purchased in the United States. In many cases military aid had to be accepted along with other aid. This tended to fortify the existing regimes in aided countries.

The various forms of "tied aid" made for continuing American involvement. Harvesters, tractors, transmitters, office equipment, cars, planes, machine guns all required spare parts—purchasable from the United States. In addition, transmitters needed telefilms; office machines needed paper; machine guns needed ammunition. Much "aid" was thus, in effect, a subsidy of American exports, and tended to create a continuing dependence on the part of the "aided" country.

In the mid-1950's, television, like missionary expeditions of another era, seemed to serve as an advance herald of empire. Implicit in its arrival was a web of relationships involving cultural, economic, and military aspects, and forming the basis for a new kind of empire.*

Inevitably the television invasion brought strains of many sorts. Reports from telefilm salesmen usually reflected an enthusiastic reception of all that was offered. Sales figures suggested complete acceptance of the avalanche of action films. But this picture was incomplete.

* Among 1975 allegations concerning the CIA was that it had occasionally used J. Walter Thompson personnel abroad as "cover."

The telefilms that distributors—CBS, NBC, MCA, Screen Gems, and others—sold to Australia in the late 1950's had already earned back their production cost—in some cases, several times the production cost. Any price paid by the Australians would be profit. And it would further profit American companies to get the Australians started. Prices were therefore set at a most attractive level. "We gave them some series," said John McCarthy of the Television Program Export Association at a UNESCO conference in New York, "for as little as a thousand dollars for a one-hour program, for all of Australia."

The price scale was unquestionably helpful to Australians; television station managers and advertisers were delighted. After a few years the price edged up to $3000 per one-hour episode, $1500 per half-hour episode—still reasonable.

The same sequence of events was experienced quite differently by writers, directors, and producers in Australia's small film industry. Inspired by the advent of television, they began—American-fashion—to make proposals to Australian sponsors. A series of half-hour films could be produced for $20,000 per episode, they explained—if every possible economy was used. Magnificent themes from Australian history and present-day life were available. But the sponsor—perhaps a subsidiary of an American company—received such offers with comments like: "Look—I can get *Restless Gun* for $1400 an episode. It had a Videodex rating of 31.1 in the United States. According to *Sponsor* magazine, it had a CPMHPCM rating of $2.34. That's some CPMHPCM rating, isn't it? Now what can you offer?"* The Australian film maker could offer ideas, perhaps talent, but certainly not a bargain certified by Videodex and CPMHPCM ratings.

In Canada, with its brilliant record of film production, the situ-

---

* *Sponsor* magazine listed CPMHPCM (cost-per-thousand-homes-per-commercial-minute) ratings as a basis for comparing program costs. Videodex ratings were based on viewing diaries maintained by a fixed sample of homes, via arrangements made by the rating organization.

ation was similar and perhaps even more tragic. In the late 1950's American telefilm series were being sold in Canada for $2000 per half-hour episode—for Canada-wide rights. No Canadian film maker could quote a price lower than ten times that sum. In Canada, as in Australia, sponsors moved into prime-time periods with American telefilms about cowboys, crime-fighters, and spies. The writer-director Henry A. Comor, president of the Association of Canadian Television and Radio Artists, told a New York forum of the Academy of Television Arts and Sciences: "You've made it impossible for us to earn a living." He added with a studied casualness: "By the way, my young son thinks he lives in the United States."

Both Australia and Canada introduced quota systems to limit foreign programming and protect home programming. But native-content rules could be taken care of with football matches, round-table discussions, cooking lessons—rather than by expensive drama. Film drama tended to become largely a United States preserve, taking the best hours. Before long, many people tended to take the situation for granted.

The prices that were winning for American telefilms a dominant position in half the world were profitable prices because of the large economic base from which they came. But to foreign producers they seemed "cut-throat" prices, stifling possible competition. Britain, with a very stringent quota system—only 14 per cent of British schedules could originate outside the British Commonwealth—had some success in holding back the television invasion and even in finding foreign markets for its telefilms. Japan later achieved a similar position.

In Toronto in the early 1950's a brilliant group of television artists was at work—Lorne Greene, Norman Jewison, Harry Rasky, Reuven Frank, Christopher Plummer, Art Hiller, and others. Like similar groups elsewhere, they knew the exhilaration of discovery, and saw talents recognized. But the waves of telefilms swept around them. To escape being stranded, they migrated to Hollywood and New York. Soon Art Hiller learned to direct programs like *Gun-*

Bonanza—at right, Lorne Greene.   NBC

smoke, Reuven Frank and Harry Rasky entered the New York documentary field, and Shakespearian actor Lorne Greene became the cowboy-patriarch of *Bonanza*, soon seen in prime time around the world along with *Cheyenne*, *Wyatt Earp*, *Hawaiian Eye*, 77 *Sunset Strip*.

If artists in many lands grew restive, so did educators. The vision of a country united by a television schoolroom was replaced by a different reality. Instead of scientific farming, a mythology of violent struggle riveted attention, followed by cola drinks, cigarettes, headache tablets, soaps, laxatives, hair tonics, deodorants.

In every country American television tended to create a division. It won enthusiastic adherents among station entrepreneurs, advertisers, advertising agencies, distributors, merchandisers, retail outlets—the whole complex of modern distribution—and captured large segments of audience. On the other side were artists, teachers, social workers. They tended to feel a culture was being wrenched loose from its moorings. There were also isolated local businessmen, facing a razzle-dazzle competition linked with overseas enterprise of unimaginable resources.

But their fears and objections were not very audible, even at home. For one thing, they were not on television. And their objections, which seemed petulant and small-spirited, were waved aside by others. These films, were they not merely entertainment?

The divisions abroad were counterparts of those at home. The networks, surveying television interests that were becoming world-wide, were increasingly confident. As their telefilms flowed into ever-expanding markets, the rising prosperity was shared by others —stockholders, advertisers, advertising agencies, distributors, producers—who firmly supported the prevailing order.

It was in mid-1958 that William Paley felt he could get along without *See It Now*, and dropped it. Among series that served a safety-valve purpose, *See It Now* with its $90,000-per-program budget was by far the most expensive. In contrast, such a series as *Face the Nation*—a press-conference type program—was cheap, and often made news. In the confident atmosphere of 1958, *See It Now* seemed expendable.

John Crosby, television critic for the New York *Herald-Tribune*, commented:

> *See It Now* . . . is by every criterion television's most brilliant, most decorated, most imaginative, most courageous and most important program. The fact that CBS cannot afford it but can afford *Beat the Clock* is shocking.

Edward R. Murrow, though still prosperously busy with *Person to Person*, was deeply troubled over the trend. He compared prime-time schedules to Nero and his fiddle.

But empire television continued to spread. In thatched huts and villas men watched cattle stampedes and gunfights, amid the clatter of hoofs and the ricochet of bullets. Precisely what it all meant to them, no one could be sure. Perhaps they had a sense of sharing a destiny with a breed of men who could make decisions and make them stick.

American telefilms, radio transmitters, consumer goods, military bases—much of the world was living in an atmosphere shaped by them. The orientation of all this toward peace was assumed by most Americans and many allies.

To Russians and Chinese, hearing and seeing, the purpose often seemed different. Nikita Khrushchev, gradually emerging as the leading figure in the post-Stalin Soviet regime, was telling Jawaharlal Nehru of India: "We feel like a besieged people."

THE NEW DIPLOMACY

In 1957 Nikita Khrushchev, to the amazement of practically everyone, accepted an invitation to appear on the CBS-TV series *Face the Nation*. Allowing his Moscow office to be turned into a film studio tangled in cables and ablaze with lights, he answered questions from Daniel Schorr and Stuart Novins of CBS and B. J. Cutler of the New York *Herald-Tribune*, while CBS cameramen shot 5400 feet of film and a Soviet crew made its own footage.

The rotund Khrushchev chose the role of genial persuader and, according to Roscoe Drummond, "played it like a Barrymore." His theme was "peaceful competition." America preferred capitalism and the Soviets preferred communism—very well, let them enter into peaceful competition. He and other Soviet leaders were confident of the result. The program went on the CBS-TV network on June 2 at 3:30 p.m. It was not prime time but a fringe period in the slack time of the year; yet it was a first step, and caused a sensation. *Time* called it "the season's most extraordinary hour of broadcasting." President Eisenhower did not quite know what to make of it. He called it a "unique performance" but intimated that CBS was merely trying to improve its commercial standing. Murrow considered the President's remarks "ill-chosen, uninformed."

Some congressmen were outraged that CBS had given a propaganda platform to the Soviet leader, but the majority—along with most of the press—acclaimed the network for its journalistic initiative. Senator Lyndon B. Johnson, Majority Leader of the Senate, said there should be regular exchange programs of this sort, an "open curtain" in place of an iron curtain. Secretary John Foster Dulles, apparently taken aback by the applause greeting this suggestion, said he had been trying for eighteen months to promote something of this sort. Senator J. William Fulbright of Arkansas, a member of the Senate foreign relations committee, scoffed at this remark: if the State Department had been pressing Russia with an "open curtain" proposal for eighteen months, he said, "it is the best kept secret since the first atomic bomb was made." CBS, flushed with praise, arranged further interviews with unorthodox leaders, including Nehru of India. It was a fine idea, many people agreed, to be familiar with the attitudes of foreign leaders. President Frank Stanton was asked if CBS had plans to interview a leader of communist China. "We have no such plans," he said firmly.

Khrushchev was meanwhile traveling. He turned up in various capitals, always available to reporters and cameramen. He became one of the most photographed of leaders, a familiar television figure around the world. From some angles he could look like Eisenhower, but in profile his sagging chin and figure gave a different impression. With somewhat baggy pants, outstretched hand, jovial manner, he looked more like a traveling salesman than a mysterious dictator. He was ready to put on funny hats for cameramen. He had a large supply of aphorisms. He displayed a ready familiarity with American affairs. Telling an American reporter that their conversation would probably lead to a subpoena from the House committee on un-American activities, he promised smilingly to vouch for the reporter's orthodox character. Ready for questions, Khrushchev slipped in his own messages. In good humor, he reminded questioners that the United States had sent troops to Russia in 1917 in an effort to stifle the Soviet Union at the hour of its birth, and currently had bases all around the Soviet Union without any similar provocation from her. But that, he seemed to say, was foolishness. War would solve nothing. Both nations were advanced and mighty and could learn from each other. They should compete and trade.

Competition—trade—they were honored words in the capitalist lexicon. Khrushchev was making them his own, along with *peace* and *negotiation.*

With neat timing, and underlining his apparent confidence, the Soviet Union on October 4 put the first man-made satellite—Sputnik I—in orbit around the earth. The world marveled and the United States was stunned.

In a matter of weeks Khrushchev seemed to have made a mockery of the Dulles depiction of the Soviet world. It did not seem on the point of collapse. It was not rigid. It exhibited a wish for peace and friendly competition.

In 1958 Khrushchev became Premier of the Soviet Union. Late that year John Foster Dulles became ill and began a series of checkups and treatments. The job of Secretary of State fell to Christian Herter, who was himself not in good health; foreign-policy problems fell increasingly on President Eisenhower and Vice President Nixon. Eisenhower was troubled; he wanted to be thought of as a man of peace. In January 1958 he approved a cultural exchange program, and the United States decided to stage an exhibit in Moscow in the summer of 1959. It would include color television, videotape, and other marvels of modern America. Vice President Richard Nixon—who could not be attacked at home as "soft on communism"—would open the exhibit and would meet with Khrushchev. Nixon would be accompanied by George V. Allen, career diplomat who had become director of USIA.

Diplomacy, Allen told an audience before leaving for Moscow, used to be conducted by diplomats.

They were sent abroad to various countries, sometimes supplied with a pair of striped pants and a top hat. They dwelt in foreign capitals and dealt with a small group of people in the foreign office of that country; and that was the link between nations.

All that had changed, said Allen. A great nation now addressed people of other nations over the heads of their rulers, appealing to public opinion.

The new diplomacy had for years used the radio medium but now, as Nixon and Allen left for Moscow, they were thinking especially of television—as was Khrushchev. Nixon and Allen hoped to create an event that would find a place on Soviet television. Khrushchev had his eye on American television. The world was entering a period when the planning of television spectaculars was becoming a central activity of rulers.

When Nixon arrived in Moscow in July, he was received by Khrushchev at his office and shown a cantaloupe-sized ball—a duplicate of Sputnik I. Nixon expressed interest. When Khrushchev later visited the American exhibit, Nixon was the host. He guided Khrushchev first to a building housing an RCA closed-circuit color television set-up and Ampex videotape equipment. It was in a room with an overhead gallery, crowded with Russian spectators and a few visiting Americans.

Below, as Nixon and Khrushchev entered, the color cameras were on them, and they could see themselves on a monitor. They were also being videotaped, so that they would immediately be able to see a replay of their live performance. Nixon, well briefed, began an explanation of the marvels.

Khrushchev, seeing the cameras, the tape, the rapt attention of Russians in the gallery, clearly did not relish the role in which he was being cast—a mute country bumpkin listening to explanations from the centers of progress and civilization.

He interrupted. The Soviet Union had such marvels too, he said, and then began to discuss something he felt was of greater interest: America's foreign bases. Russians did not maintain bases around the world, so why should Americans? Nixon tried to steer the discussion back to the marvels of RCA color television, but Khrushchev plowed ahead, getting occasional applause from the gallery. He asked why America held back on trade with the Soviet Union. Why did it permit only limited cultural exchange? By way of emphasis, he wagged a finger at Nixon.

But now Nixon, too—with a sense of being trapped on videotape —saw the need for resolute action, and began jabbing a finger toward Khrushchev. Meaningful competition, said Nixon, required a free exchange of ideas. "You must not be afraid of ideas. . . . You don't know everything." Nixon again brought the discussion back to color television and videotape, and recommended them as ideal instruments for an exchange of ideas. Khrushchev was dubious, saying Americans habitually suppressed things. Nixon rose to the challenge. He suggested that both countries televise the taped discussion in full, without cuts. Khrushchev grinned. "Shake!" Their right hands met in a resounding clasp.

So they were off on a running debate. The 16-minute taped harangue in the television exhibit hall was followed by further tangles elsewhere, starting with the kitchen exhibit. The encounter thus became known as the "kitchen debate," and became the basis for Nixon's claim of "standing up" to Russian leaders.

But the big show was not over. At the Moscow airport, inspecting an American plane, Khrushchev was asked by a reporter: "Would you like to fly to the United States in a plane like this?"

"This one or some other one."

"When?"

"When the time is ripe."

Within weeks the time was considered ripe, and American television prepared for its greatest spectacular to date: the American tour of Nikita Khrushchev.

But before it began, the television industry faced a painful crisis.

Kitchen debate—Moscow, 1959.   Wide World

A TERRIBLE THING TO DO

During the rise of Khrushchev as television personality, the smol-
dering rumors of quiz program corruptions blazed into scandal.
The revelations were dismaying to the industry and the nation,
and the timing was embarrassing.

There had long been hints and allegations. In August 1958 Her-
bert Stempel, an early winner on *Twenty-One*, said the program
was "fixed." At this time Charles Van Doren, most famous of the
Twenty-One winners, was presiding over the *Today* series on
NBC-TV as summer replacement for its host, David Garroway.
On the air, Van Doren said he knew of no irregularities. But a New
York grand jury began to look into the matter. In January 1959

Van Doren, along with many others, again gave assurance that all was on the level, but the grand jury found discrepancies in their statements. Meanwhile, the House of Representatives special sub-committee on legislative oversight became interested and called witnesses.

Early that fall, amid charges and denials, Charles Van Doren dropped from sight, and then suddenly reappeared. Before the oversight subcommittee, in deep anguish, he read a long statement.

> I would give almost anything I have to reverse the course of my life in the last three years . . . I have deceived my friends, and I had millions of them.

He recounted how he, being good at games, had been urged by friends to appear on a quiz program and had gone to the office of Barry & Enright, producers of *Tic Tac Dough* and other programs. He had passed a written examination and then another, much harder, and had been chosen to appear on the company's new night-time series, *Twenty-One*. This was regarded as a high honor. He began earnestly to memorize miscellaneous facts and attended several broadcasts as "stand-by contestant." But before his first appearance on the air he was asked by Albert Freedman, producer of the series, to come to his apartment.

> He took me into his bedroom where we could talk alone. He told me that Herbert Stempel, the current champion, was an "unbeatable" contestant because he knew too much. He said that Stempel was unpopular, and was defeating opponents right and left to the detriment of the program. He asked me if, as a favor to him, I would agree to make an arrangement whereby I would tie Stempel and thus increase the entertainment value of the program.

> I asked him to let me go on the program honestly, without receiving help. He said that was impossible. He told me that I would not have a chance to defeat Stempel because he was too knowledgeable. He also told me that the show was merely entertainment and that giving help to quiz contestants was a common practice and merely a part of show business. This of course was not true, but perhaps I wanted to believe him.

"I would give almost anything . . ." Charles Van Doren, Washington, 1959.
Wide World

It became the practice for Freedman, before each program, to go over the scheduled questions with Van Doren and give him the answers. Van Doren found he knew the answers to some questions, not to others.

> A foolish sort of pride made me want to look up the answers when I could, and learn as much about the subject as possible.

Freedman was concerned about the manner of answering. He suggested—said the Van Doren statement—that he pause before some answers, skip parts and return to them, hesitate, build up suspense. After the first program, on which he tied Stempel three times, Van Doren was told he would win the next week, and be the new champion. At this point he had won $20,000, but the earnings mounted rapidly. So did his fame. Thousands of letters poured in: invitations to lecture, write articles, appear in films. He almost persuaded himself he was enhancing the national attitude to teachers and "the intellectual life." But at the same time the tensions within him mounted. He testified that after several months, which earned him $129,000, he pleaded for release. When finally informed that he would lose to Mrs. Vivienne Nearing—after a few ties, to build suspense—he described his own reaction as: "Thank God!"

The celebrity aura clung to him. He read poetry on the *Today* series, discussing it as he might in a freshman English class. At Columbia University he finished his Ph.D. and became assistant professor of English.

When Stempel's accusations were reported in the press, Van Doren was "horror-struck." Thousands of letters, including many from school children, were expressing confidence in him. "I could not bear to betray that faith and hope." Newsmen waited for him, besieging him with questions. After long indecision, he decided to tell the truth.

Many quiz figures had lied to the grand jury. A number were now disclosing the facts, and the revelations ripped into various quiz series. Production personnel of *The $64,000 Question* and *The $64,000 Challenge* told the oversight subcommittee that the sponsor, Revlon, had often instructed them which contestants should be disposed of, and which allowed to continue. If they were dull, they had to be eliminated. Details were left to the producers, but they could expect angry reprimand if they failed to follow instructions.

Albert Freedman, who after early evasion had been frank with the grand jury, defended quiz programs as a breath of fresh air in schedules "saturated with murder and violence," and pointed to other prevailing deceptions:

> Is it any great shock to learn that important national figures generally hire "ghost writers" to write their speeches, and in many instances to write their books?

The probes prompted lawsuits by losing contestants, which remained in litigation for years.

The year 1959 also brought revelations of "payola"—bribes to disk-jockeys. Disk-jockey Stan Richards of WILD, Boston, admitted accepting money and other gifts but, like Freedman, pointed to precedent. It was like a political contribution, he said. The giver pays "in the hope that something good will happen." He said he had not been influenced.

To those who heard this testimony, the members of the House oversight subcommittee, it must have had a familiar ring. Its own probe conducted by the energetic Professor Bernard Schwartz had —in spite of obstructions by the subcommittee itself—recently led to the resignation of FCC Chairman John C. Doerfer, whose constant acceptance of "amenities" was found imprudent; also of FCC Commissioner Richard Mack, who had accepted a bribe for his vote on a disputed Florida channel; and finally, of Sherman Adams, assistant to the President, whose pressure on the Federal Trade Commission on behalf of a man from whom he had accepted gifts embarrassed the White House.

These men were all Eisenhower appointees. But the President, who expressed deep shock over the quiz and payola revelations, did not link them with the political scandals. Instead he thought of the White Sox baseball scandals of 1919, when the World Series was fixed, and of the fan who said to one of the players, Shoeless Joe Jackson, "Say it ain't so, Joe." The quiz deceptions, said the President, were a "terrible thing to do to the American people."

At the networks, the scandals seemed to call for desperate measures. Amid a wave of government inquiries, CBS president Frank Stanton announced that his network, in the fall of 1959, would start a new series of documentaries on important subjects. The network that only a few months earlier had felt confident enough to wash out *See It Now* hurried to prepare a similar series—*CBS Reports*, to be produced by Fred W. Friendly. NBC likewise moved to organize a "creative projects" unit in its news division.

Among other reform moves, Stanton also announced that thenceforth everything on CBS would be "what it purports to be." For example, canned laughter and applause would have to be identified

	% TV Homes	
Gunsmoke (CBS)	30.8	
Have Gun—Will Travel (CBS)	26.0	Nielsen ratings for August 1959 reflected stampede to westerns, and rise of ABC to competitive position. Game programs survived, but big-money quizzes had vanished.
Rifleman (ABC)	24.3	
I've Got a Secret (CBS)	21.7	
Peter Gunn (NBC)	21.5	
Best of Groucho (NBC)	21.3	
Alfred Hitchcock (CBS)	21.2	
Joseph Cotton (CBS)	20.0	
Wyatt Earp (ABC)	20.0	
Frontier Justice (CBS)	19.8	

as such. However, this radical idea was abandoned a few weeks later.

Meanwhile, statesmanlike pronouncements of a familiar sort were heard in hearing rooms. Legislation was not the answer. Self-regulation in the American tradition was called for. There was some reorganizing and renaming of network surveillance units. At NBC the "continuity acceptance" unit became the "standards and practices" unit.

Possibly the most telling result of the scandals was that the networks scrapped big-prize quiz programs and filled the gaps mainly with telefilms. Thus one of the principal remnants of New York television disappeared. The 1959 fall schedules brought forth more than thirty new Hollywood series. Prime-time television settled to a steady diet of telefilms—with spectacular interruptions.

SUMMITRY ON THE MOVE

When Nikita Khrushchev in September 1959, at Andrews Air Force Base in Maryland, stepped from a Soviet plane into two weeks of prime-time television, he faced enormous risks, as great as those involved in his denunciation of Joseph Stalin.

Emerging from an era in which the Soviet ruler had been a Kremlin recluse, the new leader was exposing himself in a land regarded by many in Russia as its mortal enemy. He was facing questions he could not censor, risking answers he could neither edit nor call back. He was doing so over the objections of some leaders in the Soviet Union and of the leadership of its most important ally, China.

If Khrushchev commanded American prime-time television, it was precisely because of the risks involved in the drama—and because he was prepared to give every act a bravura performance. Seemingly heedless of pitfalls, he joked, argued, clowned, denounced. Irrepressible good humor at times gave way to bursts of anger; but, as suddenly, good humor rebounded. His fund of maxims seemed inexhaustible. "Two mountains never meet, but two people can."

The Khrushchev gamble was that he could puncture stereotypes of American political thinking, ease the cold war and the arms race, and free Russian resources for consumer goods. His political future depended on the degree of his success.

Once more, in a triumph of timing, scientific achievement set the stage. Three days before his arrival a Soviet missile hit the moon, depositing on its surface a Soviet flag. It enabled Khrushchev during the arrival ceremonies, in the presence of President Eisenhower and other American dignitaries—political and military—to strike a magnanimous and at the same time condescending note:

KHRUSHCHEV: We have come to you with an open heart and good intentions . . . We entertain no doubt that the splendid scientists, engineers, and workers of the United States of America who are engaged in the field of conquering Cosmos will also carry their flag to the moon. The Soviet flag, as an old resident of the moon, will welcome your pennant and they will live there together in peace and friendship as we both should live together on the earth in peace and friendship, as should live in peace and friendship all peoples who inhabit our common Mother Earth—who so generously gives us her gifts.

Scores of cameras turned and clicked, along with videotape machines, which were becoming a prominent tool in television reporting. A floating army of some 375 reporters began to follow Khrushchev and remained with him almost continuously during the next two weeks. The result was scores of short sequences on regularly scheduled news programs, plus dozens of special programs under such titles as *Mr. Khrushchev Abroad* (ABC-TV), *Eyewitness to History* (CBS-TV), and *Khrushchev in America* (NBC-TV). The hordes of reporters, photographers and technicians trailing behind Khrushchev as he visited farm, supermarket, museum, and film studio became almost ludicrous. Those at the edges of the swarm hardly knew what was happening. Some carried transistor radios to keep up with the news.

A climax of the visit was the great Hollywood banquet—an extravaganza of hypocrisy. A recent Oscar for "best screenplay" had gone to one "Robert Rich," who had never come forward to receive his prize because he was really Dalton Trumbo, a writer who had been publicly untouchable since the Hollywood hearings, in which he had been one of the "unfriendly ten." Since his jail term he had been blacklisted but had survived by writing behind "fronts" —a practice ignored by the Hollywood hierarchy so long as no "trouble" erupted, such as protests or boycotts. Dalton Trumbo, not on the guest list for the Khrushchev banquet, was expected to keep well out of sight while the movie elite took charge of honoring the Soviet leader. Presiding at the white-tie affair was the tycoon Spyros Skouras, who decided to inform Khrushchev about democracy. Skouras explained that he came from an obscure family of Greek immigrants.

SKOURAS: When we came to this country, my two brothers and I worked as humble busboys. But because of the American system of opportunity for all, now I am president of Twentieth Century-Fox, an international organization employing 10,000 people.

Khrushchev visits a farm . . .

TV DIPLOMACY

. . . and a packing plant.

Khrushchev absorbed this and said he was not greatly surprised. He himself had worked from the time he could walk, had been a sheep herder till the age of twelve, worked in mines and factories, and now, thanks to the Soviet system, was the Prime Minister of a nation of 200,000,000 people.

Skouras felt challenged and stood up, holding the microphone. "How many Prime Ministers in Russia?"

Khrushchev looked puzzled. "How many Presidents in the United States?" This brought some laughter and applause.

Skouras shouted: "We have two million presidents—presidents of American corporations . . . their stockholders!"

It threatened for a time to escalate into hot debate. Skouras spoke of American relief efforts in Russia after the Russian revolution. Khrushchev said America should by all means continue to live under capitalism. "But don't inflict it on us."

Later, Khrushchev had a good time about Disneyland. On the spur of the moment he suggested a visit there, but the State Department, with no time for security arrangements, vetoed it. Khrushchev asked reporters, armed with their notebooks and cameras and tape recorders: "What do they have there—rocket launching pads? . . . Have gangsters taken control of the place?"

Wherever he went, Khrushchev could expect hostile questions. Queried about Soviet jamming of American broadcasts, he gave varied answers. If stones are thrown in a window, he said on one occasion, isn't it logical to protect oneself? Questions about Soviet suppression of a 1956 Hungarian uprising nettled him more, and brought angry retorts. "We also have some dead cats we can throw at you."

All in all, Khrushchev won what the business-oriented *Broadcasting* magazine called "million-dollar coverage." Film footage of the visit was widely shown, not only in the United States but also in many other countries, including the Soviet Union. Voice of America transmissions to the Soviet Union were not jammed during the Khrushchev visit; the jamming was later resumed selectively, on a reduced scale. Clearly Khrushchev had set changes in motion, both in the United States and the Soviet Union.

Some weeks after his departure, the White House announced that American, Russian, British, and French leaders would join in a summit meeting in Paris in May 1960, and that President Eisenhower would afterwards make a goodwill tour of the Soviet Union. The White House chose the 1959 Christmas season to make the announcement, and it was received as a message of peace and hope. Television networks began planning fantastic coverage of the coming events.

Eisenhower depended heavily on staff work. Plans were presented to him and approved or disapproved. In the army, where there was usually agreement on the objective—defeat of the enemy —this had worked well: it was a choice between alternative methods. Now he was surrounded by assistants—able men—who seemed to work in totally different directions. The disparity of objectives was constantly left unresolved.

Early in 1960, as one group worked on peace moves, another pressed him about Fidel Castro, who during the previous year had seized control in Cuba. His revolt, begun as a small guerrilla operation, had captured the imagination of many Americans, and Washington had recognized his regime and offered aid. But Castro felt that its terms assured continuance of Cuba's state of economic vassalage; he proclaimed that his Cuba was to be built for the exploited Cuban, not the foreign investor and those of the Cuban middle class who fed at his table. Castro planned expropriation of various United States holdings and of Cuban interests linked to them—including television and film. Castro's policy toward these media affected their subsequent history in Latin America.

Cuba already had a large television system—the largest of any Latin American country—firmly launched on United States lines. Its leading magnate, Goar Mestre, happened to be entertaining a visiting Screen Gems executive, William Fineshriber, when news came that Castro had taken power, and that his predecessor, Batista, had fled. Mestre said he would certainly have to leave the country, and he soon took off for Argentina. Cuban television became an instrument of the Castro revolution. So did its film studios, which had been a major center for pornographic production and now turned to documentaries in support of Castro's reforms.

Washington, protesting Castro expropriations, backed the protests with economic pressure: it cut sugar import quotas. Castro apparently faced ruin or retreat, but he showed no sign of accepting either. Visits by Soviet diplomats suggested that Castro was depending on Soviet aid to underwrite his declaration of independence from United States hegemony.

But President Eisenhower was already—only few knew of this—embarking on steps to retain that hegemony by military means. In March 1960, two months before the Paris summit meeting, he approved plans drawn up by the CIA for invading Cuba and overthrowing Castro. No hint of this disturbed the search-for-peace talk on television.

In April, along back streets of Miami, the CIA began quietly recruiting an army among Cuban refugees. It included ex-Batista adherents, disenchanted ex-Castro followers and others. The recruiters said they had nothing to do with the United States government but were employed by a group of wealthy capitalists who were fighting communism and had friends in Washington. Recruits were offered $175 a month, plus extra sums for dependents. They were assured of "all the weapons you need." Tanks and airplanes were mentioned. Some recruits felt the United States government must be behind it and this reassured them. There were jokes about the Cuban billionaire, perhaps named "Uncle Sam." Recruits were taken in closed vans in the dark of night to a disused airport—Opa Locka—and hurried into a plane with windows blacked out. The planes took off quickly, and when they landed they were at a training camp high in rugged mountains. They learned later it was in Guatemala, which was now ruled by President Miguel Ydigoras Fuentes. He had aided the CIA in the 1954 Guatemala coup, which was the model for the anti-Castro venture. This time there was an added feature: a CIA radio station was being built on a small Caribbean island, Swan Island. This would be a "liberation" station to foment rebellion in Cuba. It went on the air with 50,000 watts in May 1960—about the time the dignitaries of the great powers converged on Paris to defuse the cold war and usher in peaceful competition.

Another platoon of Eisenhower aides was busy with Vietnam. American efforts to build Ngo Dinh Diem as a popular rival to Ho Chi Minh had met with no success; Diem was widely hated. But the CIA was training and equipping a South Vietnamese internal-security police force to help Diem suppress political opposition. State Department policy statements still proclaimed Diem as Vietnam representative of the free world.

As the leaders assembled in Paris, another platoon of Eisenhower aides made an unscheduled appearance in newscasts. On May 1, 1960, a CIA spy plane, on a flight over the Soviet Union from a United States base in Pakistan, failed to return. The CIA had a cover story—fabrication, lie—ready for this. An "official" government bulletin—issued, to its discredit, by the National Aeronautics and Space Administration—announced that a weather observation plane flying over Turkey had apparently had "oxygen difficulties" and might have made a forced landing. Three days later Khrushchev announced that an American spy plane had been shot down over the Soviet Union.

Most Americans at this time knew nothing about U-2 spy planes. These planes had been used for several years for reconnaissance over the Soviet Union, flying at 80,000 feet, but were still a hush-hush subject. Eisenhower had been repeatedly assured by John Foster Dulles that the flights involved no diplomatic risks because the Russians, humiliated by inability to shoot down planes at this height, would never make public protest. Top officials—the few who knew about the U-2 flights—had clung to this confidence even after a Soviet missile had hit the moon. Besides, the U-2 planes had

". . . absolutely no—N-O . . . never has been." — Lincoln White, May 7, 1960. UPI

a self-destruct mechanism. If anything went wrong, not a fragment of evidence was supposed to remain.

This confidence led the State Department, even after the Khrushchev announcement, to stick to the CIA fabrication. In a crucial moment in American diplomatic history, millions of American television viewers saw Lincoln White, State Department press chief, appear before a battery of cameras and declare that there had been *"absolutely no—N-O—deliberate attempt to violate Soviet air space . . . never has been!"* The President had told an earlier press conference that he personally had forbidden provocative flights over the Soviet Union. Viewers were left with the impression that the Soviet talk about a spy plane had been another outrageous Russian falsehood.

The United States had walked into a trap. The pilot, Francis Gary Powers, was not dead. His plane had not been obliterated. He had been captured and had confessed the nature of his mission. Presently television viewers in many lands were treated to a filmed tour of the U-2 wreckage, guided by Khrushchev himself.

The unfolding drama included poignant details. The captured pilot, according to word from Moscow, had with him his social security card, a half-used pack of filter cigarettes, an unused suicide needle, currency of several countries, a girlie magazine, two watches, and seven gold rings. Khrushchev, whose spirits were at their highest, quipped: "Maybe the pilot was to have flown still higher to Mars and was going to lead astray Martian ladies."

The administration, having been exposed in a lie, compounded it with confusion and further lies. The State Department now admitted the U-2 was a spy plane but said the flight had not been authorized. The President contradicted this and said he had authorized all such flights. He defended the flights as a duty and said they would continue. When Khrushchev demanded an end to the flights, Vice President Nixon, interviewed by David Susskind on the television series *Open End*, scoffed at the demand and said the United States would certainly not discontinue them. Then the President in a press-conference statement said that he had already discontinued them.

To some people the government's confusion was more dismaying than its falsehoods, but not to everyone. Most Americans had always assumed that a government bulletin, while perhaps not giving the whole truth, was true. For many, the U-2 incident was the first in their memory in which their government had clearly been shown lying.

The incident had a fantastic television climax. Audiences throughout the world saw Paris pageantry: the arrival of the dignitaries. But Khrushchev took the spotlight. He announced that the summit conference could not begin until Eisenhower had apologized and punished the guilty. When this brought no results, a Khrushchev press conference was scheduled.

Khrushchev had the world's attention and made the most—or the worst—of it. Translated by the able young interpreter Victor Sukhodrev, who had an exceptional feeling for idiom, Khrushchev excoriated the United States as a war-mongering power, denounced Eisenhower, reviewed the history of US-USSR relations, fumed, raged. He withdrew the invitation to Eisenhower to visit the Soviet Union. The summit conference had apparently ground to a halt. One by one, the leaders headed for home.

But the floating spectacular had one more sequence. In the sum-

mer of 1960 Castro began to claim that the United States was training an army in Central America to overthrow his regime, and asked
that the matter be put on the United Nations agenda for September.
He himself would speak for Cuba. At the meeting a number of new
African nations were to be admitted and the admission of communist China was to be debated. The combination of items brought an
extraordinary representation. Khrushchev announced he would
head the Soviet delegation. The United States announced an address by Eisenhower. Other world leaders decided to attend: Tito,
Nehru, Nasser—the array was unprecedented, unbelievable. In mid-
September they began to arrive and to drift back and forth across
the television screen. Khrushchev and Castro were notified by the
State Department that they would be confined to Manhattan. Castro had disputes with a midtown hotel; he said his rooms were
bugged. Others—including Hearst writers—said he was turning his
suite into a bordello. In the midst of the dispute Castro adopted a
bold videogenic stratagem. He moved his delegation to the Hotel
Theresa on 125th Street, in the heart of Harlem, a hotel seldom
seen by white men. Nikita Khrushchev immediately decided to
visit Castro in Harlem. In view of farflung television audiences, and
surrounded by crowds of blacks on the Harlem sidewalk before the
Hotel Theresa, the two leaders embraced, laughed, pummeled each
other, talked eagerly, waved to the Harlem crowd and—via television—to blacks and whites of the world. Sandwiched between
lily-white telefilms and toothpaste and deodorant commercials, the
scene was dumbfounding—a strange intrusion into the accepted
world of cowboys, detectives, and other heroes.

But the interruption did not last long. Khrushchev had played
his cards. On this visit, flattering attentions of another day were replaced by official hostility and much unofficial truculence. The
State Department went so far as to urge broadcasters to play down
his reappearance. Khrushchev, for his part, became more edgy; like
a comedian who feels he is slipping, he overplayed. At a televised
United Nations session he ranted and blustered; as rulings went

against him he took off his shoe and pounded the desk. It was a spectacle that delighted his enemies.

In the end, many who had deplored giving Khrushchev a "platform" were delighted with the result. Hearst reporters noted with satisfaction that the public had come to know his "every twitch, every obscenity, every evasion, every declaration, determination, disarming gambit." And this, they felt, was good. The American media should not ignore Khrushchev, said the reporters, merely because of disagreement with him.

Apparently wisdom of this sort was not to be applied to Castro. Castro, perhaps assuming that his United Nations appearance would give him a chance to tell the American audience something about United States-Cuba relations, prepared a long address. But the television industry felt it could ignore Castro and the United Nations proceedings, and returned to profit-making. It perhaps felt virtuous in doing so.

In not carrying the Castro speech, the networks missed a historic opportunity. Castro ranged over much Caribbean history from a Castroite point of view. It was often a diatribe and would have been unpalatable to many, but would also have given them some understanding of revolutionary pressures facing them in Latin America— a subject scarcely hinted at in prime-time television. It would also have given them a scoop, for Castro told of an invasion force being paid, armed, and trained at the expense of the American taxpayer, in violation of American law and treaty obligations. The speech was not telecast, scarcely even quoted. Its charges were denied by American spokesmen. In some newscasts they were mentioned as ravings of a madman.

Castro's journey to the United States thus had little impact on American opinion. Meanwhile the Cuban airliner that had brought him was impounded by legal action of those whose properties he had expropriated. He accepted the offer of a Russian plane to take him back to Cuba. Every aspect of the journey seemed to push him closer to Khrushchev.

For Khrushchev, the itinerant television spectacular was over. It had failed in its first purpose. The United States rapprochement had collapsed.

His final United Nations oratory made clear the complete redirection of his strategy. Praising communist China and "courageous Cuba," he denounced American interventionism. He was trying to mend fences at home and in China.

By 1960 the networks had learned that explosions of special events, though interrupting normal business, could be a boon as well as a burden. Specials and documentaries *might* mean financial loss—but then again, they might not. CBS had persuaded Firestone to sponsor some of the Khrushchev documentaries. It seemed possible that such programs might not, in due time, be loss leaders after all, but profitable items. Meanwhile they were considered a necessary service.

Thus, in the wake of the quiz scandals, a split-personality pattern was becoming the network norm. One part, the news division, was always preparing for, and welcoming, the grandstand interruptions that had become its specialty, and that gave scope to its developing resources and skills. The other part, the real money-making part, was thereby enabled to go ahead with normal business, such as telefilms.

In 1960 the news half was preparing, among other matters, coverage of a presidential election that promised to be hard-fought. The other was locked in an inter-network battle that was suddenly turning savage.

UNTOUCHABLES

The big 1960 telefilm news was the rise of *The Untouchables*. The series had started in October of the year before and by mid-April was pushing into top position with a 35.1 Arbitron rating.* A sur-

* Arbitron used, in a fixed sample of homes, electronic devices which measured the tune-in every 90 seconds and sent it to a central office of the Amer-

prising aspect of all this was that the program was on ABC-TV, the also-ran network. The industry noted that *The Untouchables*, depicting struggles against gangsters, was probably the most violent show on television.

ABC-TV had other rating successes to trumpet in trade-press advertising. Its third-place position had stemmed partly from its late arrival on the television scene. In some cities ABC-TV had no regular outlet and could only place occasional programs on affiliates of other networks—usually in unfavorable periods. But in cities that had three or more stations, and in which all networks were represented, ABC-TV had surprising successes. In these cities it was winning rating battles regularly—on Thursdays with *The Untouchables*, on Fridays with 77 *Sunset Strip*, on Sundays with *The Rebel*, on Mondays with *Cheyenne*, on Tuesdays with *Rifleman*, on Wednesdays with *Hawaiian Eye*.

All of these were violent. ABC-TV did not mention this in trade-press advertising, but the other networks were aware of it—and responded in kind.

ABC-TV, ever since its breakthrough success with *Cheyenne*, had been devoted to "action-adventure"; now this policy was paying off in profits.

It happened to be a moment when executive shuffles brought ABC executives to top positions at both CBS and NBC. The quiz scandals had made telefilms the main battleground; CBS, anxious for a top man with telefilm credentials, turned to James Aubrey of ABC-TV and made him vice president and then president of CBS-TV—edging out Louis Cowan who, as packager of several quiz successes, had been similarly lionized only a year earlier. Aubrey, besides canceling big-money quizzes, scrapped a CBS anthology remnant, the occasionally impressive *Playhouse 90*, and put the accent on action telefilms.

A smooth, stylish, supremely confident executive, Aubrey pre-

---

ican Research Bureau. The organization also issued "ARB ratings," which were based on interviews using a roster of program titles to prompt the interviewee's recollection.

SHARE

BUT SHARE NOT ALIKE

	*Three Network Share of Audience
ABC TELEVISION	36.5
NETWORK Y	35.5
NETWORK Z	27.9

Source: Nielsen 24 Market TV Report, average audience, week ending Aug 21, 1960, 7 nights 8-10:30 PM, Mon-Sun

The chart tells the story, except for this: ABC Television was in First Place on 4 nights out of 7. Pretty nice lead. Pretty nice week. For future success stories, watch this space.

ABC TELEVISION

dicted that he could double the CBS net income, which stood at $25,000,000 as he took office. Telefilms would be the means.

Robert Kintner, previously ABC president, had left that network for the NBC presidency. At ABC Oliver Treyz, whose salesmanship had brought many telefilm sponsors to the network, became ABC-TV president. Thus all three networks were led by men who had had a part in the rise of ABC; all proceeded to push the successful formula.

Along with ratings, other factors contributed to the trend. The 1950's had seen new developments in "executive compensation" to counteract the rising tax bite. A much-desired benefit was the stock option. Thus Aubrey as CBS-TV president acquired options to buy a number of shares of CBS stock at a fixed price. A rise in the CBS stock quotation could put him in position to make instant money. With such a policy, an executive could hardly eliminate awareness of stock prices from programming decisions. Stock prices were becoming increasingly sensitive to successes like that of *The Untouchables*. Stocks could be nudged up or down, it seemed, by shifts in Arbitron, Nielsen, or Videodex ratings.

It also happened to be a moment when network chiefs acquired powers they had not had before. The quiz scandals had brought this on. Networks had promised to take firmer control of programming. CBS, said corporation president Frank Stanton, would be absolute master in its own house. No longer would sponsors control periods and determine how they would be used. The network would do the scheduling and let the sponsor know what was available.

To many critics of television, this had sounded promising. Sponsors had seemed to be guided by merchandizing considerations; networks at least had split personalities. But at the networks the decisions were now being made by Aubrey, Kintner, and Treyz.

Controlling schedules, the three executives began to juggle them for advantage in the rating war. ABC-TV had developed the technique of "counter-programming." If CBS-TV and NBC-TV had competing comedies, ABC-TV felt it could "knock them off" with a sharply contrasting western. Action programs became the principal weapon in the struggle. In their orders to Hollywood studios the networks demanded more action. They never—or seldom—said "violence," but that is what they got.

The Untouchables was produced by Quinn Martin at the Desilu Studios under contract with ABC-TV. A network script supervisor combed through each script to make sure it was active enough. Scripts of insufficient vigor would bring complaints from network headquarters in New York to Quinn Martin. These would bring memoranda from Martin to his assistants and writers, demanding more action—"or we are all going to get clobbered." At the same time, Martin was hard put to avoid repetitiousness. He wrote to one writer:

I wish you would come up with a different device than running the man down with a car, as we have done this now in three different shows. I like the idea of sadism, but I hope we can come up with another approach to it.

The Untouchables, heading rating lists, was estimated to reach 5,000,000 to 8,000,000 juvenile viewers with each program. Evidence of its popularity came from diverse sources. A juvenile gang in Cleveland called itself "the Untouchables" and its leader said he was the "second Al Capone." When some were rounded up on an assault-to-kill charge, one said: "We're untouchable—you can't do anything with us." A Department of Justice survey at two correctional institutions found that almost all listed as their favorite programs *The Untouchables, Thriller, Route 66, Rebel, Have Gun—Will Travel.* Most had spent three to five hours a day watching television.

The ABC-TV concentration on action, which later became known in government circles as the "Treyz trend," was rivaled at CBS-TV by an "Aubrey dictum." Aubrey demanded action but wanted girls to be a part of it. One staff member summarized the dictum as "broads, bosoms, and fun." NBC apparently dared not leave the field to its rivals and this led, according to later government studies, to a "Kintner edict." Robert Kintner, former newspaper columnist, had a strong interest in news programming and was pushing NBC into a lead in that field. For telefilms he had a realist's contempt; they were "entertainment" and served their purpose if they won audiences and sponsors. So he too began a push for action. NBC-TV's chief supplier, MCA, was ready to provide it. One of the most violent contributions was *Whispering Smith,* the story of a soft-talking gunman.

A group in Los Angeles surveying night-time television during one week—November 12-19, 1960—tabulated:

144 murders (scenes of mass murder not tabulated), 143 attempted murders, 52 justifiable killings, 14 cases of drugging, 12 jailbreaks, 36 robberies, 6 thefts, 13 kidnappings (1 of a small boy), 6 burglaries, 7 cases of torture, 6 extortion cases, 5 blackmail, 11 planned murders, 4 attempted lynchings, 1 massacre scene with hundreds killed, 1 mass murder of homesteaders, 1 planned mass murder by arson, 3 scenes of shooting between gangland posses, many killed, 1 other mass gun battle, 1 program with over 50 women kidnapped, this one including an hour of violence, kidnapping, murder, brutal fighting. These figures do not include the innumerable prolonged and brutal fights, the threats to kill, the sluggings or the many times when characters in the crime programs manhandled the victims, the forced confessions, and dynamiting to illegally destroy.

The group also noted that ABC-TV used film-clips of its most violent scenes as promotion material at station breaks throughout the day.

The precise effects of all this were not known. With juvenile delinquency rates constantly rising, some conjectured that television was a factor; but others said that television was obviously mirroring an increasingly violent world. The debate received only limited attention in 1960.

While many watched the murder parade with fixed gaze, something else was more widely publicized. It was interruption time: the other half of the split personality was demanding attention. This was election year.

VÉRITÉ

When forty-one-year-old Senator John F. Kennedy of Massachusetts, campaigning for the Democratic nomination for President, announced his intention to enter the Wisconsin primary, he received a flying visit from Robert Drew of Time, Inc. They had a talk in Detroit.

Drew had a suggestion. He was a film enthusiast and had brought with him Richard Leacock, the cameraman who had done magnificent photography for *Louisiana Story*, produced by Robert Flaherty. Drew and "Ricky" Leacock wanted, during the primary, to be everywhere with Kennedy: in and out of cars, in hotel rooms, on speech platforms. Throughout the marathon they would never, at any time, ask him to *do* anything. They would never say, "Would you come through that door again, we missed that?" They wanted to be ignored, but wanted access.

Kennedy, who had grown up surrounded by reporters and cameramen and whose father, ex-Ambassador Joseph P. Kennedy, had once headed Pathé, was aware that the arrangement could damage him. Leacock and Drew did not argue the point. Drew merely said, "You'll have to trust us." Kennedy had to fly back to Washington. The film makers got seats on the same plane and kept talking.

The Drew film obsession was, in a sense, a logical outgrowth of the candid photography that had established *Life*, where he had served briefly as an assistant picture editor. But Drew was also a television watcher. He was appalled at the sterility of most news programs, but had seen some telecasts he could not shake off.

He remembered an early *See It Now* program, which had shown Senator Robert A. Taft and Senator Leverett Saltonstall campaigning in a New England town. Normally the speeches, or tidbits of them, would have been the meat of newsfilm coverage. But the *See It Now* camera showed the end of each speech, then followed the speaker down the platform stairs. Senator Taft came to a group of small children with autograph books, and moved them all aside with sweeping gesture. Later Senator Saltonstall, coming down the same steps, noted the same group with amused interest and stopped to enjoy a moment with them. No narration commented on this. After seeing this program, Drew went to Murrow and offered himself "body and soul" to work in the Murrow unit. Not finding a place with Murrow, Drew badgered Time, Inc., for funds for "candid" motion picture experiments. The first experiments pleased no one.

An interval as a Nieman Fellow at Harvard gave him a chance to look into the reasons.

Studying films he had admired, he got in touch with Leacock, and their views coalesced. Both hated narration that sought to direct—and thereby control—the viewer's observation. They wanted the audience to see for itself, to make discoveries and inferences. This might make a film more difficult—sometimes perplexing—in the end, more meaningful. This became the guiding principle of the film work at Time, Inc.

On the flight to Washington, Drew suggested to Kennedy that the proposed film would have extraordinary historic interest—especially if he were elected. Kennedy did not respond directly to this. But at the end of the trip he said abruptly, "If you don't hear from me, assume it's on."

The same arrangements were made with Senator Hubert Humphrey, who had also entered the Wisconsin primary.

A remarkable film team got to work. Besides Drew and Leacock, it included Donn Pennebaker, Terence McCartney-Filgate, and Albert Maysles. All were young and searching for their role as film artists. All shared the purpose that animated Drew—to capture significant moments, letting viewers experience them without *ex cathedra* guidance. Some called this *cinéma vérité*, others *direct cinema*. So it was with a "movement" feeling that the Drew unit, as a division of Time, Inc., began to trail the Kennedy and Humphrey forces across Wisconsin.

They made a film of endless fascination—and historic interest. To public awareness of two leaders on the rise, and of the mechanics of a campaign, the film contributed a rich array of sights and sounds—informative, puzzling, disturbing, amusing, provocative. No previous film had so caught the pressure, noise, euphoria, and sweaty maneuvering. Detail and long-shot, noise and privacy, alternated rapidly.

Across a misty, rolling countryside the viewer saw a lonely motorcade of half a dozen Humphrey cars en route to their next stop;

at a reception, an extreme close-up of John Kennedy's hands in a long handshaking sequence, as citizen after citizen—unseen except for the hands—is propelled down the line; on a platform, during a speech by Kennedy, the neatly gloved hand of Jacqueline Kennedy twiddling behind her; in a barren room, Hubert Humphrey talking to a sprinkling of farmers, telling them the big boys back East don't like him much because they know his heart is with the farmer. Humphrey plugs his coming telethon over WEAU-TV, Lacrosse, urging people to phone in.

> HUMPHREY: Tell them you want to ask a question to that Humphrey fellow. And make them tough. That's what they like. They like to see me squirm.

Then the viewer is suddenly right behind Kennedy as he pushes through an endless, screaming crowd, acknowledging shouted questions, laughing, pushing on.

Film technology was not fully ready for such a sequence. Leacock and his camera were behind Kennedy; behind Leacock came Drew and a tape recorder. To keep film and tape synchronized, a short length of cable had to connect the two. As Leacock moved, Drew squirmed along at his heels at the end of a four-foot umbilical cord. It was mad and impossible: they squeezed together through a revolving door, upstairs, downstairs, into limousines. When they began editing, they found disaster: the connection had been broken. Pennebaker spent weeks going over the material frame by frame, to put sound and picture *in sync*. One thing they knew: the umbilical cord had to go; some other synchronizing system must be found. In 1960 various groups were working desperately to that end.

On primary day, as the returns came in, McCartney-Filgate was covering Humphrey, who led in the early vote-count. But in the end victory was in a Milwaukee hotel room where Leacock and Drew maneuvered around John and Jacqueline Kennedy and Bobby Kennedy and other relatives and co-workers, milling, grinning, planning.

Primary, an extraordinary achievement, was telecast on a few stations owned by Time, Inc. It was rejected by all three networks. The rejection involved a newly developed—and perilous—policy of the networks.

All were now fostering their own documentary units, which might or might not prove financial assets. Each considered such a unit a government-relations necessity, but hoped to recoup costs through commercial sponsorship. Each was working on documentaries on a range of topics: space travel, election campaigns, Latin America, the cold war.

Early in 1960 an enterprising independent producer, David Wolper, completed a film titled *The Race for Space*, and secured a sponsor, Shulton, who was ready to buy time for it on any network. But each network was developing similar projects, which would be less salable if the film were accepted. Each network announced that it would, as a matter of policy, carry only news documentaries produced by the network itself. Independent producers were stunned, dismayed. The network action seemed a move toward a documentary monopoly of three producing companies. Since network exposure influenced use in all other markets, the decision had a bearing on the whole documentary field.

Some loopholes remained. Shulton, having contracted to sponsor *The Race for Space*, bought time in many parts of the country, station by station. *The Race for Space* was thus, with much difficulty, able to reach an audience. But documentary writers and directors were hardly reassured.

The networks explained the policy as a matter of responsibility. John Charles Daly, vice president for news at ABC-TV—where documentary was in a rudimentary stage—answered a Writers Guild of America protest by writing: "The standards of production and presentation which apply to a professional network news department would not necessarily apply to, for instance, an independent Hollywood producer." NBC-TV explained that its obligation "for objective, fair, and responsible presentation of news developments and public issues" required that it do all news documentaries itself. CBS-TV similarly ascribed its decision to a need for standards. "Since *The Race for Space* was not produced by CBS News and used a newsman not on the CBS News staff, our policy required its rejection."

The film *Primary*, coming on the heels of such policy statements, again raised the issue. Film artists wondered whether Time, Inc., might perhaps lead a crusade against a policy they saw as dangerously monopolistic. But the possibility of such a crusade was averted by a compromise.

American Broadcasting-Paramount Theaters president Leonard Goldenson, after screening work of the Drew unit, was so impressed that he made a deal with Time, Inc. Its Drew unit would make a series of films for ABC-TV and function, in effect, as an ABC-TV documentary unit. The move purported to uphold the new policy, but sidestepped it insofar as the Drew unit was concerned. The policy remained, but the Drew unit was able to go on to higher things. Goldenson asked the group to begin with a film on the Latin American turmoil. With no inkling of United States invasion preparations, Drew sent Albert Maysles to Cuba, accompanied by William Worthy, the Baltimore *Afro-American* writer who had angered the State Department by going to China. Leacock was assigned to Venezuela and Costa Rica, and Drew went with him.

The Drew productions were to be telecast under the series title *Close-Up*. ABC-TV secured Bell & Howell as sponsor for a number of *Close-Up* programs. *Cinéma vérité* won a foothold in prime time.

BAREFACED

The year 1960 was crucial for documentaries, but above all it was the year of the Great Debates.

Even before the Democrats at their Los Angeles convention nominated John F. Kennedy and Lyndon B. Johnson, and the Republicans at Chicago nominated Richard M. Nixon and Henry Cabot Lodge, the networks were agitating for television confrontations between major candidates. Quite aside from the dramatic possibilities, the networks had a special purpose. They hoped to rid themselves of Section 315 of the Communications Act, which they regarded as tyrannous.

Section 315 provided that if a station licensee let a legally qualified candidate "use" the station, other candidates for the same office had to be given "equal opportunities" to use the station. This was assumed to mean that if one candidate got free time, rival candidates were entitled to free time; if one paid for time, the same rates and conditions had to apply to the rivals.

The law had not been difficult to interpret in regard to candidates' speeches, but campaigns invaded many other kinds of programming. Many a candidate was ready to dedicate a playground with a "nonpolitical" speech which he hoped stations would cover in newscasts; to appear on a quiz program; to visit a late-night variety program for a human-interest chat and a piano solo; to perform in a documentary. Such programs made licensees uncertain about their obligations, and the FCC had contributed to this uncertainty with interpretations that sometimes seemed contradictory.

In 1959 Congress, seeking to clarify the situation, amended Section 315 by exempting "bona fide" newscasts, "bona fide" news interviews, "bona fide" news documentaries, and broadcasts relating to political conventions. But the networks, hoping for more, urged outright repeal. Immediately after the conventions they added pressure by wiring debate invitations to Nixon and Kennedy—subject to favorable legislative action.

Kennedy at once wired his acceptance; Nixon delayed a few days. He had little to gain, much to lose, by appearances with Kennedy, the lesser-known candidate. Eisenhower advised Nixon not to debate. But Nixon, with a reputation for "standing up to Khrushchev," could not afford to seem afraid of Kennedy. And Kennedy's acceptance speech, which Nixon had watched at home on television, had reassured him; it had seemed to Nixon "way over people's heads." Nixon felt he would not make that mistake, and decided to accept. Spokesmen for the two candidates and the networks worked out a plan for four debates—still subject to favorable legislative action.

With the candidates in agreement, Congress finally acted. It did not go as far as the networks had hoped; it merely suspended Section 315 for the 1960 presidential drive. But the networks hoped, through success of the plan, to accomplish the final extinction of Section 315. President Eisenhower signed the bill on August 24, 1960.

Late in September the candidates and their retinues converged on Chicago in an atmosphere of tension. At CBS station WBBM, site of the first debate—scheduled for September 26—the Nixon advisers found the studio background too pale. Their candidate's light-colored suit would merge with it. It was repainted but the new paint dried lighter than had been expected and an additional coat was required. The paint was still tacky at debate time. There was also argument—and suspicion—about lighting and camera positions. The Republicans did not want Nixon photographed from the left. This was satisfactory to all concerned, including the Democrats.

Don Hewitt of CBS News, the agreed-on director for the first telecast, was still juggling arrangements when he found Nixon entering from one side, Kennedy from the other. The occasion seemed to call for initiative on his part so he said: "I assume you two gentlemen know each other?" The candidates shook hands.

To keep things moving, Hewitt asked Kennedy: "Do you want makeup?" Kennedy had been campaigning in California and looked tanned, incredibly vigorous, and in full bloom. He promptly said, "No!" Nixon looked pale. He had made a vow to campaign in all fifty states and had been trying to carry it out. Besides, he had had

"I assume you two gentlemen know each other?" John F. Kennedy, Don
Hewitt, Richard M. Nixon.   CBS

a brief illness and had lost a few pounds; his collar looked loose
around his neck. But after Kennedy's "no" he replied with an
equally firm "no." Later his advisers, worried about his appearance, applied some Lazy-Shave, a product recommended for "five-
o'clock shadow."

The first debate was disastrous for Nixon. This had little to do
with what was said, which on both sides consisted of almost ritualized campaign ploys and slogans. What television audiences noted
chiefly was the air of confidence, the nimbleness of mind that ex-
uded from the young Kennedy. It emerged not only from crisp
statements emphasized by sparse gestures, but also from glimpses
of Kennedy not talking. Don Hewitt used occasional "reaction
shots" showing each candidate listening to the other. A glimpse of

The Great Debates.

the listening Kennedy showed him attentive, alert, with a suggestion of a smile on his lips. A Nixon glimpse showed him haggard; the lines on his face seemed like gashes and gave a fearful look. Toward the end, perspiration streaked the Lazy-Shave.

Edward A. ("Ted") Rogers, principal television adviser to Nixon, protested the reaction shots. But Hewitt said they were a normal television technique and that viewers would feel cheated without them. Such elements may have played a decisive part in the Nixon catastrophe. Among those who heard the first debate on radio, Nixon apparently held his own. Only on television had he seemed to lose.

In the second, third, and fourth debates—held on October 6, 13, and 21—Nixon looked better and fared far better. The second was in Washington; for the third, Kennedy was in New York, Nixon in California; the fourth was held in New York. All the debates had vast audiences.* Polls tended to show that the most crucial impact was on previously undecided voters; a larger share of these went to Kennedy. Fence-sitting politicians swung to him; he had clearly created a victory psychology. After the first debate increasingly large crowds gathered at Kennedy campaign stops.

Critics of the Great Debates said that they measured coolness

* The American Research Bureau estimated the television audiences of the four debates at 75,000,000, 61,000,000, 70,000,000, and 63,000,000.

and adroitness, not wisdom. The Great Debates, said historian Henry Steele Commager, glorified traits having no relationship to the presidency; he was sure George Washington would have lost a television Great Debate. But enthusiasts saw in the public ordeal of the debates a relevance to leadership in an age of instant crisis and instant communication.

Time periods for the Great Debates were made available free by networks and stations, but the debates were only one element in a furiously contested campaign. Both parties also bought time—in each case, more than in any previous campaign. The Republicans spent $7,558,809, the Democrats $6,204,986, on television and radio.

The Democrats, perhaps remembering their 1956 difficulties in finding an advertising agency, made the unusual move of selecting a San Francisco-based agency, Guild, Bascom & Bonfigli—thirty-fifth in standing among advertising agencies. But Robert F. Kennedy, thirty-four-year-old brother of the candidate, was definitely in charge of strategy, abetted by the still younger Ted Kennedy and other Kennedy relatives, friends, and associates.

For the Republicans, the television and radio campaign was again supervised by Batten, Barton, Durstine & Osborn personnel, but Nixon wanted to avoid a Madison Avenue stigma, so BBD&O executive Carroll Newton left his Madison Avenue quarters for a Vanderbilt Avenue office a block away, where a temporary agency, Campaign Associates, was created, with recruits from a number of organizations.

Among them was Gene Wyckoff of NBC, who had considerable difficulty with a film for Henry Cabot Lodge. Lodge looked statesmanlike, but when he spoke, something else came through —a patrician condescension. A filmed talk by Lodge was considered a disaster, and was scrapped. Instead Wyckoff assembled a 4¼-minute film—to be used as a hitchhiker—composed largely of still photos from Lodge family albums. Stills used with camera motion had been an avant-garde preoccupation for some years, having been popularized by the Canadian film *City of Gold*, a 1957

Oscar winner. The Lodge campaign film helped to make the technique a fixture in politics. A similar film was made for Nixon. For both, narration was pieced together from President Eisenhower's press conferences, using laudatory references to Lodge and Nixon.

For Kennedy the most important campaign film dealt with the religious issue. Attacks on him as a Catholic had been widespread, and he knew he must, at some stage, meet them head-on. An invitation from Texas to address the Houston Ministerial Association provided a springboard. He appeared before the ministers on September 12.

> KENNEDY: I believe in an America where the separation of Church and State is absolute—where no Catholic would tell the President (should he be a Catholic) how to act, and no Protestant minister would tell his parishioners for whom to vote—where no church or church school is granted any public funds or political preference. . . .

Last-minute staff research had culled from the names of those who died at the Alamo a few who *might* have been Catholic—although no one could find out if they were. This resulted in the astute lines:

> KENNEDY: . . . side by side with Bowie and Crockett died McCafferty and Bailey and Carey, but no one knows if they were Catholics or not. For there was no religious test at the Alamo.

Seasoned Texas politician Sam Rayburn considered the session a triumph and said that Kennedy "ate 'em blood raw." Filmed highlights of the confrontation became a basic campaign weapon. Time was bought on television stations across the country, with special concentration where the message seemed most needed.

The campaign had suddenly thrust a new personality on the consciousness of television audiences. Like Lucy and Van Doren and the *Bonanza* group and *The Untouchables*, John Kennedy had caught on suddenly with a spectacular rise in ratings. He did not belong to the regularly scheduled world but seemed as professional as a regular. He had wit and drama. He went after an adversary with style. He said: "Mr. Nixon may be very experienced in kitchen debates, but so are a great many other married men I know." When Nixon accused him of a "bare-faced lie," Kennedy replied that he could not accuse Nixon of anything bare-faced because "I've seen him in a television studio, with his makeup on." With utmost brevity, he sometimes made statements that rang out. Concerning the developing world he said: "More energy is released by the awakening of these new nations than by the fission of the atom itself."

He had an air of confidence that to some people, including Adlai Stevenson and Edward R. Murrow, had an element of arrogance. He seemed to have a lot of information on many problems, and ready statistics on them. Perhaps he reacted to them as fields for political action rather than as deeply felt personal concerns; yet he was aware, alert, growing. In the fall of 1960 his vitality crackled from the television tube.

Reviewing a videotape of one of his own television appearances, John F. Kennedy commented: "We wouldn't have had a prayer without that gadget." He won by a popular vote of 34,221,463 to 34,108,582, and an electoral vote of 303 to 219. Crucial states had been won by a hair.

TOP PRIORITIES

On November 18 President-elect Kennedy, then at Palm Beach, was briefed by CIA director Allen Dulles on activities of his agency. Kennedy now learned for the first time of the Cuban invasion plan—in very general terms. The information was kept even from close campaign associates.

Visitors to the Kennedy Palm Beach headquarters during following days included Robert Drew of the *Time* film unit. He was invited to show *Primary*, which Kennedy had not yet seen. He also brought "Yanki No!" the program on Latin American tensions just shot for the ABC-TV *Close-Up* series.

John and Jacqueline Kennedy expressed delight with *Primary*. The President-elect spoke of having his presidential administration documented in similar fashion. On the following evening they looked at "Yanki No!"—this time with two other visitors to the Palm Beach quarters, Senator and Mrs. J. William Fulbright.

Shot *cinéma-vérité* style, "Yanki No!" announced itself as a warning, to the United States, of a widening gulf. The viewer received the impression of military regimes, fortified by United States support, holding against wide unrest—except in Cuba, where Maysles's camera followed Castro through surging, delirious, admiring throngs. Here the dam had burst.

At the end of the film Kennedy paced up and down restlessly. He and Fulbright appeared to respect the film and its disturbing portrayal. Kennedy walked up to Drew, and with his face three inches away, said, "So what do we do about it?"

Drew was nonplussed at the question. "All I can do," he said, "is try to show the problem."

About this time Edward R. Murrow at CBS had a visit from a journalist he had known during World War II. The man said he had details about a coming invasion of Cuba, which he insisted was being organized by the United States. Murrow discussed it with Fred Friendly as a possible *CBS Reports* subject. Friendly could scarcely believe the story, already denied on various occasions. Murrow seemed to have more faith in it, but they hardly knew how to proceed. "It just seemed to us we were getting mixed up with something we couldn't handle," said Friendly later. Soon afterwards Murrow was offered the directorship of the United States Information Agency, and accepted; he and Friendly had no further discussions on Cuba.

The Cuban government still talked about a threatened invasion. In January 1961 President Eisenhower, saying that United States endurance was at an end, severed diplomatic relations with Cuba.

Yanki No!—1960.   Drew Associates

It was two weeks before the end of his presidency. At about the same time a spokesman for refugee groups in Miami flatly denied the invasion rumor.

At the isolated CIA training camp in Guatemala, trainees were splintering into factions. The CIA mistrusted some of the recruits; to prevent leaks, a number were transferred by the CIA to a jungle prison accessible only by helicopter.

The CIA was thus managing to keep its activity well submerged. In the United States only two periodicals, *The Hispanic-American Report* and *The Nation,* both with small circulation, had treated the rumors with any seriousness. Their effect was negligible. Television and radio were being kept almost spotless. Allen Dulles, in later memoirs, explained his policy toward the mass media.

I always considered, first, how the operation could be kept from the opponent and, second, how it could be kept from the press. Often the priority was reversed.

The high-priority task of keeping it from the press—and the public —was being performed with impressive success as the new administration prepared for office.

With the election interruption out of the way the industry—the main part, the regularly scheduled part—could resume full force. There was no let-up in the boom. Evening schedules were practically sold out. New advertisers were coming in.

ABC-TV, for added profit, decided to stretch the 30-second break between programs to a 40-second break. This would allow four instead of three 10-second commercials at station-break time, and mean millions in additional revenue. The stations of the network were pressing for the innovation.

There was some anxiety that it would be denounced as commercialism. "Why don't we explain," said one ABC-TV executive, "that it will seem *less* commercial? Wherever possible there will be two 20-second commercials, not four 10-second commercials."

"Why don't we explain," said vice president Giraud Chester, who sometimes made irreverent suggestions, "that we want to make more money? That will strengthen capitalism and be a blow to communism."

In 1960 a new institution made a flourishing start: a film festival for commercials. It was so successful that a thousand entries were expected for the following year. Entries would be eligible for election to a Commercial Classics Hall of Fame and for awards—the CLIO awards—in numerous categories: apparel, automobiles, cake mixes, cigarettes and cigars, coffees and teas, cosmetics and toiletries, laundry soaps and detergents, paper products and wraps, pet foods, pharmaceuticals, soft drinks, and twenty other categories.

Commercials were becoming lavish. While budgets in the telefilm field had risen to about $2000 per minute, budgets for commercials were running to $10,000 and $20,000 per minute and were climbing rapidly. Major Hollywood studios, including Metro-Goldwyn-Mayer, were competing for a share of this business. Animated commercials were especially costly but avoided residual payments to on-camera actors and the problem of obsolescence of clothing and hair styles. For lower costs, some agencies were having animated sequences done in Japan, Spain, and other countries where costs were low. Impressive talents were drawn into the making of commercials, which sometimes—in the opinion of some viewers—outshone the entertainment. Observers noted that among the young, television talk focused as often on commercials as on programs.

The 1960-61 season brought its new crop of telefilm series. *The Roaring Twenties* was somewhat like *The Untouchables, Surfside 6* like *77 Sunset Strip, The Aquanauts* like *Seahunt, The Man from Interpol* like *The Man Called X.*

CBS executive William Morwood once explained his technique for persuading an advertising agency or sponsor of the virtues of a proposed script or series. He always began by saying, "This is something that's never been done before. . . ." Here he would identify the novel element—a setting or occupation or plot device. Then he would add: "And it's *exactly* like. . . ." Here he would point out the similarity to a well-known success. In 1960-61 the "completely new . . . exactly like" syndrome still dominated the telefilm field —at all networks.

Business was good but the industry was wary of the new administration; budgets for news, special events, and documentaries were pushed up.

THE CAMELOT MOMENT

The 1960-61 season brought to the documentary field a sense of a renascence. The documentary spurt, which owed some of its impetus to the quiz scandals, had been further stimulated by disasters like the U-2 affair, which brought foreign policy under more earnest public scrutiny. The new critical atmosphere prompted NBC, for example, to undertake a documentary on the U-2 incident and to schedule it in the closing weeks of the Eisenhower administration—behavior that seemed uncharacteristic of NBC.

But the feeling of renascence acquired more positive momentum from the tone set by the Kennedy administration as it gathered the reins of government. That tone emerged from interviews, appointments and—unforgettably—from the Kennedy inaugural.

In interviews Kennedy said he did not plan fireside chats in the Roosevelt tradition but believed strongly in documentaries. He felt that the motion picture camera could help keep citizens informed about activities of government and should be allowed to do so. Documentary producers sensed they had a spokesman in the White House—where the western had held a place of honor.

The appointment of Edward R. Murrow to head the U.S. Information Agency confirmed their sense of representation. Plans for the inaugural further encouraged expectations of a new dawn. Kennedy wanted "The Star Spangled Banner" sung by Marian Anderson, who had once been barred from singing in Constitution Hall by the Daughters of the American Revolution. Whereas President Eisenhower had asked the Negro to be patient, his successor clearly intended to move forward.

The inauguration, held on a bitterly cold day in a city all but paralyzed by eight inches of snow, produced warm and memorable moments on the television screen. There was the eighty-five-year-old Robert Frost, who had been asked to read a poem—again, a symbolic moment, since poets had not recently been noticed in high places. He began to read words he had written for the occasion.

FROST: . . . a Golden Age of poetry and power,
Of which this noonday's the beginning hour . . .

Blinded by the glare of sun and snow, he could hardly read the words, and faltered briefly. But those words were only a prologue

Robert Frost–Kennedy inauguration, 1961.   Wide World

to an older poem he knew well. He held his head high and the words rang out.

Striking was the contrast between outgoing and incoming Presidents—one, the oldest to serve; the other, the youngest ever to be elected. The contrast gave emphasis to a passage in the inaugural address:

> KENNEDY: Let the word go forth from this time and place, to friend and foe alike, that the torch has been passed to a new generation of Americans, born in this century, tempered by war, disciplined by a hard and bitter peace, proud of our ancient heritage, and unwilling to witness or permit the slow undoing of those human rights to which this nation has always been committed, and to which we are committed today at home and around the world.

What actions were foreshadowed by these ringing words? No one could even guess, but their rhythm and eloquence, the verve of their delivery, won extraordinary response from the young. Kennedy's address included standard cold-war language, but also departed from it. He dared to use a term John Foster Dulles had considered equivalent to *appease—negotiate.*

KENNEDY: Let us never negotiate out of fear, but let us never fear to negotiate.

The whole day was a dazzling series of telecasts—a glorious interruption. Next day, for most of the industry, it was time to get back to regular schedules. But many in news and documentary units felt they had an agenda; they had heard some sort of call. The Kennedy aura seemed to encourage unthinkable thoughts and impossible dreams. Kennedy enthusiasts were reminded of the legendary Camelot—subject of a current musical.

The rise of the documentary was now stimulated by three-network rivalry. No longer did CBS, as in the *See It Now* years, totally dominate the field. NBC president Kintner had lured Irving Gitlin from CBS to head the "creative projects" unit in NBC News; it began a series of specials titled *NBC White Paper*—of which "The U-2 Affair" was the first.

In the same week—on November 25—*CBS Reports* came up with "Harvest of Shame," produced by David Lowe under Fred Friendly's supervision, and narrated by Edward R. Murrow shortly before his departure from CBS. It portrayed the plight of migrant workers—so vividly that many people rejected its truth. Such poverty and human erosion could not easily be fitted into the world as seen in prime time. This reaction became a familiar one to documentary producers.

A week later, on December 7, ABC-TV's *Close-Up* series presented "Yanki No!" and followed it a few weeks later with "The Children Were Watching," which gave viewers a sense of how it felt to be a six-year-old black child attending the first integrated school in New Orleans. The competition was keen—and produced moments of brilliance.

USIA, too, began to experience a feeling of renascence. Murrow felt that candid reporting of the American scene would, in the long run, do honor to the United States; thus he considered integrity, not salesmanship, to be at the heart of good propaganda. His arrival brought a lift to USIA morale.*

It was not yet a golden age. The network news divisions—which had jurisdiction over the network documentary activity—were aware of their second-class citizenship. Network news, at this critical juncture of American history, still had as its main achievement an early-evening 15-minute telecast of news-film items threaded by one or more anchor-men. Its scheduling made it a preliminary to the real business of the evening. As for network documentaries, they *might* get into prime time, but this usually depended on Aubrey, Kintner, Treyz. Documentaries were made in news divisions but scheduled by executives outside the news divisions. The scheduling decisions often seemed to depend on how things looked in Washington. In 1960-61 the omens were good for documentaries.

In March 1961 NBC offered one of its finest documentary works, *The Real West*—made, like *City of Gold*, from historic photographs, often presenting sharp contrasts to the West of the telefilm. The researcher for *The Real West*, Daniel Jones, ransacked historical societies and attics in a score of states for photographs of the westward push of the late nineteenth century; a script by Philip Reisman, Jr., matched them in poignance, drama, comedy, irony, tragedy. In his search for photographs, Daniel Jones discovered so many of Indians of the period that NBC decided on another film, to tell the same story from the point of view of the Indian. It eventually became *End of the Trail*.

---

* Murrow's first days at USIA were, however, marred by a lapse of judgment. He asked BBC director general Hugh Carlton Greene, as a "personal favor," not to broadcast "Harvest of Shame," which the BBC had purchased. Intensive badgering at the Senate foreign relations committee confirmation hearing, over his alleged overemphasis on the "seamy" side of American life, apparently led to this action by Murrow; he later regretted and deplored his request. The BBC refused to honor it.

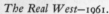 *The Real West*—1961.   NBC   *The Virginian*—1962.   Universal

Another product of brilliance and patience erupted on CBS-TV in 1961. This was "Biography of a Bookie Joint," seen on *CBS Reports* on November 30. It was chiefly the work of Jay McMullen, who was becoming known as an "investigative reporter." CBS had become so confident of his talents that it sometimes permitted him to disappear for months without telling anyone exactly what he was up to. The results were usually good. In 1960 he began photographing the entrance to a Boston bookie parlor—from a window across the street.

The bookie joint was disguised as a key shop, but it had as many as a thousand visitors a day, including members of the Boston police, who sometimes left their patrol cars double-parked during their visits. McMullen, with help from Palmer Williams, developed a lunch box with a concealed 8mm camera, and completed sequences inside the bookie parlor. The film provided a detailed look at a gambling operation, its customers, and its protective machinery. It led to the resignation of a police commissioner.

Meanwhile the *NBC White Paper* series had triumphs of its own. Its "Sit-In" featured newsfilm of Negro resistance to restaurant and department store segregation in Nashville, and the resulting violence. But the film makers—Albert Wasserman and Robert Young—used this material merely as a starting point. Robert Young sought out identifiable participants, then filmed and recorded their accounts of the incidents. The two strands of material, edited together, gave an illuminating picture of the trickiness of human testimony. Again and again a participant could be seen reshaping an episode to fit his own biases, purposes, and self-image.

The film made Robert Young something of a hero in the black community, and led to another *NBC White Paper*. In northern Angola in West Africa—still in colonial status—the Portuguese were attempting to subdue a native uprising. Foreign newsmen were not allowed to enter Angola for direct observation. Robert Young persuaded NBC to let him—along with black cameraman Charles Dorkins—go to the Congo to try to enter the Angola war area from there. Armed with recommendations from American black leaders they walked 300 miles through jungle—carrying Arriflex camera, film, and tape—and returned with footage that became "Angola: Journey to a War." The war they had seen and photographed was savagely fought. They were especially troubled to find, in a native village demolished from the air, napalm bomb fragments with instructions in the English language. They photographed the evidence and took a bomb nose-cone with them. Back home, American manufacture of the napalm bomb was confirmed. Was it part of American military aid to Portugal? Or was it NATO matériel, supplied for protection against communist aggression? The issue remained unresolved, but NBC made a decision. The bomb sequence was removed from the film because, said Gitlin, the Russians would "use it against us." "Angola: Journey to a War" won awards, but the film makers felt deeply disturbed over the decision.

Film makers were becoming acutely aware of the ambiguity of

the film image. It had the ability to arouse strong emotions, but these emotions could be steered in various directions. Narration could, to some extent, control what the viewer saw and how he responded. In 1960 the San Francisco hearings of the House committee on un-American activities were picketed by students protesting the committee's procedure. The students were driven off with fire hoses, and many were beaten. San Francisco television stations covered these events; the footage was later subpoenaed by the House committee and turned over to film producer Fulton Lewis III, who used it to make *Operation Abolition*. Its narration tells a story of violent students manipulated by a communist conspiracy and posing a threat to law and order. The film had wide use during 1960-61 among conservative groups and on television stations. But another film maker took the same footage and wrote another narration, making it a case history of police brutality and the stifling of democratic processes.

An element in the documentary upsurge was the development of new equipment. The 16mm camera was becoming standard for television news and documentaries. Whereas *See It Now* had used bulky 35mm equipment, *CBS Reports* used 16mm. NBC News had also made the transition from 35mm to 16mm, gaining maneuverability.

For the documentary producer who wanted to record synchronized sound on location—as the Drew unit, against all odds, had done in *Primary*—there was an especially notable advance. In 1960 the umbilical cord between camera and recorder became obsolete with the invention of methods for synchronizing them without wire connection.* The wire between microphone and recording equipment could likewise be abolished by use of the wireless microphone, which communicated its signals to the recording equipment via a miniature transmitter. Murrow's *Person to Person* series had pioneered the use of this device in television. Now the per-

* The first such system was based on the use of tuning forks, but these were soon superseded by crystal-controlled motors.

former with his microphone, the cameraman with his camera, the sound engineer with his recording equipment, could all be free agents. To the *cinéma vérité* movement all this was especially important.

But technical advances menaced as well as aided the documentarist. The videotape recorder made it easy for affiliate stations to tape a prime-time documentary and use it in a fringe period. Some stations made a habit of this.

Kennedy, pursuing his policy of accessibility to the camera, made an historic innovation in presidential press conferences. They could be filmed or telecast live, without strings. Prerelease scrutiny was abolished. Kennedy at once proved fantastically nimble and effective—and sometimes witty—in his ad-lib replies and exchanges. He prepared carefully, letting aides hurl questions at him on every conceivable current question. They enjoyed mimicking prominent newsmen in anticipated questions.

The Kennedy innovation was a smashing success for everyone but the newspaper correspondent, whose role was further reduced by the change. There seemed little point in phoning a report afterwards to the newspaper—the office could get it all on television. The newspaperman survived partly as a publicity agent for his paper: he could get up, be seen on television, and ask a question—after mentioning his name and that of his newspaper.

President Kennedy also pursued promptly his interest in the documentary. He invited Drew and his group to document the beginnings of the regime, in a film that acquired the title *Adventures on the New Frontier*. Drew, with Pennebaker at the camera, even followed Kennedy into a meeting with the Joint Chiefs of Staff. This was the President's idea. He would let them know, he said, when it was time to leave. Entering the meeting, he explained to the Chiefs, "These men are with me." There was brief organizational talk; then came the real agenda. It was time, someone said, to discuss "Caribbean maneuvers." The President nodded to Drew to indicate that it was time to leave.

At this point, government withdrew from public scrutiny. Soon the sense of a golden age was harshly shattered.

DECEPTION, INC.

The invasion of Cuba at the Bay of Pigs, so long planned by the CIA, began in April 1961 and failed quickly. Many details that became known about the venture came to light only *because* it failed. The failure spread on the record a monumental case history of deceptions—of government leaders by government leaders, of news media by government leaders, of the public by government leaders, and of the public by news media—including television.

By 1960 approximately half the people in the United States depended for their news primarily on television; thus television played a crucial role in shaping public ideas about world events. But few viewers realized that the networks, through which this world news came to them, had only thin channels of information concerning many foreign events, such as those in Cuba and Guatemala. Networks depended heavily on wire services—mainly the Associated Press and United Press International. The AP stringer in Guatemala, when asked by AP to check the training camp rumors, merely consulted the Ydigoras government and relayed its denials.

Many network news items were based on the information that reporters—their own and those of the wire services—gathered in Washington from the White House, the State Department, and the Defense Department—via press conferences, releases, background sessions. In the Cuban affair the government spokesmen at these agencies gave out data that had come, in the first place, from the CIA.

Other sources of information available to reporters included two of particular interest. The various Cuban exile groups had set up a Cuban Revolutionary Council, which was calling on the people of Cuba to overthrow Castro. It was considered the genesis of a government in exile. It issued bulletins through the New York public relations firm of Lem Jones. Though these bulletins were all issued in the name of the Cuban Revolutionary Council, all were dictated to Jones over the phone by the CIA, which actually employed him at the expense of the American taxpayer—a fact not revealed until much later. The CIA had, in fact, organized and financed the Cuban Revolutionary Council.

Another source was Radio Swan, the 50,000-watt transmitter broadcasting from Swan Island in the Caribbean and also claiming to represent Cuban exiles. Reporters sometimes checked it for information, unaware that it too was a covert CIA project, under absolute CIA control.*

As the Cuban situation grew hotter, these various voices—a well-orchestrated ensemble—gave a coherent impression. Their story was passed on to the American people via television, radio, and the press, and seemed to be "the facts."

A few discordant notes sounded through the music. Rumors heard in Miami did not quite agree with the handouts. The efforts of reporters—including network reporters—to track these rumors down eventually gained some headway.

On April 6, 1961, CBS broadcast a short statement from Stuart Novins in Miami, suggesting that the United States was, in spite of denials, deeply involved in preparations for a Cuban invasion and that the invasion was "imminent." He had worked with Tad Szulc of the New York *Times*, which on April 7 published a similar, more cautious dispatch—omitting "imminent." Five days later President Kennedy seemed to sweep the story aside, telling the cameras and microphones that there would not be, "under any conditions, an intervention in Cuba by the United States." His words seemed to repudiate Novins and Szulc.

President Kennedy had actually—it was later revealed—approved the invasion plan two days before the Novins bulletin. He had stip-

* It was headed by Thomas Dudley Cabot, former president of United Fruit.

ulated that no United States "armed forces" should take part in the landings, and perhaps felt that this stipulation reduced the American role to less than "intervention." The stipulation had been accepted by the CIA.

Among the President's top-level advisers, only Senator J. William Fulbright appears to have protested the plan, calling it "of a piece with the hypocrisy and cynicism for which the United States is constantly denouncing the Soviet Union in the United Nations and elsewhere." Allen Dulles was supremely sure of results—even surer, he said, than he had been of the Guatemala intervention. Secretary of State Dean Rusk and Secretary of Defense Robert McNamara approved the plan, along with the Joint Chiefs of Staff. USIA chief Edward R. Murrow, who would have the task of explaining it all to the world, was not consulted. He is said to have been aghast when he learned the facts.

Kennedy faced the choice of approving—or scuttling—a plan in preparation for a year and approved by President Eisenhower, the most celebrated military leader of the age. Kennedy was told delay would be fatal because Cuba would soon get Soviet MIG's and pilots trained in Czechoslovakia, and because the rainy season would soon turn the Guatemalan training sites into a sea of mud. Besides, the bitterness that would result from cancellation was portrayed as unimaginable. The trainees could not be left in Guatemala; they would have to be brought to the United States. There would be, as Allen Dulles put it, "a disposal problem."

In the end it seemed easiest to proceed. And it might just turn out to be grand and glorious. So far, Kennedy had been lucky.

The invasion force was transferred by plane from Guatemala to an embarkation point in Nicaragua, which was cooperating with the CIA, as in the overthrow of Arbenz. In Nicaragua the CIA had assembled an invasion fleet of seven ships. President Luis Somoza of Nicaragua, surrounded by bodyguards, came to wave goodbye to the fleet. He called out, "Bring me a couple of hairs from Castro's beard!" As the ships sailed, late on April 14, trainees were comforted by the sight of U.S. destroyers and one or two larger ships. A U.S. submarine was seen circling. The men were told by their CIA trainers that they would have "protection by sea, by air, and even from under the sea," and that marines would be near by if needed.

The CIA also had thirty-six planes available and had trained exile pilots to fly them. Before dawn on April 15, nine planes took off—B-26's of World War II design. They had been chosen by the CIA because many nations had such planes and their source would be difficult to establish. More importantly, Castro's own air force included B-26's. The CIA planes had been repainted with the insignia of Castro's FAR—Fuerza Aerea Revolucionaria.

Eight of the disguised planes headed for Cuba. Their mission was to bomb Castro's air force into extinction by the first light of dawn—before the FAR planes could get off the ground.

The ninth plane, which had already been provided with photogenic bullet holes, headed for Florida. A "cover story" was unfolding.

Its pilot, Mario Zuniga, who had been recruited a few weeks earlier in Miami, landed at Miami International Airport and announced that he was one of a number of FAR pilots who had revolted and were devastating Castro's air bases. He himself had been hit during these operations, he said, but had managed to reach Miami. Press photographers took pictures of the plane and bullet holes. Then Zuniga was hurried into seclusion. Story and pictures went out over the press wires. An April 14 Associated Press bulletin began: "Pilots of Prime Minister Fidel Castro's air force revolted today and attacked three of the Castro regime's key air bases with bombs and rockets." The bulletin was broadcast by stations throughout the nation and the world, including those of the Voice of America—whose news announcers assumed it was the truth.

The Cuban Revolutionary Council in New York released a statement acclaiming the "heroic blow for Cuban freedom." The council said it had been in touch with the brave pilots in Cuba and had encouraged the move. The statement was quoted on radio and television.

White House press secretary Pierre Salinger said he knew nothing about it and that the United States was trying to get information. He was duly quoted.

That same afternoon at 3 p.m. Ambassador Raul Roa of Cuba spoke in the General Assembly of the United Nations. He was angry. He said the United States had launched a surprise attack on Cuba with mercenaries trained by "experts of the Pentagon and the Central Intelligence Agency," and that seven people had been killed. The United States, he said, was scandalously passing this off as an attack by FAR defectors.

U.S. Ambassador Adlai Stevenson, who did not know the truth but thought he did, rose in shocked indignation. Television cameras were on him as he spoke.

STEVENSON: No United States personnel participated. No United States government airplanes of any kind participated.

He held up a photograph of United Press International.

STEVENSON: I have here a picture of one of these planes. It has the markings of the Castro air force right on the tail, which everyone can see for himself. The Cuban star and initials FAR—Fuerza Aerea Revolucionaria—are clearly visible. Let me read the statement which has just arrived over the wire from the pilot who landed in Miami . . .

Stevenson repeated the full CIA fabrication. That evening and on the following day—Sunday, April 16—his firm rejection of "wild" Cuban charges was widely reported and applauded on the air and in newspapers. Kennedy is said to have been aghast at the realization that the credibility of the principal American spokesman at the United Nations was being placed in jeopardy before the world. But in hope of quick developments in Cuba, Stevenson was still allowed to remain in ignorance.

On Monday Raul Roa again rose in the General Assembly. He

stated that the CIA had organized the invasion, that it was using Opa Locka air field, and that the CIA had poured $500,000 into invasion preparations. He apparently underestimated the cost; otherwise, his statements were correct. But for the second time in forty-eight hours Ambassador Stevenson stood up before the cameras and delegates and flatly denied the charges.

Lem Jones, on CIA instructions, was meanwhile releasing a bulletin dated April 17, 1961, and marked *for immediate release.*

CUBAN REVOLUTIONARY COUNCIL
via: Lem Jones Associates, Inc.
280 Madison Avenue
New York, New York

Bulletin No. 1

The following statement was issued this morning by Dr. Jose Miro Cardona, president of the Cuban Revolutionary Council.

"Before dawn Cuban patriots in the cities and in the hills began the battle to liberate our homeland . . ."

Dr. Miro Cardona, in whose name this was issued, actually knew nothing about it. But he heard it broadcast over a Florida radio station, and was furious. He was in a small building near Opa Locka, held incommunicado. The CIA had whisked him from New York the day before so that he could be flown to Cuba as soon as a beachhead was secured. Then his government was to be recognized at once as a sovereign nation; this, it was understood, would remove obstacles to overt military help. But meanwhile he was neither informed nor consulted; he was virtually held prisoner.

The same No. 1 bulletin was also being broadcast by Radio Swan, along with mysterious action calls: "Alert, Alert! . . . the fish will rise . . . the fish is red!"—apparently code signals to an underground. Then Radio Swan broadcast further prefabricated items.

VOICE: Forces loyal to the Revolutionary Council have carried out a general uprising on a large scale on the island of Cuba . . . the militia in which Castro placed his confidence appears to be possessed by a state of panic. . . . To victory, Cubans!

The invasion had in fact begun, but not on the lines of the pre-planned CIA bulletins. In violation of the President's orders, the first man ashore at each of the two main landing places was a United States frogman. Two of the ships were quickly sunk by the FAR air force, which had not been knocked out. Two other ships, carrying supplies for the landing parties, fled south. They were later intercepted and turned back by the U.S. Navy. Meanwhile the landing parties were in peril. Six CIA planes were shot down the first day; the second air strike was called off, then reinstated. The invaders had been told that the defenders would not have tanks, but this proved incorrect; the CIA tanks of the invaders clashed with defending tanks on the beaches. Falsely marked CIA planes caused confusion and unforgettable bitterness. A convoy of Castro militiamen waved caps at a plane with familiar FAR markings. As they waved, machine guns and rockets hit them full. An ambulance exploded. In some encounters the invaders used United States phosphorus grenades. "Everything was on fire" an invader said later. The screaming of the defenders was "just like hell."

In Washington a State Department spokesman, Joseph Reap, who perhaps did not know he was lying, announced: "The State Department is unaware of any invasion."

White House press secretary Pierre Salinger, who may also have been ignorant, was likewise uninformative. An AP bulletin quoted him as saying: "All we know about Cuba is what we read on the wire services."

Secretary of State Rusk was more explicitly deceptive, telling a press conference: "The American people are entitled to know whether we are intervening in Cuba or intend to do so in the future. The answer to that question is no."

Over the phone the CIA dictated to Lem Jones a second bulletin, announcing a successful landing; a third, reporting "a wave of sabotage and rebellion"; and a fourth, in which it was charged that the defenders were using MIG aircraft. The statement about the MIG's proved untrue; no MIG's were seen during the invasion.

With a sense of showmanship, Castro gave many of these American bulletins added circulation. A funeral for those killed in the first raid was broadcast throughout Cuba and heard in Miami. Castro himself made the funeral address, comparing the attack to Pearl Harbor. He read various CIA-inspired news bulletins, calling them "pure fantasy. . . . Even Hollywood would not try to film such a story." Without question, the occasion consolidated his position in Cuba.

On Tuesday, April 18, Soviet Premier Nikita Khrushchev repeated the charge that the United States had armed and trained the exiles. He said the Soviet Union would give Cuba "all necessary assistance" unless Washington halted the invasion. In reply, Kennedy warned Khrushchev to stay out of Western Hemisphere affairs. Kennedy said he did not intend to be lectured "by those whose character was stamped for all time on the bloody streets of Budapest." It was a statement curiously reminiscent of Khrushchev's retort: "We also have some dead cats we can throw at you."

On April 18 the exile air force was exhausted and rebellious. In violation of President Kennedy's orders, United States instructors began to fly bombing missions from Nicaragua. By the end of the day ten Cuban and four American pilots had been killed. Catastrophe was near. On April 19 the invasion collapsed. One by one the invaders were hunted down. Some escaped via rescue ships and planes.

Reactions to the collapse and the revelations that followed were varied. To a Fair Play for Cuba Rally sociologist C. Wright Mills telegraphed: "I feel a desperate shame for my country." While he attacked American policy as a moral disgrace, network newsmen generally used the term "fiasco." In busy discussion of planning errors, the horrifying implications of the Bay of Pigs venture were shunted aside. There was little discussion of the precariousness of our news sources—a matter the networks were probably too embarrassed to examine in public—and the demonstrated effectiveness with which the CIA, to conceal its activities, could corrupt them and maneuver other government agencies—and the news media—into helping them do so. Discussion of the illegality of the venture and its violation of treaty obligations was also minimal. The very term "Bay of Pigs fiasco," used repeatedly on the air, was a face-saving term. It made the failure, not the action, the subject of discussion.

In this spirit ex-President Eisenhower advised at Gettysburg: "Don't go back and rake over the ashes. . . . To say you're going into methods and practices of the administration—I would say the last thing you want is to have a full investigation and lay all this out on the record." A few days later all records of the Guatemala camp were put in a freshly dug hole and bulldozed over.

A committee appointed by Kennedy to find out "what went wrong" came up with the answer that it was "a shortage of ammunition." This preposterous four-man committee of inquiry included two people who had had a leading part in planning the venture and its web of deceptions. One was Allen Dulles.

The disaster brought few changes. Allen Dulles was replaced. But the Central Intelligence Agency, and the charter of deceit under which it had acted—the Central Intelligence Agency Act of 1949*—remained intact, available for other ventures.

The events were a severe setback for the Kennedy leadership. Liberals blamed him for having approved the invasion; right-wing elements, for failing to give it more military muscle.

Liberals were quicker to come back. They did so because of Kennedy's actions in a number of directions including the Peace Corps, civil rights—and television.

---

* The Act had transformed the agency, originally a fact-gathering organization, into something different. Authorizing unspecified activities abroad, the new Act—with dubious constitutionality—exempted the CIA from "publication or disclosure of the organization, functions, names, official titles, salaries, or number of personnel employed by the agency." It could spend money "without regard to the provisions of law and regulations relating to the expenditure of Government funds." The Constitution requires public reports of federal disbursements.

VAST WASTELAND

When President Kennedy accepted an invitation to address the 1961 meeting of the National Association of Broadcasters, many broadcasters speculated that he would have censorship proposals, to prevent such things as the Stuart Novins bulletin on the "imminent" invasion of Cuba. Trade-press discussion had predicted such proposals. But Kennedy surprised them: his remarks had an opposite thrust:

> The essence of free communication must be that our failures as well as our successes will be broadcast around the world. . . . That is why I am here with you today. For the flow of ideas, the capacity to make informed choices, the ability to criticize, all the assumptions on which political democracy rests, depend largely upon communication. And you are the guardians of the most powerful and effective means of communication ever designed.

If such views were welcome, and brought cheers, the jubilation soon faded. The program included an address by Newton Minow, a lawyer whom Kennedy had just appointed chairman of the Federal Communications Commission. He was an unknown quantity to the convention delegates; they had no idea what to expect. He looked mild-mannered and clerkish. He began with words of admiration.

> Yours is a most honorable profession. Anyone who is in the broadcasting business has a tough row to hoe. You earn your bread by using public property. When you work in broadcasting you volunteer for public service, public pressure, and public regulation. . . . I can think of easier ways to make a living. . . .

> I admire your courage—but that doesn't mean I would make life easier for you.

He was happy to find their "health" good. A 1960 gross revenue of $1,268,000,000 had given broadcasters a profit, he noted, of $243,-900,000 before taxes—a return of 19.2 per cent. "For your investors the price has indeed been right."

He said television had had great achievements and delightful moments, and mentioned some in the course of his speech. Except for the fantasy of *Peter Pan* and *Twilight Zone*, his choices were oriented toward reality. They included *Project Twenty, Victory At Sea, See It Now, CBS Reports,* the Army-McCarthy hearings, convention and campaign broadcasts, the Great Debates, *Kraft Television Theater, Studio One, Playhouse 90.* When television was good, he said, nothing was better.

> But when television is bad, nothing is worse. I invite you to sit down in front of your television set when your station goes on the air and stay there without a book, magazine, newspaper, profit and loss sheet or rating book to distract you—and keep your eyes glued to that set until the station signs off. I can assure you that you will observe a vast wasteland. You will see a procession of game shows, violence, audience participation shows, formula comedies about totally unbelievable families, blood and thunder, mayhem, violence, sadism, murder, western badmen, western good men, private eyes, gangsters, more violence, and cartoons. And endlessly, commercials—many screaming, cajoling, and offending. . . .

> Is there one person in this room who claims that broadcasting can't do better? . . .

> Gentlemen, your trust accounting with your beneficiaries is overdue. Never have so few owed so much to so many.

Near the end he said:

> I understand that many people feel that in the past licenses were often renewed *pro forma.* I say to you now: renewal will not be *pro forma* in the future. There is nothing permanent or sacred about a broadcast license.

In the corridors, reporters for *Broadcasting* sampled reactions. "A young smart alec." "I think he's bucking for a bigger government job." "A naïve young man who has read all the books but hasn't had to meet a payroll." "I can watch any TV station all day long and enjoy it." "It's a sneaky kind of censorship. . . ."

Minow proved to be more than a phrase-maker. In his efforts to

Newton N. Minow.

strengthen noncommercial television, he showed himself a dexterous bureaucrat.

Noncommercial television was clearly in a bad plight. Producing on starvation budgets, it still lacked outlets in New York, Los Angeles, Washington. It had scarcely begun to make an impact on the national life.

In 1961 National Telefilm Associates, licensee for WNTA-TV —operating on channel 13 in the New York metropolitan area— announced that it would sell its facilities and transfer the license. It was offered $6.6 million by a group headed by David Susskind and backed by Paramount Pictures. Another group, headed by Ely Landau, offered $8 million for WNTA-TV and a related radio station, WNTA. A spirited auction seemed to have begun.

National Educational Television was desperately anxious to have channel 13 as New York outlet for its noncommercial programming. Pledges from foundations scraped together an offer of $4 million, but it was quickly rejected by National Telefilm Associates.

Chairman Minow was equally anxious for channel 13 to go non-commercial, but his hands appeared tied. In 1952 an ingenious amendment had been grafted onto the Communications Act. It *forbade* the FCC, when acting on transfer proposals, to consider

... whether the public interest, convenience, and necessity might be served by the transfer, assignment, and disposal of the permit or license to a person other than the proposed transferee or assignee.

National Telefilm Associates was thus in a position to hold its auction, submit the name of the winning bidder to the FCC, and insist that his qualifications be assessed without reference to any other question. Judged by precedent, Susskind and Landau were qualified.

But the auction spectacle was a disgrace. The station facilities were modest, perhaps worth a half million. It was the eyes and ears of a world metropolis that were on the auction block. Theoretically the channel was public property; under the law the licensee, National Telefilm Associates, had no ownership in it. Yet it was auctioning the channel. The 1952 amendment made the spectacle possible.

This apparently blocked any possible action on behalf of noncommercial television, but Minow saw one possible weapon. National Telefilm Associates was anxious for cash and wanted a quick deal.

Minow now persuaded the FCC to schedule hearings—an "inquiry"—on the desirability of securing noncommercial outlets in New York and Los Angeles. During the inquiry applications for license transfers in those cities would be held in abeyance.

National Telefilm Associates and the commercial bidders fumed. Minow was offering them a prospect of months—perhaps more than a year—of delay. Funds might have to be held in escrow awaiting FCC action. Bids began to be withdrawn. National Telefilm Associates finally asked the FCC to approve transfer to the noncommercial group.

Educational television received another important boost in 1962 through legislation advocated by Minow. It authorized federal grants—for station construction, not programming.

Later Minow moves had an anti-monopoly flavor. Network affiliation contracts had long contained clauses giving the network virtual control over blocks of time on affiliate stations. Some lawyers had argued that these "network option" clauses were equivalent to the block booking through which major Hollywood studios had controlled theaters, and which the U.S. Supreme Court had outlawed in 1948 in *U.S.* v. *Paramount et al.* In 1963 the FCC, led by Minow, banned "network option" clauses as an improper surrender of licensee responsibility. Although strongly opposed by the networks—which made prophecies of disaster—the move had only minimal effects on schedules and profits.

In another move, Minow persuaded Congress to require that sets manufactured after January 1963 be equipped to receive UHF as well as VHF channels. Set manufacturers, many of whom had VHF stations, had been in no hurry to spread the competition. The move was of crucial importance to noncommercial television.

Kennedy is said to have given Minow continual encouragement, telling him, "You keep this up! This is one of the really important things." This firm support for Minow kept the industry in a state of uneasiness.

One other public figure seized the spotlight in 1961 as a warrior on the battlefield of television: Senator Thomas J. Dodd of Connecticut. In this case the outcome was different—and mysterious.

Thomas J. Dodd, who had entered the Senate in 1959, was an impressive figure with classic profile. He had considered a career as actor or priest before turning to law, and had served a year as an FBI agent. He once told an aide that he wanted, above all, to become director of the FBI or the CIA.

He began his Senate career with cold-war speeches but leaped into national prominence when, as chairman of the Senate subcommittee on juvenile delinquency, he took up a subject that had troubled Senator Kefauver—television violence. He hit pay dirt when he subpoenaed voluminous files from networks and producers, uncovering the violence obsessions behind *The Untouchables* and other series. It was the Dodd subcommittee that documented, via numerous instructions and policy memoranda, the "Treyz trend," the "Aubrey dictum," and the "Kintner edict."

Dodd was in his glory. The life roles to which he had aspired—priest, actor, spy, lawyer—all seemed to unite in the crusading Senator Dodd. His handsome head, prematurely white, became familiar in front-page photos and occasionally in television newscasts. He was a national figure, mentioned as vice presidential material.

After triumphant hearings of June-July 1961, Dodd was so busy that he left things more and more to the subcommittee staff. At his direction it prepared for further hearings and drafted a summary of committee findings.

But things were changing, especially with Dodd. As a member of important committees he received many blandishments and gifts, to which he responded warmly. He had entered politics with modest means, but he soon converted his Connecticut farm into a baronial estate—with private road, artificial lake, waterfall, stables, guest house—and lived on a lavish scale. Company planes took him to vacation resorts. As his tastes became more expansive, so did his financial needs, and he became anxious for "campaign contributions," which often arrived in bundles of cash. His staff, once dedicated and even hero-worshiping, began to feel uneasy about him.

He was on friendly terms with executives of Metromedia, a company that had suddenly risen to power with valuable frequencies, including channel 5 in New York (WNEW-TV) and channel 5 in Washington (WTTG-TV). Dodd received campaign contributions and other gifts from Metromedia officials. Metromedia executive Florence Lowe sent him a de luxe television set.

Meanwhile the subcommittee staff was planning further hearings. They noted that many network series mentioned in earlier testimony as especially violent were being syndicated, and shown on

New York World-Telegram
The Sun
Local Forecast: Mostly sunny and pleasant today and tomorrow. Clear, cool tonight. Details on Page 2.

VOL. 131—NO. 279—   NEW YORK, THURSDAY, JULY 30, 1964   TEN CENTS

DODD RAPS TV CRIME
Senator Calls Violence Excessive

**Networks
Called
To Explain**

By STEVEN GERSTEL

WASHINGTON, July 30
—Sen. Thomas J. Dodd (D.,
Conn.) charged today that
prime television time is still
"permeated with programs
featuring excessive crime,
violence and debased moral

independent stations throughout the country. One committee aide
observed: "It's as if they used our 1961 hearings as a shopping list!"
Many of the programs were scheduled at earlier hours than before,
and were reaching younger audiences. The staff felt that the extension of the violence wave through syndication was worthy of study.
In Washington they considered channel 5 a glaring example; they
suggested this as a starting point for new inquiries.

But Dodd said abruptly: "Channel 5 is out." To the astonishment
of the committee, he appointed Mrs. Lowe's son to the subcommittee staff.

Meanwhile there were other surprises. In November 1961 Senator Dodd arranged with NBC that its chairman, Robert Sarnoff,
should testify in secret. On the day of the hearings Dodd sum-
moned Paul Laskin, subcommittee counsel, to his office. Laskin
found Sarnoff and his attorney already there. In front of Sarnoff,
whom Laskin was presumably to cross-examine, he found himself
berated by Dodd for pressing the investigation too hard. Such ag-
gressiveness, said Dodd in a booming voice, would no longer be

tolerated. After a brief hearing, Dodd ordered the transcript of the session locked up. There were further hearings, but *Variety*—May 16, 1962—commented on their "hot and cold running nature"; Dodd seemed a "reluctant dragon." No report on his violence probe was ever published. An interim report was mimeographed in a watered-down version for subcommittee members, but never released to the public. According to James Boyd, long-time aide and speech-writer to Dodd, staff members deplored it as a "sell-out."

By the end of 1962 the broadcasting industry felt easier about the Dodd menace. Minow still caused worry, and this brought defensive measures in the form of more varied programming. Some was in fringe periods and included informational children's series like *Exploring* and *Discovery*. But the pressure also affected prime time, bringing a rash of new comedy telefilms. The 1961-62 arrivals also included more meaty drama. Notable was *The Defenders*, a series with legal background created by Reginald Rose of *Twelve Angry Men*. With stories that often touched current issues, it stirred memories of anthology drama. There were also impressive series with a medical background including *Ben Casey*, *Dr. Kildare*, and *The Nurses*. To the apparent surprise of network officialdom, these were extremely successful in terms of ratings. The success of *Ben Casey* and *Dr. Kildare* threatened a television stampede to the operating table. A social worker was featured in *East Side—West Side*, a teacher in *Mr. Novak*.

Among comedy series, the deft and genial *Dick Van Dyke Show* exhibited exceptional talents, and Lucille Ball arrived with a new series, *The Lucy Show*. But these were overwhelmed by two other phenomena. One was the clattering arrival, in September 1962, of *The Beverly Hillbillies*, which by the end of the year headed all rating lists and diverted indignation from the subject of violence. The series concerned a mountain clan from the Ozarks that had struck oil and moved to Beverly Hills on an old flatbed truck loaded with jugs of corn liquor and $25,000,000. The family remained unchanged by the new environment, and this was the source of humor.

The series popped jokes with abandon. "Do you like Kipling?" "I don't know—I ain't never kippled." The son of a Beverly Hills banker calling on Elly May asked, "Is Elly May ready?" Granny answered, "She shore is! She's been ready since she was fourteen!" Many critics were enraged at such humor, seeing it as exploitation of old hillbilly stereotypes. To their consternation the series won admirers among sophisticates, who saw it rather as a lampoon on a money-oriented society represented by Beverly Hills. The unchanging ways of the Clampett clan seemed a kind of incorruptibility.

The Beverly Hillbillies director Richard Whorf, a former Shakespearian actor, saw another virtue in the series: "You know that no one will be killed, no one will have a brain tumor."

The Beverly Hillbillies was a creation of Filmways, which had started as producer of commercials and, after earning a small fortune, turned to telefilms as a step toward feature-film production. With money gushing in from *The Beverly Hillbillies*, Filmways began offering a series about a jet-set beauty settling on a farm—a completely new idea, and reassuringly like *The Beverly Hillbillies*. It reached the air as the Eva Gabor-Eddie Albert series *Green Acres*.

The other telefilm phenomenon of 1961-62 was the animated telefilm.

The animators who had flocked to television had become a sizable industry of small and large units. It harbored extraordinarily gifted artists, like John Hubley and Ernest Pintoff, who occasionally made award-winning theatrical shorts as a side occupation. But the main work of the industry was to depict the rapid action of decongestants on the sinuses, and similar processes. Some units survived on low-budget children's cartoons, shown mainly on Saturday morning and usually violent in a humorless way, although here and there a zany spirit emerged, as in the mock-heroic *Crusader Rabbit*.

For years frustrated animators had banged on the doors of prime time with one proposal after another. The series that finally made the leap was *The Flintstones*, produced by William Hannah and Joseph Barbera. Premiered late in 1960, it won high ratings during 1961 and became a Friday night leader. By 1962 it had established animation as a prime-time commodity.

Like *The Beverly Hillbillies*, *The Flintstones* capitalized on cultural contrasts and was aggressively plebeian. It dealt with a stoneage family which was at the same time controlled by current middle-class mores and loaded with modern artifacts. The series began with hints of social satire but settled for easier forms of comedy. Its extensive dialogue used a simplified form of lip-synchronization, which facilitated mass production. But it represented no renascence in the art of the cartoon film.

By 1962 the Hannah-Barbera organization was said to be reaping an annual profit of over a million dollars from merchandising tie-ups—toys and other articles using animated characters. It was ready to launch *The Jetsons*, the story of a space-age family—a completely new idea, and reassuringly like *The Flintstones*.

During 1961-62 action series did not go into limbo. They were too deeply ingrained in industry habits and were still winning ratings, and residuals from syndication at home and abroad. There were even new arrivals: in 1961, *The Gunslinger, Two Faces West, Whiplash;* in 1962, *Brenner, Sam Benedict, The Virginian.*

The broadcasting industry was fighting off interference not by changing money-making ways but by trying to protect them with an increasing diversity of services. An expanding schedule of news, special events, and documentaries was among the benefits. In 1962 a new factor began to contribute to this. Television was entering the space age.

INTO ORBIT

In 1962 the United States lunged forward in space development, and thrust television into a new era.

The United States, President Kennedy had said a few months earlier, should determine to "put a man on the moon" by the end of the decade. His aim was to "beat the Soviets," and for this purpose space research budgets were sharply increased. The President's statement seemed at first a flight of rhetoric, but in 1962 developments came so fast that the dream began to seem plausible.

In February 1962, when Lieutenant Colonel John H. Glenn, Jr., became the first American to be shot into orbit around the earth, the United States won world prestige by permitting live television coverage. Within months Lieutenant Commander M. Scott Carpenter repeated the achievement. Again television viewers had front-row seats, both at blast-off and in recovery operations. Films were flown to television stations and theaters throughout the world —by networks, newsreels, and the USIA.

Within weeks another Cape Canaveral blast-off involved television more directly. In July 1962 Telstar I, a communication satellite, was boosted into orbit. Culminating several earlier experiments, it was the first communication satellite that could relay all forms of communication, including television. The event was thus comparable to the laying of the first Atlantic cable or the sending of the first radio signal across the Atlantic. David Brinkley, honoring the new era with a telecast from Paris, indulged his puckish humor by announcing solemnly "via Telstar" that there was no important news. But the possibility of transmitting events "live" to and from all parts of the globe clearly suggested momentous vistas.

The event contributed to an important decision by each network —to expand its 15-minute evening newscast to 30 minutes in 1963. It was scarcely the millennium, but seemed to news divisions a promising forward stride.

Telstar I was launched by the National Aeronautics and Space Administration "for AT&T" and was described as "paid for" by AT&T. But its existence was of course made possible by space experimentation that had cost billions in public funds. That public investments should thus be channeled into a private preserve agitated some observers, although it was hardly discussed on television.

Since the beginnings of network broadcasting, the relaying of programs from station to station had been the province of AT&T, and AT&T now appeared set to play a comparable role in the relaying of programs from continent to continent. But delicate issues were involved. Who would decide what programs would flow—and on what terms—from continent to continent? A new communication highway had been opened—and with it, new tollgates. The operation of these tollgates involved relations between nations.

In spite of the touchiness of the issues the Kennedy administration wanted to push ahead as rapidly as possible with satellite communication, as a key to international prestige and power. It was anxious to set up a functioning organization that could press ahead, and most congressmen shared the sense of urgency. The result was the Communications Satellite Act of 1962, which became law a month after Telstar I.

The bill placed international satellite communication firmly in the private sector. It authorized the creation of COMSAT—the Communications Satellite Corporation—a private corporation. Half the stock would be offered to the general public. The other half would be owned by AT&T and other major communications companies, with the proviso that no company could own a majority.

The law called for a fifteen-man board of directors—three to be chosen by the President, six by the public stockholders, six by the communications companies investing in COMSAT. However, no one company was to have more than two representatives on the board. The arrangement was reminiscent of the way RCA had been established in 1919 under navy auspices, with provision for government representation on the board but with control lodged in four companies—among them, AT&T. In that case, as in the case of COMSAT, the result was an accommodation of existing power groups.

By February 1963 COMSAT was organized. On the board AT&T was joined by representatives of RCA, Western Union International, and the International Telephone and Telegraph Company—a conglomerate that had grown especially powerful through foreign operations.

COMSAT stock, when offered to the public, was sold overnight and quickly doubled in value. To many observers it was a triumphant demonstration of private investment serving a public purpose. Others were uneasy that so prominent a role in international affairs would revolve around the profit motive.

One function of COMSAT was to negotiate with foreign governments concerning ground stations, to implement their participation in a global system. Such international diplomacy was at once begun, but the private status of COMSAT proved an obstacle. This was solved by another compromise: a consortium was created —INTELSAT, the International Telecommunications Satellite Consortium—which would be titular owner of the evolving satellite system. But all management functions were delegated to COMSAT.

Telstar I, though highly successful, was already obsolete when it went into orbit around the globe. It could link only areas which were, at any moment, in its line of sight. As early as 1945 Arthur C. Clarke, British scientist and science fiction writer, had outlined —in an article in *Wireless World*—the possibility of a different kind of satellite—one that would move in an orbit so synchronized with the earth's rotation that it would seem to hover in a fixed spot. In 1962, as Telstar I began its career, a *synchronous* satellite was already being built by Hughes Aircraft Corporation, and early in 1963 it was blasted into space. Its electronic equipment failed, but a second synchronous satellite, lofted a few months later, functioned perfectly. Synchronous satellites became the focus of COMSAT planning—for global television and other communication.

The whole development was being pushed forward with staggering speed. One of COMSAT's organizers, contemplating its tasks, said: "It is like being ordered to organize a worldwide airline six months after the Wright brothers first flew."

Even as COMSAT plunged ahead, great uncertainties sur-

Early Bird communications satellite— launched 1965. Comsat

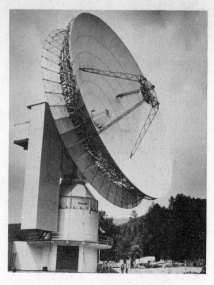

Earth station—Etam, West Virginia. Comsat

ORBIT

Via Early Bird: global round table, 1965, with former President Dwight D. Eisenhower and Field Marshall Sir Bernard Montgomery. At left, Walter Cronkite as moderator.

Comsat

rounded it. Its synchronous satellites would be linked to participating countries by ground stations. A standard ground station, using a dish approximately 100 feet in diameter, cost between three and seven million dollars. To some countries this seemed a modest entry fee; to others it was formidable. But the Kennedy administration was anxious that many countries join the system as promptly as possible, for there might soon be competing systems sponsored by rival powers using other technology. Thus United States economic aid as well as military aid were invoked to help developing countries join up. Though COMSAT was private, Kennedy policy sought its quick success.

But the thoughts of Arthur Clarke, who had led scientists to the synchronous satellite, were already outrunning the COMSAT system. In the September 1959 issue of *Holiday* he outlined ideas on "how to conquer the world without anyone noticing." He felt the means were available to the United States and the Soviet Union alike. He pointed out that ground stations were not really necessary. The Soviet Union might, for example, put a synchronous satellite high over Asia, reaching the entire continent. If through Soviet trade missions it could then flood the continent—perhaps at a slight profit—with low-cost sets designed to receive the satellite directly, the ground stations would pass into limbo. The same technique could be applied to Africa and elsewhere. From the satellite would flow exciting drama, sports events, quiz programs, brisk newscasts —everything to enthrall nations in the way that "even ostensibly educated nations have been unable to resist." First prize on quiz programs would always be a free trip to the Soviet Union. Before long, uncommitted nations would become committed. Priority in establishing such a system, said Arthur Clarke, "may determine whether, fifty years from now, Russian or English is the main language of mankind."

Officials at COMSAT did not talk that way; it was not designated as a propaganda agency. It was private and its assignment was to perform a service at a profit. But such thoughts were in the air.

	% TV Homes	
Beverly Hillbillies (CBS)	38.8	Nielsen reports for February
Andy Griffith Show		1963 reflected a retreat from
(CBS)	33.2	violence, with rural humor—and
Red Skelton Hour (CBS)	33.1	CBS—dominating the ratings.
Candid Camera (CBS)	32.3	
Ben Casey (ABC)	31.4	
Bonanza (NBC)	30.9	
Lucy Show (CBS)	30.8	
Dick Van Dyke Show		
(CBS)	29.6	
Danny Thomas Show		
(CBS)	29.5	
Gunsmoke (CBS)	29.1	

In 1963, for the first time, a majority of people told Roper researchers that their chief source of news was television rather than newspapers.* Spectacular blast-offs from Cape Canaveral, news bulletins "by satellite," news specials on the age of the missile, must have helped to produce such a result.

In 1962 American television presented bizarre juxtapositions. There were *The Beverly Hillbillies* and other Nielsen pacemakers; and there were news specials that seemed to come from another world. The two worlds often seemed incompatible. They represented the two worlds into which television had fissioned. Within television they were interdependent, but antagonistic.

There was no doubt which commanded the chief loyalty of audiences. Such series as *Bonanza, The Red Skelton Hour, Ben Casey,*

* The research firm Roper and Associates asked people periodically from what source "you get most of your news about what's going on in the world today—from the newspapers or radio or television or magazines or talking to people or where?" Some people named two or more media. In November 1963 the answers ran: television 55, newspapers 53, radio 29, magazines 6, people 4, don't know 3. In November 1961 the answers had been: television 52, newspapers 57, radio 34, magazines 9, people 5, don't know 3.

The Andy Griffith Show, The Flintstones, Gunsmoke hovered near the top of most rating lists. But now and then the other world broke in.

In October the most sensational interruption featured John F. Kennedy. It was an international ultimatum delivered by television —about missiles in Cuba.

ULTIMATUM VIA TV

While Kennedy was campaigning in the midwest, boosting Democrats in state and local elections, he suddenly canceled his schedule and returned to Washington. He asked for television time on all networks for Monday, October 22, 1962, at 7 p.m. eastern time.

The CIA had presented him with photographic evidence that missile sites were being built in Cuba with Russian help, not only for surface-to-air missiles for use against aircraft, but also for missiles of longer range, able to reach cities on the continent. There was no evidence of nuclear warheads, but it was supposed that they might be on hand or en route.

In days of feverish behind-the-scenes debate, alternative plans for United States action were proposed and developed by various units within the administration. A central role for television was so much taken for granted that each group recommended not only what should be done, but what President Kennedy should say on the air. Participants referred to the plans as "scenarios."

The Joint Chiefs of Staff all felt that the United States should at once demolish the missile bases with a massive air-strike. They assumed the communists would use atomic weapons and therefore felt the United States should go ahead with atomic weapons. Robert Kennedy later commented that the recommendations of the military leaders always had the advantage that if they proved mistaken, no one would be around to know.

An alternative plan, which Robert Kennedy and Secretary of

Defense McNamara favored, was a blockade of Cuba. They argued
that an attack would still be possible if the blockade proved unable
to remove the missiles.

The blockade scenario—using the term "quarantine" because a
"blockade" is an act of war—was adopted. The quarantine would
be coupled with an ultimatum to be addressed not to Cuba but to
the Soviet Union. Kennedy would demand that the Soviet Union
remove its missiles from Cuba. Failure to do so would bring United
States military action against Cuba. Meanwhile Soviet ships en
route to Cuba would be stopped and searched for military supplies.

To give the ultimatum maximum force, it would be delivered via
television—not merely through diplomatic channels. The televised
commitment, relayed throughout the world by satellite, would
create a situation from which retreat would appear impossible.

To the group around Kennedy, the impossibility of retreat was
obvious for many reasons. One was the current election campaign.
The Bay of Pigs debacle had given Kennedy, in many eyes, a "soft
on communism" image which was proving a factor in the present
campaign. He had tried to neutralize this with increased military
deployments—for example, he had sharply increased the number of
so-called military advisers in Vietnam—but these moves made little
public impact. It was assumed by those around Kennedy that any
halfway resolution of the missile situation would destroy Kennedy
politically.

Kennedy needed an atmosphere of victory. Ironically, Khrushchev, by his perilous gamble, had offered a chance for a victory.
Kennedy saw the chance.

The ultimatum telecast of October 22 and the moves surrounding
it showed Kennedy a brilliant technician in the consolidation and
use of political power. He checked all details with minute precision;
he was fully in control. Meanwhile his coolness astonished observers. A few minutes before the telecast NBC correspondent Robert
Goralski was in the office of Evelyn Lincoln, Kennedy's secretary,
to check some information. Through the open door of the wash-

room he saw Kennedy calmly combing his hair; makeup was already on.

A minute or two later Kennedy, speaking on television in his rapid, clipped style, was preparing his worldwide audience for atomic war. Referring to the bases under construction, he said:

KENNEDY: The purpose of these bases can be none other than to provide a nuclear strike capability against the Western hemisphere. . . . Several of them include medium-range ballistic missiles capable of carrying a nuclear warhead for a distance of more than 1000 nautical miles. Each of these missiles, in short, is capable of striking Washington, D.C., the Panama Canal, Cape Canaveral, Mexico City, or any other city in the southeastern part of the United States, in Central America, or in the Caribbean area. Additional sites not yet completed appear to be designed for intermediate-range ballistic missiles capable of traveling more than twice as far —and thus capable of striking most of the major cities of the Western hemisphere, ranging as far north as Hudson Bay, Canada, and as far south as Lima, Peru. In addition, jet bombers, capable of carrying nuclear weapons, are now being uncrated and assembled in Cuba, while the necessary air bases are being prepared.

Using the word "nuclear" eleven times, Kennedy drew a panorama of devastation enveloping the whole hemisphere. The moves that had made such things possible, said Kennedy, could not be accepted by the United States "if our courage and our commitments are ever to be trusted again by either friend or foe." He asserted:

We will not prematurely or unnecessarily risk the costs of world-wide nuclear war in which the fruits of victory would be ashes in our mouth—but neither will we shrink from that risk at any time it must be faced.

Then he turned to Khrushchev:

I call upon Chairman Khrushchev to halt and eliminate this clandestine, reckless, and provocative threat to world peace and to stable relations between our two nations. I call upon him further to abandon this course of world domination and to join in an historic effort to end the perilous arms race and transform the history of man. He has an opportunity now to move the world back from the abyss of destruction. . . .

He told the American people:

Many months of sacrifice and self-discipline lie ahead.

Although Kennedy prepared his audience for a long crisis, it proved short. So effective had been Kennedy's bludgeoning attack, coupled with vast moves of navy, army, and air force units and intensive diplomatic maneuvers, that the crisis came quickly. Soviet ships en route to Cuba halted in the Atlantic. A series of Soviet messages to the United States offered a basis for settlement. In two weeks the crisis was largely over. Dismantling of the missile sites was begun, and the blockade was removed. Kennedy gave assurance that Cuba would not be invaded.

Kennedy in his television ultimatum showed a complete sense of assurance about the United States position and its moral rightness, but his own feelings were not so unclouded. He had been furious to learn, during the intensive writing of scenarios, that the United States still maintained missile bases in Turkey, ready to rain atomic destruction on major Russian cities. He had ordered Rusk months earlier to withdraw those missiles, considering them an unnecessary and ultimately useless provocation. But Rusk, delaying, had not done so. Kennedy was furious because he considered those missiles, in the words of Assistant Secretary of State Roger Hilsman, a "political albatross." They raised such questions as: if American missiles in Turkey were "defensive," why were Russian missiles in Cuba not also "defensive"?

Khrushchev at first justified missiles in Cuba on the ground that the United States had attacked Cuba, and that many United States leaders had called for a new attack. The Soviet Union had not attacked Turkey.

The comparative situations of Cuba and Turkey troubled Kennedy. They also worried Adlai Stevenson, who this time was brought into administration councils.* Stevenson, approving the quarantine plan, suggested that withdrawal of missiles based in Turkey—and also in Italy—could be elements in a settlement. Kennedy agreed with this but did not wish to mention such concessions in his ultimatum. Thus all troublesome details were swept under the rug to make the television address as unified and powerful as possible. It proved so powerful that the Turkish and Italian missile bases were ignored in the speedy resolution.

Television audiences were thus left with the misleading picture of a good buy/bad guy crisis. A villain had been caught in a fiendish plan and had been stopped by a good guy. It was an oversimplification—a defect not uncommon in television messages.

But few were inclined to criticize Kennedy on these grounds, for his strategy, so effectively executed, had apparently accomplished miracles. Holding the Joint Chiefs in check, it had removed the Cuban missiles without atomic attack. For this all liberals were thankful. At the same time Kennedy had, through his anti-communist success, neutralized attacks from the right.

The end of the crisis was not marked by any television event. Kennedy was insistent that he wanted no "victory" statement, no gloating. Humiliation of Khrushchev and the Soviet Union would, he feared, stimulate the arms race, and he hoped to prevent that.

Of course he could not. The events had doomed Khrushchev. His misadventure opened him to attack from the Soviet military-industrial complex and the rulers of China. Khrushchev, in self-defense, tried for a rapprochement with the United States. He halted all jamming; in return the United States curtailed, then stopped, its ten-year encroachment on the Moscow frequency of 173 kc. The nuclear test-ban treaty was another move toward better relations. But Khrushchev could no longer control events. In the end the arms race intensified.

* Also invited to confer at an early stage was Edward R. Murrow, but he was ill, apparently already suffering from the lung cancer to which he later succumbed.

Meanwhile Kennedy had achieved an extraordinary unification. The sense of Camelot returned. Kennedy, feeling more secure internationally, could hammer at domestic issues on which he wanted action—such as civil rights. His rapport with artists and writers increased. He was surrounded with an aura of history in the making. He seemed to have America "moving again." All this had its impact on television.

VENTURE VIDEO

Conscious of new dignity, the network news divisions expanded. Their staffs did not inquire what had given them a warmer place in the sun. They were vaguely aware that Kennedy activism, international rivalries, and network tremors over Washington contributed to a changed situation. Meanwhile it was enough that budgets rose and scheduling was more favorable—sometimes.

The new affluence gave rise to a fascinating diversity of projects—among them *The Tunnel*, an NBC documentary that raised international controversy.

Reuven Frank, who had moved from Toronto to New York and who had become an executive producer for NBC News, wanted to do a film about East German escapees, who eluded the communist-built Berlin wall by jumping across roofs, wading through sewers, and digging tunnels. During a European trip he asked the NBC Berlin staff to shoot anything interesting on escapees.

In June 1962 Piers Anderton of the NBC Berlin bureau came to New York with a proposal for action. The bureau was in touch with three West Berlin students who were starting a tunnel to help friends and relatives in East Berlin escape. The students were willing to have cameramen join them. A sticky problem was that the tunnelers wanted $50,000. Reuven Frank said, "They're crazy!" But he agreed to a smaller sum, later reported as $7500.

Only a few at NBC were told of the project, and these carried on in cloak-and-dagger fashion. Funds were disbursed "outside the NBC channels." An agreement signed with the diggers was not seen by an NBC lawyer. The project was never mentioned on the phone. Reuven Frank, though in charge, stayed away from Berlin until the digging was finished, because his presence might cause speculation. No film left Berlin until it was all over. Processing was done in a local Berlin laboratory considered politically trustworthy. Two young Berlin cameramen, often lying flat on their backs, did the shooting for NBC. A tape recorder in the tunnel could pick up footsteps fifteen feet above them in the street.

The film was not pure *cinéma vérité*. Under Anderton's direction the group leaders reenacted planning phases for the NBC cameras.

On September 13 Reuven Frank, alerted by Anderton, flew to Berlin with a film editor. The following day the tunnel was completed and the escape of twenty-six people—including five babies—was filmed. The NBC group rushed the editing of twenty hours of accumulated film. By phone to William McAndrew, head of NBC News, Frank said cautiously, "I think we need ninety minutes." He carried the film to New York as hand-luggage.

A surprise message from McAndrew awaited Reuven Frank at the airport in New York: he was to fly on to Pittsburgh. There in a hotel room he met with representatives of Gulf Oil to tell them about *The Tunnel*, and they agreed to sponsor it, assuring prime time.

Although originally announced for October 31, *The Tunnel* was not shown until December 10. The missile crisis and the imminence of elections played a part in the postponement, along with crises over the film itself. The State Department, learning of the project, criticized it as imperiling international relations. The $7500 payment to the tunnel leaders had become known in East Germany and had given it valuable propaganda ammunition. In the United States some critics charged that NBC by providing funds had in fact financed the completion of the tunnel.

Jack Gould of the New York *Times*, probably the most influen-

The Tunnel—1962   NBC

tial of television critics, felt that NBC's initiative had been understandable, but he added: "With peace hanging by a thread it is no time for adventurous laymen to turn up in the front lines of world tension."

Such objections were largely forgotten when *The Tunnel* was shown on NBC-TV on December 10, 8:30-10 p.m. eastern time, sponsored by Gulf. It matched *The Lucy Show* in ratings, and won awards. Amid the hosannas the State Department decided it was useful cold-war propaganda and permitted USIA to show it abroad. Questions about private cold-war initiatives were no less valid than before, but were left hanging.

Television was often accused of timidity but became less timid in 1962-63. Along with the adventurous air of the Kennedy regime, a dramatic legal event contributed to the new spirit. In June 1962 the lawsuit of John Henry Faulk against Aware, Inc., Vincent Hartnett, and Syracuse supermarket executive Laurence Johnson reached its climax in a New York court. A parade of witnesses had laid bare methods by which self-styled patriots had conducted a purge of the industry, with much help from within the industry. Executives who had at first taken the "security" claims seriously, but had since sickened of the operation, testified in illuminating detail. As a climax Louis Nizer, attorney for Faulk, sought testimony from defendant Laurence Johnson, who through legal maneuvers and medical bulletins had staved off appearance in court. As the case was ready to go to the jury, word arrived that Laurence Johnson had been found dead in a Bronx motel. He had apparently taken barbiturates, vomited, and choked to death. The court ordered that the estate of Laurence Johnson be substituted for the deceased as a defendant in the case. A few hours later the jury awarded unprecedented damages of $3,500,000 to John Henry Faulk.

It was an extraordinary vindication for Faulk, who had given six years of his life to clear his name; also for those who, like Edward R. Murrow, had not hesitated to help him finance his suit. The verdict was upheld at every level, although the award was eventually scaled down.

Thousands in the television industry breathed a sigh of relief. The blacklist machinery appeared to be disintegrating. Many an artist emerged from long obscurity. Topics that would have been considered too controversial a year or two earlier were now welcomed. Treatment became less fearful. "Meet Comrade Student," a *Close-Up* program produced by John Secondari and written by Robert Lewis Shayon, examined Russian education with a minimum of standard polemics; it noted that Russian schools had their successes and failures and that it was important for Americans to understand both. Increasing courage also erupted in local programming, where the documentary was winning a foothold. Surveying local documentaries of this period, the writer William Bluem found many worthy of praise, among them *Suspect* (KING-TV, Seattle), an examination of a right-wing extremist group; *The Wasted Years* (WBBM-TV, Chicago), on the human erosion of prison life; *Superfluous People* (WCBS-TV, New York), on New York's staggering welfare problems; and *Block Busting—Atlanta Style* (WSB-TV, Atlanta), on segregationist tactics.

Race issues were ever-present and lurked behind many other problems. The year 1963 produced moments that seemed to offer extraordinary promise. After a sequence of violence in Birmingham, Martin Luther King was able to negotiate a desegregation agreement with white Birmingham leaders. Because prominent businessmen participated, the resolution gave hope of a new era, especially when King—by now often seen in television statements—told his followers: "We must not see the present victory as a victory for the Negro. It is a victory for democracy. . . . We must not be overbearing or haughty in spirit."

But uglier currents were also at work. Several buildings used by Negro leadership groups were bombed. Medgar Evers, black civil rights leader, was murdered in Mississippi. Such events brought more militant black leaders to the fore, notably Malcolm X, who was interviewed at length over National Educational Television. Martin Luther King, though assailed from one direction as "communist," was increasingly denounced by others as too moderate.

Amid such tensions, the announcement that Martin Luther King would lead a mammoth march on Washington in August 1963, with people coming from all states to petition Congress for equal rights, posed elements of a crisis. Some government leaders felt the plan must be halted as a threat to law and order. Memories of the Herbert Hoover era, when a march of veterans demanding a bonus had been driven back by mounted troops, stirred deep fears. But Kennedy decided to encourage the march. The result was one of the most inspiring of television spectaculars. An incredibly disciplined migration had its climax on August 28 when Martin Luther

King spoke to 200,000 people at the Lincoln Memorial in Washington. He told them—and millions of others via television and radio:

KING: I have a dream. It is a dream deeply rooted in the American Dream. I have a dream that one day this nation will rise up and live out the true meaning of its creed: "We hold these truths to be self-evident, that all men are created equal."

I have a dream that one day on the red hills of Georgia sons of former slaves and sons of former slave owners will be able to sit down together at the table of brotherhood. I have a dream that even the state of Mississippi, a state sweltering with the heat of injustice, sweltering with the heat of oppression, will be transformed into an oasis of freedom and justice. . . .

The networks—television and radio—had no doubts about the necessity of relaying these events, in whole or part, to the American public. Through live and delayed coverage, millions shared the experience.

The USIA had its own decision to make. The story of a protest march required some word on what was being protested. Former USIA regimes, shell-shocked by the McCarthy attacks, would have handled such an event in gingerly style, reporting it as a triumph of democracy while saying as little as possible about issues involved. The New Frontier atmosphere permitted a more venturesome approach.

George Stevens, Jr., USIA film chief under Edward R. Murrow, had a policy of encouraging young film makers, and entrusted film coverage of the march to James Blue, a University of Southern California film graduate who had later studied in Paris at the Institut des Hautes Études Cinématographiques, and had made a film about the Algerian revolt. In his hands, the event became a major USIA film—*The March*.

The March began with shots of hordes en route to Washington by all conceivable means of travel.

NARRATOR: They came from Los Angeles and San Francisco or about the distance from Moscow to Bombay. They came from

Cleveland, from Chicago or about the distance from Buenos Aires to Rio de Janeiro. They came from Birmingham, Alabama, from Jackson, Mississippi, or about the distance from Johannesburg to Dar-es-Salaam.

He had been insulted, beaten, jailed, drenched with water, chased by dogs, but he was coming to Washington, he said, to swallow up hatred with love, to overcome violence by peaceful protest.

There were glimpses of fantastic preparations—the making of 80,-000 cheese sandwiches, the network of walkie-talkies, the distribution of pins: "I MARCH FOR JOBS AND FREEDOM." At the end came the King speech, and "We Shall Overcome" sung by a sea of humanity, and final words by the narrator.

NARRATOR: There were many who praised this day and said that there had been a new awakening in the conscience of the nation. Others called it a disgrace. In the wake of this day, more violence was to come, more hatred, but in the long history of man's cruelty to man, this was a day of hope.

Some congressmen who previewed the film were determined to block its distribution. But test showings in India and Africa yielded eloquent evidence. Here was a nation, said viewers in astonishment, that could admit its errors, discuss them openly, and move to correct them. After delays the film went into wide distribution and won recognition as one of USIA's finest hours.

The shifting climate of 1963 put pressure on producers of television drama and commercials to change their largely lily-white world. There was response but also nimble foot-dragging. The daytime serial remained almost untouched. Progress was more noticeable in other areas. Inclusion of a Negro or two in crowd scenes was becoming standard. Some series went further. *The Defenders*, often breaking new ground, featured black actor Ossie Davis as a prosecutor. Medical shows occasionally had a black doctor or nurse. The Jackie Gleason program engaged a black dancer—granddaughter of Duke Ellington—for its formerly all-white chorus line. The Ed Sullivan program welcomed Negro acts. *East Side/West Side* and

Mr. Novak used stories about Negroes. But resistance appeared constantly. CBS found two of its southern affiliates refusing to carry an *East Side/West Side* episode because of its black roles. When a *Bonanza* episode introduced a black character, General Motors considered withdrawing its commercial—but was dissuaded by NBC.

A National Urban League study revealed that the ten leading New York advertising agencies had, among 23,600 employees, only eleven blacks. Four years of persuasive efforts by the League had produced one new hiring—in the research division of Foote, Cone & Belding. On the other hand, a Manufacturers Hanover Trust Company commercial featuring the beautiful Diahann Carroll created enough stir to encourage bandwagon jumping. Statistics on Negro purchasing power got increasing attention from advertisers and their agencies. It was beginning to be argued that integration might turn out to be good business. The box-office success of theatrical films on interracial themes encouraged the idea.

However, when NBC-TV scheduled a three-hour documentary on civil rights, produced by Robert Northshield as a 1963 Labor Day special, it found sponsors reluctant. Gulf Oil, which had been ready to back *The Tunnel* and other specials, was not interested. Such problems had to be solved by selling participations at bargain rates. ABC-TV had similar trouble with a series of five films on civil rights scheduled for late Sunday evenings.

Meanwhile each network had acquired a black on-the-air newsman. It seemed "tokenism" to some, a revolution to others. When CBS president Frank Stanton testified at a Senate communications subcommittee hearing in July 1963, Senator Strom Thurmond of South Carolina asked him, "Don't you care about white people?" Thurmond, outraged at attentions given to Martin Luther King, accused the networks of "following the NAACP line." When NBC-TV decided to cancel its telecast of the Blue-Gray football game, an annual event from which black players were barred, Governor George C. Wallace of Alabama denounced the network decision as "tragic and irresponsible." But the sponsors, Gillette and Chrysler, concurred in the cancellation.

President Kennedy, pressing hard for civil rights legislation, kept nudging the whole process forward. In October he was seen in another—somewhat bizarre—*cinéma vérité* production. The Alabama racial crisis was the subject, and Governor George C. Wallace was co-star.

In 1963 the University of Alabama, the last to remain all-white, was under federal court order to integrate. For its summer session starting June 10, its admissions office accepted two black applicants, Vivian Malone and James Hood. But Governor Wallace intervened, telling a news conference: "I am the embodiment of the sovereignty of this state and I will be present to bar the entrance of any Negro who attempts to enroll at the University of Alabama." A scrappy politician and one-time Golden Gloves bantamweight champion, he had been elected to the governorship in 1962 proclaiming "segregation now, segregation tomorrow, segregation forever!"

In June 1963, as a crisis approached, President Kennedy invited Robert Drew to document its development on film. Donn Pennebaker and his camera began to cover strategy sessions at the White House and at the home of Attorney General Robert F. Kennedy. Meanwhile, as Deputy Attorney General Nicholas Katzenbach was rushed to Alabama—with three thousand army troops kept ready near by—Alabama photography was organized by George Shuker of the Drew unit. Governor Wallace proved as ready as the Kennedys to take part; camera on shoulder, Richard Leacock and James Lipscomb were soon following him about the Alabama executive mansion, the governor's office, and the University of Alabama campus in Tuscaloosa. As events moved forward, with much telephoning between leaders in Washington and Alabama, both ends were covered by camera.

Clearly the Drew unit had scored an extraordinary coup. But the film that emerged, while full of fascinating moments, brought into focus some limitations of *cinéma vérité*. The events in *Crisis: Behind a Presidential Commitment* were a far cry from those photographed in *Primary*. In the earlier film, candidate John Kennedy, pushing through Wisconsin crowds and coping with mass meetings, tea parties, and press conferences, had been so absorbed in problems at hand that the camera could be truly forgotten—by him and audiences alike. Not so in *Crisis: Behind a Presidential Commitment*, in which the camera was often covering small groups: two or three White House advisers in shirt sleeves pacing about, discussing strategy while President Kennedy nodded thoughtfully; Robert Kennedy on the phone, instructing aides in Alabama. Television critics found themselves unable to forget the camera or to accept the notion that the participants—performers—could forget it. New York *Times* critic Jack Gould called it "managed newsfilm . . . a melodramatic peepshow."

Even the unfolding of events gave a managed feeling. As Katzenbach and the two students approached the administration building, Governor Wallace, as promised, "stood in the door" and delivered his statement defying federal authority. The students were then escorted elsewhere—to dormitory rooms already assigned to them—while Wallace capitulated off camera. He had his moment of on-camera glory, while the Kennedys had their victory. Both apparently had ammunition for future election campaigns.

A *quid pro quo* aspect touched other elements of the film. Robert Kennedy's small daughter Carrie, for some reason visiting her father's office during this crisis, was allowed to say hello on the phone to Deputy Attorney General Katzenbach in Tuscaloosa. "Hello, Uncle Nick." Perhaps to balance things, Governor George Wallace was shown hugging his small daughter. There were glimpses of his ante-bellum Southern mansion to balance shots of the Robert Kennedy home in Virginia.

There were memorable moments. Governor Wallace receiving praises from thin-lipped, elderly ladies: "We're proud of what you're doing—for Alabama. . . . Bless your heart!" The students

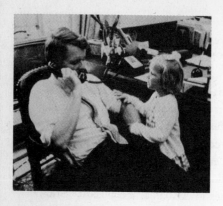

Crisis: Behind a Presidential Commitment—ABC-TV special, 1963.   Drew Associates

being advised by Katzenbach: "Dress as though you are going to church—modestly—neatly." We see the students having their pictures taken for the covers of *Newsweek* and *Time*. The students are so handsome, so firmly armed with quiet humor, one wonders whether they were "cast" for these breakthrough roles.

During the film Kennedy is considering going on television, to put the whole issue on a moral basis. There is so much talk about what to say on television, and how people will react, that the film develops a Pirandelloish atmosphere. Is it a television program about a television program about—about what? Do Wallace and Alabama actually exist?

In the film the President goes on television and says words he actually said on television. Although the context has somehow been reduced to ritual, the words are still powerful.

KENNEDY: We preach freedom around the world, and we mean it. And we cherish our freedom here at home. But are we to say to the world—and much more importantly to each other—that this is the land of the free, except for Negroes; that we have no second-class citizens, except Negroes; that we have no class or caste system,

no ghettos, no master race, except with respect to Negroes? . . .
We face, therefore, a moral crisis as a country and a people. It cannot be met by repressive police action. It cannot be left to increased demonstrations in the streets. It cannot be quieted by token
moves or talk. It is a time to act in the Congress, in your state and
local legislative body, and, above all, in all of our daily lives.

These events took place in June, but the film *Crisis: Behind a Presidential Commitment* did not reach the air until four months later.
Some thought the air showing was timed to help the unresolved
struggle for civil rights legislation, but apparently the real reason
for delay was that ABC-TV had trouble finding a sponsor. The
one-hour film was finally telecast on October 21.

Around the Kennedy family, action and entertainment were unceasing. Relations with television correspondents always had
sparkle and style. During a presidential plane ride from Hyannis-
port, reporters saw a puppy waddling along the corridor. Learning
it was a new family acquisition, a gift from father Joseph P. Kennedy, they sent a solemn questionnaire to the Kennedy compart-
ment. Jacqueline Kennedy filled it out by hand. One question was:
"What do you feed the dog?" Jacqueline wrote: "Reporters." Kennedy's mental agility and coolness constantly amazed correspondents. They saw him as a virile political animal whose decisions
were often concerned with organizing and using power, but they
saw him grow. With insatiable curiosity, he could overwhelm them
with streams of questions, digging rapidly into almost any issue.
Actress Jean Seberg, a White House visitor with her French husband, author-producer Romain Gary, recalled a dinner with Kennedy. "He asked Romain a million questions about de Gaulle—he
was like an incredible IBM machine, digesting *everything*. I swiped
a menu and wrote Malraux a long letter about it."

A few days later Kennedy was the central figure in the most
moving spectacular ever broadcast. It lasted four days.

NOVEMBER DRUMS

There was never anything like it. At times nine out of ten Americans were watching, along with throngs in Europe, Asia, Africa, Australia—who often watched at the same time via satellite. The critic Marya Mannes wrote:

> This was not viewing. This was total involvement . . . I stayed before the set, knowing—as millions knew—that I must give myself over entirely to an appalling tragedy, and that to evade it was a treason of the spirit.

The cast of characters in the four-day telecast exceeded anything ever seen before. And it included the first "live" murder on television, the first murder ever witnessed by millions.

Early in the afternoon of November 22, 1963, a bulletin began clacking out of UPI teletype machines at television stations, radio stations, newspapers.

DALLAS, NOV 22 (UPI)—THREE SHOTS WERE FIRED AT PRESIDENT KENNEDY'S MOTORCADE TODAY IN DOWNTOWN DALLAS.

Don Gardiner at ABC Radio in New York went on the network with this announcement—six minutes after the shots. Four minutes later, on the basis of a second bulletin, Walter Cronkite broke into the television serial *As the World Turns* and appeared on CBS-TV screens.

> CRONKITE: In Dallas, Texas, three shots were fired at President Kennedy's motorcade. The first reports say the President was "seriously wounded."

The serial continued.

Within minutes radio and television audiences were growing fantastically. At 1:35 they learned that Kennedy, who had been taken to Parkland Hospital in Dallas, was dead and that Lyndon Johnson, who had been in the motorcade, had left the hospital for Love Air Field.

A fantastic kaleidoscope began to reach television screens: interviews that networks were gathering with their remote units on Capitol Hill and elsewhere; a shot of Jacqueline Kennedy accompanying the dead President's body from Parkland Hospital, leaving for Love Field; information about an arrested suspect, identified as Lee Harvey Oswald; details about Lyndon Johnson taking the oath of office at 2:38 p.m. Amid all this, videotapes of events before the shooting.

Kennedy's visit to Texas had been covered by local stations, not by networks; now these videotaped events, juxtaposed with new developments, had almost unbearable impact. Suddenly John Kennedy and a radiant Jacqueline Kennedy were on the screen, waving to crowds from their limousine. Then—more grisly—a Chamber of Commerce breakfast in Fort Worth that morning, attended by President Kennedy and Vice President Johnson. The breakfasters had gifts for the President. One was to protect him "from local enemies"—a pair of Texas boots, a shield against rattlesnakes. Each gift was presented with a local advertising plug, like a quiz prize.

In Washington, in gloomy twilight at Andrews Field, Air Force One came down and moved in strange stillness into a circle of light. The casket was seen to descend by hydraulic lift. As Jacqueline Kennedy joined the casket in the navy ambulance, a telescopic close-up showed her suit and stockings to be caked with blood. After she had left, President Johnson descended from the plane and made his first public statement. It ended:

JOHNSON: I will do my best. That is all I can do. I ask your help— and God's.

Amid such shots, the networks kept switching to Dallas. Its police were not merely cooperative, but apparently eager to surrender to television requests and whims. A manacled Lee Harvey Oswald was exhibited on a platform for cameramen and reporters. A rifle was brandished triumphantly: "The murder weapon." Asked if Oswald had a lawyer, the spokesman said he did not know. The trial-by-television continued through Saturday, with "clues" displayed on camera. That night Oswald was to be moved from city jail to county jail. To accommodate broadcasters, the police rescheduled the event for Sunday at noon—in spite of Justice Department pleas for a secret night transfer. Dallas police chief Jesse Curry was reported to be unwilling to "put anything over on" the news media.

Throughout Saturday, audiences saw planeloads of world leaders arrive in Washington, in drizzling rain. On Sunday came the solemn departure of the caisson from the White House, for transfer to the Capitol. At 12:21 eastern time ABC-TV and CBS-TV were covering this scene, but NBC-TV had switched to police headquarters in Dallas. Here audiences saw Oswald, escorted by detectives, coming from the basement to the garage, heading for an armored vehicle. A figure with a hat pushed into the picture, thrust a pistol toward Oswald, and fired. Oswald, twisting, fell out of sight. A policeman shouted, "Jack, you son of a bitch!" NBC's Tom Pettit cried out: "He's been shot! Lee Oswald has been shot!" Amid pandemonium, viewers saw the assailant overpowered, and a limp Oswald hauled to the armored car.

Only NBC-TV had shown it live, but the scene was available to the other networks via videotape, and within seconds they left the Washington scene for a Dallas replay. It was shown repeatedly, intercutting with continuing chaos at headquarters.

In front of television sets throughout the country, diverse reactions. George Reedy, assistant to President Lyndon Johnson, was busy on a telephone, watching television out of the corner of an eye; he thought that, unaccountably, NBC-TV had switched to an old Edward G. Robinson gangster movie. He told his secretary to switch it off. Then the truth penetrated—and he hung up. Later he could not remember to whom he had been talking on the phone.

In Dallas, announcers were telling about the assailant, Jack Ruby.

Shot seen round the world. Wide World

NOVEMBER

At the Capitol: the body of John F. Kennedy is moved to the Rotunda. Mrs. John F. Kennedy with children and Robert Kennedy; President and Mrs. Lyndon B. Johnson. UPI

They said he ran a striptease joint; he liked to hang around police headquarters giving out passes to his striptease parlor.

At the time of the shooting, four out of ten television sets were on. An hour later the number had almost doubled. At 2:17, in the Capitol, the world saw Mrs. Jacqueline Kennedy take daughter Caroline by the hand, as the two walked forward alone to the coffin. The mother showed perfect self-control; the daughter looked to her for cues. The mother knelt and so did Caroline. The mother leaned over to kiss the flag. The child slipped her gloved hand under it and did the same. For millions it was the most unbearable moment in four days, the most unforgettable.

NBC continued all night with coverage of the river of humanity filing past the coffin. On Monday virtually the whole nation watched the funeral procession move toward Arlington Cemetery. Some television employes had slept as little as six hours in three nights. They went on, almost welcoming the absorption in the task at hand. Their dignity, intelligence, and judgment were extraordinary. Did the networks have any conception of the talent submerged in their news divisions, squeezed into daily one-minute and two-minute capsules?

In spite of the frantically assembled facilities, slips and fluffs were few. During the processions from the Capitol to the Cathedral, from the Cathedral to Arlington, the action passed from camera to camera, newsman to newsman. The networks had only one-way communication to many of their men. William Small of the CBS Washington bureau spoke to one of his announcers via one-way phone: "Now Stan, it's moving a little closer to you now. You don't see it yet, you don't have to talk yet, just wait a few moments, then when you see the head of the cortège, then you can mention it. Now, do you have it? Don't answer me, because your mike is open, but that's what you are to do."

STAN: Okay, Bill.

The two words, spoken clearly in the midst of solemnity, were momentarily puzzling to millions.

Throughout the four days, past and present mingled. Even as cameras looked at the flag-draped coffin in St. Matthew's Cathedral, the recorded voice of John Kennedy was heard, speaking words from his inaugural:

KENNEDY: . . . ask not what your country can do for you; ask what you can do for your country.

By Monday night John Kennedy had become a legend.

The networks carried no commercials from Friday through Monday. Some stations followed the example; others did not.

Praise for the industry was widespread and warm. American television, it was felt, had helped the nation pull together. But the events had other meanings for some. The American Civil Liberties Union was aghast that police procedures in Dallas had taken on "the quality of a theatrical production for the benefit of the television cameras." Bar associations made similar statements. They blamed Dallas officials for succumbing to television, but blamed television for creating the atmosphere and pressures to which the officials had succumbed.

Other aspects of the sequence of events elicited even harsher comments:

To the Editor of the New York *Times:*

The shooting of President Kennedy was the normal method of dealing with an opponent as taught by countless television programs. This tragedy is one of the results of the corruption of people's minds and hearts by the violence of commercial television. It must not continue.

Gilbert E. Dean

Nazareth, Pa.

Concern over a climate of hate and violence came from many sources. A Dallas minister, Rev. William A. Holmes, received a visit from a fourth-grade schoolteacher who was distraught over the reaction of her class when she announced the assassination of President Kennedy. It had brought handclapping and cries of

"Goodie!" The minister mentioned the incident in a sermon and in a CBS-TV network interview, saying it apparently reflected attitudes absorbed at home.

Martin Luther King was deeply affected by the sequence of murders. When he learned of the death of Kennedy, he told his wife, "This is a sick society." He felt that he also would meet his death violently.

Talk about a "sick" society was heard on the air for a few days but soon subsided. If there was anything wrong in the climate of American life, the television industry as a whole had no feeling of having contributed to it. It emerged from the four days with a sense of achievement. It had shown its maturity, and now deserved a less regulated existence. The time had come, said numerous spokesmen, to end government harassments.

Easier times were expected. A few months before the assassination of President Kennedy, Newton Minow had left the FCC for private business, and the industry felt relieved. His youthful successor, E. William Henry, was perhaps of similar disposition, but he was not as articulate and was not expected to have comparable influence. He was also a "Robert Kennedy man" and not considered likely to remain.

In December 1963 *Sponsor* magazine noted that several "Minow-inspired programs"—the children's series *Exploring* and *Discovery* were mentioned—had already fallen by the wayside.

The industry felt comfortable about President Johnson. He was the first President to come from the ranks of broadcasting management. At the time he took office the family broadcast holdings, which had started in 1943 with a $17,500 investment in a radio station, were estimated by *Life* to be worth $8,000,000. Johnson had always taken an active part in managing the stations, and it was felt he would understand industry problems. He was considered a friend of Frank Stanton of CBS, who advised him on communication matters and seemed to have readier access to the White House than did the chairman of the FCC.

The industry, in view of its expenses and losses in the assassination period, felt justified in getting back to business. There would soon be another presidential election—conventions, campaigns, election returns. Now it was time to recoup.

In one decade—the Eisenhower and Kennedy years—American television had reached fabulous proportions. It had developed its technology and skills to a degree that earned astonishment. It had become not only a national but an international institution, helping to further and consolidate—along with other forces, such as the military—the world reach of American business.

In general television had reflected—in plots, settings, characters, taboos—the wishes and needs of business. Discordant notes had sounded at times—occasionally from drama, more often from news programming—but such intrusions had generally been muffled by economic considerations and blacklists. The Kennedy years had brought some loosening of the restraints.

On the whole, television had won a degree of acceptance that must have exceeded the dreams of a Sarnoff. For most people it had become their window on the world. The view it offered seemed to be *the* world. They trusted its validity and completeness.

The trust could be pointed to with pride by the industry, but was itself a danger. It made possible, as events had suggested, national adventures in deception and self-deception. But television itself did not warn of the danger, and so the trust remained—and with it, the danger.

As crowds poured past the bier of John Kennedy, and the world sat hypnotized, President Lyndon Johnson was already at work in the White House.

As Jacqueline and Caroline stepped back from the bier—Sunday afternoon, about 3 p.m.—the President received John McCone, who had become head of the Central Intelligence Agency. With him was Henry Cabot Lodge, just in from Vietnam. The subject was Vietnam, where things were—in their view—going badly.

Three weeks before the assassination of Kennedy, Ngo Dinh

Diem and his brother had been murdered. South Vietnam was in turmoil. The structure built around Diem with American treasure and effort faced disaster. The United States apparently had a choice of withdrawing or doubling its bets. In the way that the Cuban problem had faced Kennedy as he took office, so the problem of Vietnam now faced Johnson.

Most television viewers did not yet know where Vietnam was: there were no network bureaus there. But they would learn.

ELDER

5

"Watchman, what of the night?"

ISAIAH

Newsroom, KQED.

KQED

Early in 1964 President Johnson decided—as was later revealed in *The Pentagon Papers*—on a massive escalation of the Vietnam war. It would include large air attacks on North Vietnam and would begin in 1965. An arms buildup was begun and at once contributed to business prosperity. But the war decisions remained secret until after the 1964 presidential election.

Those around Johnson felt the escalation was essential. Truman was said to have "lost" China. If "we" lost Vietnam, it was assumed "we" would "lose" Indonesia. Oil, tin, rubber, and other resources were at stake. Halfway measures must be avoided.

For a time, the tube gave no hint of the decision, or of any change of climate. The liberal flame still burned brightly, at least occasionally. President Johnson himself kept it burning with a fervent, televised plea for a civil rights law—and startled audiences by ending with the words of the song, "We shall overcome—some day!" By thus aligning himself with the Negro rights movement as though he had been a lifelong marcher, and then applying his enormous persuasive talents to members of Congress, Johnson accomplished what Kennedy had been unable to accomplish. The bill became law in July 1964—shortly before the nominating conventions.

Throughout the early months of 1964, the civil rights drive seemed to gain momentum—with continuing effects on broadcasting. Young "freedom riders" from the North were going to Mississippi to help rebuild churches and homes of Negroes, to serve in "freedom schools," and above all, to show solidarity. In June the disappearance of two freedom riders, Michael Schwerner and Andrew Goodman, along with a local black youth, James E. Chaney, became a focus of news interest. When their bullet-ridden bodies were found, and Ku Klux Klansmen were indicted for the murder, the case won worldwide attention. Network cameramen turned up at the Chaney funeral service in the little First Union Baptist Church in Meridian, Mississippi, and the telecast brought many viewers close to the movement. In New York the young wife of Michael Schwerner remarked on television how tragic it was that it took the murder of some white boys to fasten national attention on what Negroes had long endured. The mother of Andrew Goodman said on television, "My thoughts are with Mrs. Chaney." Then Mrs. Chaney flew north from Meridian to be at the funeral of Schwerner and Goodman. She too wanted to show solidarity.

Along with freedom riders others went south. In March 1964 the communication division of the United Church of Christ, under the Reverend Everett C. Parker, began tape-recording the output of the two television stations in Jackson, Mississippi: WLBT, the NBC-TV and ABC-TV affiliate; and WJTV, the CBS-TV affiliate. On the basis of the recorded evidence, the United Church asked the FCC not to renew the station licenses. It pointed out that Negroes represented 45 per cent of the viewing area but were ignored by the stations. In addition, news about desegregation efforts, in the nation and locally, was ignored and even—in the case of network programs—eliminated by the stations of Jackson, with the result that its "entire population, Negro and white, receives a distorted picture of vital issues."

Each station was found to devote 16 per cent of its time to commercials. No black artists were used. Each station carried more than four hours of religious services—none involving Negroes. The United Church argued that the rigged program pattern, far from serving the "public interest," was a disservice to both white and black viewers.

So completely were the mores of the area taken for granted that such complaints seldom confronted the FCC formally. The commission was mildly embarrassed. By a 4 to 2 decision—the dissenters were Chairman E. William Henry and Commissioner Kenneth Cox —it renewed the licenses for one-year terms, pending good behavior. In so doing it refused public hearings demanded by the United Church and took the position that the group had in any event no rights in the case, since the "public interest" was represented by the FCC itself. The church group refused to accept this, and promptly challenged the decision in the U.S. Circuit Court of Appeals for the District of Columbia. The action precipitated legal struggles that had implications for many southern stations. Most, reassured by precedent, did not take the threat seriously, but monitoring of other southern stations was begun by the United Church and others. When the FCC was eventually reversed through court action, and was forced to vacate the WLBT license, the event brought a temporary panic, and a long-range reassessment of news policies and hiring practices among southern stations.

The agitation also put pressure on northern stations. In July 1964 the pioneer station KDKA, Pittsburgh, approaching its forty-fourth anniversary, hired its first Negro performer.

On television, programming that echoed the stirrings of the Kennedy years still turned up intermittently in 1964. On NBC-TV *That Was the Week That Was*, modeled after a British Broadcasting Corporation series, was offering lighthearted but sharp satire— a rare commodity on television. On CBS-TV *The Defenders*, produced by Herbert Brodkin, was showing special vitality, even digging into the industry's own problems—in January with a play by Ernest Kinoy, about television blacklisting; and in May with a play by Albert Ruben, about a correspondent deprived of his passport for "unauthorized" travel to China. The latter was a clear reminder of the William Worthy case. Both these scripts explored with integrity legal ramifications and nuances of their subjects.

Though some programming gave the feeling of a continuing Kennedy atmosphere, an opposite trend—encouraged by prosperity and a growing sense of ease about Washington—was increasingly evident.

THE ADVERSARY CULTURE

By 1964 James Aubrey, who had said he could double the CBS net income, was well on his way to doing it. In January the evening television schedule for the following fall was already sold out, and even fringe periods looked profitable. Preventing even grander profits were programs like *CBS Reports*, which were sometimes sold to sponsors at less than cost. Fred Friendly, who in March 1964 became president of CBS News, found he would have to battle to keep it in the schedule.

On one occasion Aubrey, according to Friendly's recollection, told him that "in this adversary system" they would of course be at each other's throats. "They say to me, 'Take your soiled little hands, get the ratings, and make as much money as you can.' They say to you, 'Take your lily-white hands, do your best, go the high road and bring us prestige.' "

The "adversary" aspect seemed to stimulate Aubrey, and he tended to make annual budget meetings an arena for combat. Presenting CBS-TV financial achievements with color slides in which the cost of news programs was depicted in—to use Friendly's term —"fire-engine red," he addressed the chair: "You can see, Mr. Chairman, how much bigger our profits could have been this year if it had not been for the drain of news." Aubrey wanted *CBS Reports* offered at a profitable figure and, if not sold, dropped.

Chairman Paley, a suave executive, disliked crude approaches of this sort. Yet Aubrey generally got his way, and the trade press carried rumors that *CBS Reports* might be scrapped.

A disdain for the "high road" trickled down through network hierarchies. When an Aubrey lieutenant engaged producer-writer William Froug, who had been producing *Twilight Zone*, for the Hollywood position of executive producer in charge of drama, it was emphasized that Froug was not to produce *Medea* but mass entertainment. The executive summarized: "Your job is to produce shit."

The view that affiliates had similar preferences was often expressed, and with some evidence. Edward W. Barrrett, former broadcasting and publishing executive who had become dean of the School of Journalism at Columbia University, attended a 1964 broadcasting convention and heard a broadcaster talking about his station. Asked what network it was affiliated with, this man answered: "NBC, damn it."

"Why do you say it that way?"

"Well, they're ruining it with all this damned news and documentary stuff. . . . We lose audiences every time we have to put that stuff in place of entertainment. Take that nonsense of extending the Huntley-Brinkley program from fifteen minutes to a full half hour. That alone costs us way over $100,000."

If there was restiveness about news programs, it was because sponsorship money was available for other things. Even Sunday afternoon, long a "cultural ghetto," was turning into a gold mine, mainly because of the sensational rise of professional football. CBS paid $28 million for television rights for the National Football League games for 1964 and 1965 and instantly recouped the investment with two $14 million sponsorship contracts—one with Ford Motor Company, the other with Philip Morris and its subsidiary the American Safety Razor Company. Additional spot announcements in station-break periods would bring large profits—both to network and affiliates.

A factor in the rise of football as television fare was the "instant replay," so tellingly used in the Oswald murder. A few weeks later, on New Year's Eve, it was used in the Army-Navy football game, and in 1964 it became a standard sports technique. While one camera showed the overall action "live," other cameras followed key players in close-up, with each camera linked to a separate videotape machine. Within seconds after a play, its crucial action could be re-examined in close-up, or even unfolded in startling slow motion. This accomplished incredible transformations: brutal collisions became ballets, and end runs and forward passes became miracles of human coordination. Football, once an unfathomable jumble on the small screen, acquired fascination for widening audiences. It eventually became evening entertainment in ABC-TV's highly successful *Monday Night Football*, presided over by Howard Cosell, a sportscaster of almost heroic brashness.

Football games were often withheld from television in cities where they were played. Such television blackouts gave rise to a new social phenomenon: sudden migrations to motels within reach of other stations.

In 1964 CBS, flush with profits, purchased a baseball team—the New York Yankees—and acquired a new stake in sports promotion. Questions of a conflict of interest were raised in government committees, argued, and quickly forgotten. The growing involvement in sports was regarded by some television executives as a useful hedge against rising talent costs. Any future strike by actors might be countered by an expanded sports schedule. Meanwhile sports were making weekend periods fabulously valuable.

Saturday mornings, once regarded as a time for do-good programs to please women's groups, were becoming profitable for a different reason. Toy manufacturers were adopting year-round rather than seasonal advertising schedules and were the main Saturday morning sponsors, backing a parade of animated films, largely violent.

Weekday mornings and afternoons were increasingly profitable. Daytime serials had at first seemed a failure on television. But when

Sunday afternoon. ABC

BIG TIME

Superbowl—1969. NBC

they were expanded from the 15-minute form inherited from radio to a 30-minute form, success followed. By 1964 daytime serials were an addiction comparable to the radio-serial addiction at its zenith, and were the mainstay of New York activity in television drama. They were especially profitable for CBS-TV.

The late evening hours were profitable far into the night. In 1962 the NBC-TV *Tonight* series became the domain of Johnny Carson, and turned into an even greater bonanza than it had been under Jack Paar. The breakfast-time hours were also highly profitable, especially for NBC-TV, with its *Today* series. Almost all hours shared in the rising affluence.

The prosperity of television had various off-shoots. When the New York Giants baseball team decided to become the San Francisco Giants and the Brooklyn Dodgers to become the Los Angeles Dodgers, it was in large part because of a television scheme—Subscription TV, Inc., organized by Matthew Fox, who had become prosperous distributing feature films to television. He brought Pat Weaver back into the spotlight as president of Subscription TV.

The company planned to supply programs to homes in San Francisco and Los Angeles by television cable. The subscriber would pay an installation fee and then pay for programs actually selected via a telephone dial system. The subscriber was promised events that would not be available on commercial television: first-run movies, major sports events, opera. The Giants and Dodgers, arriving on the West Coast with fanfare, would eventually be seen only via Subscription TV, Inc., not by commercial television. Most major motion picture companies were spellbound by the prospect of a new kind of "box office." Figures projected by Matthew Fox and Pat Weaver suggested that both film industry and major league baseball would gross revenues even exceeding those earned through "free television." Motion picture theaters were up in arms at the prospect of a new form of competition. Broadcasters were likewise alarmed. If the system proved successful, major attractions would probably become unavailable to sponsored television—they would

As the World Turns   Wisconsin Center for Theatre Research

switch to Subscription TV and other such regional systems. "Free" television might become a ghost town of the unwanted. The year 1964 loomed as the year of decision as the sale of subscriptions and the wiring of homes got under way in the Los Angeles and San Francisco areas.

One aspect of Subscription TV, Inc., was of special interest to entrepreneurs. Because it planned to operate entirely within California, its cables would not cross state lines, and the plan would apparently avoid FCC jurisdiction.

Another scheme was developing unforeseen glitter in 1964: CATV. The letters had originally stood for "community antenna television," but the industry was switching to the term "cable television."

Community antenna systems had developed early in television; they even had a history that went back to the beginnings of radio.* During the television freeze period their function was to bring programs to towns that did not yet have stations of their own. After the freeze they remained important for small isolated communities or those with bad reception, such as towns surrounded by mountains. The subscriber paid an installation fee to have his set connected by cable to the community antenna system; then a continuing subscription fee, which in 1964 was generally set at $5 a month. He needed no antenna of his own. The CATV system might bring him half a dozen to a dozen stations—in a few instances they included distant stations brought in by microwave relay. The cables to subscriber homes were usually strung on telephone poles under a contract with the local telephone company—a further involvement of AT&T affiliates with television.

At first there was no thought of additional programming created by CATV systems themselves, but the possibility existed. Such programs might be provided to subscribers as a free service or at an extra charge.

As television spread during the 1950's, the function of CATV was at first regarded as diminishing, but it was only shifting. Many communities had only one or two stations and welcomed a system that brought in others. Special reception problems persisted and multiplied. Cities had ghost images bouncing from tall buildings, and other mysterious interferences such as diathermy machines. A CATV system could solve such problems.

In the early 1960's the broadcasting industry woke up to the fact

* The first community antenna system was apparently launched in Dundee, Michigan, in 1923. Bringing in remote stations by means of a tall antenna tower, it offered their programs to local subscribers by wire at $1.50 per month. The system was described in the May 1923 issue of *Radio Broadcast* by University of Wisconsin student Grayson Kirk, later president of Columbia University.

that fortunes were being earned by the cable systems. Were they a boon to television, or a threat?

Film distributors saw a threat. United Artists, having sold a film to a television station in Scranton, supposedly for a Scranton premiere, might find the station complaining that Scranton viewers had already seen it—thanks to a CATV system that had relayed it from a Pittsburgh telecast. Clearly control of copyrights was at stake. Broadcasters planning new stations on available UHF frequencies were likewise disturbed. Success would depend on inclusion in the CATV system; they would be at its mercy. They turned to the FCC for support.

Did the FCC have jurisdiction? The CATV systems (except the few that used microwave relays) did no broadcasting. They sent no waves into the ether. They only *received* waves—as did individual viewers. As of 1964 most FCC members felt it was not a legitimate concern of the commission—an opinion revised two years later.

Meanwhile the CATV industry grew. In 1964 over a thousand systems were in operation. The majority of them were members of an aggressive National Community Television Association, later renamed National Cable Television Association. Late in 1964 Commissioner Frederick W. Ford of the FCC decided to leave the commission to accept the presidency of the NCTA. The industry had its own vigorous trade press.

There was growing awareness that a nationwide linking of cable systems could turn into a coast-to-coast subscription television system. Broadcasters were hedging their bets by investing in cable systems. So were publishers and film companies.

The promoters of all these visions moved ahead, luxuriating in a new laissez-faire era. But the center of the boom was sponsored television.

The number of commercials that could be crowded into a given time period amazed some observers, although most viewers, inured gradually, seemed to take it for granted. In 1964 a housewife who sat down for a morning television break to watch WCBS-TV, New York, could catch a Mike Wallace newscast at 10 a.m., followed by reruns of *I Love Lucy* and *The Real McCoys* and an episode of *Pete and Gladys*. The 120 minutes would include interruptions for 45 to 50 promotional messages for products and services. On a typical morning:

10:02   Beechnut Coffee ("turns lions into lambs")
10:09   Ajax ("knifes through waxed-in-dirt")
10:14   Cheerios
10:15   Betty Crocker Cake Mix
10:20   Fashion Quick Home Permanent
10:20   Hudnut Shampoo with Egg and Cream Rinse
10:25   Playtex Nurser ("less spitting up and colic")
10:26   Playtex Living Stretch Bra ("lasting stretch that won't wash out")
10:28   Cotton Producers' Institute ("the fiber you can trust")
10:29   Jack Benny program promotion
10:29   Imperial Margarine ("sniff the wonderful aroma")
10:29   Sea Mist Window Cleaner ("washes dirt away")
10:30   Scott Tissue
10:37   Action Chlorine Bleach ("three active ingredients")
10:43   Fritos Corn Chips
10:44   Glass Wax ("gobbles up window dirt")
10:50   Duranel Cookware
10:57   Playtex Living Stretch Bra
10:58   Playtex New Living Girdle ("live a little")
10:58   Red Skelton program promotion
10:59   Shambleu Shampoo
10:59   La Rosa Pizza Pie Mix
11:00   Clorox
11:08   Endust ("cuts your dusting time in half")
11:09   Vanish Toilet Bowl Cleaner ("just brush and flush")
11:12   Westinghouse Iron
11:16   Playtex Cotton Bra
11:17   Playtex Panty Girdle ("try the fingertip test")
11:23   Cotton Producers' Institute
11:27   Ajax Laundry Detergent ("stronger than dirt")
11:28   Danny Kaye program promotion

11:29 Glass Wax ("the one right cleaner for city windows")
11:29 Sandran Vinyl Floors ("you can lie down on the job")
11:30 Rexall One-Cent Sale
11:36 A. J. Orange Juice
11:44 Playtex Living Stretch Bra
11:45 Playtex New Living Girdle
11:45 Pillsbury's Best Flour
11:45 Pillsbury's Mashed Potato Flakes
11:46 Sweet 10 Sweetener ("no bitter aftertaste")
11:51 Fritos Corn Chips
11:57 Right Guard Deodorant ("24-hour protection")
11:58 Pillsbury's Best Flour
11:59 *Petticoat Junction* program promotion
11:59 SOS ("loaded with soap")
11:59 *Eye on New York* program promotion

News analyst Eric Sevareid observed in 1964:

SEVAREID: The biggest big business in America is not steel, automobiles or television. It is the manufacture, refinement and distribution of anxiety. . . .

Logically extended, this process can only terminate in a mass nervous breakdown or in a collective condition of resentment that will cause street corner Santa Clauses to be thrown down manholes, the suffering to be left to pain, and aid delegations from Ruanda-Urundi to be arrested on the White House steps.

With Sevareid all problems were sublimated into fine prose. Other observers were more indignant and pressed for action, but the regulatory spirit was on the decline. When it appeared, it was quickly squelched. On one occasion Leroy Collins, president of the National Association of Broadcasters, suggested that broadcasters should themselves restrict cigarette advertising. The NAB soon afterwards fired Collins from his $75,000-a-year job.

The experience of FCC chairman E. William Henry was even more enlightening, and also concerned the NAB. The NAB television and radio codes were constantly held up by industry spokesmen as shining examples of self-regulation, though regarded by many broadcasters as a charade. Most of its edicts had built-in escape hatches,* and the few clear rules—such as those dealing with the time to be devoted to commercials—were widely ignored. An FCC sampling of stations in 1963 found that 40 per cent had advertising exceeding the code limits. The NAB television code had an enforcement machinery which was among its more absurd features. If a subscribing station was charged with violating the code and was found guilty by an NAB review board, the station (according to the rules) would lose the right to display on the screen the NAB "seal of good practice." Since the seal meant nothing to viewers and its absence would be virtually impossible to notice, the machinery meant nothing. In fact, no station had been deprived of the seal.

Chairman E. William Henry favored a modest approach to the problem of over-commercialization. Since the industry had defined its standards in its own codes and constantly spoke of them with respect and admiration, it seemed to Henry logical that the FCC should adopt those standards officially. At license renewal time the FCC could then inquire: has the station observed the industry's own proclaimed standards?

The industry reaction to this was one of horror and outrage; it stimulated instant countermoves in Congress, where Representative Walter E. Rogers of Texas introduced a bill forbidding the FCC to take any action to limit commercials. NAB memos marked URGENT URGENT URGENT were dispatched to all stations.

> Broadcasters should immediately urge their Congressmen by phone or wire *to vote for H. R. 8316.* . . . A vote for the bill is a vote of confidence in the broadcasters in his district. A vote against the bill would open the door to unlimited governmental control of broadcasting. . . .

---

* Typical was a television code edict on *violence,* which was to be used "only as required by plot development or character delineation." The code writers seemed to pretend that plot and character were beyond the control of writer and producer. NAB Television Code, II, 2.

The bill passed, 317 to 43. The Senate ignored the affair, but the House vote served as due notice to the FCC. It dropped the notion of curbing commercials.

Chairman Henry, settling into frustration, was tempted into Minow rhetoric. That fall he referred to television schedules as an "electronic Appalachia." The words were shrugged off by the industry.

Back in the 1920's Herbert Hoover, as Secretary of Commerce, had urged broadcasters to restrain their commercial impulses; he was sure that, for their own good, they would heed his advice. He said that if a presidential message ever became "the meat in a sand-wich of two patent medicine advertisements," it would destroy broadcasting. When Hoover died on October 20, 1964, NBC broad-cast a tribute which was at once followed at its key station by a beer commercial, a political commercial, and a cigarette commer-cial. The ex-President was triple-spotted into eternity.

The broadcasting industry was in a state of almost delirious pros-perity. A Pittsburgh station—WIIC—had just changed hands for $20,500,000, the highest price ever paid for a station. Even network radio was again profitable, and radio as a whole had earned a $55 million profit during the preceding year. In mid-Manhattan a suave, impeccably dressed skyscraper designed by Eero Saarinen for CBS was rising as a monument to its role in the new era. Significantly it was almost wholly devoted to executive and sales functions, with most television program activity being banished to a rebuilt milk-bottling plant on less expensive real estate.

Against this background of prosperity, the industry was pre-paring for another presidential election.

DAISY GIRL

Many Americans, going about their business in an environment that —judged by television—was prosperous, vigorous, and forward-

Frank Stanton with model of new CBS headquarters, designed by Saarinen.
CBS

moving, first became aware of Vietnam through the 1964 presidential campaign as seen on the home screen. The awareness came not
from things President Johnson told them—he scarcely mentioned
the subject—but from issues raised by Senator Barry Goldwater of
Arizona, who was nominated by the Republicans at their San Francisco convention. Goldwater saw Vietnam as a possible issue, and
he needed issues.

Goldwater had been talking with some of the generals, and they
told him that the bogged-down action in Vietnam—which in 1963
had come close to disaster—was a disgrace that could and should be

resolved by firm measures. Goldwater seldom specified what measures should be taken, but in an ABC-TV interview with Howard K. Smith he mentioned some possibilities, one of which was to defoliate Vietnamese forests with a "low yield atomic device." The remark was widely discussed and gave the impression that Goldwater had a casual attitude toward dropping atomic "devices."

The Democratic Party in this campaign had the service of the Doyle Dane Bernbach advertising agency—a young agency with a reputation for sophistication. President Kennedy had taken a fancy to its Volkswagen advertising and to its Avis campaign: "We try harder—we have to—we're only number two." It may have reminded Kennedy of his 1960 situation. In September 1963 he asked his brother-in-law Stephen Smith to talk to the agency about working on the 1964 presidential drive; later President Johnson decided to hold to the Kennedy choice.

Although the Democrats had in the past had trouble finding an agency willing to handle their "account," Doyle Dane Bernbach was at once interested. Perhaps rising prosperity under the Democrats had something to do with it.

The Doyle Dane Bernbach campaign work was novel in several respects. Determined not to disturb viewing habits, it concentrated on spots. It even avoided the 5-minute hitch-hike programs featured in 1956, requiring partial pre-emptions. Some of the Doyle Dane Bernbach spots were less than a minute long and could be used at station-break time along with other spot commercials. The emphasis on spots was in harmony with current advertising trends. For speeches the Democrats pre-empted only eight programs throughout the campaign—in contrast to the Republicans, who pre-empted thirteen.

The Doyle Dane Bernbach spots, in addition to being the heart of the campaign, had another unusual feature. Earlier spots, such as those for Eisenhower and Stevenson, had been built around the candidate. The principal Doyle Dane Bernbach spots were not. This may have been partly a matter of necessity; the nomination of

Johnson, though a foregone conclusion, did not take place until the end of August, more than a month after the Goldwater nomination. Meanwhile the Doyle Dane Bernbach spots dealt—without mentioning him—with Goldwater.

Its most celebrated spot showed a small girl picking petals from a daisy. This was accompanied on the soundtrack by a count-down. Then came an atomic explosion, darkness, and a brief statement.

VOICE: These are the stakes. To make a world in which all God's children can live, or go into the dark.

In another spot a girl was seen eating an ice-cream cone. There was the ticking of a Geiger counter. A motherly voice was meanwhile explaining about Strontium 90, a radioactive fallout product found to concentrate itself in milk. Again a viewer was reminded of Goldwater's apparently casual attitude toward nuclear "devices" and perhaps his opposition to the test-ban treaty.

The Goldwater nomination represented a westward power shift. Goldwater backers included right-wing extremists who looked on some eastern members of the party—particularly those called "liberal"—as akin to communists. Goldwater, in a light mood, gave expression to this western chauvinism with the suggestion that someone should saw off the Atlantic seaboard and let it float out to sea. Doyle Dane Bernbach produced a spot in which someone did just that.

Though most Republicans, reversing opposition policies of earlier years, had long ago accepted Social Security, it was still anathema to some conservatives. In the New Hampshire primary Goldwater made a slighting reference to Social Security, causing speculation that he might abolish it. He denied this, but Doyle Dane Bernbach kept memories of the remark alive with a spot in which two hands were seen tearing up a Social Security card.

The Doyle Dane Bernbach strategy in all these spots was to panic Goldwater into over-reacting. They considered this strategy too subtle to explain to the Democratic National Committee and never did explain it to them. The agency dealt with the White House through Lloyd Wright and William Moyers—both Texans close to Johnson. But the strategy was apparently successful because Goldwater began fulminating against the spots. "The homes of America," he protested, "are horrified and the intelligence of Americans is insulted by weird television advertising by which this administration threatens the end of the world unless all-wise Lyndon is given the nation for his very own." Repeated assaults of this sort helped make the television spots the talk of the campaign. Astonishingly, the girl-with-a-daisy and ice-cream-cone spots were each used only once in paid time. The agency did not reschedule them, not because of orders to withdraw them—though some Democratic leaders considered them "unfortunate"—but because the attention won at first showing was so overwhelming that re-use seemed redundant. ABC News and CBS News carried news items about the daisy girl. *Time* did a cover story on her. The New York *Times* carried a news story about her. The hubbub helped reinforce the trigger-happy association pinned on Goldwater. More ironically, it also created the impression that a vote for Johnson was a vote *against* escalation —an escalation already in preparation. Johnson did nothing to counter the impression.

While the Democrats relied heavily on spots, the Republicans relied more on speeches but also on a half-hour television film—which, like the Democratic spots, became a storm center. Titled *Choice*, it was sponsored by Mothers for a Moral America and was scheduled to premiere on 145 NBC-TV stations on Thursday, October 22, at an afternoon time when the audience would be largely composed of women. Its theme was that the United States was undergoing a moral decay which the film attributed to the Democrats, including President Johnson. The decay was depicted through glimpses of topless dancers, pornographic magazines, marquees of nudist films —and rioting. The purpose, said one of its creators, was to rouse strong emotions, and to turn the anti-city feelings of rural people against the Democratic administration.

The film associated sexual emancipation and the rise of nudism with Negro protest movements; all were considered aspects of the breakdown of "law and order." The phrase "law and order" was thus turning into a coded appeal to segregationists, and the film was considered by Democrats an attempt to woo a "white backlash" vote. Rioters in the film were mostly blacks but included white teenagers.

In an attempt to pin the moral decay on President Johnson, the film had intermittent shots of a speeding Lincoln Continental screeching across the screen, with beer cans being thrown from the window. These shots were a reminder of reports that the President had driven his Lincoln at high speed near his LBJ ranch, and had been seen drinking beer at the wheel. The producers acknowledged that the shots were staged. The President was not mentioned by name.

Two hundred prints of the film were distributed throughout the United States to be ready for saturation showings after the network premiere. But before it got on the air, protests began. Democratic Party chairman John M. Bailey had a preview and called it the "sickest" program in the history of television campaigning. He suggested that its "prurient" appeal mocked its moral pretensions. NBC was reported to have qualms and to be asking for cuts. The furor persuaded Senator Goldwater to have the telecast canceled, but local showings were held.

In San Francisco, Republican Party headquarters was reported showing the film in its front window. By this time the Democrats regarded the film as an asset to their own cause, and distributed handbills announcing the "sexiest show in town . . . free . . . see Goldwater family movies . . . see them shimmy, see them shake." They also used a barker on a sound truck to send people to the Republican showings, and distributed leaflets with mock endorsements for Goldwater from "Daddies for Decent America." After the campaign, according to the *Wall Street Journal*, the Democratic Club of Washington, D.C., used a print of the Republican "feelthy pictures" as a fund-raising attraction.

The Republicans bought their television and radio time through Erwin, Wasey, Ruthrauff & Ryan. On four occasions, for campaign speeches, it pre-empted the network period occupied by the satiric series *That Was the Week That Was.* This series, returning to the air on November 10 after Johnson's landslide victory—the popular vote was 43,126,506 to 27,176,799, and the electoral vote 486 to 52 —had a mild revenge. Film footage of Goldwater talking was so cut that he *seemed* to speak the message: "Due to circumstances beyond our control, the political address originally planned for this period will not be heard."

The campaign saw the emergence of Lyndon B. Johnson as television impresario. Reporters were already familiar with his television fixation. At the White House he had three television sets lined up side by side so that he could watch all three networks simultaneously. He sometimes shouted back at the tube. When strongly displeased he might phone a network president or an offending newsman. Early in the Democratic convention he phoned about camera work. To avoid emphasis on disunity, he wanted the coverage to remain with the speaker at the rostrum, and not switched to the strife-torn Mississippi delegation. During the nominating speeches Johnson flew to Atlantic City with a plane-load of reporters, and while in flight followed the proceedings intently by television. Shoveling peanuts into his mouth, he watched Governor Connally of Texas nominating him. A reporter made a comment; the President was irked. "Shsh! he's nominatin' me!"

Among television footnotes left by the campaign, one concerned Subscription TV, Inc. On California ballots the voter had a chance to vote on Proposition 15, which declared "pay TV" to be against the public welfare. Avidly supported by theater owners, the proposition won a substantial majority of voters, who wished to keep television "free." The Subscription TV, Inc., backers planned a judicial appeal, but meanwhile the operation came to a halt and was dismantled.

Biographical campaign films played a prominent role at various stages. A curious example involved a meteoric primary drive for

Henry Cabot Lodge, who roundly defeated all Republican rivals—including Goldwater—in the New Hampshire primary. At the time, Lodge was in Saigon as U.S. Ambassador. Since he could not campaign, his backers dusted off the almost unused 4¼-minute film of 1960 based on family photos, silent footage, and endorsements by Eisenhower and others. With slight editing it was brought up to date and telecast constantly—thirty-nine times in three weeks—in paid time on New Hampshire's only television station, WMUR-TV, Manchester. The film *was* the campaign. Lodge's enormous victory, which seemed a demand for his candidacy, brought him home from Saigon to campaign in other primaries. If an absent Lodge could roll up such a vote, a campaigning Lodge was expected to sweep all before him—but somehow he failed to.

A biographical film played an important role in the transition of Robert F. Kennedy to elective politics. Entering the race for U.S. Senator from New York, he turned to film maker Charles Guggenheim, who was winning recognition as an extraordinarily skillful creator of campaign films. He had made films for various politicians including Senator George McGovern; the McGovern film brought him to Kennedy's attention.

Guggenheim studied campaign problems faced by Kennedy, who was regarded by some as a "carpet-bagger" and as "ruthless." Guggenheim said, "I'll have to humanize you," and Kennedy agreed. Guggenheim persuaded many people to record reminiscences about Kennedy at various periods. They included: a school mate who used to walk to public school with him in Bronxville, N.Y. (subtly deflecting the carpet-bagger charge as well as the rich-boy aura); a governess who described him as the most considerate of the Kennedy boys; and a high school coach who liked his team spirit. Such material was combined with a parade of pictorial items including home movies, family-album photos, college yearbook items, newsreel footage.

One of the most crucial elements was a reminiscence by author Harry Golden. He was seen talking on the steps of the New York

Guggenheim film crew—making a McGovern campaign film.   Black Star

Public Library; his voice continued over a portion of the film dealing with civil rights. Kennedy had been expected by political pun-
dits to lose the "Jewish intellectual vote" because of the ruthless
image. Golden's few words were of utmost importance in this context. Speaking of the Alabama conflict with Governor Wallace,
Golden said that Robert Kennedy had "smashed the caste system
in the South . . . ended it." This, he felt, was of the essence of humanity. "*We* know that better than anyone."

The film had saturation scheduling on television stations throughout New York State, at a probable cost of several hundred thousand dollars.

Television itself became a campaign issue. Television newsmen
underestimated Goldwater's strength before the Republican convention; the Goldwaterites, in turn, regarded the newsmen as hos-

tile to their cause. At the convention they sported buttons with such legends as "Stamp Out Huntley-Brinkley." When ex-President Eisenhower in his convention speech referred casually to "sensation-seeking columnists and commentators," he was amazed to find it producing a five-minute ovation, while Goldwater followers shook their fists at the network booths. The Goldwater forces, controlling the convention, severely restricted the movements of network newsmen, who in other conventions had freely roamed the aisles. NBC newsman John Chancellor was arrested on camera, fading out with, "This is John Chancellor, somewhere in custody."

Reporters were taken aback by the virulent attacks. The Goldwater forces seemed to regard network newsmen, along with writers of the New York *Times* and other eastern publications, as part of a conspiracy allied with "the communists." All this reflected a paranoia that also pervaded the military leadership, which readily blamed its troubles on civilian interference engineered by communists. Its frustrations in Vietnam, like the communist victory in China, seemed to require scapegoats in American government and news media. Not since the bitter conflicts of the Depression period, wrote James Reston, had correspondents been so deluged with "vulgar and personal abuse."

Paranoia has been a persistent element in American politics. In 1964 it was gathering intensity. This was not confined to speeches, tracts, and political in-fighting. It pervaded also that other and more significant political weapon—the entertainment telefilm.

PARANOID PICTURES

Sociologists Paul F. Lazarsfeld and Robert K. Merton have pointed out that even in their evasions, mass media are political. Their influence has stemmed, say these writers, "not only from what is said, but more significantly from what is not said. For these media not only continue to affirm the *status quo* but, in the same measure, they fail to raise essential questions about the structure of society."

In this sense the overwhelming absorption of tens of millions of mid-twentieth-century Americans in football games and struggles against cattle rustlers was a political achievement. Along with welfare legislation, it seemed an American equivalent of the Roman "bread and circuses."

But telefilms have been political in other ways than through evasions. Public acceptance of a foreign policy based on good guy/bad guy premises may have been reinforced by a telefilm mythology of similar obsessions. When Eisenhower described the world as "forces of good and evil arrayed as never before," he was offering a picture viewers could recognize. We and they were lined up across an international arroyo.

In the years 1964-66 telefilms turned more specifically to international struggles, with emphasis on clandestine warfare. The timing was not an accident. References to CIA action in various coups and upheavals were beginning to appear in print. Besides Cuba and Guatemala there was mention of Laos, Malaysia, Indonesia. In 1963 the drift of many rumors was confirmed by Allen Dulles himself in his book *The Craft of Intelligence*. Written in retirement, it was partly a memoir and partly a prideful justification of CIA machinations. The 1964 publication of *The Bay of Pigs* by Haynes Johnson, and *The Invisible Government* by David Wise and Thomas B. Ross, gave the public—to the consternation of the CIA and the State Department—a more detailed picture of CIA work.

To many Americans, accustomed to a national image of clean uprightness—the cowboy—the revelations were disturbing and called for some adjusting. They seemed to require either indignation or rationalization. For most people, rationalization was the easier solution. If our government had really developed a "department of dirty tricks" to organize putsches, unseat rulers, and murder when necessary, all masked by elaborate fictions, it must have been brought on by dire necessities. A deluge of spy fiction, latching onto a timely topic, provided the rationale, and got Americans used to the idea. On television it was *The Man from U.N.C.L.E.*, *The Girl from U.N.C.L.E.*, *Get Smart*, *I Spy*, *The*

Man Who Never Was, Mission: Impossible, and others—some amiable, some witty, some melodramatic. So successful was this spy cycle that its subject matter took over numerous other series. Amos Burke, millionaire cop of *Burke's Law* who rode around in a Rolls Royce, became Amos Burke the millionaire secret agent. *The FBI* became concerned chiefly with communist agents. 77 *Sunset Strip* acquired a spy-story obsession. Even comedy series like *I Dream of Jeannie, Mr. Ed,* and *The Lucy Show* took up spy themes.

Like earlier action telefilms, the new cycle concerned struggles against evil men who had to be wiped out. Bosomy girls fitted easily into the picture. But in one respect the new wave departed from precedent. Older action heroes, especially the cowboy, had maintained a code of honor and fought fairly. This tradition was rapidly vanishing. When the U.S. Navy in a 77 *Sunset Strip* episode ("The Navy Caper") hired a private eye to try to steal one of its top-secret gadgets—to test its own security arrangements against enemy powers pursuing the same objective—the hero's instructions were: "You can lie, steal, cheat—whatever the enemy might do." What followed was an epic adventure in deception and counterdeception. At the start of each *Mission: Impossible* episode an agent—member of the Impossible Missions Force—received instructions via a tape recording. The instructions included a standard passage:

> VOICE: As always, should you or any of your IMF be caught or killed, the Secretary will disavow any knowledge of your actions. This tape will self-destruct in five seconds. . . . Good luck. . . .

The official lie was thus enshrined.

Justification for deception was provided by the vastness and monstrousness of schemes devised by enemy forces, which were "arrayed as never before." An *Amos Burke* episode depicted agents of SEKOR—the enemy—as ready to paralyze Washington, D.C., by introducing a special ingredient into gasoline supplies entering the city. This ingredient, sprayed into the atmosphere through au-

tomobile exhausts, would stupify the inhabitants and allow the enemy to destroy the White House, the Pentagon, the State Department, and even—perhaps most heinous—the spy organization where
Burke worked. The paralyzing fumes would be spread through the
city unwittingly by an anti-war group that was about to demonstrate. Thus the program neatly pictured peace demonstrators as
dupes of an international anti-American conspiracy. In an *I Spy*
episode ("Weight of the World") the Red Chinese had a scheme
for dropping bubonic plague bacteria into a big-city water supply.
In a *The Man from U.N.C.L.E.* episode ("Her Master's Voice Affair") the Red Chinese had subverted the headmistress of a fashionable Long Island girls' school, and with her help put the girls—all
daughters of prominent fathers—into a state of mass hypnosis. The
daughters became obedient zombies ready to annihilate their fathers
whenever they got the verbal cue over the school's public-address
system.

Each series depicted huge enemy networks for undercover warfare. Some had names like KAOS (*Get Smart*) or THRUSH (the
U.N.C.L.E. series), or SEKOR (*Amos Burke*). Viewers, asked to
identify these, readily said "the communists." Some series used
terms like "communists," "reds," "iron curtain countries," "people's republics," or simply "the enemy," while generally avoiding
names of specific countries. *Mission: Impossible* writers were encouraged to use specific names in early drafts; nonspecific designa-
tions could be put in later. In one episode the Impossible Missions
Force masqueraded as a traveling carnival troupe that had the task
of rescuing a cardinal from a maximum-security prison behind the
iron curtain. The action was clearly located in the first draft but
was later placed "in the Balkans." All this avoided the problem of
coping with embassy protests from countries with which the United
States had diplomatic relations. This sort of problem did not apply
to China; any kind of villainy could be pinned on China. The same
applied to East Germany; the hero of *The Man Who Never Was*
assumed the identity of a dead industrial leader specifically to

The Man from U.N.C.L.E.–Robert Vaughn.   NBC

thwart East German machinations. Cuba could also be used with little inhibition.

In many ways the spy circle showed Hollywood talents in brilliant form. Each of the leading spy series had special qualities. *The Man from U.N.C.L.E.* had charm and sophistication. Against melodramatic action the heroes maintained a casual air that punctured spy-drama stereotypes of earlier years without undermining tension. Climaxes involved spectacularly graceful karate activity. *I Spy* adopted a similarly cool manner and scored an added coup: the

Get Smart—Barbara Feldon and Don Adams.   NBC

spies were a white man and a black man—played with a warm, im-
provisational quality by Robert Culp and Bill Cosby. Their "cover"
roles were a touring tennis professional and his trainer. When
Cosby was offered the role, he was wary: would this be another
second-banana part, a faithful aide like the Lone Ranger's Tonto or
the Green Hornet's Kato or Jack Benny's Rochester? Assured that
in this spy role he would have special skills, equal prominence, and
romantic interest, and aware that Culp was equally determined that
a feeling of equality and warm friendship be maintained, Cosby ac-

cepted. Virtuoso performances resulted. *Get Smart,* similarly debonair, added a running romance and a unique zany quality evolved with precision by Don Adams and Barbara Feldon. Adams's bumbling agent Smart established a catchphrase—"Oops, sorry about that"—that swept the world. *Mission: Impossible* added an element of technical expertise; its international "capers" generally involved sophisticated gadgetry, always technically plausible. This aspect exerted such fascination that science teachers suggested devices for future episodes. This series, like *I Spy,* was in the vanguard of racial shifts in television drama. It adopted a device common to a number of series—a *group* of heroes, one a black, Barney Collier, played by Greg Morris. He was a specialist, an electrical engineering genius; only Barney could defuse a time bomb.

Most of these spy series were not violent in the primitive fashion of westerns and gangster films. The means were more discreet and arcane, and seldom noisy. *Mission: Impossible* arranged, whenever possible, for one foreign agent to murder another by mistake. This was regarded as a salutary policy vis-à-vis congressional committees.

The novel surface features of these programs gained most of the critical attention. But more significant was the fact that all shared a common premise, which had to be accepted for the programs to have meaning: that Americans lived, at home and abroad, amid unscrupulous conspiracies that required response in kind. "The villains are so black," *Mission: Impossible* told its writers, "and so clever that the intricate means used to defeat them are necessary."

In its depiction of communist villains, the spy telefilm of the 1964-66 period departed from hallowed precedent. Reds had once been boorish, with a dirty look. A few years of intercultural visits may have made this less credible. On the *U.N.C.L.E.* programs as well as *I Spy* and *Mission: Impossible,* the enemy might be as svelte and handsome as "us." Female operatives were as cool and antiseptic as ours and looked as if they used the same hair sprays, skin creams, and deodorants. Our agents occasionally had passing affairs with them—a custom popularized in the James Bond books and films and adopted more circumspectly and ambiguously on television.

Mission: Impossible—Greg Morris.
Paramount

Mission: Impossible—Peter Graves.
Paramount

The standards on both sides were identical. Each saw the whole world as its arena. Conflicts were drained of principle and reduced to a question of "our side" against the other side.

The spy cycle moved high in rating charts, and its ingredients were emulated far and wide. On children's series especially, international conspiracy dominated. *The Lone Ranger*, now animated, depicted struggles with a mad scientist able to destroy mankind through control of the weather. On *Mr. Terrific* the government's Bureau of Special Projects turned to the hero to locate and thwart a defecting scientist who had invented a power paralyzer. *Tarzan* became the champion of emergent nations against communist conspiracies. On *Superman* a pet parakeet, to which a scientist had taught his devastating explosives formula, was stolen by a foreign agent. On the cartoon series *Gigantor*, Mr. Ugablob had a plan to conquer the world through a freeze ray.

A group of outer-space series was saturated with a similar atmosphere. On *Star Trek* ("Balance of Terror") the crew of the Enterprise faced a decision that might trigger an intergalactic war: should they engage the powerful alien spacecraft that had already destroyed several earth outposts? On the cartoon series *Astroboy*, an agent from the planet Xenon was recruiting brilliant earth children for some special mysterious tutoring. On *The Outer Limits* "invisibles" from space planned to take over the earth. *The Invaders* depicted each week the arrival of space creatures who could assume human form; their task was to prepare for a total take-over. When shot, they shriveled and vanished. This made for a special-effects triumph and also had plot and propaganda value. Because each vanquished invader left no trace of his existence, the dupes of the world remained unconvinced that anyone was planning the conquest of the world and the extinction of our civilization. But each week brought new landings of the mysterious infiltrators.

During this period the involvement in Vietnam skyrocketed as 15,500 "advisers" grew to an armed force approaching 500,000. U.S. spokesmen explained the need largely in rhetorical terms, speaking constantly of communist plans to "take over the world," and the need to halt aggression. Both President Lyndon Johnson and Secretary of State Dean Rusk constantly tried to recapture the consensus of World War II by depicting the Vietnam expedition as a continuation of older struggles against tyranny.

World War II had inspired a number of popular radio drama series, notably *The Man Behind the Gun*. The Vietnam war inspired no television drama series about Vietnam—producers and writers shied away from the subject. But the period did bring a television eruption of military drama about other United States wars: *McHale's Navy*, *Combat*, *Rat Patrol*, *Gomer Pyle U.S.M.C.*, *Twelve O'Clock High*, *Jericho*, *Hogan's Heroes*, *Wackiest Ship in the Army*, *Mr. Roberts*, *F Troop*, *Wild Wild West*. Most dealt with World War II; a few—*F Troop* and *Wild Wild West*—with earlier wars. Some—*Jericho* and *Wild Wild West*—featured the undercover atmosphere of spy programs. In most, military life was richly amusing as well as heroic.

Bonanza (NBC)	The fun of war, clandestine or
Get Smart (NBC)	otherwise, seemed to be the chief
The FBI (ABC)	message of 1965-66 prime-time
The Man From U.N.C.L.E. (NBC)	leaders, to judge from this Nielsen list of October 1965. *Mc-*
Wackiest Ship in the Army (NBC)	*Hale's Navy, I Spy,* and *Hogan's Heroes* were close behind the
Run for Your Life (NBC)	ten leaders. NBC had regained
Smothers Brothers (CBS)	leadership.
F Troop (ABC)	
I Dream of Jeannie (NBC)	
Gomer Pyle, U.S.M.C. (CBS)	

It was not the conscious intention of producers to buttress administration arguments linking Vietnam with World War II. But the rash of heroic and amusing World War II series, in conjunction with the flood of enemy-conspiracy drama, probably did just that.

On television the wars merged in curious ways. *Jericho* on CBS-TV dealt with an Allied team of World War II agents, usually operating behind Nazi lines in Europe or Africa and engaging in sabotage, intelligence, ambush, or rescue missions. Such names as de Gaulle and Hitler cropped up in early scripts. Producer Stanley Niss received a call from a CBS executive who wondered, "Will kids know who de Gaulle is?" Investigation tended to show that most youngsters did not know de Gaulle; in fact, many had never heard of Hitler. It seemed best to avoid these confusing names; also, to avoid constant references to Germany and Italy as enemies, since they had meanwhile become NATO allies and purchasers of telefilms. So terms like "the enemy" won preference. It became a timeless, symbolic drama: Americans once more involved in heroic action for freedom. No doubt many viewers unconsciously identified "the enemy" as communists.

For younger viewers, toy manufacturers added their contribution to the atmosphere. The Saturday morning "children's series," heavily supported by toy manufacturers, included such violence-saturated series as *Super Six*, whose superheroes smashed evil-doers throughout the universe; *Atom Ant*, about a fighting "up-and-at-'em" ant; *Secret Squirrel*, a spy series; and *Space Kidettes*, whose struggles against the "meanest pirate in the universe" required "plutonium disintegrators" and "space agitator ray guns." But a special quality of Saturday mornings came from commercials and public service announcements.

For boys there were things like Mattel's Fighting Men with machine guns and tanks—"everything real fighting men use"—and the G.I. Joe army toys, that included a "ten-inch bazooka that really works" and gas masks "to add real dimension to your play battles." For girls there were Mattel's Cheerful Tearful Dolls that could "cry real tears" as well as smile, and Kenner's automatic knitting machine—"a fast fun way to knit." A piquant addition was provided by public service announcements which included advice to "keep America beautiful," read books ("open your mind—read"), support the Young Women's Christian Association (to "help you become more interesting"), visit the United Nations, and buy U.S. Savings Bonds ("underwrite your country's might").

A visitor from another planet watching United States television for a week during the Vietnam escalation period might have concluded that viewers were being brainwashed by a cunning conspiracy determined to harness the nation—with special attention to its young—for war. Of course there was no conspiracy. Manufacturers were making things for which they saw a market, promoting them through advertising agents, producers, and broadcasters who believed in serving the client. In so doing, all avoided anything that might seem to undermine current government policy—and thereby gravitated toward its support.

Almost every segment of American business was feeling the financial injections of the 1964-66 Vietnam buildup, which created—according to U.S. Labor Department estimates—more than a million jobs during that period, with indirect effects elsewhere throughout the economy. More significantly, over half the federal tax revenue was going into war-related expenditures, and more than half of that was going directly to American corporations that were the chief suppliers. On the list of the hundred largest government suppliers, over half were companies heavily involved in broadcasting—as licensees, manufacturers, or sponsors. Restraints from these interdependencies operated all along the line. There was no conspiracy—there were merely innumerable parallel incentives. They tended to make television entertainment an integral part of the escalation machine.

Long ago, John Quincy Adams said of the United States that "she goes not abroad in search of monsters to destroy." But the telefilm told its young audience it was indeed its destiny to search out monsters—search and destroy.

NEWSROOM UPRISING

Even before the escalation there was tension in Saigon between reporters and American officialdom—military and civilian. "The brass wants you to get on the team," observed Peter Kalischer of CBS, a visitor from his post in Djakarta; "but my job is to find out what the score is." Charles Arnot of ABC charged that he had been fed lies, half-truths, and misleading information by government spokesmen. Early in 1965 Edward P. Morgan, ABC commentator, found the atmosphere "one of the most rancid I have ever seen in thirty years of reporting." Such things were said in print, not on the air.

The tensions involved problems of international justification. The "advisers" arrangement was meant to maintain a show of adherence to the Geneva accords, which the United States had pledged to honor. But as early as 1963-64 correspondents saw Americans flying jet bombers in Vietnam—"we aren't supposed to mention that," reporters were told.

The drastic escalation plan involved a decision to drop the adviser masquerade and shift to new justification. One rationale was that North Vietnam was guilty of "aggression" against South Vietnam and that Americans were helping to repel the aggression. The slipperiness of the charge did not become clear until later.

At the start of 1965, when the enormous United States troop buildup in Vietnam got under way, the Pentagon estimated the "insurgent" forces in South Vietnam at 140,000. Among these, according to the Pentagon's own estimate, were only 400 North Vietnamese—a fact revealed only much later by Senator Mike Mansfield, a member of the Senate foreign relations committee.

Meanwhile the Johnson administration had found—or created—new justification. In August 1964 the navy reported an "unprovoked" North Vietnamese attack on two United States destroyers, the *Maddox* and the *Turner Joy*, which were described as on "routine patrol" off North Vietnam. President Johnson immediately ordered retaliatory bombing of North Vietnam and obtained from Congress the so-called Tonkin Gulf resolution, which authorized "all necessary measures" to repel armed attack and prevent "further aggression." The resolution was used to justify all later escalation. Details of the alleged incident were, at the time of the resolution, extremely vague, but until later congressional inquiries the original navy version of the incident won acceptance.

The year 1965 brought, along with the troop buildup, the establishment of network bureaus in Saigon and a swelling migration of American television newsmen. Many, like young John Laurence of CBS, arrived with a strong belief in the American cause; he had asked CBS for Vietnam duty. Disenchantment came gradually. The sense of involvement in a dubious enterprise was resisted by newsmen, as by combatants. To some extent the nature of the war made this easy. Reporters seldom saw "the war" or "the enemy."

The Canadian writer-director Harry Rasky was sent by ABC-TV in 1965 to direct the film *Operation Sea War Vietnam* in the Gulf of Tonkin. Arriving in Saigon, he engaged a Vietnamese film technician to assist him, then flew to the aircraft carrier *Kitty Hawk*, which was to be the center of their activity. From there, around the clock, pilots were going on bombing missions. But they looked with intense curiosity at Rasky's assistant—the first Vietnamese most had seen. Their lives were confined to the *Kitty Hawk*. For rest periods they went to Hong Kong.

On the *Kitty Hawk* an Alice-in-Wonderland feeling enveloped a correspondent. There were 5300 people on board—a small American town afloat halfway around the world. Everyone was public-relations minded; people could not have been nicer. A ship publicity brochure revealed that the *Kitty Hawk* had three soda fountains, a barber shop with thirteen chairs, a fine drug store, and a splendid hospital including an operating room. At night there were movies. Producer Rasky was invited to sit with the admiral as they watched *Who's That Sleeping in My Bed?* While Dean Martin chased Elizabeth Montgomery (of the *Bewitched* television series) around the bed, bombs were being loaded on the *Kitty Hawk*'s planes. Soft music played over the ship's own radio station. A western was on the ship's television system.

A Vietnamese New Year truce gave occasion for a kind of water ballet by the entire strike force 77 of the Seventh Fleet. Twenty ships—carriers, cruisers, destroyers—were arranged for a picture portrait while jets formed a giant 77 in the sky overhead. That shot, Rasky kept thinking, must have cost the taxpayer millions. One admiral sent a message to another: "From the Commodore of the Tonkin Gulf Yacht Club to the Chairman of the Board, a salute." That day's program included Elizabeth Taylor in *Cleopatra*.

Rasky and his assistant went aboard a destroyer that had the task of shelling the coast. Over the hills a spotter plane called out locations and directed the guns. On the ship orders were given, and the guns rattled and shook the ship. Over the hills puffs of smoke drifted gracefully into the sky. "VC in the open," the spotter reported. The ship's guns blasted again and again: 138 rounds were fired. At one point the camera jammed and Rasky asked the captain to hold up a moment; he readily complied. The spotter, circling over the hills, asked: "What program is that you're filming down there?"

"It's for ABC."

"You know what night it will be on? . . . I'll be home soon."

"February, March, I guess."

"I'll have to see the summer reruns."

The Vietnamese technician kept saying, "What are they shooting at?"

"VC, they say."

"How do they know?" The Vietnamese later became sick and did not eat lunch.

Rasky was not allowed to write the narration. This was done in New York, where the film was also edited. ABC engaged movie actor Glenn Ford as narrator. The final film had spectacular shots of fleet maneuvers, but said almost nothing that Rasky had felt impelled to communicate. He therefore poured his feelings into a series of articles in the form of letters to his newborn daughter, which were syndicated in Canadian newspapers as *Letters to Holly*. "They conveyed more about what I felt about what I saw than my film did, and that distressed me."

This was a common experience. All along the line, the message was processed into something palatable. Things omitted, words added—these could temper meaning and even reverse it.

There was little direct censorship. Network cameramen were not permitted on North Vietnam bombing runs, and seldom on search-and-destroy missions; but correspondents could otherwise go where they liked, with a considerable sense of freedom.

Yet subtle pressures were at work. Vietnam newscast items were videotaped back home by the Defense Department and flown to Saigon for the command to see. This electronic clipping service enabled them to know exactly what each newsman was filming and reporting. If they did not like what they saw, the newsman soon learned about it.

The most startling item to reach the air in 1965 was a report by Morley Safer. A village was said to have aided the Vietcong and had to be punished. Marines moved in. The Safer report showed a Marine flicking his cigarette lighter to set its huts afire; some 120 huts were burned. This scene ignited in some viewers anger against the war; in others, anger against television. The Defense Department made it clear to CBS that Safer was *persona non grata*. CBS upheld Safer and those who had put his film on the air, but top CBS officials let Fred Friendly, president of CBS News, know that they felt uneasy about Safer. Such crises inevitably encouraged self-censorship.

By the end of 1965 the United States role in Vietnam was being denounced in a number of American magazines, and was the subject of protest meetings and marches. Criticism erupted in newspaper columns, notably those of Walter Lippmann and James Reston, and in letters to the editor. Television newsrooms, too, were the scene of debates—but during 1965 they seldom reached the air, particularly in prime time. Discussion was usually relegated to fringe periods. In newscasts a protest march was likely to be covered with a shot or two of a bearded youth, as though to categorize it as a "hippie" event.

The magazine *Commentary* had as its television critic Neil Compton, a Canadian, who covered American television from north of the border, sometimes comparing it with Canadian television. In the October 1965 issue he mentioned two overriding impressions:

> . . . first, the great networks seem to express a massive political consensus; second, they are commercial to a degree which even an outsider used to television finds overwhelming. The two phenomena are not, of course, unrelated.

Compton felt that Vietnam issues were "fiercely and frankly" discussed in American magazines and newspapers.

> But anyone who relied on NBC, ABC, and CBS television would have been far less well informed than his Canadian counterpart even though the total time devoted to Vietnam on American networks was undoubtedly greater.

He found events reported as though "in a vacuum." Comments were generally "variations on the official line." There seemed to be constant effort to insulate the viewer from world opinion through assurance that protest demonstrations in London and elsewhere were "leftist." Compton mentioned one program which seemed to him a notable exception—an August 1965 ABC-TV special titled *The Agony of Vietnam*, written by Stephen Fleischman and narrated by Edward P. Morgan. It stated, "We cannot afford to see Vietnam only through American eyes," and surveyed world opinion, pro and con.

The consensus observed by Compton was, within network news divisions, under attack by reporters but resolutely upheld at executive levels. Especially at CBS, anything that might prove unduly disturbing or inflammatory was regarded with disapproval. Demanding "objective" reporting, the policy seemed to insist on information drained of meaning.

In 1966 the surface consensus began to show signs of cracks and fissures. Two prominent members of the Senate foreign relations committee, chairman J. William Fulbright and Senator Wayne Morse, were attacking the Johnson Vietnam policy. In view of the importance of these two men they could not be ignored, and CBS News arranged a half-hour program, *Fulbright: Advice and Dissent*, in which the Senator was interviewed by Eric Sevareid and Martin Agronsky. Fulbright expressed his growing disenchantment over the Tonkin Gulf resolution and the use made of it. According to Friendly, Stanton was upset about the broadcast, saying: "What a dirty trick that was to play on the President of the United States. . . ."

The Senate attacks persisted and necessarily brought further interviews and discussions by news divisions. Both at networks and affiliate stations, scheduling conflicts often intervened. At CBS-TV they produced a major crisis.

The Senate foreign relations committee scheduled hearings which loomed as the first full-scale senatorial debate on Vietnam policy. Administration supporters and critics would be heard. Fred Friendly, urging live CBS-TV coverage, wrote an intra-network memorandum:

Broadcast journalism has, once or twice every decade, an opportunity to prove itself. Such an opportunity were the events leading up to World War II; such was the McCarthy period. The Vietnam war—its coverage in Asia and in Congress—is another such challenge.

At CBS John A. Schneider had just become president of the television network, succeeding James Aubrey. Aubrey had suddenly departed amid a flurry of rumors concerning his personal life and charges by stockholders of conflicts of interest in his program decisions. On all of this the network refused comment, but it emphasized its confidence in Schneider. He had risen in network ranks from its sales division and was considered solid and reliable. Coverage of the Vietnam hearings would be his first major decision.

As the hearings began in February 1966, CBS-TV and NBC-TV were on hand. The first testimony was on behalf of the administration and was by David Bell, the director of foreign aid programs. He was followed by retired Lieutenant General James Gavin, who opposed current strategy on military grounds.

The following testimony was to be given by former Ambassador George Kennan, considered one of the most effective critics of Vietnam policy. His objections were political rather than military. NBC-TV planned to continue coverage; Schneider reserved his decision.

As Kennan began testifying at a morning session, CBS cameras were on hand. CBS News president Fred Friendly was in his office at CBS, facing two screens—one the CBS program; the other, the NBC program. At 10 a.m. Kennan appeared on the NBC-TV screen; on the other appeared a rerun (the fifth) of *I Love Lucy*, followed by a rerun (the eighth) of a *The Real McCoys* episode. John Schneider had decided—or been instructed—not to carry the testimony.

He later explained his reasoning. Very few "decision makers" were at home in the daytime, he said. Also, the hearings would confuse the issue for many people. He had saved the company a great deal of money but said this had not been a factor in his decision.

Stanton, by way of supporting argument, pointed out that Kennan no longer held an official position—as though testimony should only be given by administration officials.

Fred Friendly, sending in his resignation, helped to make the case a front-page issue. In his letter, released to the press, he wrote:

> I am resigning because CBS News did not carry the Senate foreign relations hearings last Thursday. . . . I am resigning because the decision not to carry the hearings makes a mockery of the Paley-Stanton Columbia News division crusade of many years that demands broadest access to congressional debate. . . . We cannot, in our public utterances, demand such access and then, in one of the crucial debates of our time, abdicate that responsibility. . . . I now leave CBS News after 16 years, believing that the finest broadcast journalists anywhere will yet have the kind of leadership they deserve. . . .

Variety, referring to Friendly's exit as "cataclysmic," called it the end of the Murrow era at CBS. Murrow himself had died the year before, after surgery and lingering illness.

Although NBC-TV carried most of the hearings, and CBS-TV, stung by criticism, resumed its coverage, many affiliates of both networks failed to carry the broadcasts, or carried only portions.

Obstructions of this sort constantly muted or sidetracked television discussion about Vietnam. Under the title *ABC Scope 1966*, ABC produced a series of reports and discussions, which it offered to stations during evening time. But many affiliates failed to carry it while others—including WABC-TV, New York—videotaped the program to carry it at a less favorable time. A West Coast affiliate ran it before breakfast. A February 1966 United Nations Security Council debate on Vietnam was not carried live by any network. CBS News did prepare a half-hour summary, edited and narrated by Richard C. Hottelet and scheduled at 4:30 p.m., but WCBS-TV, New York—the network's "flagship" station—declined to carry it because it would have interfered with the movie scheduled on *The Early Show*. In November 1965 CBS commentator Eric Sevareid

Fred W. Friendly

Steve Schapiro

made a startling disclosure in an article in *Look:* he revealed that Adlai Stevenson, hours before his death, had confided to him that he was on the point of resigning in protest from his position as U.S. Ambassador to the United Nations. Stevenson's reason was that the Johnson administration had twice sabotaged peace negotiations conducted by United Nations Secretary General U Thant. Observers wondered why Sevareid revealed this sensational news in a magazine rather than on a television news program; both network and Sevareid declined to comment. Across the country most broadcasting stations, along with most newspapers, ignored the Sevareid revelations—according to a *Variety* article on the "Era of No-Guts Journalism."

Until this time Sevareid himself, in his short "think pieces" on CBS news programs, had tended to avoid the subject of Vietnam.

Eric Sevareid.   CBS

He was troubled by doubts but felt President Johnson should be given the benefit of any doubt. He told himself, "Sevareid, you don't know anything *about* this." Then he began to feel that he owed it to his viewers to find out and to speak on the subject. He began to read everything he could lay his hands on, and in the spring of 1966 he journeyed to Vietnam. Here he was soon overwhelmed by a sense of the hopelessness of the entire Vietnam intervention. He found an endless, baffling mosaic; one might pick up a tiny piece but never glimpse how it might fit into the total. No one—at any level—could see the shape or meaning of the total. He felt the same hopelessness about the machinery available for reporting the war. The bits of film appearing nightly on television screens could not possibly represent the story: "The facts didn't yield to the equipment." Returning, he was allowed a half-hour to express his dismay; it was broadcast on June 21, 1966, over CBS-TV, and entered in the *Congressional Record*.

Thus, slowly, with constant pressure, opposition to the American involvement moved forward in television and radio. Circulating on the edges, it pushed toward the center. But counterpressures were also mighty and unrelenting, and were led by the President himself.

GUARD THAT IMAGE

No President before Lyndon Johnson had worked so hard to cajole, control, and neutralize the news media. The weight of his efforts was usually directed toward television, as though he largely discounted the influence of other media. In the end his hopes seemed to hang entirely on keeping television in line.

In his first year as President, riding on extraordinary legislative successes—especially in civil rights—he had lived on good terms with the various media. Later the relationship became more edgy, particularly when his Vietnam escalation drew criticism. Hostile questions in regularly scheduled press conferences caused him to concentrate on a strategy of impromptu background sessions, to which only selected reporters were invited.

Correspondents already regarded President Johnson as a strange phenomenon. He had a deep fund of knowledge about the workings of government, but his approaches to newsmen—sometimes folksy, sometimes wheedling, sometimes angrily demanding—were often so blatant as to seem naïve. He often engaged in long, rambling soliloquies in which extraordinary vanity rose to the surface. He sometimes seemed bent on merciless self-exposure.

During 1965-66 press references to a "credibility gap" in the Johnson administration multiplied, and relations with newsmen became increasingly prickly. If he considered a question hostile, he could vent full fury or scorn on the questioner. Turning on one reporter, he said: "Why do you come and ask me, the leader of the

Western world, a chicken-shit question like that?" Television newsmen became familiar with his consuming interest in what they broadcast about him. His three-set lineup of receivers seemed to keep him aware of every word. At CBS Walter Cronkite, leaving the air after his nightly *CBS Evening News with Walter Cronkite*, often found his secretary holding the telephone aloft. "White House on the line." It might be a presidential aide, or it might be the President himself, demurring at a detail. White House correspondent Dan Rather got frequent angry phone calls at home, often laced with strong language. A protest often culminated in an inquiry about sources. "Where did you get that?"

The President did not cease for a moment his labors to control the public image of his war. In October 1966 he scheduled a trip to Manila, South Vietnam, and Thailand. The President's bubble-top limousine was flown halfway around the world for this purpose. A *Life* photographer lay on its floor as it moved through Manila crowds. From a pickup truck moving ahead of the limousine, aides frantically tossed paper flags to the crowd so that people could be seen waving them in television footage. At Camranh Bay in South Vietnam, stage management got "almost a bit too thick," thought a New York *Times* reporter, when a young man in full field pack with a grenade launcher on his back was sent to eat with the President at a mess hall table, for the benefit of the cameras. It apparently had to be documented that way because the President had already taped a radio message about his Vietnam visit to be broadcast later to the American people, in which he had said: "I went there to visit our men at our base in Camranh Bay. Many of them only recently had come from the battlefield. Some were in field dress, carrying their packs and rifles. . . ."

The Vietnam visit lasted 144 minutes, and the junket was off for Thailand, where the President took part in royal pageantry and in the presence of King Bhumibol Aduldet signed an International Education Act with eight pens, while cameras whirred.

Back home Johnson was constantly on the air. He tried various

Walter Cronkite.   CBS

techniques and gadgets: contact lenses, a new type of prompter, a slow delivery, a fast delivery. He called critics "nervous Nellies" and cast doubt on their loyalty. Dean Rusk followed suit. Castigating reporters, Rusk said: "I know what side I am on—that of the United States. All your news publications and networks won't be worth a damn unless we succeed."

Rusk, like Dulles, pursued a passport policy designed to prevent travel to mainland China, North Vietnam, North Korea, Albania, Cuba. But this policy was challenged with increasing frequency by individuals—writers, teachers, churchmen—ready to risk a court test on constitutional grounds. One ground was that the travel ban infringed freedom of the press. Another was that the right to travel was reserved "to the people" under the Tenth Amendment. Another was that the government could not invoke "war powers" because Congress had never declared war on North Vietnam. This argument challenged the legality of the war itself.

Among those who traveled to North Vietnam in 1965 was Christopher Koch of the Pacifica radio stations—WBAI, New York; KPFA, Berkeley; KPFK, Los Angeles. This group of noncommercial stations subsisted on listener subscriptions and gifts, and welcomed views from diverse sources including extremists of left and right. In so doing, the stations had won increasing attention precisely because of what *Variety* called the "no-guts journalism" of the dominant media. But in winning a cult following, the group of stations had also won indignant opposition—a fact which the FCC, under E. William Henry, had faced squarely at a 1964 license renewal:

> We recognize that as shown by the complaints here, such provocative programming as here involved may offend some listeners. But this does not mean that those offended have the right, through the commission's licensing power, to rule such programming off the air waves.

That this seemed dangerous doctrine to many commercial broadcasters was a reflection of a schism on the American scene. For the rise of Pacifica was symptomatic of a widening movement—a subculture developing across the country, especially in cities and on college campuses. Its keynote was dissent.

FRINGES

It was perhaps the most fateful development of the Vietnam war. Fateful for the nation, it had crucial implications for broadcasting.

Harold A. Innis in his *Empire and Communications* showed that media monopolies have played a central role in empires of the past; also, that the existence of such monopolies has always encouraged development of other media—which might become new power bases—on the fringes of society.

The very completeness of military-industrial control over television was, in this respect, a chink in its armor. Throughout the rise of the Vietnam war and the military atmosphere it involved, many Americans were turning from commercial television and responding to new media—or old ones in new form: underground film, off-Broadway theater, café, cabaret, folk song, poster, newsletter, demonstration, march, rock festival, sit-in, teach-in, love-in. All offered potent messages shunned by prime-time television; this was their strength. To some extent noncommercial television, along with segments of radio, became a part of this movement of dissent.

The babel of voices represented diverse groups, but dissent united them, at least temporarily. Moved by fury against a war they found repulsive, many began to question hypocrisies and self-deceptions they felt made it possible. The mechanisms of social control became an obsessive interest of many young people. On college campuses activist students were ferreting out the relationship of glossy new buildings and research programs with funding agencies in government or big business. Was it the function of colleges to develop the discerning mind or, in the words of a student in the CBS documentary *The Berkeley Rebels*, to "turn out shiny new parts for General Motors"?

Commercial television was a similar target. Virtually a symbol of the "establishment," it was lampooned in hundreds of underground films and magazines. Its routine frauds were favorite subject matter —along with Vietnam—of underground cabarets.

Television—the rejection of it—seemed to determine the life-style of the new subculture. For a generation television had showed people how to dress, talk, behave. Junior high school students had been carbon copies of heroes and heroines of commercials and telefilms. The underground reversed the process. It despised the clean-shaven hero, the office haircut, the lacquered hair, the necktie, the suburban home, the Detroit car. To many a hard-working suburban father who had for decades followed the rules and obeyed the commercials, the anarchy of style seemed to threaten social foundations. But in truth the uprising was also a return to an earlier America. The bearded Walt Whitman had said that he found the sweat of his armpits "more sweet than the perfumes of Araby." The young activist might have worded it, "than the leading deodorant." Thoreau had said that to cooperate with a government that was breaking the law was to condone its crimes. Any honest man, he said, had to "withdraw from this co-partnership." This the young activists were doing.

To the television industry the subculture seemed at first a negligible phenomenon. Broadcasters reassured themselves—and their viewers—with such terms as "hippie," "yippie," "teenie-bopper," "peacenik." Hippie activists often provided newscasts with a final one-minute light touch. But amid the condescension the subculture made inroads.

The phonograph-record field was producing anti-establishment successes—in folk-song, rock 'n' roll, and folk-rock styles—that were difficult to ignore. Stations vacillated between permitting and forbidding such songs as "Eve of Destruction" by P. F. Sloan, "The Universal Soldier" by Cree Indian folk singer Buffy Sainte-Marie, and "Waist Deep in the Big Muddy" by Pete Seeger. In 1967 CBS, having decided to end its seventeen-year blacklisting of Seeger as a performer, permitted him to be booked on *The Smothers Brothers Comedy Hour*. But the network felt new tremors when he decided to sing "Waist Deep in the Big Muddy." The song was based on an actual training-camp episode, in which some Marine trainees had died by drowning. The lyric began:

> The captain told us to ford a river,
> And that's how it all begun—
> We were waist deep in the Big Muddy
> But the big fool says push on.*

* "Waist Deep in the Big Muddy" ("The Big Muddy"), words and music by Pete Seeger. TRO—copyright © 1967 by Melody Trails, Inc., N.Y., N.Y. Used by permission.

When a sergeant protests, the captain tells him not to be a "nervous Nellie." This Lyndon Johnson phrase tended to give the maneuver and the "captain" metaphoric meanings. They do "push on," and the "big fool" himself eventually drowns. Efforts by CBS during rehearsal to make deletions were stoutly resisted by both Seeger and the Smothers Brothers, so CBS later—before the telecast—cut the entire song from the videotape. The resulting hubbub gave the song an honored status, and led to a shift. In a return engagement on the Smothers series, Seeger was allowed to sing "The Big Muddy" in full. Thus the subculture inched forward.

While hatred of the Vietnam war was the leading underground impulse, it tended to merge with other drives. "Make love, not war," a slogan displayed in every peace march, fused the peace drive with the revolt against sexual taboos. The Negro rights movement fused with both. It was in 1967 that Martin Luther King began persistently to identify the Negro rights crusade with the peace movement. He did so partly on economic grounds, since he saw war costs scuttling anti-poverty programs. He did so also on broader grounds: the readiness to slaughter Asians seemed to him of a piece with racial callousness at home. The anti-war and Negro rights movements became closely linked in underground films, plays, publications.

In the mid-1960's film-making burst out on almost all college campuses, with alienation and dissent as dominant themes. A cooperative newsreel, titled *Newsreel*, was organized in New York, dealing with such topics as draft resistance, demonstrations, police riot-control methods. Its films were welcomed by campus groups and a sprinkling of theaters. The groups also began circulating newsreels and documentaries from Vietcong and North Vietnamese sources, as well as Vietnam war footage obtained from Japan, France, Poland, East Germany. During 1966-67 the networks began intermittent use of such material, usually superimposing a warning that it was "propaganda from communist sources." The administration regarded the use of the material as little short of treason.

One of the more notable films on North Vietnam to reach the

television screen was actually commissioned by CBS, but was seen on National Educational Television. It was the work of Felix Greene, a British citizen who had been American representative of the British Broadcasting Corporation before World War II. He settled in the United States, but retained his British citizenship. This enabled him to travel to such places as mainland China and North Vietnam. His 1964 book *A Curtain of Ignorance*, the result of three sojourns in China during the 1950's and 1960's, documented the tragic results of the Chinese-American information gap. Troubled by Chinese misinformation about the United States, he was even more appalled by United States misinformation about China. In 1967 the San Francisco *Chronicle* decided to send him to North Vietnam, and CBS commissioned him to make a color-film record of his observations. The result was an 85-minute documentary, *Inside North Vietnam*. Press previews caused fervent discussion. Cleveland Amory, writing in the *Saturday Review*, found the film "superb" from start to finish.

It is objective and, if anything, understated—but it is so moving it will make you first ashamed, then angry, and finally utterly determined to make everybody you know see it.

At a preview Felix Greene fielded a barrage of questions from newsmen—some friendly and some hostile. He made it clear—as did the film—that he had not been given access to military installations. Then why did he call the film "uncensored?" "Because once I had shot something my footage was never inspected by North Vietnamese authorities. And I could go anywhere I pleased so long as it wasn't military." Why had he not also gone to South Vietnam? "I applied to go to South Vietnam and Saigon wouldn't let me." Why? "Because I'd been to China."

The film, by showing evidence of wide use of anti-personnel bombs, belied Defense Department claims of being concerned only with military targets. It also undermined the State Department version of the war by providing a close look at an "enemy" described by Rusk as living in a reign of terror and fighting at the behest of madmen. Instead the audience saw, amid bomb craters, a people smiling and laughing. Girls picked up rifles to shoot at bombers, then sat down to be demure again. Their lives were extraordinarily disrupted and their work ceaseless, but strangely joyful. This reinforced reports of various travelers, but the impression was more tellingly conveyed by camera images. To Amory, the film's most notable achievement was to show "what kind of people we are fighting—and why their record against us is bound to go down in history alongside Thermopylae, Stalingrad—or, for that matter, Valley Forge."

CBS, which had an option on the film by virtue of having provided 20,000 feet of raw film, laboratory costs, and an advance, had meanwhile decided not to use it, but only to insert fragments in *CBS Evening News with Walter Cronkite*. As a result, *Inside North Vietnam* became available to National Educational Television, which planned to use a 49-minute segment followed by a panel discussion.

The announcement caused extraordinary rumbles. Former U.S. Representative Walter Judd, who had not seen the film, wrote to congressmen.

> Dear Friend,
> I hope you will read and sign the accompanying letter protesting the proposed showing on the Educational TV network of Felix Greene's film on North Vietnam. . . . When American youth are giving their lives in a war against a ruthless enemy, surely we have an obligation to protect their families and the public against anything that strengthens that enemy.

The enclosed letter of protest, addressed to John White as president of National Educational Television and describing the film as "nothing more nor less than communist propaganda," was signed by thirty-three congressmen—not one of whom had seen the film. The letter stated that if this was NET's idea of public service, a change of management was obviously needed.

Perhaps CBS was happy to have avoided the congressional attack, but NET went ahead with its plan. The discussion following the film was between television newsman David Schoenbrun and political scientist Robert Scalapino—one a critic, the other a defender, of United States policy in Vietnam.

The *Inside North Vietnam* case exemplified—and no doubt furthered—the slippage of commercial television and the shift elsewhere. A 1967 Louis Harris poll noted "a growing television boycott" among the college-educated. The industry itself was torn by doubts. Men who had been pillars of commercial television, like Pat Weaver, were suddenly propounding the need for noncommercial television as an alternative voice. Fred Friendly, ex-president of CBS News and now a Ford Foundation consultant, had become a leading crusader for noncommercial television. Noncommercial television stations had—in 1965—finally reached a hundred in number, and more were being organized. The system had a significant coverage and, in spite of pinched budgets, was building a loyal following. In February 1967 a commission established by a Carnegie Corporation grant urged establishment of a Corporation for Public Broadcasting, aided by a tax on television sets, to promote noncommercial television. It mentioned the need for sums of at least $100 million a year to finance a meaningful network. NET had seldom had a tenth of that sum.

In the spring of 1967 the Ford Foundation stimulated the hubbub by earmarking $10 million for a Public Broadcast Laboratory. It was to produce a major Sunday evening series, *PBL*, to be available to the 100-odd educational stations, most of which would be linked by AT&T cables—at a cost of several million. The series was to explore the possibilities, in theme and treatment, of an adequately financed system released from commercial restraints.

PBL, debuting in November 1967, at once reflected a world in sharp contrast to that of prime-time television. Mindful of its function as an alternative voice, it dipped into work of fringe theaters, cabarets, and underground films, and inevitably reflected the angry

PBL examines life on welfare in "None of My Business." WNET

PBL

The Living Theater, off-Broadway troupe, makes appearance on *PBL*.

WNET

subculture. The thrust of the message was anti-war, anti-racist, anti-establishment; the techniques, sometimes drawing on the absurdist theater, were strange and seemed outrageous to many television viewers.

The very first *PBL* program presented an off-Broadway success by Douglas Turner Ward, titled *Day of Absence*, about a southern town from which all blacks have suddenly vanished. Finding itself unable to function, the town begs them to return. To many viewers the most jolting aspect of the production was that whites were played by Negroes in "whiteface," with makeup applied in the blatant style of the blackface comics of another era. The enactments were likewise in a brutal cartoon style. Some southern stations, informed by advance rumor, declined to carry the program.

The crisis made it clear that noncommercial television, working under boards often selected for fund-raising potential and political influence, could be as tightly tethered as commercial stations. Yet noncommercial television was to some extent giving expression to the ferment of the subculture—not only through *PBL* but also through *NET Journal, Black Journal, NET Playhouse, The Creative Person,* and various local series.

Many observers were puzzled when President Johnson, obsessed with maintaining a Vietnam consensus—or the appearance of a consensus—boarded the noncommercial television bandwagon. He espoused the idea of a Corporation for Public Broadcasting and urged its adoption. With astonishing smoothness the idea moved through the legislative process and became law on November 7, 1967—two days after *PBL*'s shock debut. The meaning of the President's sudden interest in noncommercial television was not clear but observers soon felt they saw straws in the wind. He recommended an appropriation of only $4,500,000 for the first year, and followed this with an appointment that stunned noncommercial television enthusiasts. As chairman of the new corporation he chose Frank Pace, Jr., a former Secretary of the Army and a former chief executive officer of General Dynamics—an embodiment of the military-industrial alliance. Chairman Pace at once expressed his enthusiasm for his new post and said he had already commissioned research on an important idea—how public television might be used for riot control. The President's support had created vast expectations among supporters of noncommercial television. Now they wondered if it was being hugged to death.

During 1966-67 every subject tended to become Vietnam. Networks, with a haunted intensity, looked for safe documentary subjects that might lure a sponsor, and came up with such topics as *A Bird's Eye View of Scotland, An Essay on Women, Gauguin in Tahiti, Nurses,* and *Venice.* But some seemingly remote topics turned out to be, in the context of the day, Vietnam. NBC-TV scheduled *The Investigation,* by Peter Weiss, adapted from a Broadway production by its director, Ulu Grosbard. It was a "documentary drama" in which all dialogue was from Nazi war crimes trials relating to Auschwitz extermination operations. But the words offered familiar echoes.

> I only did my duty. . . . I believe in my country. . . . Personally, I have always behaved decently. . . . We were dealing with the annihilation of an ideology. . . . It was my duty as a soldier. . . .

Not surprisingly, the NBC-TV special of *The Investigation* found no sponsor.

Yet a sense of the horror of the war was creeping slowly toward the center of television. It did so in a 1967 CBS-TV special, *Morley Safer's Vietnam.* A subtle and complex work, it stuck to CBS rules of objectivity, while providing rich food for thought. Safer showed a helicopter crew just back from a mission. Its members were asked how it felt to "make a kill like that."

> CAPTAIN: I feel real good when we do it. It's kind of a feeling of accomplishment. It's the only way you're going to win, I guess, is to kill 'em.
>
> PILOT: I just feel like it's just another target. You know, like in the

States you shot at dummies, over here you shoot at Vietnamese. Vietnamese Cong.

ANOTHER (*off*, *interrupting*): Cong. You shoot at Cong. You don't shoot at Vietnamese.

PILOT (*laughing*): All right. You shoot at Cong. Anyway, when you come out on the run and then you see them, and they come into your sights, it's just like a wooden dummy or something there, you just thumb off a couple pair of rockets. Like they weren't people at all.

In January 1968 the American command was making predictions of an early victory. Shortly afterwards guerrillas began lobbing mortars and rockets into major South Vietnamese cities, including Saigon and Hue, and followed by seizing footholds in them. To eradicate the infiltrators, American airpower began a block-by-block destruction of the very cities that had been the basis of the American position in Vietnam. The problem of refugees became catastrophic. General Westmoreland asked for 200,000 more troops. President Johnson, already hard pressed by opposition at home, now faced military peril abroad.

In February the Senate foreign relations committee held hearings, carried by CBS-TV and NBC-TV, on the background of the Tonkin Gulf resolution. The Tonkin Gulf "incident" began to be seen as a trumped-up pretext for attacks long planned.

It was election year. The renomination of Lyndon Johnson had been a foregone conclusion, but Senator Eugene McCarthy made plans to enter the New Hampshire primary, contesting Johnson on the basis of the Vietnam war. Senator Robert Kennedy was moving toward opposition to the President.

Mounting bitterness marked the home front. Ghetto areas and college campuses were torn with riots and demonstrations. Attacks on ROTC offices, recruiting offices, draft boards were routine newscast items. Recruiters for Dow, makers of napalm—among many other products—were blocked from campuses by demonstrators. Countless young men were resolving to go to jail rather than into uniform. Thousands had moved to Canada to avoid the draft. A colony of deserters was forming in Sweden. Use of drugs was on the rise at home and in Vietnam. Colonies of runaway teenagers congregated on New York's lower East Side, in San Francisco's Haight-Ashbury section, and in slum areas in other cities. The girls painted flowers on their foreheads, meaning "make love, not war."

But some of the young were not ready to flee or "freak out." The unhysterical, reasoned anti-war candidacy of Senator Eugene McCarthy drew many to his banner. They became McCarthy volunteers and painted flowers on the family car.

According to Gallup polls taken in the early months of 1968, supporters and opponents of the war had become evenly balanced. On television the early-evening network newscasts seemed to assume the task of keeping America on an even keel. Chet Huntley on NBC relayed official statements and body-counts of killed Vietcong without hint of approval or disapproval. David Brinkley sometimes twitched an eyebrow; he had said in *TV Guide* that he opposed the war, but he did not say it on the air. On *CBS Evening News with Walter Cronkite*, anchorman Cronkite gave all news items the same weight, seeming to avoid intonations that might imply degrees of significance.

The organizations behind these network news programs had grown enormous, and the years of crisis had given them a growing following. In the late 1950's they had found sponsors elusive, but now they were well sponsored. By expanding to half-hour length in 1963 they had taken a small step toward peak time. The shift to color film in 1965-66 had affected some topics, including war. Mud and blood were indistinguishable in black and white; in color, blood was blood. In color, misty Vietnamese landscapes hung with indescribable beauty behind gory actions.

Some television executives, like James Hagerty of ABC—former press aide to Eisenhower—were convinced that television had brought the face of war home to the American people. Many others

felt with syndicated columnist John Horn that television had triv-
ialized the war, making it "of no more consequence than a movie
star's latest marriage, the arrival of the Beatles, a Senator's pronouncement, a three-alarm fire"—all links in a chain of unevaluated
events used to sell mouthwash, pills, and cigarettes.

In January 1968 Walter Cronkite decided he had to see for himself. He had not been into Vietnam since 1965. "This time," he told
CBS executives, "let's say what I think about it." When he returned
he appeared on television saying that the United States might have
to accept a stalemate in Vietnam. Two weeks later, on an NBC telecast, Frank McGee said that the United States was losing the war
in Vietnam. To destroy Vietnam in order to "save" it, he implied,
might not be wisdom.

These moments marked a divide for television and Lyndon Johnson. According to some observers, the defection of Cronkite especially shook the President.

On March 12 he was shaken again. In the first presidential primary of the year, New Hampshire voters showed massive support
for Senator Eugene McCarthy; a McCarthy triumph was also predicted in the Wisconsin primary.

About this time the President requested television time to address
the nation, and his aides began writing the speech. The first drafts
were like all the other speeches: justification, denunciation of
Hanoi, scorn for critics, pleas for unity, and touches of the "Abraham Lincoln syndrome" that was overtaking Johnson. He seemed
constantly to see his ordeal—or to try to see it—in terms of the vigils
of other wartime leaders, especially Lincoln. But all of this had
been said, and some advisers felt it would not do. Finally the President made his decision. Characteristically, he "kept his options
open" until the last moment. As the speech went on the air on the
evening of March 31, it gave no hint of its bombshell ending. An
advance text had not included the ending. This contributed to its
impact.

The words near the end had been written by Johnson himself.

He expressed confidence that the United States would be a "land of greater opportunity and fulfillment" because of what his presidency had achieved. Those gains were important, he said, and must not now be jeopardized by "suspicion and distrust and selfishness and politics." Therefore—

> JOHNSON: I have concluded that I should not permit the presidency to become involved in the partisan divisions that are developing in this political year. Accordingly, I shall not seek, and I will not accept, the nomination of my party for another term as your President.

Lyndon Johnson had removed himself from the eye of the storm. But the storm was not over. Peace talks were begun in Paris, but the war went on. Meanwhile the United States prepared for bitter election struggles.

THE FORTRESS

Most Americans during the 1966-68 upheavals were not demonstrating, marching, or rioting. Most were doing their jobs and relaxing over television. In homes with children the set was likely to be on sixty hours a week. The breadwinner watched after dinner. He might catch the early-evening news, or part of it, but the rest of the evening was the main thing.

There was also some radio listening by individual members of the family, usually as background to other activity.

These media were for many a psychological refuge, a fortress. Except for the occasionally disturbing documentaries, evening television confirmed the average man's view of the world. It presented the America he wanted and believed in and had labored to be part of. It was alive with handsome men and women, and symbols of the good life. It invited and drew him into its charmed circle. If the circle was threatened, it was surely not by flaws within itself but by outside evildoers.

Hollywood, where most of this was made, was also a kind of refuge and a fortress—although a troubled one. It had its dissident spirits who made independent features that seemed to belong to the subculture. But much of the solid part of Hollywood was busy with telefilms. The activity was now firmly established at Metro-Goldwyn-Mayer, Paramount, Twentieth Century-Fox, Warner, Columbia, Universal—the old aristocracy. At some studios, television executives were moving into top positions.

From television, huge sums were pouring into the studios; program budgets were reaching a scale not dreamed of in earlier television years. By 1968 the 90-minute *The Virginian* and *The Name of the Game* were each budgeted at $275,000 per episode. The 60-minute programs *Bonanza, Mission: Impossible, Land of the Giants, Star Trek* were budgeted at $180,000 or more per episode. The 30-minute series *Bewitched, Hogan's Heroes, Green Acres, Get Smart* were budgeted at $80,000 or more per episode.* It was a land of milk and honey but also of tensions. Everything depended on decisions of networks and, beyond them, of advertisers and their agencies. On the basis of ratings, fortunes rose and fell, and heads rolled with unnerving suddenness. Contempt for the needs of "the market" was often heard, especially from writers, directors, and actors, but the rhetoric of denunciation seldom changed anything. The machine had its momentum; the stakes were huge. Escape into "independent production" for theaters was a favorite fantasy; a few achieved it.

In the 1950's the informal relation between writer and producer

---

* Expenditures on a typical one-hour program may be suggested by outlays on one 1968 *Star Trek* episode: script (writer and consultants) $8783, cast $22,650, director $3825, camera $3066, production facilities $23,550, production staff $2983, set design $1832, set construction $3153, set operations $3634, wardrobe $3198, makeup and hair stylists $3311, electrical expenses $4082, rushes $9221, editing $7351, optical effects $15,030, music $3250, lab processing $7946, payroll benefits $7448, producer $10,427, and additional overhead allocations. "Wink of an Eye," *Star Trek,* Paramount Television.

had enabled many a writer to turn out dozens of scripts a year. Now this had vanished, overwhelmed by protocol. The network as underwriter of a series generally had the right to review each episode at several stages: synopsis, teleplay, revised pages, and screenings of roughly edited workprint and final print. Advertising agency representatives and sponsors might also see copies of the teleplay; a CBS policy statement permitted them to "participate in the creative process." All this encouraged memo-writing. Directors and writers were inclined to feel that the Xerox machine had complicated their lives. A producer issuing policy instructions to a director could easily send "information copies" to a dozen agency representatives and sometimes seemed to have written the memo for this purpose—or perhaps for any government agency that might care to subpoena it. A surging tide of paper flowed back and forth.

Scripts were in constant revision. Each time a page was revised, it appeared on paper of a different color. Some pages of the script might remain white in each version of the script while others became blue, pink, yellow, red, green—each indicating a new revision. The final script was always multi-hued.

The telefilm exhibited a number of persistent themes. Heroes with special magic powers were numerous, and seemed to observers a metaphor for the national obsession with secret weapons. The atom bomb had been thought by many to be a key to world control, and perhaps the dream persisted in the super-heroes. They represented, according to Beverly Hills psychiatrist Murray Korengold, "the American ethic of hegemony and supremacy." Women were included in the magic powers. In *I Dream of Jeannie* the heroine was a genie in a bottle found by an astronaut after splashdown near a tropical island. She becomes his constant companion, often frustrating foreign agents trying to obtain American space secrets. *Bewitched* and *The Flying Nun*—from the same studio, Columbia—also featured women with special powers. The trend coincided with a wave of magic characters in commercials, dramatizing the occult powers of detergents and cleansers, and made

Deanna Lund and Kurt Kasznar in *Land of the Giants*. Twentieth Century-Fox

HOSTILE UNIVERSE

Adam West in *Batman*.
Twentieth Century-Fox

Mark Goddard in *Lost in Space*.
Twentieth Century-Fox

drama and commercial highly compatible. Animal heroes satisfied similar power obsessions and, like all supermen, inevitably became involved in international struggles. In a 1968 *Flipper* episode the dolphin-hero helps to prevent a spy from delivering an aborted rocket's instrument package to a hostile power. Television animals had sound instincts about enemies.

In contrast to the paranoia and hostility of the power programs, many family series were uncompromisingly wholesome and offered a reassuringly warm view of the American home. Two monster-family series, *The Addams Family* and *The Munsters*, perhaps represented a countertrend, but even they were wholesome and lovable.

Imitation of success, especially one's own, was a persistent trend, and seemed to be an inevitable result of the huge stakes involved. The multiplicity of sponsors was also credited with a homogenizing effect. By 1968 the single-sponsor series had almost vanished; many had a dozen sponsors; ABC-TV's *The Big Valley* had twenty-six.

If all went well, investment funds flowed back in profusion—from American and foreign use. By 1968 there were 140 million television sets abroad—almost twice as many as in the United States. More than a hundred countries had become markets for American telefilms. A successful one-hour telefilm series could expect up to $7000 per episode from the United Kingdom, $6500 from Canada, $6000 from West Germany, $6000 from Japan, $4400 from France, $4250 from Australia, $4000 from Brazil—and, at the other end of the scale, $180 per episode from Kuwait, $150 from Hong Kong, $120 from Saudi Arabia, $110 from Guatemala, $90 from Taiwan, $60 from Nicaragua.

United States foreign earnings from telefilms were climbing:

1958	$15 million		
1959	25	1964	70
1960	30	1965	76
1961	45	1966	70
1962	55	1967	78
1963	66	1968	80

Some sales were being made in communist countries: Bulgaria, East Germany, Hungary, Poland, Romania, Yugoslavia. Their motives were often a subject for speculation. Did Poland buy *The Untouchables* out of sheer enthusiasm, or because it confirmed a Polish conception of American life? A similar question was raised when Sweden, strongly anti-American in respect to war policies, promptly bought *Mission: Impossible*.

In numerous countries United States programming took the prime-time spotlight. This was made fairly inevitable by the dearth of rival products. In 1968 the Motion Picture Export Association was pleased to inform its members that in Italy "only a few films are being produced locally for television, since American-made TV films are available at far below what it would cost RAI to produce similar films or series."

If this was true of Italy, a major film-producing country, it was all the more true of scores of other countries. The Motion Picture Export Association could report: "Very little TV material is filmed in Argentina." "There is no film production in Chile except news flashes and TV commercials." From one country to another, film schedules showed similarities. And prime time was a psychological bond uniting like-minded people.

American prime-time devotees, like those abroad, accepted the idea that what they saw during most evening hours was "entertainment"—perhaps because it confirmed their beliefs and views. This was true of most drama and most comedy—except for a few oddments like the Smothers Brothers. The comedians who dominated television year after year were court jesters who knew the line.

Bob Hope, a great man in radio and television for thirty years, played golf with Presidents and was a perennial toastmaster at award ceremonies. His one-liners, enlivened by an ever-present leer, had earned him fantastic wealth. A 1968 *Fortune* survey of millionaires put him in the $150 to $200 million group. He had begun entertaining troops in World War II, and had never stopped. During the Vietnam war his appearances were filmed and became the substance of prime-time telecasts at home and a potent element of support for the American involvement. In December 1967, as domestic discord over the war was approaching a climax of indignation, Hope was on one of his Vietnam visits, bringing roars from 12,000 troops at Danang. His jokes—war after war—seemed to proclaim that all were the same war: "I hope your grandfather heard me at Appomattox. I was great." At Danang Bob Hope and the singer Phil Crosby came out wearing long-haired wigs and carrying antiwar signs, and got roars of laughter. "Don't worry about the riots in the States," Hope told the troops. "You'll be sent to survival school before you go back there."

All this was lively stuff, but left no doubt where he stood. The long-haired people, with signs and so on, were fools or dupes. They were outsiders, not part of the prime-time world.

On April 1, 1968, as America was agog over the withdrawal of Lyndon Johnson, Jack Benny was on television with Lucille Ball, queen of comediennes for almost two decades. The Desilu she had built with Desi Arnaz had been sold to the conglomerate Gulf & Western—the new owners of Paramount—for $17 million. Jack Benny had been a ratings leader even longer than Hope. For thirty-five years he had refined the same jokes. One concerned his famous $100 Stradivarius—"it's one of the few *ever* made in Japan." Even more celebrated was his supposed miserliness. In the program with Lucy she worked in a bank which wanted a celebrity depositor, and her job was to persuade Benny to give up the cavernous underground vault beneath his house where he was said to guard his accumulated hoard of millions. For this program the Paramount scenic crews constructed an underground defense labyrinth that would have stymied the heroes of *Mission: Impossible*.

All of this—fortunes, success, glittering decor, beautiful people, and the jokes that kept them all in the public mind—were a continuing celebration of the American way. Viewers who stuck to prime time could dwell in that splendid world. Outside its orbit—pushing into newscasts but seldom beyond—were shouters, protesters, attackers. The very sight of them aroused deepening fury. With the withdrawal of Johnson, many viewers already knew what they wanted. The man who had stood up to Khrushchev could take care of the hippies.

HIGH NOON

By early 1968 Richard Nixon seemed certain of the Republican nomination, and this was a miracle. In 1962—two years after defeat by John Kennedy—he had tried to reactivate his career by running for election to the governorship of California but had been defeated by the incumbent Democratic governor, Edmund ("Pat") Brown. It was for Nixon an ignominious event, for he considered Brown a second-rater. When the outcome became clear at Nixon headquarters, his press aide Herbert Klein read a concession statement to reporters, and said the candidate would not be available for questions. But as he spoke there was commotion in the corridor and Nixon pushed in, surrounded by red-eyed followers. Quivering, he vented his frustration. "As I leave you, I want you to know, just think how much you'll be missing. You won't have Nixon to kick around any more. . . ." Leaving, he muttered to aides, "It had to be said, it had to be said." It was considered his farewell to politics.

He went into private law practice. In 1964 he said on *Today* over NBC-TV that he was not a candidate for the presidency but might accept a vice presidential nomination if his party wished him to. Then he went on a world tour, described as private. He was accompanied by a Pepsi-Cola executive and was serving as an international envoy for the company; he is said to have ironed out Pepsi-Cola distribution problems in Taiwan. But it was also a chance to visit world leaders and was regarded by some observers as a try at re-establishing himself as a major figure. The wire services did not feel it worthwhile to send a reporter with him, nor did newspapers. Only NBC News felt the tour called for coverage and sent correspondent Herbert Kaplow and a camera crew with Nixon and the Pepsi-Cola entourage. Occasional filmed items and statements appeared in NBC newscasts, generated some press attention, and helped Nixon to maintain a continued visibility. During his tour he called for vigorous military action against North Vietnam and rebels in Laos. On his return he backed Goldwater, which may have been crucial to his fortunes. Republican leaders who shunned Goldwater, as Governor Nelson Rockefeller did, aroused much party resentment. The defeat suffered by Goldwater brought party stalwarts back to Nixon.

While fury over the Vietnam war raged around Johnson, Nixon could afford to say little or nothing on the subject; it was not his war. He spoke widely at Republican fund-raising rallies.

Meanwhile the Democrats were tearing each other apart. Johnson war policies were defended by some, angrily attacked by others.

Among the angry men was Martin Luther King. His nonviolent crusade had seemed to move within sight of the promised land, but now he saw his cohorts breaking. Wartime inflation was widening the gap between rich and poor. Among black youth, said King, unemployment ran as high as 40 per cent. On newscasts, voices for "black power" outshouted the pleas for nonviolence. None of the causes of riots, warned King, were being solved. "Why have we substituted the arrogant undertaking of policing the whole world for the high risk of putting our own house in order?" he saw the United States as the chief generator of violence around the world. He planned a Poor People's March on Washington, for white and black. Against growing odds, he said it must be nonviolent.

On April 4, 1968, he walked out onto the balcony of a Memphis motel and was felled by a sniper. A bullet ripped into him, throwing him against a wall; blood spurted from his neck as he went down. Riots and looting quickly broke out in all major cities. Men and women wept—over the loss of a loved leader and over the tidal wave of violence it had let loose. In South Vietnam servicemen

Martin Luther King, Jr.   Wide World

were described as stunned, although one said: "We have three hundred people dying here each week." In Saigon the Armed Forces
Radio and Television Service canceled rock 'n' roll programs and
substituted music by Morton Gould, Montavani, and Kostelanetz—
quieter, but scarcely a tribute to King or his cause. On the hour
AFRTS brought bulletins, telling of troop movements from various
locations to Washington, Chicago, and other danger areas.

Once more television audiences throughout the world participated in an extraordinary funeral. In the course of a seven-hour telecast, sent across the ocean by satellite, they joined mourners in an Atlanta ghetto church, and among them glimpsed faces they knew—Jacqueline Kennedy, Robert Kennedy, Ted Kennedy, Richard Nixon, Hubert Humphrey, Eugene McCarthy, and many of the entertainment world. Then they watched spellbound as King's coffin, on a farm wagon drawn by two Georgia mules, moved toward the cemetery followed by crowds on foot—crowds estimated at two hundred thousand people.

The presidential campaign resumed—on television, a thread of frenetic counterpoint to "regular" programming. Robert Kennedy had decided to run. The New Hampshire primary had clinched his decision—to the dismay and anger of McCarthy supporters. But Kennedy felt that the quiet-spoken, sometimes mystical McCarthy could not be elected. The need of the hour, as Kennedy saw it, was to unite the disaffected—the young, the black, the poor—and Kennedy felt he could. During the next two months he was constantly in motion. Day by day television newscasts showed glimpses of him —hair wild and allowed to grow longer—as he pushed through frenzied crowds of people screaming, jumping, wanting to touch him. He responded with an ecstasy of his own. In his entourage now were people like Jack Newfield, a youth twice jailed in civil rights demonstrations, who had once picketed Attorney General Robert Kennedy but now felt that Bobby had discovered his true character and destiny. Clearly Kennedy, who had a capacity to arouse hate, also had a capacity to stir extraordinary hopes.

On the night of June 5, in a back corridor of the Ambassador Hotel in Los Angeles, surrounded by jubilant supporters celebrating his victory in the California primary, Robert Kennedy was shot down. A guest screamed: "Not *again!*" As celebrities crowded around the sprawled figure, a member of the ABC-TV production staff, William Weisel, found he too was wounded, bleeding. Within minutes the scene of pandemonium and consternation was on tele-

Funeral: wagon drawn by mules.   Wide World

Mrs. Martin Luther King, Jr., with daughter Bernice.   Wide World

vision, as the unconscious Kennedy was rushed to a hospital. Later a solemn President Johnson appeared on the home screen.

JOHNSON: Let us put an end to violence. . . . Let us begin in the aftermath of this great tragedy to find a way to reverence life, to protect it. . . .

He said he had appointed a commission headed by ex-President Eisenhower's brother, Milton Eisenhower, to study the phenomenon of rising violence and find out "what in the nature of our people and the environment of our society makes possible such murder and such violence."

The following day. Arthur Schlesinger, Jr,. commented: "We are today the most frightening people on the planet." He considered the Vietnam war the main factor in the trend to violence but noted that "the atrocities we commit trouble so little our official self-righteousness, our invincible conviction of our moral superiority." Some attacked the indiscriminate sale of guns; others, the role of television as merchandiser of violence. Attorney Morris L. Ernst, interviewed on television on *The Merv Griffin Show*, said: "We're being murdered by TV, not by the guns." Networks began a frantic pruning and juggling of programs. Scheduled segments of *Bonanza*, *Mannix*, *The Avengers*, *Big Valley*, and *The Guns of Will Sonnett* were canceled. The producer of *Get Smart* blue-penciled a number of scripts ready for production. Scripts of *The Mod Squad* and *It Takes a Thief*—in production for the fall—were likewise revised. Network spokesmen said again that there was no demonstrated causal connection between entertainment and crime, but many in the industry no longer felt reassured by such statements. Several hundred Hollywood actors and writers signed a published statement in *Variety* and other trade papers: "We will no longer lend our talents in any way to add to the creation of a climate for murder. . . ."

Once more, hundreds of millions of television viewers witnessed a ritual beyond belief. They saw the center of New York City paralyzed as throngs passed the bier in St. Patrick's Cathedral. Then came a fantastic migration to the interment in Washington. A camera poised at a Pennsylvania station escalator in New York watched celebrity faces, in close-up, drift by in dream-like motion—political leaders, social leaders, media leaders.

Then programs, commercials, and campaigns resumed. Richard Nixon was duly nominated at a convention in Miami. In his acceptance speech viewers found an uncanny resemblance to the oratory of Martin Luther King. Where King had said, "I have a dream," Nixon said, "I see a day," and he used the refrain eight times. The same kinds of visions were used—an attempt, apparently, to offset the conservative-Southern aura of men around Nixon, as exemplified by the selection of Spiro Agnew as vice presidential candidate.

But greater tension surrounded Chicago, where the Democratic convention would be held weeks later—in August. City authorities anticipated trouble and prepared for it. Police received special riot-control drills. Fences and barbed wire were erected around the convention area. As television engineers prepared their installations, they felt they were in an armed camp.

For many Americans, especially the young, the democratic process itself was facing a test. To many it seemed that issues were being settled by a shoot-out. However, there was still Eugene McCarthy.

He confounded observers. His campaigning remained easy-going —some said indolent. The delirium that had surrounded Kennedy campaigns was missing. Followers who hoped for anti-Johnson invective were disappointed. McCarthy seemed almost to try to dampen audiences with broad philosophic arguments. On a California telecast he said that America during the 1950's and 1960's had built up for itself a mission "to judge the political systems of other nations—nearly all the other nations of the world—accepting that we had the right to interfere with all those systems if we found them wanting." He said all this with such calm detachment—without teleprompter—that it was difficult to realize he was setting aside

Republican convention, 1968—Howard K. Smith reporting.   ABC

assumptions that had governed American foreign policy for two decades. The absence of theatrics troubled politicos but delighted many others. Students came to him by thousands.

But the delegates heading for Chicago included many politicians who had backed Johnson war policies and were not eager to repudiate their own records. Although Kennedy and McCarthy—the anti-war candidates—had polled 80 per cent of the Democratic votes in the primaries and had far out-polled war supporters, it was clear long before Chicago that many delegates leaned to Hubert Humphrey; he, too, had gone down the line with Johnson.

The crowds that converged on Chicago came with diverse motives. A delegation of the Poor People's March—now led by Ralph Abernathy, Martin Luther King's deputy—came for nonviolent protest. So did many McCarthy supporters, still hoping that massive demonstrations would stop Humphrey and turn the tide toward their candidate—or perhaps Ted Kennedy—and a repudiation of the Vietnam war. Some had no illusions and came to disrupt. A few young people came to Chicago because it seemed, suddenly, the place to be. The migrants numbered less than ten thousand, but seemed likely to make news—if only because of the huge police power mobilized to confront them.

The hundreds of television people who arrived with several hundred tons of television equipment faced extraordinary problems. The arrangements made by the city, under the direction of Mayor Richard J. Daley, virtually confined live coverage to the hall itself. Demonstrators were to be kept in areas remote from the convention hall, such as Grant Park and Lincoln Park, where they were apparently to demonstrate for their own satisfaction. Television coverage of any demonstration would have to be done mainly by videotape mobile units or by cameramen on foot, with film and tape being rushed by courier to the convention hall facilities. Use of film would involve additional time-lags for development.

Under the Daley arrangements the convention would be completely insulated from demonstrators. The television viewer would be aware of them only if networks were able to film and tape their activity and intercut it with convention hall proceedings. *Variety* predicted that the arrangements would clinch Humphrey's nomination "but contrariwise would cast a pall over his election chances . . . his victory at Chicago is bound to look like a political steamroller."

The arrangements caused broadcasters and convention management to have an edgy relationship from the start. This was aggravated when NBC newsmen were found to have planted an electronic eavesdropping device in a secret platform committee meeting. Their action was at once repudiated by network executives, but it may have helped them learn that the platform, in its first draft, contained a clause denouncing television violence. Network remonstrances eliminated the clause.

Network newsmen encountered further hostility when they moved their mobile units toward police lines facing protesters near Grant Park. The police clearly considered the cameras an unwelcome presence, but the protesters cheered them. Taunting the police, they shouted, "The whole world is watching! The whole world is watching!" As a long, sleek NBC mobile unit, with camera and men perched on its roof, pushed toward the area of confrontation, the protesters continued to goad the phalanxes of policemen. "Sieg heil! Sieg heil!" Demonstrators were resolved on a protest march to the convention; police, who outnumbered them and were armed with nightsticks, guns, tear-gas, and mace, and reinforced by National Guard units, were resolved to stop them. Groups began to form marches and to attempt to bypass police lines at various points to enter the Loop area.

The film and tape arriving at the television control room suddenly began to look like slaughter. Networks threw it on the air as fast as they could. Viewers saw a dizzying kaleidoscope: nominating speech, headcracking, speech, tear gas, shouting crowd, wounded, paddy wagons, balloting, ambulances, speeches. Viewers sensed that the delegates were unaware of the bloody events; then, suddenly, that they were becoming aware. Rumor swept through the hall. Some got the news via phone calls from downtown hotels. Some listened on transistor radios or left to look at monitors. The convention managers plowed ahead with proceedings. Some delegates wanted to recess, but protests and questions were ruled out of order. The hall became a wild rumble. Senator Abraham Ribicoff of Connecticut, in the midst of a nominating speech, digressed to speak of "turmoil and violence competing with this great convention for the attention of the American people." As he spoke bitterly of "Gestapo tactics in the streets of Chicago," television cameras focused on a furious Mayor Richard Daley, in close-up.

Among the hundreds injured in the melees were twenty-one reporters and photographers, clubbed by police while trying to cover the events. Violence spread to the hall itself. Television viewers saw

NBC

Democratic convention, 1968.

CBS newsman Dan Rather assaulted by security police. The flare-up was rapidly suppressed, but not before anchorman Walter Cronkite had expressed fury.

As the convention rumbled on, bitter charge and countercharge overshadowed the proceedings. Frank Sullivan, information officer for the Chicago police, spoke angrily of the demonstrators as "allies of the men who are killing American soldiers." Dismissing the indignation against Mayor Daley, he said: "The intellectuals of America hate Richard J. Daley because he was elected by the people—unlike Walter Cronkite."

The world saw Hubert Humphrey nominated in what appeared to be a fortified stockade, and guessed he had very little chance of election. Choice of the highly respected Senator Edmund S. Muskie as his running mate improved his chances.

Richard Nixon seemed to his campaign advisers to be sure of election. But they felt that his campaign had to be managed with care. He appeared mainly before selected audiences of the committed, and also filmed a number of spots:

NIXON: The administration has struck out on keeping the peace abroad, on keeping the peace at home, on providing prosperity without inflation. I say three strikes are enough. Let's get a new batter up there!

On poverty:

NIXON: Instead of more millions on welfare rolls, let's have more millions on payrolls!

On Vietnam:

NIXON: We need new leadership that will not only end the war in Vietnam but keep the nation out of other wars for eight years.

Nixon appeared so certain of victory, said court jester Bob Hope, that Whittier, California—Nixon's home town—had already started building a log cabin for him.

After all the violence, the campaign itself seemed anticlimactic. The young people had gone home. The Republicans spent over $25 million on television and radio; the Democrats, more than $15 million. Broadcast expenditures had almost doubled since 1964, tripled since 1960, quadrupled since 1956.

Yet in 1968 40 per cent of eligible voters stayed away from the polls—the highest abstention rate since 1956. Richard Nixon was elected by about 27 per cent of the eligible voters; he faced a nation in which faith in government processes had been dangerously eroded.

The violence remained an issue for some months. The Milton Eisenhower commission, which had acquired the title National Commission on the Causes and Prevention of Violence, was studying television programming as a possible factor. Senator John A. Pastore, chairman of the Senate subcommittee on communications, was planning hearings on television violence and sex. The U.S. Public Health Service was studying mental health implications of television brutality. Networks scrapped some of the violent cartoon series still crowding Saturday morning schedules. Scripts for telefilms continued to be pruned of expendable mayhem. Hollywood's two hundred stunt men, who lived by being hurled from balconies and automobiles, encountered a sudden decline in employment. Many fights were reduced to a punch or two. The shoot-out on a dusty street that had opened *Gunsmoke* for years was scrapped for a quiet opening; the west was tamed again. Though the procedure of counting acts of violence had never seemed valid to CBS, the network adopted it and announced a 30 per cent reduction "in the number of violent incidents in our prime-time programs" for the following season. Some producers felt it would all blow over soon. They hoped so; they had other matters on their minds.

COSMIC NIELSEN

Among the industry's concerns was the most extraordinary spectacular ever conceived. It would take men outside their present habitat to a climax on the moon. From the start it was all planned as a series of television shows.

On-the-air tests of the Apollo spacecraft, which also functioned as television studio and transmitter, began late in 1968. During the first manned Apollo flight—163 times around the earth—television viewers shared the view of earth from orbit, and became acquainted with the euphoria that seemed to overtake men in weightlessness. Floating around their studio-capsule, Walter M. Schirra, Jr., and Donn F. Eisele clowned for the camera and held up a sign: "KEEP THOSE CARDS AND LETTERS COMING IN FOLKS."

Late in December, during the first manned flight around the moon, viewers shared with astronauts the sight of its bleak and forbidding surface. Then on Christmas Eve, from the vicinity of the moon, the men staged a reading of Genesis. It was begun by William A. Anders.

ANDERS: In the beginning God created the heaven and the earth. And the earth was without form, and void. And darkness was upon the face of the deep. . . .

After a few lines, James Lovell took up the reading. Frank Borman concluded it with, ". . . and God saw that it was good." It was reminiscent of another Christmas Eve—1906—when wireless operators on ships in the Atlantic, accustomed to hearing dots and dashes on their earphones, were flabbergasted to hear, instead, Reginald Fessenden reading a Bible passage. It called to mind also the fantastic changes the intervening decades had brought.

In March 1969 astronauts tested a spidery "bug" of the sort that would later take men to the moon's surface from an orbiting spaceship. During this flight Russell L. Schweickart also spent forty minutes outside a spacecraft taking pictures while doctors in Houston studied the curve of his heartbeat and other biological data sent by radio transmitters inside his space suit. In May astronauts took a bug to within eight miles of the moon, and viewers watched its departure from the spaceship via a color camera on the spaceship. The

Promotional message from outer space. Donn F. Eisele, left; Walter M. Schirra, Jr., right.

Wide World

camera had been built by Westinghouse, the company that had precipitated the broadcasting era.

But now it was July and time to make history. A bug named Eagle would take two men to the moon—to an area known as the Sea of Tranquillity. With astonishing and frightening confidence, the planners released an advance scenario. A week before the event, viewers could read details in their newspapers.

The greatest show in the history of television begins when Armstrong starts down the nine-rung ladder leading from Eagle's hatch to the surface. When he reaches the third rung from the top, the astronaut will reach out with his left arm and pull a D-shaped handle, opening a storage bay and exposing the lens of a black-and-white TV camera.

In 1.3 seconds, the time it takes light to reach the earth, we will see Armstrong's legs carefully moving down the ladder.

A moment later, men on earth will see man walking on the moon.

Everything went by the script. Even words were ready beforehand. The occasion needed a touch of magic, like the words used by Alexander Morse to click the first telegraph message from Washington to Baltimore in 1844: "What hath God wrought?" But the NASA word experts were not up to its technicians. Neil A. Armstrong, standing on the moon, said awkwardly:

ARMSTRONG: That's one small step for a man, one giant leap for mankind.

To viewers who had grown up on the radio serial *Jack Armstrong, All-American Boy* it seemed right that an Armstrong had done it. Later they saw Edwin Aldrin, Jr., join him. Together they set up a second television camera—these were both RCA-built—and viewers on earth saw the two men hop around, almost like kangaroos, gathering rocks. Then President Nixon appeared on a split-screen, ready at the telephone, in the Oval Room of the White House. The other part of the screen showed Armstrong and Aldrin in front of their spidery bug. The President said, "This certainly has to be the most historic phone call ever made." Then conversation gave way to statement.

NIXON: Because of what you have done, the heavens have become a part of man's world. And as you talk to us from the Sea of Tranquillity, it requires us to redouble our efforts to bring peace and tranquillity to earth. For one priceless moment in the whole history of man, all the people on this earth are truly one—one in their pride in what you have done and one in our prayers that you will return safely to earth.

The men planted an American flag made of nylon and stiffened at the top with an aluminum rod so that it would seem, on television, to blow in a nonexistent breeze.

When Armstrong and Aldrin, after two hours and twenty-one minutes, re-entered the bug to start the return trip, television and

Telethon

radio networks began picking up comments from points in the United States and abroad—including some behind the iron curtain.

Comments from American scientists had a curious range. No one was quite certain why the feat had been undertaken. Some said the attempt was necessary for the reason men climbed Mount Everest—"because it is there." Some said it was necessary to further the advance of knowledge in general, while others cited specific practical benefits, some of which seemed bizarre in the context of the moment; it was said the space flights were aiding development of heat-resistant paints and bath-tiles as well as world-communication instruments. One scientist considered it good to know that no matter what a mess mankind made of the earth, men would always be able to go elsewhere.

This was a chilling reminder of unsolved problems. Many scholars were stressing the precariousness of "spaceship Earth." Space flights had dramatized the importance of the life-supporting environment. Yet the earth's own "support system"—soil, water, air—was being despoiled at a staggering rate, in large part by industrial development abetted by the mass media. With population growth unchecked, some feared that the destruction of the support system would become irreversible within a few decades, dooming life on earth.

To many scientists, scientific justifications for the Apollo program seemed flimsy. In the opinion of Nobel prize winner Harold C. Urey the moon landing was to be thought of not as a scientific venture but as "something like the building of the pyramids or the Parthenon." This suggested a main function of prestige—as President Kennedy had said, "to beat the Soviets. . . ."

Perhaps that was why it had to be a television show. The emphasis on television had been deplored by some among the colony of scientists at Houston, as drawing attention from scientific pursuits, while others had defended it as assuring more congressional appropriations. But for world impact it was essential.

In relation to that purpose, the television spectacular was an epoch-making success. A key element was the American willingness to allow live coverage of what might turn into disaster. For hundreds of millions of people throughout the world, watching via satellites, the unspoken possibility of disaster must have been ever-present. Against the background of this peril, the calm assurance had an epic quality. To such men, could anything be impossible?

It was important that the operation had international aspects. The Apollo program involved "cooperative arrangements" with eighty countries—in tracking, splash-down facilities, satellite schedules, ground-station operations. All over the world, the moon landing took the Vietnam war off the front pages and—at least momentarily—out of the minds of men.

Among the half-million who flocked to Cape Kennedy—formerly Cape Canaveral—to view the blast-off were newsmen, diplomats, and celebrities of many nations. It was a strange assemblage, arriving by airline, private plane and helicopter, railroad, limousine, trailer, bicycle, and on foot. There was even a mule-cart procession of the Poor People's March, led by Ralph Abernathy. They came to protest, but according to a *Time* report, as he saw the huge Apollo lift into the air as from a thundering, fiery cauldron, he forgot about poverty and prayed for the safety of the men. So it may have been around the world.

If an empire needed bread and circuses, here was the greatest circus in history. For some this was its glory, and for others its fatal flaw.

Lewis Mumford said: "It is a symbolic act of war, and the slogan the astronauts will carry, proclaiming that it is for the benefit of mankind, is on the same level as the Air Force's monstrous hypocrisy—"Our Profession Is Peace."

In the *Saturday Review* critic Robert Lewis Shayon said it more gently, but memorably:

> Wherever explorers go in the future accompanied by television cameras, they will be actors, making their nebulous exits and entrances for the benefit of multiplanetary audiences. Nowhere will there ever again be pure events (if ever there were); everything hereafter will be stage-managed for cosmic Nielsens, in the interest of national or universal establishments.

CONGLOMERATE

The International Telephone and Telegraph Company, one of the corporate members of COMSAT, was little known to the general public until the late 1960's. A huge conglomerate, ITT had foreign interests that yielded more than half its revenues.

In 1966 stockholders of ITT and ABC had voted a merger of the companies, and asked FCC approval. This was necessary because of the ABC television and radio licenses involved in the merger.

The FCC listened to executives of the two companies—and to no one else. The executives explained that ITT could provide ABC with a large infusion of cash and that this would strengthen the network and serve the "public interest, convenience, and necessity." The FCC, 4-3, approved the merger.

Dissenters included Commissioner Nicholas Johnson—who, in the tradition of Clifford Durr, was a frequent FCC dissenter. In a long written statement, Johnson raised the question of whether ITT interests abroad might at some time affect ABC news policies. This issue was causing some concern. U.S. Senator Gaylord Nelson of Wisconsin asked for postponement of the merger to give the Justice Department time to study antitrust aspects.

At this stage, ITT actions provided striking dramatization of the point raised by Johnson. The writer Eileen Shanahan, after discussing the controversy in the New York *Times,* reported being "badgered" by an ITT vice president. Did she not care that stockholders might lose money because of her dispatches? He warned that Senator Nelson was working with Commissioner Johnson on a bill to strip newspapers, including the New York *Times,* of their broadcasting interests. (Senator Nelson said he had never met Commissioner Johnson.) Eileen Shanahan then found that ITT investigators were probing her private life. The writer James Ridgeway, after a *New Republic* article about the Shanahan affair, likewise found his private life being investigated by ITT sleuths.

Meanwhile the Justice Department was finding that ABC, far from being pinched for cash, was extremely prosperous. The Justice Department also discovered an internal ITT memo that illuminated its motives and flatly contradicted its testimony. The memo said: "ABC's cash throw-off through 1970 will approach 100 million, almost all of which will be available for reinvestment outside the television business."

The FCC majority felt, nonetheless, that ITT should be allowed to acquire ABC, because RCA owned NBC. Johnson argued: "To say that because RCA runs NBC, ITT must be allowed to acquire ABC, is to say that things are so bad there is no point in doing anything to stop them from getting worse."

The FCC once more approved the merger, 4-3, and the minority filed another dissent:

A company whose daily activities require it to manipulate governments at the highest level is likely to be left with little more re-

spect for a free and independent press . . . than for conscientious
government officials. . . .

The Justice Department, on the ground that ABC's journalistic
independence could not be protected, asked the U.S. Court of Appeals to forbid the merger. In January 1968 ITT, faced with litigation and delays, canceled the merger.

During the following years the American public heard more frequently about ITT. The company offered the Republican Party
some $400,000 to underwrite its 1972 convention scheduled for San
Diego. When published reports linked this with settlement of an
antitrust case, in a manner favorable to ITT, the San Diego plans
were canceled, and Miami was chosen for the convention.

In 1970, when Salvador Allende Gossens, a Marxist, was elected
President of Chile, ITT offered the CIA $1,000,000 to disrupt his
regime. The CIA adopted the idea but used $8,000,000 in tax funds,
bribing Chilean legislators and supporting anti-Allende factions and
media, including broadcasting. Allende was overthrown in 1973.
The ITT and CIA actions were revealed later.

When Commissioner Nicholas Johnson's FCC term expired, he
was not reappointed by President Nixon.

ITT, in an apparent attempt to repair its public image, decided
to sponsor a series of children's programs to "promote international
understanding."

RELEVANCE

The shock waves from the 1968 turmoil and violence had reverberating effects on broadcasting. The sense that much television programming had become irrelevant was strongly felt among both executives and producers. The 1969 cry was for "relevance," and
during the following years it sent many programs into oblivion.
The "top ten" series of 1973-74 included not a single holdover from
the 1968-69 list of leaders. The replacements were almost all new
offerings.

Many *looked* different. Black, brown, yellow faces became common in drama, newscast, commercial, comedy, special event, panel. With richer ethnic mixtures came sweeping changes in clothing and hairstyles. In 1968 a young man with long hair, no tie, and a rumpled look was at once known by the audience to be a "hippie," probably a protester, and he was at once suspected of living "on welfare." A few years later such a person, whether in drama or news or round-table discussion, might be found to be a distinguished attorney, legislator, or professor. He might—as in *Mod Squad* or *The Rookies*—be a policeman. Even advertising agency personnel began to visit the studios looking like "hippies." They wanted to be in touch with "youth culture." Non-verbal communication codes were in disarray. The old cues could no longer be trusted.

Styles and roles were crossing race and sex lines. Men appearing on celebrity shows might wear magnificent, ornamental shirts and necklaces. Women, who were suddenly prominent as newscast correspondents, were no longer confined to fashion and household

Shirley Chisholm campaigns for Congress—1968.   Wide World

1968-69	% TV homes	1973-74	% TV homes
Laugh-In (NBC)	31.1	*All in the Family* (CBS)	31.2
Gomer Pyle (CBS)	27.1	*The Waltons* (CBS)	27.9
Bonanza (NBC)	27.0	*Sanford & Son* (NBC)	27.6
Mayberry R.F.D. (CBS)	25.8	*M.A.S.H.* (CBS)	25.8
Family Affair (CBS)	25.2	*Hawaii Five-O* (CBS)	23.7
Julia (NBC)	25.1	*Sonny & Cher* (CBS)	23.4
Gunsmoke (CBS)	24.8	*Maude* (CBS)	23.3
Dean Martin (NBC)	24.1	*Kojak* (CBS)	23.3
Here's Lucy (CBS)	23.7	*Mary Tyler Moore Show* (CBS)	23.2
Red Skelton (CBS)	23.6	*Cannon* (CBS)	23.0

(Nielsen averages through 4/2/69)   (Nielsen averages through 5/8/74)

Source: *Variety*

Transition. Not one of the 1968-69 top ten remained among the 1973-74 leaders. Changes involved wider ethnic distribution, increased permissiveness in language and plot, stress on "relevant" topics. But good guy/bad guy drama (*Hawaii Five-O, Kojak, Cannon*) remained a factor. Trend to videotape in place of film.

items: they reported from court-room, factory, slum, theater, Congress.

Programs *sounded* different. The upheaval brought a new permissiveness in language that startled older viewers, as well as the industry itself. A notable instance was the series *All in the Family*.* Its central figure, Archie Bunker, was a bigot who freely sprinkled his talk with references to "spics," "dagoes," "hebes," "coons"— racial epithets that had long been among the strictest of broadcasting taboos. Television, in acquiring a representative ethnic mix, seemed at last able to accommodate the verbal sparring that sometimes came with it.

The meaning and impact of all this were uncertain. A representa-

* It was modeled after a successful BBC-TV series, *Till Death Do Us Part*.

Archie Bunker.   Telethon

tive of the Anti-Defamation League, Benjamin Epstein, denounced
the series as making bigotry enjoyable and even lovable. Norman
Lear, the leading spirit behind the series, had a different and more
complex view. An ardent civil-libertarian, he had based Archie on
his own father, of whom he said: "I could never forgive him for
being a bigot—but I found there were other things to love him for."
Lear had had endless, heated arguments with his father, and had
never won them. In *All in the Family* he was, in a sense, still trying
to "reach" his father and others like him—but in a new way. He
was, he thought, enabling black and white, Jew and Gentile, to
"laugh together." The explosive welcome won by his program
among diverse groups—apparently including millions of those who
were the butt of Archie's expletives—seemed to support his claim.
The dreaded epithets had always drawn some of their voltage from
the mass-media taboos surrounding them. Their almost casual emergence in *All in the Family* was seen by Lear as a form of exorcism.
The words were in the open now—and no towers came crashing
down.

CBS-TV had launched *All in the Family* with trepidation, after ABC-TV had financed two pilot films and then abandoned the project as too risky. The quick success of the series brought a cascade of similar projects, including several from the same production group. The essential strategy was to seize on topics and relationships involving deep tensions, and introduce them in a comedy aura. In the process, innumerable taboos fell away. Interracial marriage, a young man's siege of impotence, an older woman's pregnancy and indecision about abortion, were suddenly topics of warm comedy, presented as casually as such old-time crises as: Will Dad notice the dent in the rear fender?

Lear expanded his empire ingeniously. Maude, Edith Bunker's liberated upstate cousin—the lady who had the abortion—was introduced as a character on *All in the Family* before becoming the central character of a new series, *Maude*. A black family first encountered in *All in the Family* became the subject of another new series, *The Jeffersons*. Maude's black maid became the central character of *Good Times*. The technique became a standard television stratagem. Rhoda, introduced as a character on the popular *Mary Tyler Moore Show*—whose heroine was a television news writer—became the central character of a *Rhoda* series. The technique created clusters of interrelated series, whose characters might refer to each other and visit each other. Most of the characters of the *Mary Tyler Moore Show* attended Rhoda's wedding in the *Rhoda* series —an event that momentarily eclipsed ABC-TV's *Monday Night Football* and its formidable sportscaster Howard Cosell.

Unlike a generation of action-adventure telefilms, many of the new "relevant" series were produced on videotape, and were performed before studio audiences. Advances in electronic editing equipment encouraged the trend toward videotape. Introduction of highly portable videotape cameras was beginning to make the system adaptable to outdoor as well as indoor drama. It was also affecting news production. All this foreshadowed a possibly revolutionary upheaval in equipment and production methods.

Many programming shifts of this period were, no doubt, instances of "completely new . . . and exactly like. . . ." Beyond the impact of new vocabulary, new topics, new look, *Good Times* was not unlike *The Goldbergs*, and *The Jeffersons* not unlike *Father Knows Best*. But the quick rise and fall of many new series, the atmosphere of constant change—in standards, subject matter, equipment—gave Hollywood an uneasy feeling. Such series as *I Love Lucy, Dragnet, Gunsmoke*, and such talents as Jack Benny, Dean Martin, Red Skelton, had remained leaders for decades, with little change in formula. Many industry leaders felt they were now walking on quicksand.

The feeling was abetted by developments in business and government relations. In 1967 an unusual maneuver projected the lawyer John Banzhaf III into the public spotlight. He argued before the FCC that broadcasters accepting cigarette advertising, which invariably linked cigarettes to health, vigor, romance, should also carry—free of charge—messages on the association of cigarettes with lung cancer and other diseases. He demanded this in compliance with the "fairness" doctrine, through which the FCC had tried to codify an aspect of the "public interest." When the FCC found merit in the argument, "counter-advertising" by various health agencies began to assault the cigarette—so effectively that Congress decided to ban cigarette advertising from the air after 1970. As a result, both the cigarette advertising and the free counter-advertising vanished from the air. But the events had created a precedent that broadcasters found unnerving. Numerous other products seemed to citizen groups to call for counter-advertising, as threats to the environment or to individual health. Such groups were insistently demanding not only "fairness" but "access" to the air—for ideas and interests seldom winning television recognition. Some stations tried to accommodate such pressures by scheduling "free speech messages" or "speak-out messages." The FCC subsequently required cable systems in major cities to maintain "public access" channels for such messages. Thus, along with the new permissiveness in drama, viewers began to hear arguments and manifestos from diverse protesting groups—including atheists, homosexuals, and others.

With change in the air, all programming seemed to speed in tempo. The scheduling of sequences of commercials and other messages seemed to assume an almost unlimited audience ability to absorb kaleidoscopic barrages of information and persuasion. Comedy series tended toward a new, fragmented style involving innumerable short blackouts, often resembling clusters of commercials. The staccato style, popularized in 1968-69 in the series *Rowan & Martin's Laugh-In*, was emulated the following season by the almost equally successful *Hee-Haw*, in which the zany pace was applied to barnyard humor. The leisurely tempo of most earlier television comedy, as epitomized by Jack Benny, seemed to be swept away. In 1969 the kaleidoscopic style even appeared in a series for pre-school children, *Sesame Street*.

A product of long research and experimentation, *Sesame Street* was a spirited melange of instructive exercises, games, stories, skits, and high jinks, involving people, puppets, and animated figures. Rhythm and speed were stressed. The tempo, contrasting with that of such widely approved pre-school series as the comfortable *Captain Kangaroo*, surprised many observers. Some were also surprised that pre-school children, of virtually all socio-economic levels, were spellbound by *Sesame Street*. It was as though television had fostered, in a new generation, an attention capacity to match the accelerating action of the tube.

Effects of *Sesame Street* continued to be studied by researchers, and findings seemed to indicate unusual achievements. In a sequence of tests involving comparable groups of pre-schoolers, it was found that six weeks of *Sesame Street* put viewers substantially ahead of non-viewers in recognizing letters, associating sounds with letters, and recognizing and sorting geometric forms—circles, squares, triangles, rectangles. In spite of its remarkable showing, some educators viewed the series with uneasiness, partly because its techniques

Sesame Street.   Children's Television Workshop

were so clearly derived from those of television commercials. Were
the young viewers being *taught*, or *conditioned*? But *Sesame Street*
meanwhile won a welcome in many countries; in translation, it became an international success.

Sesame Street was aimed at the underprivileged; in decor and
stylistic detail, it reflected their world. A trend in this direction was
visible also in commercial television. The former concentration on
a world of affluence, once considered so essential to the merchandising process, was weakening. The *Julia* series, which had pioneered
in 1968 by successfully launching a black romantic heroine, had
been stylistically comparable to *The Lucy Show*. Julia, played by
Diahann Carroll, was a nurse, but her life had a high-society look.
The 1973-74 black heroes and heroines lived in a different world.

"Tall"
Zero Mostel explains opposites on *Sesame Street*.

"Short"
Children's Television Workshop

Julia–Diahann Carroll and Marc Copage.   Twentieth Century-Fox

The *Sanford & Son* heroes were junk dealers; the father of *The Jeffersons* ran a dry-cleaning shop; the family of *Good Times* just managed to keep its head above water—that's what "good times" meant. In the words of its bouncy theme-song, the family lived in a world of "temporary lay-offs and easy-credit rip-offs."

The *Waltons*, taking a direction that would have frightened earlier sponsors, was set in the Great Depression, and pictured it as a time of warmth and close family ties. Launched at a time when unemployment statistics were again assuming alarming proportions, *The Waltons* almost seemed a deliberate effort to prepare Americans for harder times.

The years 1969-74—the Nixon years—witnessed the rise and fall of many programs, abrupt shifts in rating leadership, changes in content, slippage of long-established rules and standards. Sudden reversals were the hallmark of the period. If this was true of the world of programming, it reflected a political era that was also one of upheaval—much of which found its way onto the television tube.

GAME PLANS

There was good reason why Richard Nixon, veteran of televised un-American activities hearings, of the Checkers speech, the "kitchen debate," the Great Debates, countless campaign telecasts, and "the most historic phone-call," should be intent on television as an instrument of presidential power. Among all Presidents of the television age, he became its most avid practitioner—in the frequency of his appearances, and in the range of devices used to influence, cajole, and control the medium.

Throughout broadcasting history, Presidents have been given air time at their request, and under circumstances of their choosing. This has never been a legal requirement, but a practice that seemed essential to the "public interest, convenience, and necessity." All Presidents from Franklin D. Roosevelt on have been thought to misuse the privilege, exploiting it for partisan political ends; yet curtailment has seemed inconceivable.

Presidents have found many ways to use the television spotlight. The study *Presidential Television*, written in 1973 by former FCC chairman Newton N. Minow and others, summarized them succinctly:

> He may make a formal address, hold a press conference, consent to an interview, telephone an astronaut, go to a football game, receive a visiting chief of state, take a trip abroad, or play with his dog on the White House lawn. He may send his family, his cabinet members, or his political allies before the cameras. In almost every case,

he, and he alone, decides. His ability to choose when and how to appear without cost before millions of viewers is completely unmatched by his political or Congressional opponents.

Unlike Lyndon Johnson, Nixon was not a compulsive viewer. But he was devoted to televised football, and liked to offer advice on tactics to favorite teams. And he often talked of political strategy in terms of "game plans."

Many of his presidential telecasts, especially in his first term, were supremely successful in solidifying his position, as indicated in Gallup polls. Coming into office with a minimal constituency, he rapidly won wider support. Though he often seemed ill at ease on camera, his awkwardness—or lack of show-business charisma—may at times have worked in his favor in his appeals to "middle America."

He had pledged an end to the Vietnam war—a "peace with honor"—and soon after his inauguration announced a plan for removing combat ground troops from Vietnam in phased withdrawals. In numerous on-camera appearances he stressed the withdrawals.

The networks, taking their cue from this, adopted a similar stress. Av Weston, executive producer of the ABC-TV evening news, telegraphed orders to his Saigon bureau to de-emphasize battle footage in favor of material on the theme *We Are on Our Way Out of Vietnam.* A follow-up order said: "This point should be stressed to all hands." The theme thus became a pervasive one.

Unfortunately, it misrepresented events, of which the withdrawals were only a part, the televised part. While television viewers saw constant glimpses of homebound soldiers, some were still being replaced by new draftees. A few days after his inauguration, President Nixon sent a secret American sweep into Laos, and a few weeks later began secret, sustained bombing of Cambodia, a country officially recognized as neutral. The U.S. Air Force, under presidential orders, put into effect a systematic falsification of reports to conceal these attacks from the American people. Off-shore naval forces and Thailand-based air units were meanwhile strengthened for these attacks and for intensified bombing of North Vietnam

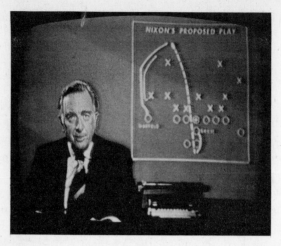

One of thousands of photos made from the television tube by Billy Adler and John Margolies for their 1971 museum exhibit *The Television Environment*.
Telethon

and Vietcong areas. Armament supplies to South Vietnam were increased to give it one of the largest air forces in the world. Thus while Americans believed that the President was "winding down the war"—a theme constantly dramatized via "going home" film sequences on the evening news—he was actually enlarging it in quest of a decisive military victory, the "peace with honor" he wanted to win, in place of the compromise available at Paris conference tables.

The "winding down" theme remained largely unchallenged in the mass media for several months, so that the President had won time for his game plan. But by mid-1969 it was clear that the war was building in fury, and that no "peace with honor" was in sight. Revelations by the New York *Times* concerning the secret Cambodia bombings helped to rekindle protest. That fall, huge demonstrations again converged on Washington and seemed to imperil the Nixon strategy. At this point he pre-empted a prime-time period on November 3 and, to an audience of more than 70 million, made one of his most potent and successful appeals. It was addressed to a "silent majority."

> And so tonight—to you, the great silent majority of my fellow Americans—I ask for your support. . . . For the more divided we are at home, the less likely the enemy is to negotiate at Paris. Let us be united for peace. Let us also be united against defeat. Because let us understand: North Vietnam cannot defeat or humiliate the United States. Only Americans can do that.

Nixon recognized that defeat, or the appearance of it, was more appalling to many Americans than war. His words did not end protest but stirred increased anger against protesters. He put protesters on the defensive, placing them outside the mainstream of American life. It was a telling maneuver, and again gained him time.

While viewer reaction to the speech was mainly favorable, there were diverse assessments from columnists and television commentators. The "instant analysis" on television seems to have been particularly infuriating to the President. He was determined to restore the more cooperative environment of earlier periods of the Vietnam war, when the broadcast media were almost automatic conduits for administration reports and rationales. The President now began to make extraordinarily effective use of Vice President Spiro Agnew, whose speaking style lent itself to smooth invective. In a speech prepared for him by White House speech writer Patrick J. Buchanan, Agnew mounted a powerful offensive against the television networks. The speech was made at a regional meeting of Republicans in Des Moines, but all three networks, forewarned of the contents, felt that the best defense was to carry the speech. Thus they gave it nationwide impact. Agnew began by referring to the President's speech of ten days earlier, and the ensuing words of commentators.

> The purpose of my remarks tonight is to focus your attention on this little group of men who not only enjoy a right of instant rebuttal to every Presidential address, but, more importantly, wield

a free hand in selecting, presenting and interpreting the great issues of our nation. . . .

The American people would rightly not tolerate this concentration of power in Government. Is it not fair and relevant to question its concentration in the hands of a tiny, enclosed fraternity of privileged men elected by no one and enjoying a monopoly sanctioned and licensed by Government? The views of the majority of this fraternity do not—and I repeat, not—represent the views of America. . . .

Perhaps the place to start looking for a credibility gap is not in the offices of Government in Washington but in the studios of the networks in New York.

As Nixon had done in his Checkers speech, Agnew triumphantly turned the telecast into a referendum. Suggesting that network "bias" be protested via mail and telephone, he managed to let loose on the networks a deluge of letters and phone calls—some reasoned and sober in tone, others vituperative, scurrilous, and ugly.

A striking aspect of the Agnew attack was that it echoed liberal complaints against the monopolistic nature of the industry. Yet the target of the attack was the one small segment of television—the news segment—that was not wholly submerged in the monopoly atmosphere, and was occasionally at odds with military-industrial views. The thrust of the speech was to smother this segment. Thus it sought to establish precisely the "concentration of power" it pretended to abhor.

Agnew, returning to the attack in the following weeks, became celebrated as a phrase-maker, especially for his alliterations. Commentators were "nattering nabobs of negativism." Bob Hope, resolute Nixon and Agnew supporter, had his gag-writers devise jokes for Agnew speeches. Car stickers proclaimed: "Spiro Is Our Hero."

In several speeches, Agnew included reminders that television was "licensed" by government. Other government spokesmen echoed the theme. FCC chairman Dean Burch, a recent Nixon appointee—and former campaign manager for Barry Goldwater—

found the Agnew attack "thoughtful" and urged broadcasters to heed it. White House aide Clay T. Whitehead, who in 1970 became presidential adviser on "telecommunications policy," added a new note. Television stations could expect more security in their licenses, he suggested—he even mentioned the possibility of *longer* licenses—if they would be more careful about news programs and documentaries they accepted from the networks. He thus turned the affiliates against the networks. According to Walter Cronkite, the Nixon-Agnew-Whitehead era brought affiliate pressures on networks for a more cautious news policy. Some affiliates even superimposed disclaimers over network commentators. The networks themselves showed a sharply reduced interest in covering protest demonstrations.

The Agnew campaign received admiring tribute from the President's daughter Tricia. She said he had had "amazing" impact and helped television "reform itself." She added: "You can't underestimate the power of fear. They're afraid if they don't shape up—"

Some months later William Paley decided that CBS would drop "instant analysis" of presidential addresses.

White House efforts during these months to control television— a "TV Blitzkrieg," *Variety* called it—went beyond overt criticism. They included also varied covert harassments of newsmen regarded as enemies. Daniel Schorr of CBS, after a dispatch that displeased the White House, found that the FBI was questioning friends and acquaintances about him. Most such operations did not become public knowledge until much later.

The chilling effect of the White House maneuvers was, however, only temporary. By the winter of 1970-71, protest was again rising in pitch. It received impetus from reports of atrocities, at My Lai and elsewhere; of horrors inflicted by "lawnmower" bombing of Vietnamese towns, leaving a swath of death hundreds of feet wide; and catastrophic defoliant operations, which were said to sport a slogan adapted from television public-service spots: "Only you can prevent forests." Amid reports of such matters, "peace with honor"

"Upstairs, Downstairs"—on *Masterpiece Theater*.   PBS

seemed not only remote; to many, the phrase began to have ghoul-
ish overtones.

On television, the new surge of protest found expression on CBS
—January 1971—in *The Selling of the Pentagon*, by Peter Davis. At
once denounced by Vice President Agnew as "disreputable," it
documented with stunning impact the cosiness between the Pentagon and its corporate contractors, and the vast sums expended by
the Pentagon on pro-war propaganda. The spirit also found expression on public television.

The public-television system had made a cautious start in its new
incarnation as a service supported in part by federal funds. Import-
ing several superb British series, too long ignored by American television—*The Forsyte Saga, Civilization, Upstairs, Downstairs*—public
television was beginning to build an ardent following. Its schedules

also included the widely applauded *Sesame Street*. But during 1970–71 it also launched the inventive, occasionally brilliant series *The Great American Dream Machine*, a composite of short items, often sardonic and even iconoclastic. White House observers seem to have been angered by its war-related items, and also outraged by *Who Invited US?*, on the interventionist tendencies of American foreign policy; and, on the series *Behind the Lines*, by a documentary about the FBI's use of *agents provocateurs* to discredit anti-war groups.

But during these months of rising opposition, President Nixon was preparing to muffle protest again with the most spectacular and successful phase of all his television operations. In the midst of the Vietnam fury he was moving for a détente with China and the Soviet Union, to be implemented and dramatized via televised journeys. It was a maneuver certain to throw the world's ideological battle lines into confusion, and to confound his opponents. Secret journeys by presidential adviser Henry Kissinger set the stage. In July 1971 the President, on a few hours' notice, requested network time—without a hint to the networks of what was in store. When he suddenly appeared on the tube—interrupting *The Dean Martin Show*, *NYPD*, and the movie *The Counterfeit Killer*—it was to announce to the world that he would start a series of diplomatic travels with a visit to Peking. Enormous plans for television coverage began.

The fact that Richard Nixon, a leading generalissimo in a quarter-century of cold war, had taken this initiative, added to the drama and its impact. His cold-war credentials may also have made the venture possible. The Chinese felt secure in his overtures, knowing they were not from a liberal who might—like Woodrow Wilson in another time—be repudiated by a conservative Congress. As a result, the Nixon move stirred worldwide feeling that a new era was at hand.

Early in 1972, plane-loads of television equipment and personnel were flown to Peking, and camera positions were prepared on the

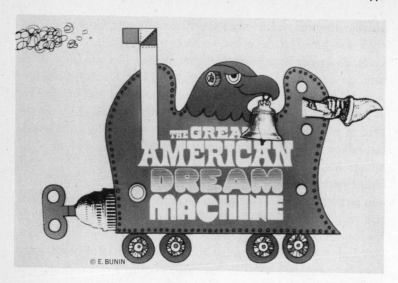

© E. BUNIN

WNET

The Great American Dream Machine—PBS series. Above, its animated opening; below, Jane Fonda in series of satirical sketches. **WNET**

China—1972.   NBC

Great Wall and elsewhere. The events aroused expectancy comparable to the first moon landing: a *terra incognita*, a world of mystery, was opening at last.

What audiences eventually saw *was* mysterious, in a fashion characteristic of television diplomacy. They saw spectacular banquets, toasts, handshakes, and smiles, but learned almost nothing of what was said in off-camera talks, beyond a report that the two powers had agreed to "normalize" relations, and to trade. But perhaps they learned what there was to learn. For this was not a television glimpse of a diplomatic maneuver. The telecast itself was the maneuver: a symbolic moment for the eyes of the world.

The venture was planned with awesome efficiency. The President knew exactly where to stop on the Great Wall to survey the world before him. It was noted that he had arranged to land in Peking in network prime time. Later his plane arrived back in Washington in prime time; it did so by waiting for some hours on the ground in Anchorage, Alaska.

Three months later came the first visit of an American President to Moscow. Again the world saw symbolic handshakes; it learned few specifics, but witnessed harmony and enthusiasm. Major network newsmen were again on hand to add descriptive details—Walter Cronkite, John Chancellor, Howard K. Smith. There was no "instant analysis." En route home, further handshakes and pageantry and waving crowds were telecast from Warsaw.

Then Nixon climaxed the travel sequence with an unprecedented video tour-de-force. Landing at Andrews Air Force Base on June 1, he went by helicopter directly to the Capitol—the first time a President had thus descended on Congress—to report to a joint session, and via television to the nation and the world, on his "journey for peace." He was interrupted repeatedly by bursts of applause.

With this sequence of summit telecasts, Nixon had scored a reverberating political coup. Those who had deplored the cold war, and generally opposed Nixon, were neutralized, in many cases won over. The anti-war forces were thrown off balance. For many people it was now impossible not to believe that the Vietnam war would be resolved within the context of Great Power amity and good-will.

A few cold-war zealots were indignant that Nixon had befriended communist China. But he was not likely to lose their support; they had nowhere else to go.

The televised journeys set the stage for the 1972 presidential elections. Nixon returned on the eve of the nominating conventions. His renomination had long been assured. On the strength of his world exploits, overwhelming reelection now seemed likely.

But Nixon was not one to settle for a likelihood. Perhaps he was haunted by memories of past defeats—in the 1960 presidential election and the 1962 California governorship race, both of which had seemed to promise victory. This time certainty would be made more certain by any means available. A Committee for the Re-election of the President was raising the greatest of all campaign war chests, swelling it—it was later revealed—by various illegal means. And clandestine espionage and sabotage operations, already set in motion before the President's journeys, were in progress against major Democratic contenders. Documents were forged to discredit Senators Hubert Humphrey, Henry Jackson, and Edmund Muskie. A unit under ex-CIA agent E. Howard Hunt, veteran of Guatemala and the Bay of Pigs and now in service at the White House, gave special attention to Edward Kennedy and the Kennedy family, past and present. Forged material was prepared for possible use in the event of his nomination. The White House hoped Senator George McGovern would win the nomination; he had campaigned almost solely on opposition to the Vietnam war and could find himself without an issue.

The covert operations, in large part conducted from the White House, proceeded with highest professional efficiency—until the night of June 17, two weeks after the President's return, when a bizarre news item erupted into headlines and television newscasts. Five intruders were arrested in the middle of the night in Democratic Party Headquarters in the Watergate apartments in Washington. Bugging equipment was confiscated; also cameras, and many $100 bills numbered in sequence, and address books which listed, among other names, "Howard Hunt, WH"—apparently, the White House.

Ronald Ziegler, Nixon press secretary, dismissed the episode as a "third-rate burglary attempt." Two days later the President scheduled a televised press conference, telling the cameras and microphones that electronic surveillance had "no place whatever in our electoral process or in our governmental process." The FBI said it was investigating. The Republicans hinted they were having similar "security" problems. Most newscasts treated the episode with a light touch—an oddity in the news.

A speculative explanation, discussed at length on the public television series *Firing Line*, featuring the writer William F. Buckley, was that the intruders—several of whom were anti-Castro Cubans and alumni of the Bay of Pigs—were seeking evidence that the Democratic Party was getting help from Castro and had made a deal with him. This theory deflected suspicion from the Republicans to the Democrats.

No network made its own inquiry into the Watergate mystery. Among news media only the Washington *Post*, at this time, felt the episode called for intensive investigative efforts. Meanwhile the break-in was pushed from the headlines by the nominating conventions. In July television viewers watched a deeply divided Democratic Party nominate McGovern; in August they saw a festive Republican convention renominate Nixon and Agnew by acclamation.

During the following months Nixon made few campaign telecasts of a conventional sort. In news telecasts he was seen receiving foreign dignitaries; the image was that of a world leader above the conflict, busy with world issues.

In October he announced that his Vietnam strategy was bearing fruit: Henry Kissinger had reached a breakthrough in talks with North Vietnam. Kissinger, on television, said a few details needed to be resolved, but peace was "within reach." He gave no further details.

Throughout these weeks the Washington *Post*—and then the New York *Times* and others—reported new Watergate clues that seemed to reach into widening circles of criminal activity. Network news programs cautiously mentioned the astonishing allegations—along with White House denunciations of them as libelous "innuendo."

McGovern, switching in his final campaign telecasts from the war issue—which seemed to be disappearing—to the rapidly accumulating Watergate reports, called the Nixon regime "the most corrupt" in American history. Republicans dismissed the accusa-

Report from Secretary of State Henry Kissinger. At left, anchorman John
Chancellor.   NBC

tions as the rantings of a desperate candidate, and they seemed so to
many voters.

On election day Nixon won 49 states; McGovern won only
Massachusetts and the District of Columbia. With an electoral
vote of 520-17, Nixon had achieved one of the greatest of land-
slides.

The first Watergate trials—of those arrested in connection with
the break-in—began early in 1973. On January 21 sequestered Watergate jurors were permitted to watch on television the jubilant inaugural festivities, without having an inkling of the President's involvement in matters they were considering. The defendants had,

at the direction of the President, received large sums for their silence. Extensive perjury was committed.

The Nixon administration had apparently weathered the Watergate episode. On January 27 an agreement "on ending the war and restoring peace in Vietnam" was signed in Paris. The President stood high in prestige throughout the world.

But during the following months further evidence accumulated, and by March began to ensnare the President. The Senate voted a Watergate inquiry, to be chaired by Senator Sam Ervin of North Carolina. It decided to open its hearings to television.

Until mid-1973 President Nixon, by exercising the prerogatives of presidential television to the full, had remained in control. Again and again he had been able to deflect criticism, stifle opposition, shift attention, set the national agenda, dramatize achievements, pillory detractors—all this supported by clandestine warfare against "enemies." But in mid-1973 presidential television was confronting something else—congressional television.

This was a phenomenon that erupted seldom but, when it did, had explosive possibilities. Congressional television rested on premises quite different from those of presidential television. Preemption of time, whether prime time or marginal time, was not a congressional privilege. Congress or its committees could only, from time to time, invite cameras and microphones into their deliberations. This might result in a 40-second newscast item—seldom more. In the case of Vietnam hearings, an *I Love Lucy* rerun had seemed to CBS a preferable offering. Occasionally, the impending drama seemed promising, as well as important.

The Watergate hearings came at a crucial moment in the history of public television. In 1972 Congress had passed a two-year authorization of $155 million for public broadcasting, but the President had vetoed it, as well as several lesser authorizations. Public broadcasting found itself living on a starvation diet. Clay Whitehead, White House spokesman on such matters, made it clear what public television should do to secure federal funds. It should stop competing for big audiences with things like *The Great American Dream Machine*. Its service should be supplementary. It should be decentralized, with the emphasis on local programs. To many this seemed a prescription for returning to the first, disastrous days of "educational television"—academic lectures, panels, interviews. During 1972-73 the field was swept by layoffs and resignations. Its conservative elements meanwhile pushed for the reforms demanded by the administration. Then came the Watergate hearings.

Public television decided to carry them—live by day, repeated via tape at night. For months its talent bills were minimal, but the response was staggering. In the way that the Army-McCarthy hearings had given ABC-TV a blood transfusion, so the Watergate hearings gave public television a new lease on life. Some of its stations gained the highest ratings in their history. To many of their executives, it seemed ironic that the President's displeasure, and their resulting poverty, had pushed them toward this salvation.

Commercial television also decided to carry the hearings, rotating live coverage among the three networks, to minimize advertising losses. They were somewhat discomfited to find that Watergate outpulled their own top-ranking daytime serials and game-shows.

Watergate became an obsession with viewers. Some watched live hearings all day, the taped repeats at night. Chairman Sam Ervin,

---

Daytime Nielsens: July 9-13, 1973

WATERGATE (NBC)	10.7	*Watergate wins.* The networks took turns carrying the Watergate hearings—and won rating battles with them. Noncommercial television, not included in Nielsen reports, was also carrying the hearings. John Dean had just completed his testimony.
Let's Make a Deal	10.0	
WATERGATE (ABC)	9.6	
Split Second	9.5	
Newlywed Game	9.4	
Girl in My Life	9.4	
As the World Turns	9.2	
WATERGATE (CBS)	9.1	
All My Children	9.1	
Days of Our Lives	8.8	

Aphorisms . . .   NBC

with his store of Bible quotations and aphorisms, became a folk
hero. The long, detailed testimony of former White House counsel
John Dean—extremely damaging to the President—riveted the national attention.

As witnesses recanted perjured testimony given earlier, and told
their stories, the vision that emerged for viewers was of a snake-pit
of duplicity and corruption guarding the Nixon presidency—espionage, sabotage, bribery, burglary, subornation of perjury. The
President's involvement became increasingly apparent.

President Nixon's "approval rating" as reported by Gallup polls
had stood at 68 per cent after the January ceasefire announcement;
by August it had fallen to 31 per cent, the lowest presidential rating
in twenty years.

RON ZIEGLER
WHITE HOUSE NEWS SECRETARY

Denials . . .   NBC

By that time a startling development had shifted the focus of attention. During testimony in July a former presidential assistant,
Alexander P. Butterfield, mentioned a voice-activated recording
system that had been in operation in various White House offices
and at Camp David since 1971, known to only a handful of people.
Tapes relevant to current inquiries were at once requested—then
subpoenaed—for the Ervin committee and Watergate grand jury.
Nixon rejected the requests and subpoenas; then released selected
tapes, one with an 18½-minute erasure; then flatly refused to surrender more, citing "presidential confidentiality" and "national security." Since much testimony in Watergate trials, past and future,
could be supported or negated by the tapes, the refusal raised an
obstruction-of-justice issue. The stage was set for legal struggle

over this issue. In the fall of 1973 it began to wind its way through the courts.

Simultaneously new Nixon administration scandals filled newscasts: Agnew's resignation, after revelations of bribery payments started during his Maryland governorship and continuing during his vice presidency; a finding that the President himself had underpaid his taxes by $432,787.13; charges that campaign contributions from dairy interests, ITT, Howard Hughes and others had been cash payments for favorable administrative decisions. Such matters received detailed comment on the three networks, and on such public television series as *Bill Moyers' Journal* and *Washington Week in Review*. CBS restored "instant analysis."

During this period of mounting reverses, Nixon made several television appearances to halt the flood. All bore resemblances to the Checkers telecast: disclosures were made, and described as unprecedented concessions, offered to lay issues to rest. In all, he pictured himself as a victim of vicious attacks. In all, he merged his cause with larger concerns—America, the world, lasting peace, history. "I want these to be the best days in America's history because I love America. . . . God bless America. And God bless each and every one of you."

It had worked in the Checkers speech. The Checkers triumph may, in a sense, have lured him to disaster, making him feel he could extricate himself from almost any dilemma by appearing on the tube and refocusing the national attention. It did not work now.

The most dramatic attempt came on April 29, 1974. The House of Representatives had voted funds for an impeachment inquiry by its judiciary committee. The President was under subpoena to deliver tapes of 141 presidential conversations to the judiciary committee—and of 64 to the Watergate prosecutor. At this juncture Nixon pre-empted prime time.

He was at a desk. Behind him viewers could see enormous stacks of bound volumes. The President said he had decided to turn over to the judiciary committee—and at the same time make public—

edited transcripts of White House conversations relating to Watergate. "As far the President's role with regard to Watergate is concerned, the entire story is here." He conceded that some passages would be seen as damaging, confusing; but overall, the massive material would show his innocence.

For the moment, it seemed a masterly performance. But within hours it had plunged his Gallup rating to a new low—below 30 per cent—and brought a renewal of demands for the tapes. There were many reasons.

The President had made his own selection; many of the requested conversations were not included in the transcripts. The transcripts, punctuated throughout with "expletive deleted" and "unintelligible," had been heavily edited. Some transcripts had to do with tapes already surrendered; the judiciary committee had its own transcripts of these, and found startling contrasts between them and the President's transcripts. In the editing process, the White House had omitted damaging passages, sometimes without any indication of an omission. Among omissions were such passages as a Nixon comment on the Washington *Post:* "The main thing is, the Washington *Post* is going to have a damnable, damnable thing out of this one. They have a TV station, you know."

The transcripts, aside from these shocking deficiencies, offered horrifying glimpses of the moral tone of discussions in the Oval Office—cynical, profane, amoral, scheming. Far from establishing the President's innocence, they suggested a ceaseless obsession with game plans for crushing enemies and thwarting investigation, often by illegal or dubious methods. If the selected passages were meant to exonerate the President, what would other passages reveal?

Apparently Nixon had hoped that the juiciness of some passages would satisfy public appetite and bring the matter to an end; also, that the sheer bulk of the material (1,308 pages, about 350,000 words) would keep it largely unread, or at least keep it off the air. But he was mistaken. Noncommercial radio stations—struggling, like public television, with marginal budgets—began marathon on-

June 13, 1974—Egypt. The last ecstasy.   UPI

the-air readings of the entire transcript, lasting some forty hours. The Pacifica radio stations did likewise, assigning roles to well-known actors, and using beeps and other symbolic sounds for "unintelligible" and "expletive omitted." Television network newscasts staged similar readings of selected passages, with montages of photographs to identify the speakers. Thus the transcripts, as edited by the White House, received saturation coverage. They set the stage for a television sequel, the beginning of the impeachment process in the House judiciary committee.

The judiciary committee decided to open its final deliberations to television, but first to hear witnesses behind closed doors. As it did so, Nixon had one more television spectacular in store—one of the most extraordinary—to seize the spotlight. He had arranged a trip to the Middle East. Once more television networks performed their miracles of coordinated coverage. Once more viewers were astounded to see screaming crowds welcoming the President—in Egypt, Syria, Israel. Then one more visit to Moscow. Once again, in this sequence, he projected the image of a world leader hard at work, in spite of lesser mortals sniping at him back home.

His return in July 1974 was very different from his previous homecoming. Instead of a joint session of Congress and thunderous applause, there was the judiciary committee preparing for the final, televised part of its impeachment deliberations. And the nation was ready to watch.

Would the presence of cameras trivialize the momentous historic occasion? Some thought it would; Ronald Ziegler called the committee a "kangaroo court." But viewers got a different impression. The thirty-eight members of the committee, one after another, assessed the evidence, weighed the balance, stated conclusions—carefully, soul-searchingly, sometimes agonizingly, often in impressive language. Some were relatively new members of Congress, unknown to the nation at large. But by the end of the week they had done much, wrote Shana Alexander in *Newsweek*, "to restore one's faith in this country's moral tone." Then, on three counts, they voted for impeachment by substantial majorities.

There was an immediate and startling epilogue—bringing more drama to the tube. While the committee deliberated, an 8-0 Supreme Court decision ordered the White House to release the subpoenaed material. When the tapes, delivered after the committee vote, were finally heard by members, their content seemed so damaging to the President's case—he had lied repeatedly, to the country, the press, and his own counsel—that Congressmen who had voted against impeachment appeared individually on television to announce that they were changing their votes. The decision became unanimous. Overwhelming ratification by the House became certain. Conviction by the Senate seemed equally inevitable. Senator Goldwater was quoted: "This man must go." A deputation of leading Republican statesmen visited the President to convey the gravity of his plight.

August 8, 1974—Washington. Resignation.   UPI

On August 8, at 9 p.m., President Nixon appeared on television to announce his resignation, effective the following day. It had become clear, he said, that he no longer had "a strong enough political base in Congress" to continue in office. There was no acknowledgement of wrongdoing.

By some perverse obsession, he wanted even the final, devastating hours of his defeat to be on the tube. On the following morning viewers watched his farewell to staff and friends. For more than an hour he rambled incoherently and irrelevantly. He spoke as though he had been visited by some catastrophe not of his making. Then a helicopter took him to Air Force One, for the flight to California. There he was briefly seen again on television, waving to airport crowds as though campaigning. Then he vanished into seclusion.

The tube was already offering glimpses of a new style of presidential television. Newsmen, waiting at dawn outside the home of Gerald Ford, recently chosen Vice President, were able to photograph him opening the front door in his dressing gown, to bring in the paper and the milk. Inaugurated at noon, he spoke briefly with relaxed simplicity.

Although his style represented sharp change, his policy decisions gave a sense of continuity. In one of his earliest television appearances, he pardoned Nixon for all criminal acts of his presidency, revealed and unrevealed. And President Ford soon urged new military aid for U.S.-supported regimes in South Vietnam and Cambodia, although both—corrupt and unpopular—seemed headed for disaster. Relations between President Ford and the mass media, having begun on a warm and cordial note, soon exhibited some of the edginess of other days.

The proper role of television in relation to government had become a tense issue. Television had played a part in the fall of a President; in the end, it had provided the arena in which the drama was played out.

There were those who thought that the news media had hounded the President of the United States out of office. Justice Potter Stewart of the U.S. Supreme Court thought differently. "On the contrary," he said; they had done what was intended by those who wrote the First Amendment to the Constitution. Through the guarantee of a free press they had meant "to create a fourth institution outside government as an additional check on the three official branches." It was never meant, he said, to be a "neutral conduit."

For some years television had edged, often reluctantly, into that

role of an "additional check," a thoughtful observer, an elder states-
man, an ombudsman. The role had earned it gratitude, but also
hatred.

The bizarre dramas of presidential television faded quickly, and
a more familiar look came over the tube. Even as the Vietnam War
ended—with the collapse of America's client regime in South Vietnam—a new season barreled in with kaleidoscopic montages of comedy, melodrama, soap opera intrigue, screaming game shows, football, cartoons, thousands of commercials. But a new digression was
already in the offing, and it seemed to be what the nation needed.

FIESTAS

For the two-hundredth birthday of the United States of America—
July 4, 1976—television was made to order. For months leading up
to the event, history was invoked in dramas long and short but also
in commercials, talk shows, quizzes, and inspirational station-break
messages. Citizens were reminded of George Washington, Abraham
Lincoln, Thomas Jefferson, Benjamin Franklin, the Roosevelt family, the Adams family, and other historic figures who seldom made
it into prime time. Their wives too got attention, with an award-
winning *Diaries of First Ladies*. Then, on July 4, a panoply of special events. The nation watched a stately, unforgettable armada of
full-rigged sailing ships gliding up the Hudson; later in the day,
firework displays from Washington, D.C., before a million people
dotting the Mall; and from far and wide, community pageants and
parades.

The nation, sharing the passing television years, had had a bad
taste in its mouth. The Vietnam War, defeat on the battlefield,
assassinations, a disgraced President and Vice President, revelations
of CIA and FBI crimes, the youth revolt, the rise of drugs—all had
jolted the nation's self-esteem and confidence. So the Bicentennial
celebrations were balm. As old glories were remembered, night-

mares faded. The forgetting process was rapid. Recent history began to be amended by a pervasive spirit of revisionism. Before long, television no longer referred to Vietnam as a mistake or a blot on American history; it became, like other wars, an ordeal that Americans had served with heroism and for noble ends.

A rising candidate for the presidency, Jimmy Carter of Georgia, peanut farmer and former governor, referred to the war in this way. He seemed to be a figure of reconciliation. Most Americans had never heard of him until they began getting frequent glimpses of him on the tube. Because he won early primaries through intensive local campaigns, the networks dubbed him a "front runner" and gave him wide news coverage. His down-to-earth manner seemed to win quick response. He was Jimmy, not James. His remoteness from national politics gave him an aura of political cleanliness, which he exploited fully in campaign spots. He said: "I'll never lie to you." The Bicentennial culminated in the election of Jimmy Carter as President with Walter Mondale as Vice President, defeating Gerald R. Ford and Robert Dole by 57 electoral votes. A few weeks later Jimmy Carter and his wife Rosalyn forsook the limousined inaugural drive down Pennsylvania Avenue to walk the final miles, smiling and hatless—a master touch of television symbolism, that seemed to announce the end of the imperial presidency.

One of Carter's assets was a record of warm relationships with blacks. His rise was widely hailed by blacks. Amy Carter, daughter of the President, entered a District of Columbia public school attended largely by black children; it provided another telling television moment, contrasting sharply with violent school-integration episodes televised in earlier years. Carter's appointee as United Nations Ambassador, the black Andrew Young, made it at once clear that closer ties with black nations of Africa were high on the Carter agenda.

As though riding the crest of this mood, ABC-TV early in 1977 launched a project that would have seemed unthinkable a few years before: on eight consecutive nights, January 23-30, it presented the mini-series *Roots*, an adaptation of author Alex Haley's account of his search for—and discovery of—the African village from which his ancestors had come. Produced by David Wolper, the series dramatized a family history: Haley's ancestor Kunta Kinte and his fellow villagers seized by slave traders and brought to America in chains, and the experience of their descendants through generations of slavery to the Emancipation.

It is a measure of the gingerliness with which such subject matter has been handled in most media—from school textbooks to television—that *Roots* had explosive impact. The eighth and final program apparently reached the largest audience of any sponsored telecast to date. This led to a new series of *Roots* programs, which followed the Haley family history to the present against the shifting tides of race relations. Meanwhile, the *Roots* explosion led NBC-TV—April 16-19, 1978—to present *Holocaust*, a four-part dramatization of the Jewish experience of the Hitler "final solution" extermination program. This won the largest audience of 1978. Both *Roots* and *Holocaust* went on to triumphant international syndication.

The wide acceptance of these projects took many in the industry by surprise. It went against accepted notions of "mass audience" preferences. Critics found both series full of stereotypes, a characteristic seldom avoided in such panoramic projects. But perhaps the important aspect of both projects was that they took steps that had long seemed beyond practical possibility. Both were in the spirit of reexamination and rededication furthered by the Bicentennial. A side effect of *Roots* was that libraries throughout the country were besieged by people wishing to explore genealogical collections for information about their own roots.

If the nation was celebrating a birthday, so was the broadcasting industry. NBC marked its fiftieth in 1976; CBS observed its in 1977. Both events called for jubilee programming and much self-congratulation. In 1976 a Museum of Broadcasting was opened in New York City, dedicated by its chief benefactor, William Paley, and headed by another broadcasting veteran, Robert Saudek, whose career had begun with a 1921 appearance on KDKA, Pittsburgh, and had included an ABC vice presidency. All networks contributed surviving radio and television treasures. A 1976 copyright law directed the Library of Congress to create an American Television and Radio Archives to preserve "the broadcasting heritage of the American people." Its organization was begun two years later. The year 1976 also marked the one-hundredth anniversary of the debut of the telephone, an event that had coincided with the nation's Centennial and that had stirred vivid imaginings of a radio and television age and hastened research to bring it into being. Thus the late 1970's were a time of unprecedented retrospection and celebration, which in turn led to a probing of the future.

The advent of television was widely compared, in its impact, with that of the Gutenberg printing press centuries earlier. Television was beginning to be seen as the more revolutionary innovation. The reasons were so obvious that they had seldom been discussed. Television viewing required no skill beyond normal human functions. Reading, on the other hand, was a skill acquired over years via effort and drilling—and not acquired by everyone. It generally involved the mediation of father, mother, grandfather, grandmother, teacher, priest, and others, a factor favoring social continuity, a transmittal of values. Television short-circuited all this. It could begin in cradle or playpen, and often did. It could bypass father, mother, grandfather, grandmother. It reached the child long before teacher and priest. Their role in the acculturation process had been sharply reduced. They had sporadically, fitfully, sought to recapture a more decisive role by seeking to control the images on the tube—but that control had slipped elsewhere, to the world of business. In a development of historic significance, television's messages had become dominant social doctrine.

In the course of the retrospective observances Vincent T. Wasilewski, president of the National Association of Broadcasters, described American television as "the most successful and universally accepted business enterprise in history," and there seemed to be no disposition to dispute him. The magazine *Advertising Age*, in its own Bicentennial assessments, said that the television years had brought "the most dizzying leap forward in American history . . . revolutionizing everything from sales pitches to politics."

Underlining these pronouncements, television advertising revenues continued upward. In 1977 network sales stood at $3.6 billion, up 21 per cent over 1976, and the rise continued. Income from foreign program sales likewise kept zooming: 1976, $180 million; 1977, $240 million; 1978, $280 million.

Yet despite the flow of cash and the public euphoria, a deep uneasiness was taking hold of American television. Its trade press kept chronicling technological developments—relating to cable, two-way television, pay-television, fiber optics, satellites, videodiscs, videocassettes, teletext—that kept the industry in constant uncertainty about its future. And in 1977, for the very first time, a Roper study showed a drop in the public's "esteem" for television. Another study showed a first-time-ever drop in viewing. Did the findings reflect a shift—the beginnings of a shift—of public affection to new things, and if so, to what? The figures could be dismissed as statistically unimportant, but they brought tremors just the same. Executive upheavals were the order of the day, especially at networks. Program plans were scrutinized, overhauled.

The new pressures aggravated an already declining morale. The sense of a pioneering venture had long slipped away from the industry. While it kept calling itself young, it felt old. All segments were affected.

In public television, crisis was a fixture. Financial problems seemed insoluble. The programming had in recent years reached high levels with such series as *Nova*, occasional *National Geographic* specials, the news analyses of the *MacNeil-Lehrer Report*, the acclaimed *Sesame Street*, and such brilliant imports as *The Ascent of Man* featuring Jacob Bronowski, directed by Adrian Malone. But every public-television station now featured endless fund appeals; at money-raising time, sales pitches were as relentless as those of commercial television, with admired artists transformed into pitchmen. To obtain federal funds, which involved stiff matching requirements, all this was necessary. But the federal funds and on-the-air appeals were never enough, and the system depended more and more on corporate financing of programs. At stations the successful fund raisers—often ex-advertising men at home in the sponsor world—were the key to survival. This pushed the system steadily toward cautious "cultural" programming. Prime time on public television became a reflection of corporate choices. The system felt—and looked—increasingly commercial.

The public radio system, which had seemed to start a radio renaissance with a rich array of national programs including the often brilliant 90-minute news series *All Things Considered*, was deep in parallel crises and efforts. With local fund marathons and sponsor appeals, the system vied with public television for the same dollars, and likewise worried about its commercial drift.

The avowedly commercial television had its own problems. Quite aside from long-range quandaries, its program planning had become a dispiriting, mechanistic exercise—no longer a release of creative energies but an application of computerized data. A quasi-scientific mystique had taken charge.

DEMOGRAPHICS

Demographics was the word of the hour. Nielsen, which had long provided audience statistics derived from audimeters—mechanisms placed in a sampling of television homes—had originally reported only audience *size*. But Nielsen had gradually added other data—obtained from diaries kept by another sampling of homes, which received a modest fee for filling out and returning the Nielsen diaries. Ratings computed from the diaries were a useful check on audimeter ratings, but also gave additional information, which sponsors especially cherished. The diaries indicated which members of a family watched which programs. Since the nature and composition of each Nielsen family was known to the Nielsen organization and the details were available in its data banks, Nielsen computers could now define a program's audience in terms of sex, age, economic and educational status, urban and rural location, and other factors. During the 1970's this demographic information began to dominate trade talk and the buying and selling of 30-second and 60-second slots for commercials.

Nielsen broke its audience information into age groups: 18-24, 25-34, 35-49, 50-64, 65-plus, etc. These same groupings were utilized by another service, the Brand Rating Index, which told a sponsor what kind of people, in demographic terms, were buying his products. For sponsors and their agents, sponsorship thus tended to become a matching game.

CBS pushed this idea. In the early 1970's it sent sponsors and agents a promotion piece entitled *Where the Girls Are*. Its cover featured a revolving disc, which could reveal at a glance the age distribution of scores of products bought primarily by women. "And the pages inside," said the brochure, "show how to apply this handy information to Nielsen's new audience reports by age of lady viewer."

Negotiations between sponsor and network, via the sponsor's advertising agency, now resembled transactions to deliver specific blocks of viewers. The agency would tell the network: "For deodorant Y, our client is prepared to invest $2 million in women 18-49. Other viewers do not interest him; he doesn't care to pay for irrelevant viewers. But for women 18-49 he is ready to pay Z dollars per thousand women. What slots can you offer?"

Gone were the days when sponsor decisions might derive from personal reactions to programs. Such decisions now seemed "elitism." Hunches were out, science in. A sponsor did not even need to watch programs. He watched charts and computer terminals. Some sponsors acquired computer terminals linked to the Nielsen

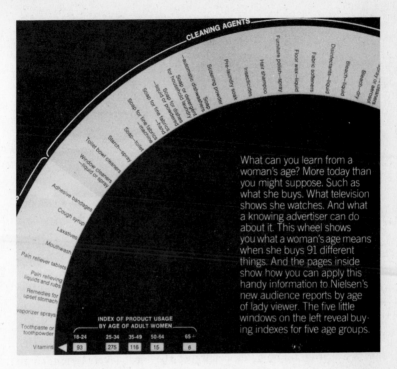

The wheel contains the following labels:

CLEANING AGENTS
Soap or detergent
for household laundry
Soap to dishes
—liquid or powdered
Soap for fine fabrics
—hand
Soap for fine fabrics
—machine
Soap—toilet
Starch—spray
Toilet bowl cleaners
Window cleaners
—liquid or spray
Adhesive bandages
Cough syrup
Laxatives
Mouthwash
Pain reliever tablets
Pain relieving
liquids and rubs
Remedies for
upset stomach
Vaporizer sprays
Toothpaste or
toothpowder
Vitamins

Soap or detergent
for automatic dishwasher
Scouring powder
Pre-laundry soak
Insecticides
Hair shampoo
Furniture polish—spray
Floor wax—liquid
Fabric softeners
Disinfectants—liquid
Bleach—liquid
Bleach—dry

What can you learn from a woman's age? More today than you might suppose. Such as what she buys. What television shows she watches. And what a knowing advertiser can do about it. This wheel shows you what a woman's age means when she buys 91 different things. And the pages inside show how you can apply this handy information to Nielsen's new audience reports by age of lady viewer. The five little windows on the left reveal buying indexes for five age groups.

INDEX OF PRODUCT USAGE
BY AGE OF ADULT WOMEN.

18-24	25-34	35-49	50-64	65+
93	275	116	15	6

Demographic dial—from CBS brochure *Where the Girls Are*, issued to help sponsors match program demographics to product demographics. Note young age spread of vitamin buyers. Laxative buyers show contrasting pattern: (18-24) 38, (25-34) 51, (35-49) 85, (50-64) 126, (65+) 210.   CBS

data bank in Dunedin, Florida, for prompt reception of Nielsen computations.

Many sponsors were intent on reaching younger, urban women, whose decisions in supermarket and drugstore spelled success or failure for scores of mass-market products—cosmetics, toiletries, processed foods, soft drinks, candies. The hold won over this audience group by such series as *Six Million Dollar Man* (premiered

1973), *Happy Days* (1974), *Starsky & Hutch* (1975), *Bionic Woman, Laverne & Shirley*, and *Charlie's Angels* (1976), *Three's Company* (1977), and *Mork & Mindy* (1978) sent the value of slots in these series as high as $50,000 to 90,000 per 30-second slot during the following years.

The makers of expensive cars, computers, and business machines had a different problem. They needed male viewers in their prime, an especially hard-to-reach group. For their attention *en masse* a 30-second slot in a Super Bowl game could be worth $100,000 or more. Newscasts and occasional documentaries, while needed by broadcasters for public relations and license protection, reached smaller, older audiences, perhaps useful for institutional spots and products aimed at older buyers—denture fixatives, pain relievers, stomach settlers, decaffeinated coffee. But the older folk were not big spenders, and their nationwide attention might be bought for as little as $10,000 to 20,000 per 30-second slot. Programs yielding such low-revenue slots seemed to network executives an obstacle to the much higher earnings that would be possible with other programming. The demographic mania produced intense efforts to jazz up news programming, especially at the local level. It tended to discourage the scheduling of documentaries unless of sensational content, or to sidetrack them to unfavorable spots in the schedule. It sometimes affected other programming also: the Red Skelton and *Gunsmoke* series, while still high in numerical ratings, were canceled because they were found to be reaching an older, rural audience, demographically unlucrative. While older people comprised a growing share of the population, their interests were not the key to large profits.

The demographic fixation was anathema to most script writers and directors. Long accustomed to tailoring their work to formula-built series, they looked on demographic litmus tests as a further outrage to the creative process.

In the mid-1970's demographic data seemed to favor heroes and heroines with magic powers—laboratory creations or people from

outer space. Such characters also populated many commercials.
What was behind the superperson surge? Was it to some extent
influenced by the "women's lib" movement? Or by news stories
about laboratory experiments with genes? Or was the nation,
nettled by its Vietnam experience, eager for new assurance of an
unlimited potential, a capacity for miracles?

Humans with god-like powers appear to be as old as storytelling
itself. In Greek mythology the hero who aspired to such powers
received a comeuppance. The wings of Icarus melted as he flew too
close to the sun, and he crashed. Prometheus, who seized fire from
the heavens, ended up chained to a rock, his liver a prey to an
eagle. Greek mythology seemed to warn that aspiration to god-like
action was *hubris*—overweening pride. But television mythology did
not recognize the idea of *hubris* and had no term for it. Its message,
in programs and commercials, was a ceaseless call to miracles. Man
and his products could repair all the deficiencies of nature. And he
could roam the universe, juggling atoms and genes. Television
supermen and superwomen did not fail: day after day they over-
came mysterious enemies and saved themselves as well as the universe from disaster.

Within the industry, the new magic era was set in motion by
ABC-TV, and this seemed in character. ABC-TV had long had

Women 18-34		*Demographics and ABC-TV.*
Laverne & Shirley (ABC)	29.2	If ABC-TV was doing well in
Happy Days (ABC)	26.9	overall ratings, it was doing
Rich Man, Poor Man (ABC)	26.8	even better in reaching demo-
Bionic Woman (ABC)	22.0	graphically profitable groups,
Starsky & Hutch (ABC)	22.0	with eight out of the ten top
Six Million Dollar Man (ABC)	21.7	favorites among women of 18
ABC Monday Movie (ABC)	21.4	to 34. Figures based on Niel-
All in the Family (CBS)	21.4	sen reports of January-April,
M*A*S*H (CBS)	21.0	1976. (*Advertising Age*, May
ABC Sunday Movie (ABC)	20.7	17, 1976)

special success with youthful audiences, and the magic trend enhanced it. If ABC-TV was doing well in quantitive audience data, it was doing even better in demographic data. The other networks were not unmindful of factors involved in this. Along with magic, they included sexual titillation and violent action, and the rivals responded in kind. Thus the recurrent problems of "sex and violence" came once more to the fore—and produced a new backlash. This resulted in a curious and revealing series of events called Family Time.

SQUEAKY CLEAN

In Washington the influential Senator John Pastore of Rhode Island, chairman of the Senate communications subcommittee that presided over broadcasting legislation and also chairman of the Senate appropriations subcommittee that controlled the FCC budget, kept telling the FCC and the industry that they should do something about television sex and violence before Congress took matters into its own hands with legislation they might not like. Similarly, FCC chairman Richard E. Wiley, who took office in 1974, kept telling industry members they should, via "self-regulation," do something about sex and violence before Congress or the FCC was forced to take actions they might not like. He even convened a meeting of network executives to convey this urgent message.

Most of the executives had a *déjà vu* feeling about this, and they doubted the feasibility—even the legality—of concerted action. But the chief CBS representative, Arthur Taylor, did not.

Arthur Taylor had recently come to CBS from the position of chief financial officer of the International Paper Company, to assume the role of President, CBS, Inc. He had no background in broadcasting, but what CBS chairman William Paley felt was needed, at a time when CBS was turning into a conglomerate with diverse interests and had a large surplus for additional ventures, was a financial wizard, a man at home in complex corporate organizations. Taylor was handsome, an effective spokesman, and only thirty-seven when he joined CBS. He was looked on as Paley's heir apparent.

His friends and relatives kept telling him he should do something about sex and violence. Taylor agreed. The task for which he had been brought to CBS, Inc., was mainly a financial and organizational one, but he felt this other matter called for top-level attention. His energetic persuasions during the following months, directed at fellow members of the industry and in frequent touch with FCC chairman Wiley, resulted in adoption by the National Association of Broadcasters Code Authority of a new "family viewing policy." During the hours 7-9 p.m. eastern time (or 6-8 p.m. central time), it would be NAB code policy that "entertainment programming inappropriate for viewing by a general family audience should not be broadcast." The period was variously called Family Time or the Family Hour.* The plan was officially endorsed by all three networks, though with foot-dragging by individual executives. It was widely publicized by the industry.

It soon became clear that the plan did not reduce violence or sexual titillation, but brought a shuffling of schedules as some early-evening programs were moved to later spots and vice versa. This attracted some sardonic comment. Young people who might be adversely affected by violent or sexual programs could not be assumed to be safely tucked in bed by 9 p.m. eastern time or 8 p.m. central time. And the policy was soon seen to be hurting ratings during the Family Time period. Perhaps the plan would prove merely a spur to later viewing.

The later hours were, in any case, changing rapidly, due to another set of circumstances. Since the mid-1950's, when the major studios began releasing feature films to television, networks and sta-

* Network executives tended to call it the Family Hour because they were mainly concerned with the 8-9 period; 7-7:30 was used for news, and 7:30-8 was locally programmed.

tions had been highly dependent on this programming. At first, it had consisted of "old movies," but the backlog had long been used up, and now features were coming to television soon after their use in theaters. The recent pictures were very different from the old. To draw people to movie theaters, studios had increasingly emphasized material *not* on television. The virtual elimination of censorship from the theatrical field during the 1950's and 1960's—following the Supreme Court decision of 1952 that films were a part of the "press" whose freedom was constitutionally guaranteed—had made this possible. The results had been diverse. There were sensitive films on long-forbidden themes. There were also violent and sexually explicit films, and some used the language of the street. Many such films had, nonetheless, won wide acceptance; American audiences were felt to have become "more sophisticated." Economic considerations strongly favored the continued scheduling of Hollywood features, in spite of the changed atmosphere of many recent releases. Their scheduling at late hours seemed a feasible solution.

It appeared to many observers that the networks had adopted Family Time to win acceptance for the shifting tone of the late hours. Television, while following the mores of the theatrical screen, was putting the public-relations spotlight on early-evening cleanliness and virtue.

While network managements apparently considered this a prudent maneuver, it enraged many creators of programs, particularly those most affected by Family Time. To the astonishment of the industry, a lawsuit was filed by the Writers Guild of America, supported by most independent producers; and another, separate suit was filed by writer-producer Norman Lear, the *All in the Family* creator. The suits charged violation of the First Amendment. The gist of that charge was that Family Time, though presented as "self-regulation," had been instituted under government threat. It was described as government action masquerading as private initiative.

If such suits, hinging on a constitutional rationale, caused astonishment, it was mainly because success seemed so unlikely. Reviewing his case, Geoffrey Cowan, counsel to the Writers Guild, summarized the prevailing skepticism as follows: "What judge would be willing, on the basis of a novel legal theory, to invalidate a policy that had the sound of motherhood, was, according to a *TV Guide* poll, supported by 82 per cent of the American public, and had the full support of the three television networks, the NAB, and the FCC?"

Nevertheless, the suits were filed. Writers Guild president David Rintels, widely admired—his one-man play *Clarence Darrow* had recently been seen on television in a brilliant performance by Henry Fonda—explained the decision: "A policy directed against sex and violence has in practice turned out to be something very different, a crusade against ideas."

In presenting their case before Judge Warren J. Ferguson, the Writers Guild offered testimony by several leading writers. One was Larry Gelbart, writer and co-producer of *M*A*S*H*. Debuted in 1972, *M*A*S*H* had won recognition as one of the most literate series on television. Focusing on an army medical unit in Korea, it built its episodes around problems of genuine concern to the army —sex, loneliness, homosexuality, drugs, venereal disease, bureaucratic infighting, crime—and had managed to do it in a manner that fascinated and delighted audiences but also won critical praise and many awards. The series style involved a light surface combined with integrity in the handling of touchy issues. Its characters had grown in complexity and clarity, and the ensemble performances achieved a rare quality of spontaneity. Its track record was an extraordinary one. Yet the inauguration of Family Time subjected *M*A*S*H* to immediate editorial harassment. A call from CBS informed Gelbart that four of the ten story proposals developed for the following season and previously approved by CBS—scripts had, in fact, been commissioned—might have to be scrapped or drastically revised. Gelbart felt that four years of *M*A*S*H* had shown that it could handle the themes meaningfully and with dignity. CBS now seemed to be telling him that those four years had been dedicated to prurience. He was determined to fight.

Another witness was writer-producer Danny Arnold of the ABC-TV series *Barney Miller*, which had debuted in 1975. It was a police series of unusual character. Built around the staff of a single big-city police department and the problems it confronted, *Barney Miller* was one of several recent series in which the people of the workplace had become a kind of family, under a benign father figure. In this respect *Barney Miller* resembled *The Mary Tyler Moore Show* and, to some extent, *M*A*S*H*. The success of such series had led to speculation that, with the erosion of family life, the workplace had for many people become the real center of "family" life. In any case, Chief Barney Miller presided over an engagingly diverse staff, each with private foibles, whose work held them together while they coped with the sometimes bizarre problems that assailed them from the outside world. Inevitably, prostitutes, thieves, and strange derelicts intruded on the family life. Like *M*A*S*H*, *Barney Miller* had a light touch but dealt with real social issues, and did so with grace and integrity. It had an educational aspect—avowedly so. Arnold told the court: "I think we're doing a tremendous disservice to the American people, to kids, if we keep telling them that life is *The Brady Bunch*."

Another witness was Allan Burns, a top writer and producer for *Rhoda*, spin-off of *The Mary Tyler Moore Show*, on which he had served in similar capacities. In earlier years he had written for the widely respected *Room 222*, which focused on problems of a schoolteacher in a big-city public school of diverse population. Like *M*A*S*H* and *Barney Miller*, these series tried to expand the subject matter of television drama but were never violent nor scabrous. To many viewers they represented network television at its best—original, tasteful, poignant. Soon after the proclamation of Family Time, Burns got a phone call from a CBS policy editor, who had begun going over scripts for the following season and had at once spotted "problems." She began to explain one of them. Burns, in his court testimony, recalled the conversation. He had asked: "Why is that a problem? We did something just like it last year." She had answered: "That was last year. You weren't in the Family Hour last year."

Still another witness was Norman Lear. While supporting the Writers Guild suit, he had filed a separate suit because *All in the Family* had, for Family Time reasons, been moved out of its long-held 8 o'clock spot to 9 o'clock on Monday evening, where it was surrounded by violence. Lear felt he had been financially injured and was suing for damages.

Lear's testimony included a curious reference to the CBS-TV news series *60 Minutes*, which had, before the start of the trial, injected itself into the dispute via an interview with Lear. The *60 Minutes* series presented CBS newsmen—Mike Wallace, Morley Safer, and later others—reporting investigations into various matters. They often put a spotlight on people "doing things in dark corners they shouldn't be doing," as producer Don Hewitt put it. The program had developed a relentless style of interviewing, in which Mike Wallace was especially adept, carefully laying a foundation with questions leading to often damaging confrontations. The interviewee would be in extreme close-up, so that any twitch or drop of perspiration would have dramatic value. To people who remembered *Dragnet,* Wallace's style resembled that of Sergeant Friday grilling a suspect. The invitation to Lear to be spotlighted on *60 Minutes* tended to cast him in this role, yet a man in Lear's position could hardly decline the invitation. *60 Minutes* had in recent years become a ratings leader, a remarkable achievement for a series technically in the news category. For Lear, the appearance was a chance to state his views to a large audience.

Wallace began by noting that Lear was involved in "liberal" causes and active in presidential politics, and a participant in such groups as the American Civil Liberties Union and Amnesty International. Wallace suggested that Lear's political perspective "creeps into your work" and that "the networks give you an opportunity to do that." Lear readily agreed. Wallace then observed that Lear apparently had "the best of all possible worlds." Wallace wondered whether the lawsuit wasn't a case of biting the hand that fed him.

Lear had an answer ready, and in his court testimony he elaborated on it. Was he really biting the hand that fed him?

LEAR: I asked Mr. Wallace to consider which is the hand and which is the biting mouth. A lot of us work very hard supplying another mouth—which is the television network—with a voracious appetite. *That* may be the biting mouth.

The writer-producers apparently impressed Judge Ferguson. In the end they were also—unintentionally—aided by network testimony. Asked to state "a general guideline that would help to express the meaning of the Family Hour," a CBS executive replied: ". . . anything that could create embarrassment among parents watching with their children." The judge appeared dumbfounded. "Did I hear this right? The standard . . . was for the purpose of protecting *parents* from embarrassment . . . ?"

His decision, issued November 4, 1976, was that Family Time, an industry policy adopted under government threat, violated the First Amendment. The ruling made clear that each network could adopt a family-viewing policy, so long as it did so individually and not through the NAB or in obedience to FCC duress. But no network moved to do so. Family Time was soon forgotten. And *All in the Family* was restored to the early-evening period.

An ironic aftermath was that in 1979 the Ninth Circuit Court of Appeals vacated Judge Ferguson's decision on procedural grounds. "The District Court should not," said the three-judge panel, "have thrust itself so hastily into the delicately balanced system of broadcast regulation." The matter was referred back to the FCC. But Richard Wiley was gone by then, replaced by a new chairman, Charles Ferris, who was dedicated to "deregulation." And Arthur Taylor was no longer at CBS. Even before Judge Ferguson's ruling was announced, Taylor had been fired by CBS chairman William

Morley Safer and Mike Wallace of *60 Minutes*—CBS News investigatory series that became a ratings leader.
CBS

Paley; he was abruptly informed that his resignation would be accepted, and he departed the premises. It was one of numerous firings of network presidents and vice presidents during the late 1970's, as the world of television felt increasingly insecure about its future, though the money still rolled in.

It was during Taylor's regime that CBS-TV lost its leadership in ratings to a resurgent ABC-TV and its youth lineup. The shift followed a 1975 move by CBS-TV programmer Fred Silverman to ABC-TV, lured by a princely salary. The ABC-TV rise was generally credited to the "genius" of Fred Silverman, though some blamed it on mistaken programming decisions he had made at CBS-TV. In any case, the Silverman phenomenon soon prompted NBC, mired in third place, to lure him to NBC for a royal salary

Who shot J.R.?		
Dallas (CBS)	37.3	
60 Minutes (CBS)	29.2	
Barbara Walters Special (ABC)	27.5	
M*A*S*H (CBS)	26.5	
NFL Football, Thursday (ABC)	25.2	
Fighting Back (ABC)	24.6	
Little House on the Prairie (NBC)	24.5	
House Calls (CBS)	24.3	
Three's Company (ABC)	24.0	
Real People (NBC)	23.5	

The shooting of "J.R.," the oil mogul viewers loved to hate, gave *Dallas* the rating leadership during the fall of 1980. In this Nielsen report, covering the first week of December, the 37.3 rating represented a 62 per cent share-of-audience. NBC lagged behind CBS and ABC.

rumored at $1,000,000. In 1978 he became NBC president, but this time no miracle followed. Within three years he was fired.

Meanwhile, programming seemed all the more obsessed with titillation and mayhem, and this now encouraged counterattacks on different lines. In 1977 more than fifty wives of senators and representatives were reported enlisting in a "crusade against TV violence." A more immediate economic peril came from groups—including one calling itself the Moral Majority—that began threatening sponsors with boycotts. Religious groups, including many represented on radio and television, blamed television for a declining national morality. They had new arguments for this. A number of cable systems were thriving on pornographic channels, specializing in feature films that the networks dared not touch even in late hours. And although most people, in interviews and polls—such as those of *TV Guide*—were ready to echo the "sex and violence" complaint, the ratings phenomenon of 1980 was the CBS series *Dallas*, a phantasmagoria of infidelities. Suspense over "who shot J.R.?," the ruthless oil tycoon (it turned out to be his sister-in-law and former mistress, Kristin Shephard) caused international speculation and sent *Dallas* to the top of the Nielsen list during the fall months. As a new presidential campaign gathered steam, the moral outcry merged with other political "family" issues, such as those relating to abortion and sex education. For the Moral Majority, one man could now save the nation—Ronald Reagan.

VOICE FROM THE WEST

When *Advertising Age* noted that television had revolutionized "everything from sales pitches to politics," it might have gone further. Politics had become sales pitches. Election campaigns belonged increasingly to the world of the television commercial. When candidates for major office went into the field to speak before crowds, it was often to obtain vivid moments of footage for 30-second and 60-second spots to be used in paid-for time—bought on the same basis as spots used for pain relievers, automobiles, cola drinks, and ski equipment. The purchased slots had become the real arena of political conflict. Alone among major democracies, the United States had incorporated election campaigns into its merchandising procedures.*

While this made for dangerously simple campaign appeals, the extraordinary escalation of time costs had made fund-raising a central concern for candidates. In the 1980 election campaign Political Action Committees, particularly those organized by business groups, played a key role. The power of such committees lay in the fact that a "reform" law of 1974, the Federal Election Campaign Act, made it illegal for a candidate to receive more than $1,000 from any one donor, but put no limit on gifts to Political Action Committees, which were also fairly free on how they could spend money. The law apparently had only minor effect on the 1976 election, but by 1980 business groups were ready to make massive use of it. Hundreds of business-related PACs, having raised unprece-

---

* In most European countries free time for election appeals was by law available to parties in proportion to party membership, or membership in a legislature, or votes in a previous election. Most barred the sale of time for political appeals.

dented war chests from employees, stockholders, clients, and others, were ready to pour tens of millions into the presidential and congressional drives. PACs mounted their own campaign drives while also making campaign donations to candidates. Pivotal candidates for Senate and House seats received $100,000 or more in donations from corporate PACs, while numerous other candidates received lesser sums. Major unions also organized PACs, and often made gifts to the same pivotal candidates. PACs formed by special-interest groups, particularly those stressing "family" issues, were another substantial factor.

PAC support proved a key ingredient in 1980 successes, and brought a sharp pro-business trend, a Republican resurgence, generally described as conservative.

As the central figure in this media-centered resurgence, Ronald Reagan had everything going for him. Beginning his career as a radio sportscaster in Des Moines, Iowa, he had—during a 1937 trip to the Catalina Island training camp of the Chicago Cubs— been offered a screen test and become a movie actor, ultimately appearing in some fifty films and rising to star rank. In films he didn't always get the girl, but he appeared regularly in nice-guy roles. He got political experience as president of the Screen Actors Guild, during which he was considered a liberal. But as he moved into television and became a series host and friend of sponsors, he turned increasingly conservative. For General Electric, sponsor of *G.E. Theater,* he served for years as company spokesman at meetings throughout the country, enunciating company views on various matters. Government interference in business— *Losing Freedom By Installments*—was a favorite topic. These years on the "chicken-à-la-king circuit," as he called it, helped to shape his political persona—vigorous, genial, with an air of common sense. As he moved into party politics, he proved a stellar fund raiser. His rise to the California governorship in 1966 made him at once a leading possibility for the presidency. In 1980 his turn came. He used it with seasoned skill.

Throughout the campaign some fifty-two Americans were hostages in Iran, where young fanatics of the Khomeini revolution had seized the American embassy in November 1979. For over fourteen months American television was itself held hostage by the crisis as nightly newscasts ticked off the days and showed "student" militants at the embassy screaming defiance and shaking their fists at the American cameras. The captors demanded that the deposed Shah Mohammed Riza Pahlevi of Iran, who had fled abroad, be returned for trial; and later, after the Shah's death from cancer, that the wealth he had transferred to the United States and elsewhere be returned to Iran. The anti-American fury was leveled especially at the CIA, which in 1953 had overthrown Iran's Premier Mohammed Mossadegh and installed the Shah, who had subsequently been strongly bolstered by American aid.

President Carter, Democratic nominee for a second term, declined to discuss Iranian demands or grievances until all hostages were free. Dedicating himself to obtaining their release through any possible channels and persuasions, he vowed to remain in the White House—i.e., above campaign politics—until the goal was achieved. Television newscasts showed him making statements from the White House, a President rather than a candidate. At first, this seemed to fortify his reelection prospects, but as months went by it seemed a weakness. The campaigning Reagan did not criticize Carter's efforts but said that he himself, as President, would not allow the United States to be "pushed around" as it had been in recent years. His assurance of a more muscular foreign policy was especially pleasing to veterans' groups.

Reagan campaign spots generally echoed themes of General Electric days. The overall message was the need to get government "off the backs of the people"—through deregulation of business, sharp cuts in taxes, and reduction of the growing burden of social services borne by the taxpayer.

That this burden had reached crisis proportions was argued by Democrat and Republican alike. But while some candidates related the crisis to unemployment, inflation, and the collapsing economy of the cities, others pictured it mainly as "welfare fraud." Efforts by administrators to defend the legitimacy of most services appeared to face an insoluble task. Tricks of "welfare chiselers" had over the years become a standard premise of televised interviews, news commentaries, and other programming including comedy programming. Johnny Carson, in monologues on the *Tonight* show, had made use of the theme:

CARSON: Did you know that coffee is up to $3 a pound? *Three dollars a pound.* . . . In New York, even the people on welfare can't afford it.

Once found certain of audience response, such a premise was likely to prove irreversible. It may have added its momentum to the conservative, anti-welfare surge of 1980.

The final campaign days saw a ritualistic Carter-Reagan debate, patterned along the lines of previous presidential encounters. The nation witnessed a stern, solemn Carter warning of catastrophe if Reagan were elected, and a Reagan who, while tense, registered confidence and goodwill. The two men stood a substantial distance from the questioning journalists, and looked somewhat like old-time quiz contestants in their isolation booths. These 1980 contestants too were armed with memorized replies. But the words were scarcely significant. The manner was the message.

Ronald Reagan, with George Bush as vice-presidential running mate, won 489-49 in electoral votes. On January 20, 1981, Reagan moved into the presidency amid spectacular ceremony, even as the hostage crisis ended. The two events shared day-long television coverage and the newspaper headlines.

The new President had been elected by less than 27 per cent of those eligible to vote. Once again, in spite of zealous PAC activity, the voting statistics seemed to reflect a persistent political apathy. Some attributed this to the declining role of political parties, as simplistic television drives assumed an increasing dominance over the political process.

Scarcely two months after the inauguration, viewers witnessed a horrifying drama replete with instant replays: Reagan felled by a would-be assassin. Rushed to a hospital, emerging for moments from semi-consciousness, he displayed a characteristic resilient humor. Seeing his wife, he said, "Honey, I forgot to duck." In the operating room, to assembled doctors and nurses: "I hope you're all Republicans." His rapid recovery, after large loss of blood, effectively scotched the argument that age clouded his presidency. In the end, the sequence of events apparently helped him to consolidate his leadership as he confronted an array of problems.

In a vigorously orchestrated exercise in presidential television, he soon pushed his program for a new international stance, which would include a vast arms buildup and deployment of new weapons, including atomic weapons. It was the honeymoon period between administration and media, and the networks provided the fullest opportunity for President Reagan, Secretary of State Alexander Haig, and Secretary of Defense Caspar Weinberger to push their arguments for the proposed five-year $1.5 trillion buildup. Special programs, newscast items, and the networks' weekly press-conference programs carried the message. But CBS served notice that it would also hold to its ombudsman role. In a move reminiscent of *The Selling of the Pentagon*, CBS-TV scheduled a five-part documentary on *The Defense of the United States*, telecast on five successive nights, June 14-18, 1981, with Howard Stringer as executive producer. Before CBS cameras, military figures at various levels demonstrated weapons and answered questions about their rationale and use. The answers sometimes had an extraordinary backfiring effect, and even suggested a kind of chaos.

With General Warren Moore, CBS newsman Bob Schieffer discussed the nightmare possibility that nuclear war might be launched by mistake, triggered by computer malfunction. During an eighteen-month period there had apparently been 147 false alarms, set off by, among other things, a Soviet training launch, a failed computer chip, a gas fire in a Siberian pipeline.

SCHIEFFER: Does that mean that the possibility exists that we could get into war by mistake or by accident?

GENERAL MOORE: Never.

SCHIEFFER: Why not?

GENERAL MOORE: First, all of these systems are—are data systems. They provide the information to us. We laugh and say the computers become more excited than we do. We don't believe them. They're good devices and it's a marvelous system, and we take that data and then a man gets into the act. He's always in the loop, analyzing, probing, testing, to find out whether it's real or not.

Other interviews, filmed in North Dakota missile installations, were with men who controlled warheads many hundreds of times more powerful than the Hiroshima bomb. Television viewers were first shown some communication training procedures, featuring arcane dialogue.

CREWMAN: I have Echo. November. Alpha. Bravo. Lima. Echo.

CREWMAN: Okay. Let's coordinate the command with everybody else.

CREWMAN: Everybody is coordinated.

CREWMAN: Okay. I'm launching at this time. (*Launching buzzer*) I have missile away.

SCHIEFFER (*to crewman*): It must be an enormous responsibility. You must—to—to be in charge, as you two gentlemen are, of the most powerful weapon, I suppose, that's ever—man has ever devised?

CREWMAN: Yes, sir, it is a definite challenge. It's more responsibility than I could obtain in a civilian world. And to me that is job satisfaction.

It seemed to be assumed by military personnel that an atomic war might have to be risked and could be won. CBS explored the question of what might be "won" in such a victory. Staging—via

Bob Schieffer with three-
headed MIRV—first television
appearance for the MIRV
(multiple independently tar-
geted reentry vehicles). From
five-part documentary *The
Defense of the United States*,
1981.   CBS

new-era special effects—an atomic hit on Omaha, Nebraska, it considered the likely consequences. The medical problems alone appeared totally insoluble.

The Defense of the United States, a documentary with an extremely equivocal impact, foreshadowed long struggles over the
issues raised. Widely telecast in Europe, the programs may have had
a role in stiffening European resistance to American military plans.

The Reagan presidency had various meanings for the broadcasting world. It seemed to symbolize the dominant role of television in
American life. But of special significance was the persistent administration theme of deregulation. Among agencies to be reduced in
power and budget, to free American business from destructive interference, were the Federal Communications Commission and the
Federal Trade Commission. With the proliferation of channels into

the home offered by American broadcasting, it seemed to the new administration that regulatory supervision had become largely unnecessary—even undesirable. Amid an evolving abundance, why should not communication be left to market forces? In this view, government support for public television and radio had likewise become a dubious holdover, due to be phased out. Viewers and listeners, not bureaucrats, would then be the judges and controllers of program services. Would this not be completely in the spirit of the First Amendment with its guarantees of free communication? So it was argued.

If this theoretic approach stirred euphoria among some, it brought alarm to others, including many established commercial broadcasters. It seemed to augur the unraveling of regulatory machinery that had governed the industry since the Radio Act of 1927 and that had brought prosperity to many. It had made the networks, in particular, a center of national power, with a kind of imperial hegemony over the industry. In recent years new technologies, often pushed by new constituencies, had begun to shadow this hegemony. Though descended from the established order, the offspring increasingly threatened to undermine and revolutionize it. The FCC, indulgent regulator of the system, had tended to hold the offspring in check in the interest of industry stability. But if deregulation and "market forces" were now to take over, what would become of the status quo and its blessings? Clearly it meant "a new ballgame"—perhaps a competitive chaos in which rival offspring would battle for dominance in a new kind of television world. What would be the shape of that world? This was a question that increasingly haunted the 1980s.

PROGENY

6

"All is flux."
HERACLITUS

"*Bring me my pipe and my bowl and the video cassette of my fiddlers three.*"

Illustration from *Channels*, May/June 1984.

Feverish change became a fixed feature of the television scene. The tube seemed likely to retain its central role in American life, but behind the tube a complex struggle was under way, spurred by different visions of the future of television, and with implications for almost every aspect of society. The long-range outcome was a subject of ceaseless discussion and speculation—rhetorical and financial. The stakes seemed enormous, and the odds shifted constantly. First one contender, then another, seemed to represent the wave of the future. A contender might fall back, then forge ahead in a new form. Each of the contending technologies was hailed—as radio and television had once been hailed—as the key to a more enlightened society and the fulfillment of democracy.

The first offspring to challenge the primacy of the networks was *cable television*. Having begun modestly, as an adjunct for improved reception of available stations, it had won an added following by offering supplementary programming of its own. This might be only a few extra movies or sports events for viewers to choose, but it was enough for continued cable growth. During the 1970s the number of local U.S. cable systems grew to some four thousand, with more than fifteen million homes subscribing. But far more spectacular developments were in store. In the late 1970s and early 1980s the arrival of such phenomena as HBO (Home Box Office), ESPN (Entertainment and Sports Programming Network), C-SPAN (Cable Satellite Public Affairs Network), CNN (Cable News Network), MTV (Music Television), a children's channel titled Nickelodeon, a family-entertainment Disney Channel, a soft-porno Playboy Channel, a round-the-clock Weather Channel—all launched in rapid succession—revolutionized the cable industry and suddenly changed the shape of American television.

The new entities were not cable systems but satellite-distributed services that enabled an existing cable system to offer, under various arrangements, not the up-to-a-dozen program choices available from early cable television but scores of choices. Cable systems with more than a hundred "channels" became feasible. A cable system assigned one such channel to each program service it decided to adopt. The satellite-distributed services might be national or even international in reach and offerings. A cable system was essentially a local operation but could now represent, in effect, a large cluster of far-reaching networks including individual stations that, like WTBS Atlanta, *became* networks (or "superstations") by distributing their offerings via satellite. The three traditional networks, NBC, CBS, ABC—chains linked for decades by AT&T—suddenly had many rivals served by satellite. Through them, cable systems could offer an overwhelming array of dialing choices.

A two-tier arrangement had evolved. Some program services, such as HBO (a *Time* subsidiary offering recent films, major sports events, night-club entertainment, and other items without commercial interruption) cost viewers "premium" charges above regular cable fees. Under this arrangement, HBO quickly became a major profit source for *Time*. Other program services were (like the "superstations") supported by advertising secured by the originating service. Thus Nickelodeon (children's programming interspersed with commercials) could be given to viewers free, as part of a cable system's basic service, although the system might have to pay Nickelodeon a nominal fee, such as 10¢-15¢ per subscriber served, to acquire the Nickelodeon service. As a lure to new cable subscribers, this price was small.

Observers saw various social meanings in the evolving system. Early network broadcasting (first radio, then television) had been praised for its unifying influence: it was said to have united the nation and even "brought the family together." The cable era obviously had a fragmenting effect. With multiple channels serving multiple tastes (and, in many homes, sets in various rooms) "the" audience had been replaced by a whole spectrum of audiences large and small. Advocates again found this a social blessing: cable, having rescued viewers from the tyranny of a three-network oligarchy, was said to have created true freedom of choice. The fact that many cable systems had "public access channels" (the FCC had for a time mandated inclusion of such channels) bolstered the argument. In some communities the access channels had in fact attracted spirited programming. All this helped cable advocates to describe cable as a new kind of democratized television. They began to speak disparagingly of old-time "broadcasting" that addressed *everyone* (with presumably a homogenizing effect) and to acclaim "narrowcasting"—which could cater to a range of tastes. Its very nature as a subscription service was felt by many to remove the need for controls. If the Playboy Channel brought glimpses of nudity into the home, it was something the home-owner had knowingly subscribed to. Television, it was argued, could now be as free as any medium: viewers were the ultimate arbiters. They were, in effect, their own programmers, selecting from a large menu of choices.

By the early 1980s business prospects for cable television looked so rosy that many jumped in for a share of the action—in some cases, disastrously. Even such seasoned enterprises as CBS and NBC miscalculated. CBS launched a satellite-based "culture channel" for the cable market, and lost tens of millions before abandoning the project. Similarly, NBC began an "entertainment channel" relying heavily on New York theatrical offerings, with similar results. By

1983 both the CBS and NBC ventures were defunct. Such failures became a familiar story in the battle of the new technologies; in this case, they brought the cable boom to a temporary slowdown. The trade magazine *Channels* even felt that "the Golden Age of cable" ended in 1983. For the moment, at least, the spotlight shifted elsewhere.

Some observers argued that the cable boom had not really been created by cable. They pointed out that the *satellite* had been the catalytic element. They felt that the satellite—control of satellites—was certain to be tomorrow's source of power and influence. In providing crucial linkages, was it not sure to acquire the kind of hegemony that network linkage had meant in yesterday's television? By 1980 up-to-date satellites—all equipped with as many as 24 "transponders" to amplify and relay communications—were providing linkages not only for cable television but for telephone systems, airlines, railroads, hotel chains, shipping companies, and the computer networks of multinational corporations, as well as an array of government agencies—especially the Pentagon, which kept putting its own satellites into orbit for military coordination, espionage, propaganda, and unannounced arcane purposes. The international ramifications of the satellite seemed mind-boggling. The very idea of national sovereignty appeared to be imperiled by it. Arthur C. Clarke, the author and theoretical scientist who had first conceived the idea of a synchronous (apparently stationary) satellite, had foreshadowed some of the possibilities. He had suggested that a satellite positioned to serve a whole continent would be able to reach its viewers without intervening cable systems or stations. Such facilities could be bypassed. A receiving dish would enable home or school or organization or business to receive satellite offerings directly. What would this mean to other media or to government agencies theoretically regulating communications? Some observers felt sure that *direct broadcast satellites* (DBS) would be the key medium of the future, and that it was ready to take its place. They noted that in rural parts of the United States a homeowner equipped with a 10-foot diameter dish could already enjoy satellite program services without subscribing to any of the cable systems for which they were intended. Thus DBS would find an audience already in place. In 1983 a number of entrepreneurs announced plans for ambitious DBS operations. They included Rupert Murdoch, an Australian who was rapidly acquiring major media holdings in America and Europe. Such announcements seemed to foreshadow an accelerating internationalization of television and other media. They also cast an ominous shadow over the future of cable television. Implementation of the DBS plans was awaited with nervousness.

In 1986 HBO and other "premium" channels began scrambling their satellite transmissions to thwart non-paying viewers. Paying subscribers received decoders for clear reception. But unauthorized decoders also appeared on the market.

Cable was meanwhile seizing on a dramatic innovation—two-way cable or *interactive television*—to recapture its momentum. This had been pioneered mainly by Warner-Amex—a Warner Brothers/American Express venture—which called its system Qube. Intent on giving it a look emphasizing revolutionary aspects, Warner-Amex avoided the term "cable television." After carefully testing the two-way system in all its technical ramifications, Warner-Amex introduced Qube in Columbus, Ohio, and found the omens good. In 1980 it was said to have won thirty thousand Columbus subscribers, and the company announced plans for similar systems in Houston, Cincinnati, Pittsburgh, and eventually other locations. Interactive television appeared to grip the public imagination and to generate waves of expectancy. For months media discussion, especially in the trade press, focused on what this new phenomenon might mean to other media and to society as a whole.

A Qube installation provided everything that any advanced cable system offered plus notable extras. A number of channels were earmarked for the two-way technology, which involved a second wire enabling subscribers to "respond." They did so via a hand-held device resembling a small calculator. By pressing its buttons, they could answer multiple-choice questions, vote on diverse issues, order merchandise displayed on the screen, and even pay for it—by punching out credit card number and other required information. The replies flowing over the response system were all recorded in a giant Qube computer and could be processed and analyzed to yield a large range of information.

Among features constantly emphasized were polling possibilities. A televised debate on an issue of the day (In rape cases, should Medicaid pay for abortions? Vote *yes* or *no*) could be climaxed by a poll of viewers, with results promptly shown on the screen. It could be done before, during, and/or after a debate, so that the impact of the debate, and of individual speakers taking part, could be measured. This suggested to some observers that truly scientific polling and rating systems would become possible. Qube, via its response system, could ascertain at any time precisely which subscribers were tuned in, and how they had voted or responded on any question. Since Qube had demographic data on all subscribers, updated at intervals, the data had considerable significance. With expansion of the system, rating services like Nielsen would seem to be doomed. Some observers suggested that the system might eventually be the basis for a truly equitable electoral procedure, in which hazards of bad weather, distance from polling places, and the impact of exit polls conducted by media organizations would no longer be able to affect the outcome.

A number of other Qube features attracted strong interest. In Columbus several of its colleges began to offer courses via Qube. Instructors sought to involve viewers frequently in the interactive process. Asking, "Am I going too fast?" an instructor could see instantly on a display panel how many answered *yes*, how many *no*, and could proceed accordingly. An almost mystical give-and-take feeling with the unseen "class" was said to develop. The instructor could test the cable-linked students at any moment on their understanding of particular points under discussion. At the end of the course students could take the exam via television, punching up their replies to multiple choice questions. Immediately afterwards a student's grade could be flashed on the screen and recorded in the Qube computer. The lectures were "open" in that any Qube subscriber could watch and take part in the Q & A responses; but for college credit, a fee would have to be paid to the college's registration office. A number of home-bound viewers (such as young mothers, invalids, and handicapped individuals) became eager participants in the Qube-delivered courses. They also were among those especially welcoming Qube's shop-by-television periods.

Off-shoots of the Qube system receiving especially wide attention were its home-security options. For an additional fee, sensors could be placed in the home, triggered to activate the return channel at any unauthorized entry and to alert a security service. A camera linked to the sensor could photograph the intruder, providing a videotaped documentation of the entry. In Columbus some five thousand Qube subscribers reportedly signed up for the home-security options during Qube's first eighteen months. "We're selling peace of mind," said a Warner-Amex spokesman.

Subscribers gradually became aware of other, less reassuring aspects of interactive television. They began to ponder the fact that information on a family's comings and goings, its specific interests, its responses on political issues, and its financial outlays, was being stored in a data base beyond the family's control. Warner-Amex was aware of the invasion-of-privacy implications and assured subscribers that the data would be protected. To what extent could it guarantee this? Would an IRS subpoena override the privacy policy? The stored information could be valuable to many—merchandisers, lobbyists, political groups. Would "computer hackers" be able to penetrate the Qube computer, as they had even the Pentagon's computers?

The Qube operation in Columbus, after a euphoric start, experienced a troubling downturn. Nonrenewals were more numerous than expected. Warner-Amex began to pull back, to reassess its position. Was apprehension about privacy the stumbling block? Or were viewers finding (as some observers had predicted they would) that pushbutton replies to pollster-type questions were something less than vibrant democracy? Cable entrepreneurs in a number of cities, having received franchises that included interactive options, postponed action on these. They had played a part in winning the franchises; cynics suggested that this had been their main purpose. In any case, interactive television went on hold. In 1984 Qube itself was halted. That same year the U.S. Supreme Court shifted the spotlight abruptly to a very different technology.

A new upheaval enveloped the world of television. The subject: *video*. Like cable television, this had begun as something very different from what it was becoming. In the 1950s U.S.-made Ampex videotape recorders—bulky and so costly that only television networks and stations seemed likely to buy them—were used mainly to record live programs for rebroadcast or file purposes. Sony and other Japanese companies began a rapid transformation of the medium. They made the equipment portable and easy to use. Prices dropped. The cassette replaced onerous reel-to-reel apparatus. When the companies developed handheld video cameras (soon acquiring sound), video became, in effect, an independent medium of expression, with remarkable advantages. A shot could be reviewed immediately, reshot if necessary. Tape could be reused. Producers could often work without special lighting. Laboratory costs and delays ceased to plague them. Small production units became the norm. At times a single video artist could be a complete crew. The term "independent producer" acquired new meaning. As quality improved, video became the standard medium of television journalism. It also became the special delight of avant-gardists and independent documentarists. It acquired a huge range of uses in education and other fields.

For millions of set-owners, however, off-the-air taping seemed the main attraction. Recording network programs, they were able to "time-shift" network schedules to serve personal convenience.

Viewers became truly their own programmers. Taping favorite movies, they also became collectors. Some made duplicates for friends. Some lent tapes to each other for viewing or perhaps further duplicating—in a process soon out of control. Film piracy boomed, finding a ready market not only in the United States but in many other countries, including the poorer countries. Many an Asian and African cafe turned into a mini-theater showing Hollywood products, including some of recent vintage. Some third-world countries had no copyright laws. Hollywood became alarmed. Its rights seemed imperiled. Jack Valenti, head of the Motion Picture Association of America, accused Sony of facilitating, abetting, and encouraging film piracy.

Some advertisements specifically promoting videocassette recorders for off-the-air taping, promising delight and inspiration, became the basis for legal action. A suit was filed by Universal and Disney. The companies won in the U.S. District Court, lost on appeal, then took the case to the U.S. Supreme Court. In 1984, the Court rendered its decision, 5-4.

For a television viewer to record a copyrighted program off the air for his or her pleasure and edification was not illegal, said the Court. "Time-shifting," which served the convenience of many viewers, could not be said to harm the producer. The Court deplored the piratical exploitation that might follow some taping, but could not place responsibility for it on the maker of the equipment. Hollywood had lost its case.

The studios, mortified by the defeat, now changed their tactics. Coding film prints so that the source of any illegal copy could be traced, they began an anti-piracy campaign that bore fruit. Meanwhile they set out to dominate the home video market. They had already experimented with releasing blockbuster films in video form—with surprising results. In 1982 Paramount had sold more than half a million cassettes of *Raiders of the Lost Ark*. With defeat in the Sony case, early video release became a basic Hollywood strategy. Theatrical use would still come first—a catalyst for all

other markets. But home video release would come next, before
HBO or any of its pay-television rivals. Through this strategy,
home owners might be induced to buy or rent the video before
having a chance to tape the film off-air. After HBO or other premium channels would come sales to the old mainstays—NBC, CBS,
ABC—for sponsored broadcasting revenue. Then would come syndication, domestic and foreign—first-run, second-run, third-run, ad
infinitum. The world television market remained omniverous.

The technology that the Hollywood hierarchy had combated
with all available legal might, in a battle it had been dismayed to
lose, had a short time later become one of its major profit sources, a
new gold mine. Jack Valenti, president of MPAA, quipped, "We
know when to lose them, don't we?" By the end of the decade a
block-buster film could be expected to yield sales of some five million cassettes. One film of this period, *Top Gun*—a 1987 video release—introduced a new device for maximizing profit. The cassette
included a commercial for Diet Pepsi, in return for Diet Pepsi's
financial help in the marketing campaign. The Hollywood cassette
became not only a product but a medium for pushing other products. Promotion for a studio's other films became a standard feature
of videocassettes for the home market.

While Hollywood became obsessed with home video revenue, a
different aspect of video was seen by some to have more far-reaching implications. With videocassette players available in homes,
schools, clubs, libraries, churches, unions, community centers, political organizations, and businesses, a new communications arena
seemed to be forming, with millions of outlets reachable directly
via cassettes, without the mediation of broadcasting or cable systems. It might conceivably accommodate ideas not considered
"mainstream." Problems of distribution—and its costs—would have
to be solved. But for the long run, some saw this possibility as especially meaningful for the democratic process.

For millions of viewers, such long-range thoughts were less compelling than a new phenomenon sweeping the country—*video*

games. It dominated many homes but also generated a nationwide eruption of video parlors featuring war games, space combat, auto races, and other contests in which the viewer operated a joystick to rescue an imperiled hero or decimate enemies, monsters, cars, planes, and spaceships. Some observers deplored the games as intolerable noise-makers and time-wasters. Others denounced them as incitements to violence and cold-war demonization of enemies. Still others, including many educators, admired the training they provided in eye-hand coordination, rapid decision-making, and coolness under pressure. They saw the games as another aspect of interactive television. It was perhaps not surprising that the craze had been precipitated by a Warner subsidiary, Atari.

Traditional networks *vs* cable *vs* direct broadcast satellites *vs* interactive television *vs* videocassettes—how went the struggle? Which would survive? Which might prevail? The venerable Nielsen reports, still based on audimeters and diaries, threw little light on what was happening. Still dividing the day into neat time segments, the reports still indicated for each network its share-of-audience for each period. But in a world of remote tuning, zappers, multi-set homes, cable, cassettes, video games, and other distractions, Nielsen was describing something that no longer existed. Yet in this field, too, new technology was evolving, and began to clarify the picture.

PEOPLE METERS

A British company, AGB Television Research, had for years been measuring audiences with devices popularly known as people meters. AGB had become the dominant system in a number of European countries. In 1984 it installed its system in Boston, in a test campaign involving several hundred homes. If successful, it planned to expand its U.S. venture nationwide, challenging Nielsen's dominance of national television ratings.

A people meter, placed atop a television set, had a series of lights, one for each member of the household. Each member was equipped with a remote-control keypad resembling a small calculator. When starting to view, her or she was to "log in" with a touch of his/her personal keypad, igniting a corresponding light on the people meter. When leaving, he or she was to "log out." The lights on the people meter were supposed to match, at any moment, the people watching—as a flashing signal periodically reminded the viewers. Each set in the home had its own people meter. Thus the people meter chronicled individual viewing—in contrast to Nielsen's audi-meters, which merely recorded set-tuning, without any indication of who or how many might be watching at a particular moment, if indeed anyone was.

AGB, like Nielsen, had demographic data on all members of a metered household, and this made possible a demographic analysis of personal viewing behavior. AGB had accepted the reality that viewing was no longer primarily a family activity. It was said to be developing other refinements, such as a unit to track off-the-air recording, and another to record the zapping of commercials.

It was a challenge Nielsen could not ignore. The company began to experiment with its own people meter. AGB successes spurred Nielsen to a rapid transition. For national ratings it announced a complete changeover to Nielsen people meters for the fall of 1987. It also devised a method for VCR playback measurement. Nielsen's rapid action virtually scuttled AGB's plans. Advertising agencies, networks, and others saw little need to subscribe to two nationwide systems, and support for AGB withered.

As with every rating system since radio days, people meters—whether AGB or Nielsen—inspired skepticism. Many an observer expounded on perceived flaws and probable biases, yet the industry closed ranks behind the Nielsen people meters. It had never really trusted any system. The important thing, apparently, was to have a system—to provide a basis for advertising charges. A conspiracy-to-believe was needed. Competing systems, with each throwing the other's statistics into doubt, would be intolerable.

The old Nielsen procedure had indicated some erosion in network audiences, which was more clearly shown by the people meters. The erosion was larger than many had suspected. Notable shifts to cable and cassette viewing were indicated. Independent stations, too, seemed to be winning a larger share of audience, at network expense. Networks worried; the new media rejoiced. Meanwhile still other technologies were claiming attention.

THE RISE OF THE LASER

Among the marvels of the age was the laser-read *videodisc*, which was soon followed by its revolutionary sibling, the compact disc or CD. The laser-read disc had been slowed in its progress by several factors, including the introduction of a competing but inferior form of videodisc played by a stylus, introduced and widely advertised by RCA—another of RCA's calamitous miscalculations during this period. The device had come and gone quickly, with loss of many millions of dollars. But the laser videodisc seemed certain to have a long-range destiny. While not likely to rival the videocassette for casual off-the-air taping, it was far superior to the cassette as a collector's medium, and ideal for long-range library and archive purposes, for which it has multimedia implications. While it could record feature films and television programming in compact and permanent form, it could reach far beyond these media. A single videodisc could accommodate all the pictures in the Louvre—or all the letters of the historic Adams family—or the entire history of sculpture—with each frame instantly retrievable on the screen. There was talk of an entire encyclopedia being stored on one laser-read disc, translated into digitalized form. Properly used, videodisc and CD seemed impervious to wear and tear. In contrast, paper records were everywhere crumbling, magnetic tape was fragile and in danger of erasure, and film, though sturdier, was not permanent. It seemed likely that today's—and yesterday's—legacy to future eras would rest heavily on laser-read discs. These, more than any other medium, would ultimately define the nature of our times.

Another laser-related medium seemed likely to have more immediate revolutionary effects, reverberating throughout society, with drastic impact on other media. This was *fiber optics*, sometimes called lightwave communication—the term preferred by AT&T, one of its principal developers.

That light waves—like radio waves—might be used as carriers of communication had long been theorized. Alexander Graham Bell had suggested such use of light waves in the 1880s. In the 1960s, experiments in this direction began to focus on the discovery that the sharp, narrow laser beam, normally traveling in a straight line, could also travel through a hair-thin glass fiber while following its curves and bends. Moreover, such a hair-thin fiber far exceeded the coaxial cable in its capacity to accommodate streams of communication. Test results almost challenged belief. They suggested that a fiber-optic bundle entering the home—far narrower and lighter than a current telephone cable—would be able to accommodate not only the needs of the telephone system but also of cable television, interactive television, two-way videophone, fax (facsimile transmission), computer systems, and inventions yet to come. Fiber optics loomed as the most extraordinary unifying invention of the communications upheaval. Naturally AT&T and its rivals plunged into fiber optics research, but so did numerous other interests, such as Corning Glass and its rivals. The basic raw material, sand, was far more available than the precious copper of coaxial cable. Equally alert to the implications were IBM and its rivals, and all cable and broadcasting interests.

By 1984 the Pentagon was said to have concluded that a fiber-optics system, unlike copper cable, had a chance of surviving a nuclear strike. Fiber also seemed to be immune to noise interfer-

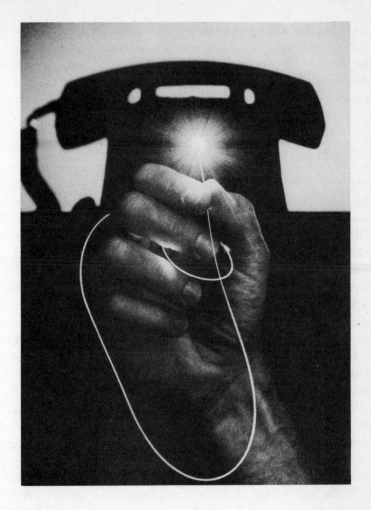

Communication superhighway—glass fiber through which a laser beam can carry numerous streams of communication, far exceeding capacity of coaxial cable.   AT&T

ence. It appeared to resist electronic eavesdropping. It was found suitable for underwater use. Construction of transatlantic and trans-pacific links was begun by the late 1980s. For intercontinental communication these were seen as ultimately more efficient and cheaper than satellites, and able to accommodate a vast telecommunications traffic.

Enthusiasts envisioned a time when home owners would be able, through the fiber-optic umbilical cords linking each of them to the world, to commandeer the farflung treasures and services of libraries, film studios, museums, public archives, universities, and data bases. Through the same umbilical cords, government agencies, the world of business, political groups, and all the program services of cable television would be able to address the home owner. It would be a single conduit for a host of functions.

Such visions seemed to face a crucial obstacle. A 1984 Cable Communications Policy Act banned "crossownership" of cable television and telephone systems. But in 1989 the FCC decided that it could, on "good cause" and to encourage technological innovation, waive the ban so as to allow a special experiment in Cerritos, California, testing precisely the kind of unification that had been forbidden. The experiment, under GTE California, was expected to last some five years. No date was set.

The "single conduit" idea now became a focus of speculation. What were its implications? Every major medium—and the societies it served—had been plagued at one time or another by issues of monopoly control. Would such issues loom again—and in an especially all-embracing way? Reassuring answers were heard: with the multiplicity of media taking shape, how could there be danger? Not everyone felt assured.

MERGERMANIA

The 1980s saw not only a battle of technologies but parallel battles at the corporate level. It was a time of unprecedented mergers, leveraged buy-outs, and hostile take-overs as one giant corporation swallowed another. Media were the choice targets; contenders included not only media organizations but conglomerates of all sorts seeking wider diversification, and convinced that communications had become the key to power and profit. Already, in Hollywood, Paramount had come under control of Gulf & Western, United Artists had been swallowed by Transamerican, Columbia Pictures by Coca-Cola—which was later supplanted by Sony. Plans for television and its progeny figured in many deals. Ted Turner, owner of baseball's Atlanta Braves and the entrepreneur behind superstation WTBS and several satellite program services (CNN, Headlines News, TNT), bought the television rights to the entire MGM library of motion pictures to serve his program needs. Soon the networks themselves, once the pivots of the industry, became engulfed.

Ironically, it was the FCC that precipitated this development. For decades, in accord with antimonopoly clauses in its charter, it has limited the number of stations that could be owned by any single owner. Seven television stations, seven radio stations, were the main limits. But Mark Fowler, FCC chairman appointed by President Reagan, shared Reagan's belief in "market forces" as a solution to most social problems, and proposed to scrap the limitations. Perhaps he considered it a boost to the networks. But as soon as he signaled his intentions, major conglomerates began to eye the networks as take-over possibilities, and Wall Street arbitrageurs began to speculate in network stocks.

ABC came first. During the 1970s it had become the No. 1 network, leading in Nielsen ratings and with demographics attractive to advertisers. ABC had a group of affiliates owned by Capital

Cities, which had grown rich during ABC's palmy days and had also made successful investments in publications and cable. ABC had once considered a takeover of Capital Cities, if ownership rules were ever changed to make it possible. On April 1, 1985, the rules *were* changed: it became possible to own twelve stations. But by this time Capital Cities was more prosperous than the floundering ABC. For $3.5 billion Capital Cities took over ABC.

Within months the other networks fell to similar circumstances and pressures. With a fortune from the real estate field, Laurence Tisch took over CBS. And General Electric, mammoth corporation with interests in nuclear technology and armaments, absorbed RCA (including NBC) for $6.3 billion. The mergers involved license transfers beyond the old limits. All the transfers were quickly approved by Fowler's FCC, as though they were merely parcels of real estate. The casual procedure seemed to observers to flout the language and spirit of the Communications Act.

The rash of mergers stirred varied worries. Many take-overs were achieved with borrowed capital. To cope with resulting debts, the take-overs were often followed by staff reductions. This happened at all three networks and affected their news staffs, each of which lost hundreds of employees.

Some mergers also raised antitrust concerns, of a sort that would have voided them in earlier years. ITT's proposed takeover of ABC—a *cause célèbre* of the 1960s—was blocked because ITT's international political involvements were felt certain to undermine the integrity of ABC's news service. GE control of NBC seemed to raise similar issues, and to do so on an even larger scale. GE was an international marketer of nuclear plants. As Pentagon contractor it was working on aspects of the so-called Star Wars plan, which (ostensibly as a defense measure) was to involve nuclear detonations in outer space. GE was represented on government planning commissions, helping to invent weaponry it might later manufacture. Its fortunes appeared closely linked to the cold war. Might an

NBC employee at some stage handle a news item in a way that would minimize conflict with perceived GE interests? Many journalists believed that self-restraint—prudence—not rocking the boat—pragmatism—self-censorship—were far more pervasive mass media problems than overt censorship.

NBC had never had a Political Action Committee (PAC), but GE, always a vigorous lobbyist, did have a PAC, and pressed NBC employees (now GE employees) to become contributors to it. The letter they received, signed by a new NBC president appointed by GE read:

> Employees that earn their living and support their families from the profits of our business must recognize a need to invest some portion of their earnings to ensure that the company is well represented in Washington, and that its important issues are clearly placed before Congress.

> Employees who elect not to participate in a giving program of this type should question their own dedication to the company and their own expectations.

NBC newsmen protested, but the protests went unheeded. As with many issues affecting broadcasting, the matter was discussed in the press but virtually ignored by the broadcast media themselves.

The mergermania seemed increasingly international in implications. Many of the mergers reached across national boundaries as well as across media and technologies. Rupert Murdoch, the Australian with international newspaper holdings and DBS plans for both America and Europe, became a U.S. citizen in order to acquire the Metromedia television stations (including important New York and Washington outlets), and then bought control of Twentieth Century-Fox to form a national Fox Network to compete with NBC, CBS, and ABC. Solidifying his publications empire, which already included the London *Times* and the prestigious publishing firm Harper & Row, he astonished observers by a $3 billion buyout of the Walter Annenberg holdings, including the fabulously profitable *TV Guide*, the lucrative *Daily Racing Form*, and miscellaneous other properties. He persuaded Disney to join his DBS plans.

The 1989 takeover by Time, Inc. of the Warner empire created another international colossus astride the media. A major motion picture studio, international theater and film distribution holdings, powerful international alignments of cable systems and satellite program services, interactive television enterprises, video games, magazines and newspapers worldwide, printing establishments, music publishing houses, recording studios, Time-Life Books and Warnerbooks.

A similar international, intermedia lineup of holdings was emerging under the flamboyant Lord Robert Maxwell, who had parlayed London's *Daily Mirror* into newspaper holdings in twenty-eight countries, meanwhile expanding into television, cable and satellite systems, and printing companies. A World War II refugee from Czechoslovakia, he had become known as the "bouncing Czech," and by the 1980s was zigzagging around the world in his own planes (or in a 175 ft. yacht) arranging new acquisitions. His Pergamon Press included a vast lineup of technical journals. In 1988 he bought the giant book publisher Macmillan. Unlike Murdoch, he was considered politically liberal. Fluent in half a dozen languages, he planned a European satellite news service with simultaneous translation in eight languages. He was considered an inveterate rival of Rupert Murdoch, but negotiated an arrangement with Murdoch under which the latter's satellite facilities would serve the Maxwell cable systems. Maxwell confidently predicted that by 1995 there would be "only ten global corporations of communications." He expected to control one of them.

The struggle among technologies, the huge stakes involved, uncertainties about the outcome, the rise of deregulation, had all stirred the pot. Some asked, how would all this affect programming? What did it mean, in what audiences would see and hear?

PRODUCT

Amid the clash of battle, producers, directors, writers, actors, cameramen, lighting specialists, scene designers, costumers and others continued to grind out the needed programs. Vast quantities were required to fill the schedules. Popular wisdom had it that expanding opportunities plus deregulation would spur innovation and bring on a television renascence. Few saw this happening. The glut of programming apparently did not guarantee increased diversity. Cable systems produced little that was new; most felt they did not need to. Each was a supermarket of items made largely by others. Each held a local monopoly. Spokesmen for the networks—still dominant but increasingly edgy—were fond of pointing out that cable schedules, when not featuring old movies, were often filled up with old television series—network hand-me-downs. Cable offerings of the mid-1980s included *Dragnet, Blondie, Naked City, Flipper, Bewitched, The Life of Riley, Lassie, Rifleman, I Married Joan, Cisco Kid, Dennis the Menace, Beverly Hillbillies, Father Knows Best*, and other items of the 1950s and 1960s. Cable spokesmen, in response, expressed satisfaction that they were helping television "classics" find a new audience, and noted that many viewers apparently found them preferable to current network fare.

The networks were caught on a treadmill of their own. Increasingly insecure, they recycled long-trusted genres—domestic sitcoms, often zany, increasingly obsessed with sex; and dramas of the tracking, subduing, and killing of enemies foreign and domestic. Violence was pervasive and increasingly ritualized, as in *Miami Vice*. Its locale, once a retirement and convention mecca, was acquiring a new image, which *Miami Vice* did much to crystallize. A restless anti-Castro Latino population, including Bay of Pigs survivors and other veteran soldiers of fortune, were making it a cauldron of agitation. On *Miami Vice*, drugs, smuggling and prostitution were constant themes—not as social problems challenging public policy but as occasions for lavishly choreographed sequences of violence and pursuit, always accompanied by loud, pulsating music. *Miami Vice* made melodrama into a species of popular musical. It was, as one critic put it, MTV with cops.

With the start of the Reagan years, U.S. diplomacy was marked by a new surge of cold-war rhetoric. His administration became intent on efforts (secret at first) to undermine and perhaps topple leftist regimes in Cuba, Nicaragua, Grenada, Afghanistan, Angola, and Cambodia considered inimical to U.S. interests. Such efforts were meant as indirect attacks on the Soviet Union, which Reagan called "the evil empire." All this echoed the Dulles era. Programmers took their cue from the new hostility. *Mission: Impossible*, the series that had epitomized cold-war drama, had been dropped during the more decorous Carter years but came back in the Reagan era, still glorifying covert action and rationalizing government lies (as strategies for "deniability"). *The A-Team* joined the roster with a similar dedication, featuring a group of ex-convicts, wrongly convicted, who became international vigilantes carrying out noble missions that governments were too wimpish to carry out. Series like *Hawaii Five-O* gravitated to similar themes. The *Rambo* films added their particular psychopathic drive, first in movie theaters, then on the home screen. A bizarre climax to the cold-war drama was provided by a 14-hour ABC miniseries titled *Amerika*, unveiled in 1988. It purported to depict the United States as of 1997, after years of Soviet occupation. Soviet-controlled forces wearing United Nations peacekeeping helmets and insignia were shown in full control, having already blown up the Capitol, massacred most Congressmen, raped and killed innocent Americans, and reduced the population to slavery and passivity. Featuring a mix of Nazi and Russian show-business accents, the occupation forces were now contemplating "the final solution of the American problem." Assailed by critics—on the one hand for absurdity; on the other for incitement to hatred and hysteria—author Donald Wrye denied any political implications. It was just "entertainment," he said. An ABC spokesman echoed this, saying it was "pure fiction." A United Nations spokesman called it a grievous insult to the U.N. forces who even then were risking their lives in peacekeeping missions in various parts of the world, including Lebanon. A Soviet spokesman, predictably, denounced the project. Under Mikhail Gorbachev the USSR was proclaiming *glasnost*—a policy of openness—which some in the United States hoped would become the basis for a relaxation of the cold war. Others saw *glasnost* as a mere sham, a tactic, and declared that nothing in the USSR had changed. *Amerika* clearly took this view—and Reagan was felt to share it.

As in every period of television history, a few drama offerings rose above the average and became media landmarks. Such a series was *The Cosby Show*, a weekly series focusing on the Huxtables, a large middle-class black family. Written with perception, shrewdness, and wit, it managed to avoid most show-business preconceptions of black life. Cosby resolved to shoot the series in New York, drawing performers from New York neighborhoods. They quickly achieved an exceptional psychological coherence. Black-white relations were an implicit factor in many situations but seldom the main focus. A series without rancor, it was felt to have made a significant contribution to interracial enlightenment. Launched on NBC in 1984 (CBS and ABC had rejected the project), it remained among Nielsen leaders for five years, and in the process made Cosby wealthy. In 1988 he donated twenty million dollars to Spelman, a black women's college in Atlanta.

The producers responsible for *The Cosby Show* were Tom Werner and Marcy Carsey, who had left positions at a floundering ABC to start an independent production unit. They did not seek financing from a Hollywood studio—a standard route for "independents" but always involving some loss of independence—and instead mortgaged their respective homes. "We really bet on ourselves," Werner explained. When *The Cosby Show* proved a runaway success, the Carsey-Werner team followed it with *A Different World*,

Top 5—December 12-18, 1988

		Nielsen rating	Audience share
The Cosby Show*	NBC	25.9	42%
A Very Brady Christmas	CBS	25.1	39
A Different World*	NBC	24.2	39
Cheers	NBC	23.7	37
Roseanne*	ABC	22.9	35

* Produced by Carsey-Werner

NBC had strongly resumed the lead. A rating point was said to represent 904,000 homes.

Source: A. C. Nielsen reports

which focused on one of the Huxtable girls at an upscale college. The two series remained interrelated, with characters moving between them. *A Different World* proved almost as successful as *The Cosby Show.* In 1988 Carsey-Werner followed with *Roseanne,* in which the comedienne Roseanne Barr ruled a somewhat disordered family with a combination of sardonic wit and loving support. She herself ate too much and left dirty dishes in the sink—elements that may have endeared her to many viewers. Roseanne seemed to relieve others of guilt feelings—including viewers. Within months the series joined *The Cosby Show* and *A Different World* among Nielsen leaders.

Another series that stretched a familiar genre was *LA Law.* Like *M*A*S*H* and *Barney Miller,* it focused on a workplace in which workers had become a large quasi-family, locked in a range of interrelationships as they pursued the legal cases assigned to each. The series was compelling on a human-interest (occasionally soap opera) level, and at the same time illuminating on legal issues and processes. Relying on the freedom made possible by deregulation, it offered frank treatment on topics that in earlier years would have been approached with euphemisms. This same freedom was seen by other producers as a go-ahead for nonstop titillation—as in *The Golden Girls*, about senior citizens obsessed with giddy sex talk and implied goings-on, and *Nightingales*, about nurses in and out of bed with doctors and others. This trend brought protests from conservative pressure groups. Such groups, however, seemed more intent on attacking documentaries.

The Reagan years were not good for the documentary. Distinguished work emerged mainly on public television, and came largely from independent producers, even though they were hemmed in by shrinking production funds. Reagan appointees to such agencies as the Corporation for Public Broadcasting and the National Endowments seemed to take a dim view of documentaries, particularly when they treated topics on which the administration held strong views. Not only funding, but import and export of documentaries were affected.

Notable series emerging during these years included some that had been planned and funded in earlier years. Among them was *Vietnam: A Television History*, released in 1982, produced by Richard Ellison of WGBH-TV, Boston. A painstaking review of the nation's Vietnam nightmare via archive footage, reminiscence, and analysis, it inevitably invited protest, especially from some who had initiated or championed Vietnam policies. But for many it provided a valuable clearing of the air, and won praise and awards as a highly responsible summation of a tragic chapter in American history. A similarly impressive project was *Eyes on the Prize*, a six-part review of the struggle for civil rights as seen from a black perspective. Unveiled in 1986, it had required years of exploration in footage files, skillful editing, and writing of rare integrity. Produced under the supervision of Henry Hampton and quietly narrated by Julian Bond, it seemed certain to win a place as a permanent educational treasure. Still another offering of high quality was *The Constitution: That Delicate Balance*, a series of programs aired intermittently during the 1980s, bringing producer Fred Friendly back into the television spotlight—this time on public television.

Each program was a kind of social psychodrama built on a fictional case history agreed on by the participants. These might include, on a typical program, an actual ex-President (e.g., Gerald Ford or Jimmy Carter), a U.S. Supreme Court Justice (Thurgood Marshall), a television journalist (Dan Rather), a newspaper magnate (Katherine Graham), all of whom were led by a moderator through the legal and ethical crises posed by the scenario and asked to decide their actions at specific junctures. The series managed to lay bare, with exceptional vividness, issues and dilemmas facing American society and the policy problems posed by them.

Documentaries imported from abroad had in the past contributed valuably to public television schedules, but such imports encountered new obstructions. In an unusual move, three environmental films of the National Film Board of Canada including *If You Love This Planet* (an Academy Award nominee), touching on effects of nuclear weapons, and two films on acid rain, ran into opposition from the Justice Department, which ruled, under authority of the Foreign Agents Registration Act, that the films would have to carry prefatory warnings labeling them as "propaganda." This extraordinary ruling, widely assailed, may have won the films a wider audience.

Export of documentaries ran into similar difficulties. In 1948 thirty nations had agreed on a plan "to facilitate the international circulation of visual and auditory materials of educational, scientific, and cultural character" by waiving stiff tariffs and procedures imposed on commercial products. The educational character of the material was to be certified by the exporting country. For over three decades this had worked well, with USIA issuing the needed certificates. Beginning in 1981 a succession of documentaries was denied certification for apparently ideological reasons. They included *In Our Own Backyards*, documenting the hazards of uranium mining; *The Killing Ground*, a survey of the problem of toxic wastes, and *Soldier Girls*, on U.S. army training of recruits. The Justice Department and USIA actions seemed to reflect coordinated administration policy. Its appropriateness to a nation proclaiming the blessings of an open society and of "getting the government off our backs" was widely questioned.

At the commercial networks the documentary tradition was going through drastic changes. Deregulation was again a factor. Many network officials had long considered documentaries an unprofitable genre needed for license renewal. But license renewals had become automatic. No longer did the FCC ask for reports on a broadcaster's "public service" achievements. As a result, documentary probes such as those of the Murrow-Friendly *See It Now* series were scarcely contemplated. The networks now tended to avoid the term *documentary* and to speak instead of *reality programming*. This encompassed series adopting the investigative structure of *Sixty Minutes* and *Twenty/Twenty* but often veering toward the seamy, scabrous, and bizarre. The genre began to be compared to publications sold at checkout counters—and appeared to be similarly profitable. Some of the series, of which *Entertainment Tonight* was the most glitzy, focused on the media world itself, but seldom looked beyond patio and bedroom. On others, such as *Unsolved Mysteries*, *America's Most Wanted*, and *A Current Affair*, the pursuit of missing criminals was the focus. Still other forms of reality programming included pickups of actual trials (*On Trial*); re-enactments of trials (*The Judge*); and court cases resolved, by agreement, in a television studio before a retired judge (*The People's Court*).

Television programming became increasingly intertwined with the judicial system. In 1977, Florida had become the first state to permit cameras in the courtroom. Later a defendant, losing his case, claimed that the presence of cameras had made a fair trial impossible. In 1981 the U.S. Supreme Court rejected this protest and empowered individual states to set their own guidelines on electronic coverage. Within a few years most states abolished rules against cameras in the courtroom, but the process quickly moved further. Videotape footage obtained by undercover police in "sting" operations began to be made available to television. Then Station WSYX-TV, Columbus, Ohio, became the first station to conduct its own sting operation. Via concealed equipment it managed to photograph and record a U.S. Congressman conferring in a Mac-Donald's restaurant with the angry mother of a teenaged daughter seduced by the Congressman. The tape proved a television sensation and later helped convict the Congressman of contributing to the delinquency of a minor. Such victories were loudly celebrated. *America's Most Wanted*, broadcasting re-enactments of crimes plus photos and interviews, claimed to have brought a number of criminals to justice. *Unsolved Mysteries* was credited with the recapture of a clinic owner guilty of a major Medicaid fraud. In 1989 judicial activism by the media reached a new dimension. According to a press report, a U.S. diplomat had been videotaped passing a briefcase to a Soviet agent. The diplomat had not been charged or arrested, and the alleged tape was not shown. But on July 21, ABC-TV filled the gap with a "simulated" version of the passing of the alleged briefcase. Crosshairs in the picture created a convincing impression of counterespionage photography. ABC neglected to mention that its shot was simulated, a fact for which it later apologized. The diplomat had still not been indicted or tried—except, in a sense, on the television screen.

Judicial activism by television roused conflicting feelings. Some said it was bringing the law closer to the people. Others said it was cheapening the judicial process and creating new problems in legal and media ethics.

Another genre of reality programming evoked a similar range of opinion. This was the panel show attended by large studio audiences, as on the much-admired *Oprah Winfrey Show*. The procedure generally called for Winfrey, who had achieved celebrity through her performance in the motion picture *The Color Purple*, to interview several special guests associated with a current problem or topic. After this the audience was invited to participate in the questioning and discussion as Winfrey moved among them, microphone in hand. Her selection of guests was sometimes sensational. One program featured several guests whose spouses had been murdered; and, on the same program, several people who had committed murder under similar circumstances, been convicted, and served sentences. Another program featured the multiple wives of con-men who had left trails of defrauded "wives." Winfrey's theme-setting interviews were probing but always judicious, sympathetic, tactful—in search of understanding rather than melodrama. Her sagacity set the tone. The *Oprah Winfrey Show* seemed to attract an unusually intelligent studio audience. Other series, such as *The Donahue Show*, were somewhat different in this respect. Like Winfrey, Donahue showed a serious concern for social problems, but was far more intent on producing a clash of opinions. Sprinting with microphone among tiers of guests, sometimes feverishly, he prodded, encouraged, always fanning any sign of dissension. On still other series of the genre, such as *Geraldo* and the *Morton Downey, Jr. Show*, dissension had apparently become the main goal. Downey was provocateur rather than host. His own hostility set the tone. He seemed to enjoy berating his special guests as well as the studio audience. "Shut up, you old hag!" To one of his guests, a candidate for office, he said: "If I had a slime like you in the White House, I'd puke on you!" His style attracted studio audiences intent on similar boorishness and vehemence. Brawls resulted.

Some observers deplored the rancor, recalling the decorum that once dominated panel shows. But "trash TV" also had its defenders. Downey himself scorned the "elitism" of old-style discussion shows, through which the elect too often communicated only with the elect. He said his own brand of television drew in the politically uninvolved, serving to stretch democracy. Van Gordon Sauter, a former president of CBS News, wrote in *TV Guide:* "These tabloid talk shows can be great fun. Sometimes they are relevant. Sometimes they are even—brace yourself—good journalism."

The contentiousness of the day was even invading the intimate panels not attended by studio audiences. Such political discussion shows as *Crossfire* and *The McLaughlin Group* regularly culminated in shouting matches.

The same trend took over the world of advertising, which during the 1980s became addicted to so-called "negative advertising." Damaging insinuations about rival products, mentioned by name, became prevalent in television commercials. The same was true of political campaign messages, which had virtually become a domain of the advertising business. Here, too, attacks on opponents received increasing attention, and during the presidential campaigns of 1984 and 1988 achieved a new level of rancor.

One theme was recurrent among observers: deregulation and a hands-off FCC had encouraged a free-for-all. That was the risk of freedom. Democracy had always had its boorish moments, but perhaps they made their contribution.

Yet if an administration hands-off policy was a potent factor, giving free rein to many, it did not liberate all branches of programming. A notable exception was network (as opposed to local) news, especially the half-hour early-evening series *CBS Evening News*, *NBC Nightly News*, and ABC's *World News Tonight*—broadcast before the main entertainment of the evening and serving millions as their window on the world. In this one area the Reagan administration, involved in covert warfare and other secret operations in many parts of the world, was implacably determined to control the view—and did so with extraordinary success for eight years. The success, and the way it was achieved, go far to define the presidency of the "great communicator."

TWILIGHT NEWS

Early evening news roundups on the state of the world had evolved into an international genre. Each nation had its variations, but common characteristics were more striking.

Each drew on essentially the same raw material. This included information distributed by international news agencies—AP, UPI, Reuters, Agence France-Presse, and a few others—all services of pre-television origin that had served the newspaper world since the colonial era. But the core of the matter had become something different—pictures.

The generating, gathering, sifting, distributing, refining, processing, editing, scheduling, and presenting of this pictorial element had become the obsession of artists, technicians, editors, producers, administrators, and rulers worldwide. It was the essence of the evening news.

The process began at dawn each day as camera people throughout the world went to work making images of "news." They took cues from news agencies and newspapers but also from announcements of planned events: proclamations, meetings, press conferences, celebrations, anniversaries, award ceremonies, cornerstone layings, battleship christenings, and revelations of new inventions and products. Since the advent of television most of its news images had been of events created for cameras. Daniel Boorstin had dubbed them "pseudoevents" but viewers had become fairly oblivious to this aspect of the invented event. Camera people also rushed to unplanned events such as hurricanes and forest fires—disasters lasting long enough for image-takers to get there and do their work. But the most common disasters, such as murders and car crashes, were likely to be symbolized by events created afterwards as photo opportunities: officials inspecting the scene; television newsfolk visiting the victims. A "news" item of this sort was less an event than an artifact.

Much of the imagery recorded during a day on film or tape was earmarked for local use. Items that might have commercial value elsewhere were forwarded to distributing agencies to be sorted and dispatched where appropriate, via still other sorting, distributing, and editing agencies.

The U.S. networks, while supplied with material by their own staffs, were served by a number of other sources. A choice of still pictures was always available from AP and UPI, while moving images came mainly from agencies created for television. The most prominent of these was Visnews, which served NBC and other television systems throughout the world and was in turn served by them. By this means the USSR had access to footage from NBC as well as from Britain's BBC, Japan's NHK, and other systems—and vice versa. "We don't take sides," said Visnews. "We take pictures." Similarly organized was Worldwide Television News, which served ABC and was partly owned by it, and likewise served and was served by many other systems. CBS owned its own international service, syndicating CBS footage. These various services maintained camera crews in major world centers—somewhat automatically conferring on happenings in or near those centers a status of special importance. Events in remote parts of Asia, Africa, and South America had less chance of erupting onto the home screen.

By and large, television news was something that erupted. This was a frequent criticism of television news: it demonstrated results, seldom causes, or world crises. To clarify causes, words were needed, and words had been devalued. Word-based programs were edged to the periphery of the schedule. When a festering problem reached a point of explosion, television evening news would show the havoc it had caused—and go on to other things. It had little time for historic context. Havoc was more photogenic, and quickly perceived.

Images from a network's own crews and from Visnews or other agencies were supplemented at times by images from "stringers" and from amateurs who had happened on crucial or curious happenings. All this might further be supplemented by images relayed and transmitted "live" via cable or microwave relay, usually of events of timely significance.

Throughout the day, producers and editors of an evening news series weighed and reweighed available items, live, filmed, or taped. Early in the day they would arrive at a tentative "routine." Showmanship played a part. They looked for a compelling opening number to hold and seize attention. They liked to end on a warm human-interest item. A catastrophe of world interest had to have its moment, even if "bad news." Overall, producers favored a selection that confirmed the rightness of the national culture. In every nation, the evening news emerged as confirmation. The brief words of anchorpersons and their smiles, gestures, shrugs or other signals conscious or unconscious played an important part in this. Such matters seldom needed discussion. In the United States most television news personnel of the 1980s had grown up on television; their view of the world and "our" place in it had been shaped mainly by television. It was in their psyches, in a subliminal and self-perpetuating pattern. So standardized were the habits and pressures that, night after night, ABC, CBS, and NBC evening news programs tended to choose the same items and routines.

Outside of commercials, less than 23 minutes was available to producers. To many people—including newsmen—this seemed a bizarre and even arrogant allotment for the activities of a world of some six billion people. It was defended only in terms of "realism." Within this framework, foreign relations could seldom receive more than a few minutes. From the start of the Reagan years the White House became determined to shape this segment to the fullest possible extent.

The group of men who, years earlier, had seen in actor Ronald Reagan attributes of a President and guided him through preparatory years including the California governorship, had found him a dexterous apprentice. As their chosen star, he came through test after test. At crucial times he could perform in bravura style. It was a *straight* style, never actorish. He felt like a star, which helped the image. He was well aware that he had never been a major star, but sensed that he would be treated as a star, proclaimed a star, so long as he appeared on schedule, knew his lines, observed his toe marks, and performed to the hilt when required.

As in Hollywood, Reagan showed little inclination to argue about scripts or directorial decisions. As candidate and office holder he relied on speech writers, public relations specialists, photographers, political mentors, makeup artists and all their heterogeneous assistants to know and do their jobs. Often he seemed hardly conscious of the identity of many of the people in his entourage, and he seldom showed curiosity about them. As always, his mind was on the show.

Early in his presidency he told a reporter, in a guileless moment he might not have risked in later years: "Each morning they give me a list that shows exactly what I'm going to be doing the rest of the day." He was not being ironic about his presidential role. On the contrary, he was pleased that everything was clicking along smoothly. It was like Hollywood at its best.

The President's tendency to accept staff recommendations—even on matters like cabinet appointments—with few questions asked sometimes worried his mentors. As a matter of policy they constantly depicted Reagan as a hands-on President, aware of every detail. It was staff policy. They knew that the President's credibility was their chief asset.

They were well aware of his limitations, and from the start scheduled him accordingly. Reagan had fixed ideas about history but his knowledge on the subject was scant—and fuzzy, even weird, at the edges. He could not be trusted in many ad lib encounters. On the other hand he was a very quick study. Briefed and rehearsed for a press conference, he could come through in virtuoso style. Informal meetings with the press were risky. Throughout the Reagan presidency the television audience had the sense of seeing and hearing him constantly and being reassured by him on many issues. Actually, he held fewer press conferences than any recent President. Franklin D. Roosevelt averaged 6.9 news conferences a month, Truman 3.4, Eisenhower 2, Kennedy 1.9, Nixon 0.5, Ford 1.3, Carter 1.2. With Reagan the frequency dropped below the Nixon level. What the public saw was an ample succession of controlled events: clips of speeches before friendly audiences; a parade of foreign dignitaries in rose-garden photography (at which press queries were generally taboo); and appearances rich in symbolism like Reagan in flak jacket at the border between South and North Korea—leader of the free world peering at the enemy through field glasses. A member of the White House team—usually Michael Deaver—visited such sites in advance and planned all details, chalking the toe marks. There were also arrivals and departures by helicopter, when the noise level ruled out colloquies with reporters. Reagan, with a gesture, explained he couldn't hear.

Steven V. Roberts, *New York Times* Washington correspondent who appeared frequently on the PBS series *Washington Week in Review*, recalled that in twenty weeks of "covering the President" he was able to ask him exactly three questions. The protective shield seemed to him an extraordinary achievement. The attempted assassination soon after the Reagan inaugural had helped justify the shield. Some reporters had complained of the security measures—which kept them, among others, at a distance—but the complaints did not endear them to the public. Sympathy went to Reagan. Persistent reporters were felt to be harassing the President. Most reporters sensed this and refrained. Michael Deaver, a key figure in the Reagan entourage during the early years—others were James Baker, Edwin Meese, David Gergen, Richard Darman—felt that Reagan had "enjoyed the most generous treatment by the press of any President of the postwar era." According to Deaver, Reagan was aware of this and pleased with the distinction.

The Reagan team was successful in avoiding the adversarial atmosphere that had dominated relations between media and White House in preceding administrations. Baker urged his staff, "Don't

"Mr. President . . . !"   Dirk Halstead/Gamma-Liaison © 1988

get paranoid and draw the wagons around the White House." An all-out shoot-out with the media, he warned, could not be won. Relationships were to be controlled but always friendly. Sandy Socolow, of *CBS Evening News*, felt that the White House some-how gave reporters a sense of being part of an inner circle. Reagan himself might not be as available as they wished but was always genial. An unfriendly news item never seemed to be resented. The cordial atmosphere made it hard to think of "going after him."

Along with a damage-control environment, the Reagan White House sought continuously to pre-empt—to control—the few min-utes allotted to the international scene. To this end the Reagan team—this was Deaver's specialty—provided a constant supply of news items of a sort the media would not be able to resist. If they were informed that the President would make a dramatic disclosure (with photo opportunity) *re* Nicaragua, Cambodia, or Afghanistan, no network dared to be unrepresented. Advance word to top network executives, plus staff briefings for individual reporters (often providing an advance nugget or two) helped further to align network schedules with White House objectives—and edge reporters away from areas that might mean trouble. What the President disclosed on such occasions might involve matters on which the media themselves had little direct information. The President was assumed to have knowledge inaccessible to others. Reports trickling in from around the world might later amend, even contradict, what had been said. The important thing, to White House tacticians, was to get their own version out first. Contrary versions could later be ignored or dismissed as "fantasy." At worst they would appear in back pages of newspapers. Television news seldom had time for such followups. And the White House kept reiterating its version.

Throughout the Reagan years there were puzzling discrepancies between various versions of events. As early as March 1982 the *New York Times* carried a report to the effect that U.S. arms were going to Iran via Israel. It caused little to-do because few believed it. In one administration statement after another, Iran had been called a "terrorist" nation. Reagan had vowed never to deal with terrorists. Iran's Ayatollah Khomeini had called the United States "the Great Satan." An Israel-Iran link seemed equally implausible. In any case, there was no follow-up—certainly not on television. The administration repeated its determination to have nothing to do with terrorists.

Almost a year later, in March 1983, the administration decreed that during any investigation of news leaks all government employees must agree to lie detector tests or "face the consequences." Few observers linked it with the strange bulletin of the year before. The order went further. Any employee with access to sensitive information must thenceforth get official approval—for the rest of his or her life—before writing anything about work done in government. It was a gag order unprecedented in twentieth-century

U.S. history. Perhaps to minimize its impact, it was issued on a Friday afternoon, likely to be buried in weekend sports news.

In July 1983 a *Time* article again spoke of U.S. arms going to Iran via Israel. Again, it caused little stir; the White House ignored the report. A few small-circulation magazines like *The Nation* and *The Progressive* were pursuing their own investigations. Television viewers had little reason to doubt the firmness of Reagan policy or the validity of his on-camera statements.

Two years later, on June 10, 1985, an AP story by Robert Parry again mentioned arms sales to Iran and added a startling detail. Profits from the arms sales were said to be going to the "contras" in Nicaragua—whom Reagan called "freedom fighters"—via a "private aid network" run by a Colonel Oliver North, a largely unknown figure until this time. Because all U.S. aid to the contras had been outlawed by Congress in October 1984, the report awakened curiosity. On August 8 the *New York Times* added a further detail: "White House officials on the National Security Council" were said to be providing strategic as well as financial help to the contras. The implication of serious illegalities—under both U.S. and international law—could no longer be merely ignored. In a televised "photo opportunity," Reagan told viewers that in his opinion the freedom fighters should still get U.S. support. But he added, with apparently total conviction: "*We are not violating any laws.*"

A year later a Jack Anderson syndicated column placed the value of the reported arms sales to Iran during 1981-85 at $250 million. Despite denials and gag orders, the story was expanding and winning adherents.

It was administration policy to place Reagan before the cameras for celebratory news; damaging admissions, when apparently necessary, came from others. With the Iran-Israel-contra story unraveling day by day, a move came from Edwin Meese, who was U.S. Attorney General as well as a long-time Reagan adviser and confidant. On November 25, 1987, he announced in a press conference that profits from certain arms sales were apparently going to the contras and he would investigate. The mystery was now on the public agenda. In 1988 the Senate-House Iran contra hearings began—another televised spectacular on the Watergate model. Now the public would learn startling facts—though far from all the facts. It would hear of cabals in White House and cabinet, mutual suspicions and deceptions, private arms-dealer profits far beyond sums allotted to the contras, hasty shredding of official documents, coded Swiss bank accounts, delivery of thousands of TOW antitank missiles to Iran via Israel and other secretly co-operating nations (referred to at first by code numbers) and subsequent release of hostages. It would eventually be informed of such intriguing details as a gift from Saudi Arabia to the contras at U.S. urging; of a similar gift by the Sultan of Brunei at the suggestion of Secretary of State George Shultz, who, however, pictured himself as uninvolved in the complex imbroglio; and a gift from Ronald Reagan to the Ayatollah Khomeini—a Bible with a presidential inscription, hand-delivered by a U.S. emissary. It would finally learn that the government of Argentina, one of the most ruthless of terrorist regimes, had obliged the White House by helping to train the contras, and that the CIA had furthered the training with an instructional picture book on assassination techniques. The President told television viewers and radio listeners that "mistakes" might have been made but he said firmly that he knew of nothing illegal. He insisted there had been no "arms-for-hostages deal" and that he would never deal with terrorists.

Throughout the long unraveling, Reagan had appeared vulnerable on a number of issues, but perils had been deflected by the administration's persistent initiative in news management. It was control "by saturation." A notable example was a sequence of events in midsummer 1983, when charges relating to Iran and Nicaragua were beginning to pile up. On August 30 the USSR downed a Korean airliner—KAL 007—flying over Soviet territory. All 269 people aboard died, including many Americans. With only scant information on hand, the administration came out with its version of the event. "The United States reacts with revulsion," said Secretary of State Shultz, on camera. "We can see no excuse whatsoever for this appalling act." Reagan followed with several appearances.

> They deny the deed, but in their conflicting and misleading protestations the Soviets reveal that, yes, shooting down a plane, even one with hundreds of innocent men, women, children and babies is a part of their normal procedure if that plane is in what they claim as their airspace. This was the Soviet Union against the world and the moral precepts which guide human relations among people everywhere. It was an act of barbarism born of a society which wantonly disregards individual rights and the value of human life and seeks constantly to expand and dominate other nations. The brutality of this act should not be compounded through silence or the cynical distortion of the evidence now at hand.

His invective was promptly echoed by U.S. allies, bringing US-USSR relations to a new point of tension. With follow-up statements the matter was kept at fever pitch for many days, dominating the news. The Soviets had explanations, which some papers—including the *Wall Street Journal*—discussed in detail. But network newscasts had no time for this. The nation and much of the world rallied to the President, whose status as anti-terrorist champion remained unchallenged except in fringe media. The administration's activities in Nicaragua and elsewhere were, for the time being, blotted from public awareness.

Even with disclosure of further administration illegalities, such as the CIA's 1984 mining of Nicaragua harbors (subsequently condemned by the World Court), the major media continued to spare the President. On network evening news programs White House pronouncements continued to be treated with full deference. Media often referred to President Reagan as the "Teflon President," meaning that blame somehow failed to stick to him. The term seemed to ascribe the phenomenon to some characteristic of Reagan himself, but many reporters were well aware that it was the failure of the media to disclose painful and embarrassing facts that was responsible for the Teflon effect. Many journalists were, in fact, beginning to feel uncomfortable about their own role in the process— the media failure to hold the President and his administration responsible for their actions. During the final years of the Reagan regime, books by reporters began to document the long-hidden story, and to make clear their chagrin. Mark Hertsgaard called his account *On Bended Knee*, a title meant to epitomize what he saw as the posture of most media during the Reagan reign. Hertsgaard quotes Chris Wallace of CBS: "I guess I didn't have a good enough imagination to envision Ronald Reagan selling arms to Khomeini."

While tending to spare Reagan, the media focused on those around him. Here Reagan's detached approach to the presidency, starring as on-camera spokesman while leaving many key decisions to others, came to his aid. Besides, the media had little desire to participate in bringing down another President. They treated with utmost respect his eleventh-hour visit to the Soviet Union, in which he had a chance to play one of the most dramatic scenes of his presidency: Ronald Reagan strolling through Red Square with Mikhail Gorbachev, chatting with Soviet citizens amid the fluttering pigeons. Screens throughout the world displayed cordiality and spectacle. The "evil empire" seemed forgotten. Interviewed, the President admitted he no longer considered the USSR an evil empire. Characteristically, he could explain it only in individual, anecdotal terms. Gorbachev seemed to him a good man.

And so Ronald Reagan was allowed to depart ceremoniously. The last television vignettes were of Reagan as peacemaker. And in spite of all the weird and sinister revelations of past months, many people retained a warm feeling toward him. In a roundup of opinions on National Public Radio's *All Things Considered*, a college student from Kansas said: "He said things that made me feel good about being an American and all that." In a more complex reaction, a Californian said:

Ronald Reagan taught me that politics is, above all, irony and para-dox. It was Ronald Reagan who opened to the Soviet Union—something a liberal Democrat would have proposed, although none of them could have accomplished it. Does it mean that those favor-ing progressive solutions to the nation's and the world's ills must vote for retrograde candidates in the knowledge that in the curi-ous world of politics, wrong sometimes makes right?

If the networks spared Reagan, they showed during the transi-tion between the Reagan and Bush regimes moments of the inde-pendence that had long been missing. On the heels of the 1988 election of George Bush as President and Dan Quayle as Vice President came a number of television specials that would have seemed unimaginable a few months earlier.

On November 28, 1988, barely three weeks after election day, NBC broadcast *Shootdown*, a drama that painstakingly examined the events of five years earlier, when the 269 people on a Korean airliner had lost their lives. It was based on the book *Shootdown: Flight 007 and the American Connection*, by R. W. Johnson, and like the book, focused on the long efforts of families of victims to learn the truth behind the tragedy. A leading figure in the group was Nan Moore, a U.S. government worker whose son had been killed. The broadcast changed names of individuals but stuck closely to the personal histories. The group's search for clues had been pursued in Washington, Korea, and elsewhere, and had ended in troublesome questions. Why were the events still obscured by government secrecy? Why had the plane been 300 miles off its proper course, and over a Soviet military base? Since U.S. radar had apparently tracked the plane during its hours of flight, why had U.S. authorities not warned the plane that it was dangerously off course? When warned by the Soviets to change course, why had it not complied? Why had the U.S. air force destroyed radar tapes relating to the flight? Why were hundreds of relevant U.S. records still classified secret? Above all, why had there been no con-

Shootdown: Angela Lansbury (left) as a government worker learning that her son has died aboard KAL 007.   NBC

gressional investigation? This fact especially angered the American group.

The Soviet Union said that on radar the plane's contour (it was flying without lights) resembled that of a U.S. reconnaissance plane previously seen in the area; that the blacked-out plane had not responded to warnings but engaged in evasive maneuvers. Experts consulted by the group had diverse interpretations. Some felt the plane's pilot was somehow unaware of his off-bounds course. In contrast, others felt that the plane was (as speculated by the Soviets) on a U.S.-Korean intelligence mission designed to reveal Soviet defenses by "tickling" its radar installations; that a Korean airliner (flown by a pilot with a military background) had been recruited for the task with the assumption that the Soviets would not shoot down a passenger plane. During earlier accidental intrusions they had not done so.

The script for the independent production had gone through twenty-seven revisions before final acceptance by NBC. It had been a marathon negotiation with many compromises between producer and network censors. Many cuts were made. Inasmuch as the truth remained unknown, the drama necessarily ended on an inconclusive note. Yet the broadcast, so carefully documenting the uncertainties, had its impact. For those who remembered the Reagan broadcasts of 1983, *Shootdown* constituted a strong rebuke to his hasty political exploitation of a tragedy. The fact that *Shootdown* was broadcast seemed remarkable, after the years of network passivity.

Of similar impact was NBC's 1989 broadcast, *Roe vs Wade*, dramatizing a landmark case in the abortion dispute. On television, this issue had been represented again and again via demonstrations (sometimes violent) at abortion clinics and, during the election drive, via vitriolic one-liners in campaign commercials. *Roe vs Wade* pursued the human, medical, and legal ramifications in far more responsible fashion. Again the broadcast was a culmination of scene-by-scene, word-by-word negotiation, this time through nineteen revisions, amid "side-bar" consultations with pressure groups. "Truth" in the age of television had become an entity to be negotiated.

Perhaps the most remarkable offering of the interregnum period was *Secret Intelligence*, a series of four one-hour documentaries carried by PBS during the 1988-89 winter months, tracing CIA covert warfare and related activities since creation of the agency in 1947. Perhaps reflecting nervousness surrounding the offering, it was broadcast with virtually no promotion. With historic footage

and photos, along with valuable on-camera testimony by participants in various parts of the world, it recounted events in Indonesia,
Congo, Laos, Italy, and numerous other places. Most of the actions
had been mentioned in print media of various sorts, but television
had tended to treat such matters as hallowed mysteries not to be
violated. CIA attempts to assassinate Castro with help recruited
from the underworld (after failure of the CIA's Bay of Pigs invasion) received due attention. More significant was the forthright
look at CIA interventions in Iran (1953), Guatemala (1954), and
Chile, (1973), in each of which it achieved the overthrow of an
elected leader and his replacement by a military dictator favored
by the U.S. administration—the Shah in Iran, Colonel Castillo-
Armas in Guatemala, General Augusto Pinochet in Chile, all of
whom proved among the most repressive and murderous of rulers,
all disastrous in their consequences and leading, in the case of Iran,
to the Khomeini revolution, in the course of which the United
States became "the Great Satan." The CIA interventions seemed
to have garnered a harvest of havoc.

Secret Intelligence, produced by Blaine Baggott, was never po-
lemical. It chronicled events and left it to viewers to draw conclusions, and perhaps to wonder how the nation (or at least its leaders)
could still cling to the notion that secret international violence,
defying law and principle, was somehow an essential tool to promote "democracy" and "freedom." The actions detailed in *Secret
Intelligence* had all been accompanied by "cover stories" meant to
mislead public and press—muddying and distorting the flow of public communication for as long as the facts could be kept secret.
U.S. television networks, which liked to be thought of as bastions
of a free press, had done little or nothing to stem this trend. Instead
they had, in their entertainment features, regularly treated CIA-
style deceptions and exploits as charming "capers."

Ironically, the *Secret Intelligence* broadcasts coincided with the
launching of the presidency of George Bush, who had recently
served a term as CIA director. This fact had not been a campaign

TOE MARKS

President Bush and Japanese Prime Minister Takeshita, as they prepare
for a photo opportunity (2/3/89), seem to differ momentarily on
where they are supposed to stand. But international harmony prevails.
                                                        The New York Times

issue, and had scarcely been mentioned—perhaps for good reason.
Virtually no information was available.

As U.S. television entered the 1990s, it neared the completion of
the first hundred years of broadcasting. This had been a century
of extraordinary achievement in communications, with American
television playing a spectacular role. It had become a world phenomenon. Its programs and commercials dominated television in
many parts of the world. It was so interlocked with other media
that it was often referred to as "the media"—a plural form that had

become singular in many people's vocabulary. Its influence was affecting life styles, commerce, clothing, diet, music, and speech on all continents. Yet it was torn by struggles technological and corporate, and faced with huge uncertainties about its future. So was the world it served, which increasingly saw its habitat, the planet, imperiled—by pollution, armaments, and widening poverty. Could American television, with its fantastic reach and power, help to see the planet through those perils? Some leaders challenged it to do so.

But a new element had entered the situation. To many people the American system of broadcasting—and its very success—were part of the problem, contributing in many ways to the planet's dilemmas. Clearly a crucial juncture lay ahead, for media and planet alike.

CROSSROADS

A catalyst in U.S. broadcasting annals had been the 1920s decision to hitch its destiny to advertising. The expansion fueled by that step carried the industry through the television boom into an era of worldwide multimedia hegemony. Its progress had meshed with the equally spectacular rise of U.S.-based multinational corporations—always prominent customers of the U.S. media and eventually chief owners of media conglomerates. Along the way, U.S. advertising agencies had likewise become global entities.

The naïve, primitive sales pitches that had interrupted programs of the 1920s had become centerpieces of a fabulous media world. More money was spent on commercials—some meant for international use—than on programming. The lavish commercial mini-epics drew on talents of leading designers, directors, writers, composers, choreographers. The U.S. acting profession earned more from television commercials than from all other performing arts combined. Commercials provided crucial leverage not only for merchandising but for politics, religion, and social movements of all sorts.

Meanwhile a striking shift in attitudes had taken place. In the 1920s and 1930s many performers had refused to do sales messages. They proclaimed themselves artists or journalists—not pitchmen. But within decades Hollywood stars, billionaire industrialists, elder statesmen, opera divas, sports champions, and members of European nobility all seemed equally available for the salesmanship role. It appeared to confer a new kind of celebrity. Salesmanship was a dominant strain of the culture. Elementary school teachers were struck with how eagerly many children responded to the assignment to "do a commercial." It seemed a supreme motivation—an entering wedge for the learning process. A half-century of commercials had sold many things including, it seemed, the elixir of selling.

Salesmanship was not confined to commercials. Their aura overflowed surrounding programming. A commercial for a luxury sedan or exotic perfume was a jewel that needed a suitable setting, such as a drama series featuring mouth-watering women and decor. For sports cars or shaving lotions more rugged, even violent programming served well. The entertainment industry provided what was needed. Some observers had begun to speak of the "consciousness industry."

Above all, its component media emphasized products. Products seemed the key to success in business, romance, community status, and the well-being of the nation. Problems ranging from headaches to loneliness to obesity to failure to dangerous addictions were solved by products. The avalanche of products rolling off assembly lines was fueled by energy sources old and new. The United States, once a place of Puritan frugality, had entered on an era of buying and spending. "I think, therefore I am," Descartes had said. Americans had changed it to: "I spend, therefore I am."

New products permeated society with astonishing speed. It had taken the telephone decades to become a fixture in average homes. Radio, television, and the twentieth-century wonders they proclaimed—electric refrigerators, airconditioning, freezers, tape recording, video, computers, organ transplants, magic medicines for health and beauty, and the miracles of atomic energy—took roots overnight. For much of the century the public was spellbound by the parade of wonders. But a new theme began to be heard. Success, it seemed, had its troublesome byproducts: overflowing garbage dumps, toxic rivers and lakes, polluted ocean beaches, smog, acid rain, deforestation, leaking atomic reactors, a depleted ozone layer, dangerous climate changes, and mysterious ailments threatening flora and fauna, including humankind. Amid areas of affluence were stretches of poverty and hunger. A new message began to permeate the consciousness industry: not all was well. Adjustments were needed. In an epoch of change, more change was due.

In the United States, confidence remained strong that a powerful democracy that had faced and surmounted many problems would make its way successfully through the new challenges. Yet democracy itself faced new dilemmas, which likewise stemmed from the radio decision of the 1920s.

Having opted for a commercial future, the industry also decided that candidates for public office should not receive free time for campaign speeches. For election appeals they must buy time on a businesslike basis. Was it not, after all, a form of advertising? Compliant government regulators—the Federal Radio Commission, later the Federal Communications Commission—acceded to the industry resolve. So did Congress and President. American society had embarked on a path that was scarcely foreseen.

Most of Europe did not follow the U.S. example. Almost all European nations (Luxembourg was, for a time, the sole exception) forbade the sale of time for electioneering, and found other solutions: allocating time to competing parties in proportion to their representation in a legislature, or their votes in a previous election, or the party's membership enrollment, or a combination of such measures. While a few later veered toward aspects of the U.S. system, most have held to their first decision.

In the United States the consequences of its course became clear with time. As radio and then television began to dominate American society, broadcast campaigning became essential. A "stump speech"—once delivered from a tree stump—now required a large cash payment. By the 1980s several million dollars were generally needed to become a Senator, scores of millions to become President. Fund raising dominated electoral politics and often meant commitments—spoken or unspoken, explicit or implicit—to major donors. To counter dangers, "reforms" were introduced. Limits on individual contributions were enacted—but were struck down in March 1985 by the U.S. Supreme Court as a violation of the First Amendment. A campaign donation, said the Court, was a form of free speech, not to be abridged. Wealth acquired a special Court-sanctioned role in the electoral system. A further "reform" permitted organization of political action committees or PACs, which could be formed by all sorts of organizations or groups—a chance, it was said, for the lowly to participate with their gifts. But the PACs inevitably channeled power toward the more affluent groups. Some U.S. budget appropriations tended to become revolving funds: contracts went to companies throughout the nation; a share returned to legislators in the form of campaign contributions.

At the dawn of U.S. history, elections had been far from democratic. The right to vote was at first confined to property owners, provided they were also male and white. U.S. political beginnings were thus dominated by a mere fraction of the populace. During the following decades a constant expansion of the electorate began. As industrialization got under way the worker without property (if male and white) won the vote. After the Civil War the race barrier was outlawed; long decades of struggle, including litigation, gradually translated this into actuality. World War I brought the vote to women. Later wars led to lowering of the voting age. All these moves created a more representative democracy.

Campaigns dominated by television war chests unfortunately brought a reverse trend. Fund raising involved processes out of sight of average voters, and pressures beyond their ken. Many politicians now seemed more concerned with major donors than with constituents; the donors had, in effect, become the real constituents. As costs forced campaigning into ever-shorter "commercials," campaigns deteriorated in other ways. They often became sloganeering hit-and-run attacks. Issues seemed remote. In every federal election of the 1980s, less than half the eligible voters took the trouble to vote—the lowest proportion for any major democracy. What did their abstinence mean?

Historians saw in the trend a peril to American democracy. And it was one in which television and its progeny had a dangerous complicity.

Could such an industry help the nation to face the dilemmas of a new era? This was the challenge that faced the consciousness industry as it moved toward its own second century and into a new millennium.

QUESTIONS FOR A NEW MILLENNIUM

"The wrong way always seems the more reasonable."

GEORGE MOORE

1. The pattern of tomorrow's television cannot be foreseen by anyone, but change is inevitable. On the basis of the past record, what aspects of today's television should at all costs be retained, and which should be abolished or changed?

2. Radio, television, and each of their offspring were hailed as likely to lead to a better informed and more vital democracy. What government communications policies can help bring about such a result?

3. What is meant by the "consciousness industry"? Is this something new in human history? What are the components of this industry? What influences determine its trends and its assumed impact on public consciousness?

4. Television brought onto the same screen such varied interests and activities as drama, journalism, religion, entertainment, sports, music, politics, education—each of which used to have its own arena or outlet. As a consequence, observers have noted an increasing tendency for each to take over functions of the other, so that drama, journalism, politics, etc., are deeply involved in each other's business. Is this a useful or a perilous trend?

5. Scholars have long warned that any communications monopoly or oligopoly, whether public or private, endangers democracy. Some feel that today's multiplicity of media makes such concerns obsolete. On the other hand, some feel that the danger of private monopoly control is increased by the trend toward unified ownership of media, while still others see the danger of government monopoly control increased by licensing requirements governing almost all the new media. Does communications monopoly seem likely to remain an issue of concern? If so, why?

6. Some observers, including leaders of the broadcasting industry, feel that deregulation has gone too far, and press for reregulation. What are the reasons behind their demand? Do their concerns relate to the general welfare, or rather to problems affecting particular media? Is regulation still necessary? If so, by whom?

7. In an era of direct broadcast satellites, privately owned by multinational corporations and serving viewers in a number of countries, how can one nation's regulatory agency effectively regulate? Is an international regulatory entity necessary, and is it feasible?

8. Some observers wonder whether national sovereignty can survive such phenomena as multinational conglomerates making efficient use of their satellites and other global communication systems. Some corporate spokesmen have suggested that nationalism is obsolete. They see their own enterprises as world-unifying systems, elements of stability amid increasing chaos. Is it possible that the future will be organized on the basis of multinational enterprises instead of nation states, and that the media revolution leads in that direction?

9. Some observers emphasize a world trend toward fragmentation, as ever smaller ethnic and linguistic minorities seek autonomy and nationhood. Most have developed their own media, including television. Has the explosion of new media played a role in the fragmentation? If so, where is this likely to lead?

10. The news and picture agencies serving the television systems of the world are based largely in leading industrial nations, and many are holdovers from the colonial era. So-called third world countries often complain that the services of the agencies are neo-imperialistic, emphasizing interests of the industrialized world while tending to obliterate

third-world concerns from world consciousness. To what extent is this a valid concern and what remedies are available?

11. The highly developed U.S. television system is less dependent on imported programming than are most systems of the world. Perhaps as a result, young people in the United States have been found in many tests to be less well informed about other parts of the world than are their counterparts in other leading nations. Is this a legitimate area of concern for programmers and regulators? If so, how can it be attacked?

12. Sociologists see all kinds of television programming as able to influence levels of information, attitudes, ideas, and actions—in ways that may include socially desirable and socially undesirable effects. Television executives have tended to discount such social effects, and prefer to describe most television as "entertainment." What do they mean by this? What sort of programming can be considered value-neutral?

13. The "pornography of violence" has been an almost constant subject of debate. The prominence of violence in U.S. television has been justified as reflecting a violent world; proposals to limit it have been dismissed as meaningless and denounced as unconstitutional attacks on freedom of expression. Yet many institutions and groups have passed anti-violence resolutions, and U.S. programs have at times been excluded from other countries on grounds of excessive violence. How do you explain the persistence of this issue?

14. An aspect of U.S. television frequently criticized is its commercialized role in the U.S. electoral system. What can be done about this link to high finance, and toward re-establishing a more democratic tradition?

15. A persistent concern over advertising dominance of U.S. television has been the effect on children, exposed to ceaseless messages they are scarcely equipped to evaluate. As an example, they hear from infancy that products are available that quickly make you feel better, end pain, help you sleep, make you popular, keep you alert, build muscles, keep you strong, assure success. The educator S. I. Hayakawa has warned: "Drugs are the natural refuge of a child nurtured on television." To what extent should social policy be governed by such concerns, and in what way?

CHRONOLOGY

1876 Alexander Graham Bell demonstrates the telephone and stimulates visions of the broadcasting age, including television.

1884 Invention of the Nipkow disk establishes scanning technique, as step toward transmission of images.

1894 Thomas Edison's peep-show kinetoscope inspires intensified experimentation in motion pictures.

1895 Guglielmo Marconi sends wireless messages on family estate.
The Lumière brothers' *cinématographe* launches the motion picture age.

1897 Marconi company formed in England.

1899 Marconi visits United States to report the *America*'s Cup Race via wireless, forms American Marconi, demonstrates for army and navy, precipitates wireless mania.

1901 Reginald A. Fessenden experiments with voice transmission, achieves his first successes.

1904 John Ambrose Fleming in England develops glass-bulb detector of radio waves.

1906 Lee de Forest develops three-element Audion tube.
Use of various crystals as detectors demonstrated.
Fessenden broadcasts Christmas Eve program of music and readings.

1907 De Forest Radio Telephone Company begins broadcasts in New York.
Word *television* used in *Scientific American*.

1908 De Forest broadcasts from Eiffel Tower.

1910 De Forest presents opera broadcast with Enrico Caruso from stage of Metropolitan.

1912 News of *Titanic* disaster reaches United States through Marconi operator David Sarnoff.

Extensive experiments in transmission of images, using Nipkow disk.

Broadcasting licenses required by new law.

1913 AT&T begins purchase of De Forest patents.

Edwin H. Armstrong develops feedback circuit.

1915 AT&T long-distance service reaches San Francisco, using vacuum-tube amplifiers.

1916 De Forest broadcasts music and election returns in New York.

David Sarnoff urges American Marconi to market radio music boxes.

1917 After United States declaration of war on Germany, radio equipment—commercial and amateur—is sealed or taken over by navy.

Patent struggles shelved for war production, by government order.

1918 President Wilson's Fourteen Points broadcast throughout Europe from New Brunswick, N.J.

Navy seeks permanent control of radio in the United States; rebuffed by Congress, it urges private monopoly.

1919 GE forms Radio Corporation of America to take over assets of American Marconi.

Amateurs resume activity.

1920 Vladimir Zworykin and others resume television experiments.

AT&T becomes RCA partner; AT&T-GE-RCA cross-licensing agreement.

Amateur stations broadcasting in many parts of United States.

Westinghouse buys various Armstrong patents.

Westinghouse station KDKA broadcasts election returns.

1921 Westinghouse and United Fruit become RCA partners, join cross-licensing pact.

1922 More than 500 broadcasting stations licensed during year.

First Washington Radio Conference.

AT&T introduces "toll" broadcasting—i.e., commercials.

ASCAP demands royalties from radio stations for use of music.

1923 Federal Trade Commission starts radio-monopoly investigation.

NAB formed.

Opening of Congress broadcast for first time.

Zworykin demonstrates partly electronic television system.

1924 WEAF drops Kaltenborn under State Department pressure.

AT&T and "radio group" begin secret arbitration.

FTC files monopoly complaint against patent allies.

Coolidge campaign speech on 26-station coast-to-coast hookup.

1925 Thirty-seven educational stations give up.

1926 GE, Westinghouse, RCA organize National Broadcasting Company.

NBC buys WEAF for $1,000,000; contracts to use AT&T wires.

Government defeat in *U.S.* v. *Zenith* leads to period of "wave piracy."

1927 Two NBC networks, "red" and "blue," in operation.

Herbert Hoover appears on experimental telecast for AT&T.

Formation of Columbia Phonograph Broadcasting System—later CBS.

Philo T. Farnsworth applies for patent on electronic television system—granted three years later.

Radio Act of 1927 passed; Federal Radio Commission formed.

Jazz Singer debut brings hasty conversion of film industry to sound.

1928 FRC shifts most stations, abolishes eighty-three.

William Paley takes over CBS.

GE presents *The Queen's Messenger*, first television drama, in Schenectady.

RKO formed by GE-Westinghouse-RCA and film interests.

1929 *Amos 'n' Andy* becomes NBC network series.

Paramount buys 49 per cent of CBS.

RCA buys Victor Talking Machine Company.

Wall Street boom—with spectacular rise of RCA stock—followed by crash.

1930 Collapse of vaudeville brings radio vaudeville era.

Start of Crossley ratings, based on telephone calls.

David Sarnoff becomes RCA president.

United States antitrust suit against RCA and patent allies.

1931 Increase in commercial announcements, contests, premiums, merchandising schemes.

AT&T withdraws from patent alliance.

1932 GE-Westinghouse-RCA divorce plan brings consent decree, terminates antitrust suit.

NBC becomes wholly owned RCA subsidiary.

NBC starts television station in Empire State Building.

Paley buys back Paramount holdings in CBS.

Radio City under construction.

1933 Banking crisis leads to first Fireside Chat.

Armstrong demonstrates FM for RCA executives.

1934 Proposal to reserve 25 per cent of channels for education (Wagner-Hatfield bill) defeated.

Communications Act is passed.

1935 Audimeter appears as research tool, becomes basis of Nielsen ratings.

Armstrong demonstrates FM for press.

1936 RCA launches $1,000,000 television field tests.

Kaltenborn describes the battle of Irun over CBS.

New York-Philadelphia coaxial cable ready for use.

1937 NBC Symphony formed with Toscanini as conductor.

NBC television mobile unit in action in New York City.

1938 Murrow describes annexation of Austria over CBS.

World news roundup programs begin.

Munich crisis broadcasts by Kaltenborn.

Orson Welles broadcast of "War of the Worlds" on *Mercury Theater on the Air*.

CBS buys Columbia Records.

1939 Armstrong completes FM station at Alpine, New Jersey.

RCA television demonstration at New York World's Fair.

Television on limited-commercial basis.

Radar production begins.

1940 FCC decides television will have FM sound.

Republican and Democratic conventions telecast.

Election returns telecast first time.

Murrow describes the London blitz over CBS radio.

1941 Television goes on commercial basis.

1942 Manufacture of receivers halted.

Television schedules curtailed.

Office of War Information formed.

Armed Forces Radio Service formed.

1943 U.S. Supreme Court decision requires NBC to sell one of its networks.

Noble buys Blue Network, renames it American Broadcasting Company.

Wire recorders in use on Italian front.

1944 Normandy landings described via wire recorders.
Sponsors experiment with television commercials.

1945 German tape recorders captured.
FCC moves FM "upstairs" in radio spectrum.
Set manufacture approved as war ends.

1946 Stanton becomes CBS president.
Murrow, new CBS vice-president, starts documentary unit.
Television sets go on sale.
Opening of United Nations Security Council televised.
Color television demonstrations by CBS and NBC.

1947 Congress opening televised for first time.
Blue baby operation televised.
Kraft Television Theater series begins.
FCC denies CBS color-television petition.
Durr questions value of undocumented, unsolicited FBI data.
Counterattack newsletter launched.
HUAC hearings on Hollywood.

1948 Frieda Hennock becomes first FCC woman commissioner.
33 1/3 and 45 RPM records appear.
Philadelphia becomes convention site because of television cable.
Truman stresses barnstorming tour instead of broadcasts.
CBS talent raids on NBC based on capital-gains tax rate.
Armstrong sues RCA over FM patent infringement.
U.S. v. *Paramount et al.*, won by government.
FCC starts "freeze" on television licenses.
Rise of Negro radio stations.

1949 Inauguration telecast for first time.
I Can Hear It Now LP album appears.

1950 Paul Draper appearance on *Toast of the Town* attacked.
Red Channels appears.
Cases of Jean Muir, Philip Loeb, and many others.
Laurence Johnson of Syracuse enters the blacklist field.
CBS institutes a loyalty oath.
Hear It Now radio series launched by Murrow.

1951 Movie attendance dropping sharply in television cities.
Wave of movie theater closings.
ABC-Paramount Theaters merger negotiated.
NBC launches *Today* television series.
CBS starts Murrow-Friendly *See It Now* television series.

Blacklisting institutionalized at networks and agencies.

1952 FCC reserves television channels for education.

Amendments to Communications Act.

FCC lifts "freeze" and processes license applications.

Nixon "Checkers" speech.

Eisenhower 20-second spot campaign.

Hundreds of television stations rush to reach air.

1953 ABC and Paramount Theaters merge.

Noncommercial television begins in Houston.

Senator Joseph R. McCarthy directs purges and appointments at Voice of America and FCC.

Marty broadcast on *Goodyear Television Playhouse.*

Radio Liberation launched.

Formation of Aware, Inc.

1954 *See It Now* documentary on Senator McCarthy, and his reply.

Army-McCarthy hearings carried live by ABC-TV.

Increase in censorship disputes on anthology series.

Rise of filmed episodic series.

Disney and Warner Brothers contract to produce for ABC-TV.

Armed Forces Radio Service launches television outlets.

1955 Filming of Eisenhower press conferences permitted, subject to pre-release review.

The $64,000 Question precipitates big-money quiz boom.

Commercial television in Britain and Japan widens market for telefilms.

Robert Sarnoff takes over NBC presidency.

1956 John Henry Faulk files suit over Aware attack and blacklist conspiracy.

Cheyenne stirs avalanche of television westerns.

Release of hundreds of pre-1948 features brings decline in local television production.

Huntley-Brinkley team formed for NBC convention telecasts.

Eisenhower-Stevenson campaign features five-minute "hitch-hike" programs.

1957 Inauguration recorded for first time by videotape.

William Worthy broadcasts over CBS from Peking and Shanghai and is deprived of passport by State Department.

American Cancer Society report on smoking brings advertising emphasis on long and filter cigarettes.

Nikita Khrushchev on *Face the Nation* over CBS.

John C. Doerfer becomes FCC chairman.

1958 Bribery evidence brings resignation of FCC commissioner Richard A. Mack.

CBS ends *See It Now*.

Robert Kintner becomes NBC president as Robert Sarnoff assumes chairmanship.

1959 Nixon-Khrushchev "kitchen debate" in Moscow.

Khrushchev tour of United States widely covered by television.

Revelations of quiz rigging bring rise in public-service budgets and debut of *CBS Reports*.

James T. Aubrey becomes CBS-TV president.

1960 Radio Swan launched by CIA to prepare for invasion of Cuba.

Time documentary *Primary* stirs *cinéma vérité* movement.

FCC chairman John C. Doerfer resigns on request over issue of fraternization with industry.

Networks ban news documentaries other than their own.

The Untouchables leads trend to violence in telefilms.

Khrushchev-Castro meeting on Harlem sidewalk televised.

Richard M. Nixon and John F. Kennedy meet in *The Great Debates*.

1961 Eisenhower, in television farewell, warns against military-industrial complex.

Kennedy inaugural signals policy of encouragement to arts.

Edward R. Murrow heads USIA.

Kennedy allows filming and televising of presidential press conferences without restriction.

Wide falsification of Bay of Pigs news by CIA fronts.

Senator Thomas J. Dodd studies television violence.

ABC-TV inaugurates 40-second station break for extra commercial, and other networks follow example.

FCC chairman Newton N. Minow finds a vast wasteland.

1962 Non-commercial television acquires New York Channel 13.

John Henry Faulk wins unprecedented award over blacklist conspiracy.

Telstar I inaugurates satellite relays of television programs.

Growth of noncommercial television aided by federal grants for facilities.

Cuban missile crisis brings televised ultimatum.

NBC-TV broadcasts *The Tunnel*.

Rise of *The Beverly Hillbillies*.

1963 E. William Henry succeeds Newton Minow as FCC chairman.

"I Have a Dream" speech by Martin Luther King climaxes March on Washington telecasts.

Westward move by baseball Giants and Dodgers linked to plans of Subscription TV, Inc.

Networks start half-hour evening newscasts.

Assassination and funeral of President Kennedy and murder of Lee Harvey Oswald rivet world attention through four days of coverage.

1964 United Church monitors television stations in Jackson, Mississippi.

Fred W. Friendly becomes CBS News president.

Instant replay adds new dimension to sport telecasts.

CBS buys New York Yankees baseball team.

Johnson-Goldwater campaign features girl-with-a-daisy and other spots.

Subscription TV, Inc., halted by California referendum.

1965 Former FCC commissioner Frederick W. Ford heads National Community Television Association.

Early Bird synchronous satellite makes debut.

Increased coverage of Vietnam as war escalates.

John A. Schneider succeeds James Aubrey as CBS-TV president.

Television network news shifting to color.

CBS occupies new skyscraper headquarters.

1966 Referendum outlawing pay-television declared unconstitutional by California Supreme Court.

Friendly resigns over CBS decision to halt coverage of Senate hearings on Vietnam war.

FCC assumes jurisdiction over cable television.

Spies and war dominate telefilms.

Asian tour by President Johnson receives wide coverage.

1967 Anti-war marches and demonstrations seen with increasing frequency on newcasts.

Occasional use of newsfilm from North Vietnam.

PBL series launched over NET stations.

Corporation for Public Broadcasting formed.

1968 NET schedules portion of Felix Greene film *Inside North Vietnam* and is assailed by congressmen.

Television coverage of New Hampshire primary indicates strong support for anti-war stand of Senator Eugene McCarthy.

Martin Luther King announces Poor People's March as war protest.

President Johnson broadcasts decision not to be a candidate for re-election.

Rowan & Martin's Laugh-In popularizes kaleidoscopic comedy style.

ITT-ABC merger blocked.

Televised funeral of Martin Luther King, killed by sniper.

CBS-TV broadcast of *Hunger in America* stirs wide response.

Televised funeral of Senator Robert Kennedy, assassinated after primary victory.

Scenes of violence mark Democratic convention coverage.

Record sums spent on Nixon-Humphrey television campaigns, but many voters abstain.

Television films temporarily pruned of violence.

1969 CBS cancels *Smothers Brothers Comedy Hour* after frequent censorship clashes

Apollo flights climaxed by televised moon landings.

Dean Burch becomes FCC chairman.

Debut of *Sesame Street*.

President Nixon makes televised appeal to "silent majority."

Vice President Agnew begins attacks on network news.

1970 Robert Sarnoff becomes RCA board chairman.

Widespread Earth Day telecasts.

Whitehead becomes White House adviser on "telecommunications policy."

Fiftieth anniversary of KDKA debut that launched broadcasting era.

Who Invited Us?, on public television, irks White House.

1971 Ban on broadcast cigarette advertising goes into effect.

New surge of protest against Vietnam war, on and off air.

The Selling of the Pentagon on CBS.

All in the Family, emulating British comedy series about a bigot, scores success on CBS.

The Great American Dream Machine on public television.

President Nixon announces plans for Peking and Moscow visits.

1972 Telecasts of Nixon visits to Peking, Moscow, Warsaw.

Watergate break-in dismissed by White House spokesman as "third-rate burglary attempt."

Kissinger tells nation that peace is "within reach."

Landslide victory for Nixon over McGovern.

Nixon veto of public-television appropriation precipitates reorganization and decentralization of system.

1973 Accumulating evidence leads to televised Watergate inquiry by Senate committee.

Watergate hearings give public television record ratings.

Existence of White House tape recordings revealed. Agnew resigns after revelations of income tax fraud and bribery.

British import *Upstairs, Downstairs* wins kudos on public television in *Masterpiece Theater* series.

1974 Widespread telecasts and radio broadcasts of White House tape transcripts.

Nixon visits to Middle East and Moscow televised.

Televised impeachment deliberations by House judiciary committee.

Nixon telecasts resignation statement, is succeeded by President Gerald Ford.

1975 World audiences watch United States evacuation of Cambodia and Vietnam, and the collapse of its "client" regimes.

Bionic heroes and heroines bring new wave of omnipotence drama and rise of ABC-TV to competitive position.

Nielsen's demographic ratings increasingly important in sponsorship decisions.

1976 Nation celebrates two-hundredth birthday with television spectaculars.

World views Martian landscape via American television.

Presidential victory of Jimmy Carter, new face on the tube, reflects disillusionment with "Washington."

ABC-TV wins season lead with Olympics coverage.

Lawsuit by Writers Guild of America voids "family viewing policy" of NAB code.

1977 First indications of slump in television popularity and viewing.

AT&T starts Chicago test of glass fiber as substitute for copper wires in telephone, television, computer, and other communication services, and plans further tests.

Roots series of eight programs, family saga depicting history of slavery in America, breaks audience records.

1978 *Holocaust* series wins largest audience of year.

Public Broadcasting System launches plan for satellite interconnection of its stations via Western Union satellite, giving stations program choice.

Library of Congress announces plans for television and radio archive to "preserve the broadcasting heritage of the American people."

1979 NBC-TV bid wins right to televise 1980 Moscow Olympics.

U.S. Postal Service conducts Washington-London electronic mail experiments, looking to eventual integration into home and office telecommunication systems.

COMSAT announces plans for satellite programming direct to the home, via rooftop dishes to be marketed by Sears, Roebuck.

Moral Majority and other groups threaten sponsor boycotts over sex-and-violence issue.

1980 U.S. boycott of Moscow Olympics in protest of Soviet troops in Afghanistan cancels NBC television coverage.

Political Action Committees play prominent role in presidential and congressional television campaigns.

Warner's two-way cable-television system, Qube, quickly wins a following in Columbus, Ohio.

"Who shot J. R.?" mystery sends *Dallas* to top of Nielsen ratings.

American hostages in Iran, newscast topic throughout year, a factor in undermining Carter reelection drive.

Reagan and Bush win election landslide.

1981 Reagan inaugural and return of hostages share headlines and television spotlight.

Nation horrified by attempted assassination of Reagan on Washington sidewalk, seen widely via instant replays.

First National Video Festival organized in Washington by American Film Institute, spotlighting a decade of video production.

CBS-TV broadcasts five-part documentary on *The Defense of the United States*, with global view of problems and plans.

1982 Reagan administration stress on broadcasting deregulation augurs era of fierce competition among new technologies.

Cable television experiencing boom period via numerous new satellite program services.

Allegations of illegal U.S. arms sales to Iran appear in press but are generally ignored by electronic media.

1983 Rupert Murdoch announces plans for DBS (direct broadcast satellite) program services.

1984 Qube, troubled by nonrenewals in Columbus interactive cable system, pulls back from its plans.

The Cosby Show debuts on NBC and moves quickly toward ratings leadership.

U.S. Supreme Court sanctions noncommercial off-air home taping, upholding Sony against Hollywood suit.

1985 Amid rash of mergers and take-overs ABC, CBS, and NBC pass to new ownership. Multimedia conglomerates increasingly dominate media world.

1986 *Eyes on the Prize*, film series chronicling civil-rights struggles, wins many honors via PBS telecasts.

1987 Home video rentals boom amid further innovations: *Top Gun* cassette includes a commercial for Pepsi Cola.

Nielsen switches from audimeters to people meters, pioneered by British research firm; new research procedure documents shift away from networks toward other program choices.

1988 ABC's *Amerika* miniseries assailed and ridiculed.

Televised congressional Iran/contra hearings probe wide spectrum of governmental deceptions and related private frauds.

Negative advertising and PACs play prominent role in presidential election campaign.

President Reagan visits Moscow in new televised spectacular.

1989 President George Bush and Vice President Dan Quayle take office amid worldwide political upheavals, economic pressures, and environmental crises.

Time, Inc. absorbs Warner Brothers to create new multimedia colossus.

Rise of "trash TV."

U.S. media face unprecedented uncertainties and challenges.

BIBLIOGRAPHICAL NOTES

The following notes indicate the principal sources of each section of this work, and suggest additional readings. For more detailed information on sources, see the extensive bibliographies in the author's *A History of Broadcasting in the United States*, which appeared in three volumes (New York, Oxford University Press, 1966, 1968, 1970). The first volume, *A Tower in Babel*, carries the story to 1933; the second volume, *The Golden Web*, covers the period 1933-1953; the third volume, *The Image Empire*, takes the story from 1953. *Tube of Plenty* is a condensed and updated version of this larger history.

1. FOREBEARS

For the early history of the telephone and its influence on other media see Rhodes, Frederick Leland, *Beginnings of Telephony* (New York, Harper, 1929); and Harlow, Alvin F., *Old Wires and New Waves: the history of the telegraph, telephone, and wireless* (New York, Appleton-Century, 1936).

Black Box No. 1

The Marconi story is told with special eloquence in Marconi, Degna, *My Father, Marconi* (New York, McGraw-Hill, 1962). For a somewhat more technical account, see Dunlap, Orrin E., Jr., *Marconi: the man and his wireless* (New York, Macmillan, 1937).

Voices in the Ether

For the Fessenden story see Fessenden, Helen M., *Fessenden: builder of tomorrows* (New York, Coward-McCann, 1940). De Forest's frequently fluctuating fortunes are absorbingly recounted in his *Father of Radio: the autobiography of Lee de Forest* (Chicago, Wilcox & Follett, 1950), and in Carneal, Georgette, *A Conqueror of Space: an authorized biography of the life and work of Lee de Forest* (New York, Liveright, 1930). The role of the amateurs during the early radio period is richly illuminated by numerous accounts in the Columbia University Oral History Collection, also available in the Broadcast Pioneers History Project library, National Association of Broadcasters, Washington. See especially reminiscences of Everett L. Bragdon, Edgar H. Felix, Edgar J. Love, Stanley R. Manning, Ray Newby, William Edmund Scripps.

We Need a Monopoly

Schubert, Paul, *The Electric Word: the rise of radio* (New York, Macmillan, 1928) provides a highly readable account of navy contributions to early radio. The official *History of Communications-Electronics in the United States Navy* (Washington, Government Printing Office, 1963), written under the auspices of the Bureau of Ships and Office of Naval History in the U.S. Navy Department, presents the story in greater detail, from a bureaucratic vantage point. For a personal view of naval radio in wartime, see the fascinating *Papers 1906-47* of Malcolm P. Hanson in the Mass Communication History Center of the Wisconsin Historical Society. Congressional debates on the proposed navy control over radio will be found in *Government Control of Radio Communication: hearings before the committee on merchant marine and fisheries*, U.S. House of Representatives, 65th Congress, 3rd session, December 12-19, 1918 (Washington, Government Printing Office, 1919). For the formation of RCA see Archer, Gleason L., *History of Radio: to 1926* (New York, American Historical Society, 1938) and

Tarbell, Ida M., *Owen D. Young: a new type of industrial leader* (New York, Macmillan, 1932). An additional, unpublished source is Clark, George H., *The Formation of RCA*, in the Radioana Collection, Smithsonian Institution, Washington.

2. TODDLER

The story of Frank Conrad is told vividly in the reminiscences of his co-worker Donald G. Little, in the Columbia University Oral History Collection, also available in the Broadcast Pioneers History Project library, National Association of Broadcasters, Washington. See also *Dr. Conrad and His Work*, a long Westinghouse press release of 1942, in the Mass Communication History Center of the Wisconsin Historical Society; also, Archer, Gleason L., *History of Radio: to 1926*, mentioned above.

Merchandising Concept

The genesis of KDKA and other Westinghouse stations is told from a management point of view in Davis, H. P., "The Early History of Broadcasting in the United States," *The Radio Industry* (Chicago, A. W. Shaw, 1928).

Raggle-taggle Mob

Lessing, Lawrence, *Man of High Fidelity: Edwin Howard Armstrong* (Philadelphia, Lippincott, 1956) portrays tellingly the revolt of upstart "amateurs" against RCA hegemony. The chief government study of the controversy is *Report of the Federal Trade Commission on the Radio Industry* (Washington, Government Printing Office, 1924). See also Jome, Hiram L., *Economics of the Radio Industry* (Chicago, A. W. Shaw, 1925).

Come Into Our Phone Booth

The issue of "ether advertising" is discussed in various early issues of *Radio Broadcast*, published monthly 1922-30 by Doubleday, Page, in Garden City, N.Y. The genesis of the sponsored-broadcasting idea within AT&T is told in the unpublished Espenschied, Lloyd, *Recollec-*

tions of the Radio Industry, available in the Columbia University Oral History Collection and in the Broadcast Pioneers History Project library, National Association of Broadcasters, Washington. The birth of WEAF is chronicled in Banning, William Peck, *Commercial Broadcasting Pioneer: the WEAF experiment 1922-1926* (Cambridge, Harvard University Press, 1946).

The Birth of NBC

The indispensable source on the feud between the RCA partners, and the détente which brought the birth of NBC, is Archer, Gleason L., *Big Business and Radio* (New York, American Historical Company, 1939). Based on material made available to Archer by David Sarnoff in 1938, it goes over events already covered by Archer in *History of Radio: to 1926*, but presents a different view of them.

But Not the Ownership Thereof

For the text of the 1927 Radio Act, see Public Law No. 632, 69th Congress. For the debates see *Congressional Record*, v. 67.

Flickering Snapshot

Hubbell, Richard W., *4000 Years of Television: the story of seeing at a distance* (New York, Putnam, 1942). For the Wall Street boom in radio stocks, see Allen, Frederick Lewis, *Only Yesterday: an informal history of the nineteen-twenties* (New York, Harper, 1951). For the rise of CBS see Landry, Robert J., *This Fascinating Radio Business* (Indianapolis, Bobbs-Merrill, 1946).

A Bill of Divorcement

The principal source is the already-mentioned Archer, *Big Business and Radio*. For a vivid glimpse of the negotiations see the reminiscences of Walter C. Evans in the Columbia University Oral History Collection and the Broadcast Pioneers History Project library, National Association of Broadcasters, Washington.

Fifty-third Floor

Zworykin, Vladimir K., "The Early Days," *Television Quarterly*, November 1962. For the protest movement against the broadcasting status quo see *Report of the Advisory Committee on Education by Radio* (Columbus, F. J. Heer Printing Company, 1930) and Rorty, James, *Our Master's Voice: advertising* (New York, John Day, 1934). For the Brinkley story see the enlightening Carson, Gerald, *The Roguish World of Doctor Brinkley* (New York, Holt, Rinehart & Winston, 1960). For the debates on the 1934 Communications Act, see *Congressional Record*, v. 78.

Of Attics and Back Rooms

For the Farnsworth story, Everson, George, *The Story of Television: the life of Philo T. Farnsworth* (New York, Norton, 1949). On the Armstrong-Sarnoff feud see Lessing, Lawrence, *Man of High Fidelity: Edwin Howard Armstrong* (Philadelphia, Lippincott, 1956).

Target Date

Porterfield, John, and Kay Reynolds (eds.), *We Present Television,* gives a comprehensive picture of television production on the eve of World War II. De Forest, Lee, *Television: today and tomorrow* (New York, Dial, 1942) summarizes its technical status. For a portrait of David Sarnoff, his career and style of leadership, see Tebbel, John, *David Sarnoff: putting electrons to work* (Chicago, Encyclopedia Britannica Press, 1963); also Lyons, Eugene, *David Sarnoff: a biography* (New York, Harper & Row, 1966).

3. PLASTIC YEARS

The blow-by-blow struggle over color systems can be traced in *Broadcasting*, published in Washington since 1931—at first semi-monthly, then weekly.

Mosaic

The NBC memorandum was *Prospects for NBC Telecasting 1946-50.* A copy is in Hedges, *Papers*, Broadcast Pioneers History Project, National Association of Broadcasters, Washington. Reviews in the entertainment weekly *Variety* (New York, published since 1905) provide a vivid overview of television program developments of the period.

Or Affiliated Sympathetically

The Durr-FBI contest erupts in the *Minutes* of the Federal Communications Commission, December 1, 1947. The various Durr statements are quoted in Cook, Fred J., *The FBI Nobody Knows* (New York, Macmillan, 1964). The Hollywood hearings testimony will be found in *Hearings: before committee on un-American activities on communist infiltration of Hollywood motion picture industry* (Washington, Government Printing Office, 1947). *Counterattack: the newsletter of facts on communism* was published monthly, 1947-55, by American Business Consultants, New York.

Freeze

The Truman comments on the "kept press and paid radio" are in Truman, Harry S., *Memoirs: years of trial and hope* (Garden City, N.Y., Doubleday, 1956). The impact of television in the "television cities" was surveyed by the New York *Times* in a series of articles published on seven consecutive days starting June 24, 1951.

Panic City

The "Paramount case"—*U.S. v. Paramount et al.*, 334 U.S. 131 (1948)—is exhaustively reviewed in Conant, Michael, *Antitrust in the Motion Picture Industry* (New York, Macmillan, 1946). For screen-writer Ardrey's close-up of the panic, see Ardrey, Robert, "Hollywood: the toll of the frenzied forties," *Reporter*, March 21, 1957.

It Will Be a Great Show

Revealing sources on the Ed Sullivan brouhaha include: Kahn, E. J., "The Greenwich Tea Party," *New Yorker*, April 15, 1950; Miller, Merle, *The Judges and the Judged* (Garden City, N.Y., Doubleday, 1952). The Kenyon & Eckhardt agency prepared for its sponsor, the Ford Motor Company, a document entitled *A Report on the Results of Paul Draper's Appearance on "Toast of the Town" Sunday, January*

22, 1950. The Ed Sullivan column on Kirkpatrick and the coming "bombshell" was in New York *Daily News,* June 21, 1950.

Handy Reference

Red Channels: the report of communist influence in radio and television (New York, American Business Consultants, 1950) was the starting point of most broadcasting blacklists. The mushroom growth of the blacklist movement is well told in Cogley, John, *Report on Blacklisting, II: radio-television* (Fund for the Republic, 1956), and in Miller, Merle, *The Judges and the Judged,* mentioned above.

Crusade in the Supermarkets

Much information on Laurence Johnson emerged in testimony in a lawsuit filed in 1956 by John Henry Faulk against Laurence Johnson and others. See Nizer, Louis, *The Jury Returns* (Garden City, N.Y., Doubleday, 1966); and Faulk, John Henry, *Fear on Trial* (New York, Simon & Schuster, 1964).

Crime Automated

Two illuminating sources on the live episodic series are the reminiscences of Philip Reisman, Jr. and Ralph Bellamy in the Columbia University Oral History Project.

Ike and Ikon

For the 1952 presidential campaign see Mayer, Martin, *Madison Avenue, U.S.A.* (New York, Harper, 1958); Nixon, Richard M., *Six Crises* (Garden City, N.Y., Doubleday, 1962); Mazo, Earl, *Richard Nixon: a political and personal portrait* (New York, Harper, 1959); Eisenhower, Dwight D., *The White House Years: mandate for change* (Garden City, N.Y., Doubleday, 1963).

Sixth Report and Order

For the *Broadcasting* attack on the educational television reservations, see the issue of November 10, 1952. The results of the New York monitoring studies were reported in Smythe, Dallas W., *Three Years of*

New York Television 1951-1953 (Urbana, Ill., National Association of Educational Broadcasters). This was No. 6 in a series of such studies, which also reported on "acts and threats" of violence on Los Angeles television.

High Level

The tragedy is superbly told in Lessing, Lawrence, *Man of High Fidelity: Edwin Howard Armstrong* (Philadelphia, Lippincott, 1956).

Maelstrom

See the kaleidoscopic chronicle by Schulman, Arthur, and Roger Youman, *The Television Years* (New York, Popular Library, 1973); also Green, Gerald, "What Does the Monkey Do?", in Barrett, Edward W. (ed.), *Journalists in Action* (Manhasset, N.Y., Channel Press, 1963).

4. PRIME

For Senator Joseph R. McCarthy on the rise, see Wilson, Richard, "The Ring Around McCarthy," *Look*, December 1, 1953; and Rovere, Richard H., *Senator Joe McCarthy* (Cleveland, World, 1960). Also Lamb, Edward, *No Lamb for Slaughter* (New York, Harcourt, Brace & World, 1963).

Television Theater

Among the most illuminating comments on the anthology drama period are the Chayefsky prefaces to his plays, published in Chayefsky, Paddy, *Television Plays* (New York, Simon & Schuster, 1955). See also Rose, Reginald, *Six Television Plays* (New York, Simon & Schuster, 1956), and Vidal, Gore (ed.), *Best Television Plays* (New York, Ballantine, 1956). For rising control problems see Rice, Elmer, "The Biography of a Play," *Theatre Arts*, November 1959. The Hartnett correspondence concerning Aware, Inc., read at a meeting of the American Federation of Radio and Television Artists (AFTRA), was entered in the union minutes, and later became evidence in the case of *Faulk* v. *Aware et al.* Quoted, Nizer, Louis, *The Jury Returns* (Garden City, N.Y., Doubleday, 1966).

Hopscotching

For *Broadcasting*'s admiration of Swayze, see the issue of March 2, 1953.

The Murrow Moment

The indispensable source is the eloquent Friendly, Fred W., *Due to Circumstances Beyond Our Control* . . . (New York, Random House, 1967. See also Kendrick, Alexander, *Prime Time: the life of Edward R. Murrow* (Boston, Little, Brown, 1969).

Biggest Money

The account by Walter Craig is from a recorded interview in the Broadcast Pioneers History Project library, National Association of Broadcasters, Washington.

Executive Suites

The Robert Sarnoff testimony is quoted from FCC Docket No. 12782, *Hearings*, p. 3386.

Go Western

The NBC-MCA liaison is described in *Fortune*, July 1960.

Boom Land

The Dichter periodical, *Motivations*, was published by Motivational Publications, Inc., Croton-on-Hudson, N.Y.; see the issue of September 1957. For the scandals unearthed by Professor Schwartz, see Schwartz, Bernard, *The Professor and the Commissions* (New York, Knopf, 1959). The Carl Watson memo appeared in *Hearings of Antitrust Subcommittee of the Committee on the Judiciary*, House of Representatives, 84th Congress, 2nd session (Washington, Government Printing Office, 1956). The Edmerson study, a master's essay written in 1954 at the University of California in Los Angeles, was titled Edmerson, Estelle, *A Descriptive Study of the American Negro in United States Pro-*

fessional Radio 1922-1953. The Aware, Inc. bulletins appeared from 1954 to 1956.

Telefilm

For the Kefauver criticisms of television violence, see "Let's Get Rid of Tele-Violence," *Reader's Digest,* April 1956. For industry replies, see *Broadcasting,* April 9 and 23, 1956. See also Liebert, Robert M., with John M. Neale and Emily S. Davidson, *The Early Window: effects of television on children and youth* (New York, Pergamon, 1973).

Dynamic Duo

Quotations are from Dulles, *Papers,* and from oral-history reminiscences in the Dulles Collection, Princeton University. Quoted reminiscences include those of George V. Allen, David Schoenbrun, David Waters. Additional valuable sources: Sorensen, Thomas C., *The Word War: the story of American propaganda* (New York, Harper, 1968); Dulles, Allen W., *The Craft of Intelligence* (New York, Harper & Row, 1963); Drummond, Roscoe, and Gaston Coblentz, *Duel at the Brink: John Foster Dulles' command of American power* (Garden City, N.Y., Doubleday, 1960); Wise, David, and Thomas B. Ross, *The Invisible Government* (New York, Random House, 1964).

Bonanza Globe

The campaign to commercialize British television was described in Wilson, H. H., *Pressure Group* (New Brunswick, N.J., Rutgers University Press, 1961). For the comments by Robert E. Button, see New York *Times,* February 26, 1956. On the demise of *See It Now* see Crosby, John, *With Love and Loathing* (New York, McGraw-Hill, 1963).

The New Diplomacy

A lively description of Khrushchev diplomacy will be found in Hearst, William Randolph, Jr., Bob Considine, and Frank Conniff, *Khrushchev and the Russian Challenge* (New York, Avon, 1961).

A Terrible Thing To Do

For the full Charles Van Doren disclosure, see New York *Times*, November 3, 1959. See also *Broadcasting*, November 9, 1959.

Summitry on the Move

For sidelights on the Khrushchev visit see especially Crankshaw, Edward, *Khrushchev: a career* (New York, Viking, 1966); Schumach, Murray, *The Face on the Cutting Room Floor: the story of movie and television censorship* (New York, Morrow, 1964).

Untouchables

The principal documents relating to the editorial policies of *The Untouchables* are in the unpublished *Television and Juvenile Delinquency: interim report of the subcommittee to investigate juvenile delinquency, committee on the judiciary*, U.S. Senate, 88th Congress, 2nd session; a copy is in FCC library. For testimony see *Juvenile Delinquency: hearings before the subcommittee to investigate juvenile delinquency, committee on the judiciary*, U.S. Senate, 87th Congress, Part 10: effects on young people of violence and crime portrayed on television (Washington, Government Printing Office, 1963).

Vérité

For the genesis of *cinéma vérité* see Barnouw, Erik, *Documentary: a history of the non-fiction film* (New York, Oxford University Press, 1974); also Mamber, Stephen, *Cinema Verite in America: studies in uncontrolled documentary* (Cambridge, Mass., MIT Press, 1947).

Barefaced

For the television campaign of 1960, see especially Sorensen, Theodore C., *Kennedy* (New York, Harper, 1965); White, Theodore H., *The Making of the President 1960* (New York, Atheneum, 1961); and Wyckoff, Gene, *The Image Candidates: American politics in the age of television* (New York, Macmillan, 1968). The temporary amendment to the Communications Act, making the Great Debates possible, was Public Law 86-677, signed August 24, 1960.

Top Priorities

For the Bay of Pigs invasion preparations, see Johnson, Haynes, with Manuel Artime, José Peréz San Román, Erneido Oliva, and Enrique Ruiz-Williams, *The Bay of Pigs: the leaders' story of brigade 2506* (New York, Norton, 1964).

The Camelot Moment

The mystique of the period is splendidly conveyed in Schlesinger, Arthur M., Jr., *A Thousand Days: John F. Kennedy in the White House* (Boston, Houghton Mifflin, 1965). Numerous documentaries of the period are discussed in Bluem, A. William, *Documentary in American Television* (New York, Hastings, 1965).

Deception, Inc.

The media corruptions involved in the Bay of Pigs invasion plans are detailed in Wise and Ross, *The Invisible Government*, previously mentioned. See also Szulc, Tad, and Karl E. Meyer, *The Cuban Invasion: the chronicle of a disaster* (New York, Ballantine, 1962).

Vast Wasteland

The stunning impact of the "vast wasteland" speech is tellingly reported in *Broadcasting*, May 15, 1961. The story of Thomas J. Dodd, the corrupted crusader, is well told in Boyd, James, *Above the Law: the rise and fall of Senator Thomas J. Dodd* (New York, New American Library, 1968).

Into Orbit

Two articles by Arthur C. Clarke, British scientist and science fiction writer, proved to be milestones in the evolution of ideas about communication satellites: "Extraterrestrial Relays," *Wireless World*, October 1945; and "Faces from the Sky," *Holiday*, September 1959.

Ultimatum Via TV

The missile crisis and its television involvement receive special attention in Abel, Elie, *The Missile Crisis* (New York, Bantam, 1966); and in

Kennedy, Robert F., *Thirteen Days: a memoir of the Cuban missile crisis* (New York, Signet, 1969). See also Hilsman, Roger, *To Move a Nation: the politics of foreign policy in the administration of John F. Kennedy* (New York, Delta, 1968).

Venture Video

The making of *The Tunnel* is traced in Frank, Reuven, "The Making of *The Tunnel*," *Television Quarterly*, Fall 1963. For the triumphant conclusion of the John Henry Faulk ordeal, see Faulk, John Henry, *Fear on Trial* (New York, Simon & Schuster, 1964).

November Drums

Sources of special interest: Manchester, William, *The Death of a President* (New York, Harper & Row, 1967); Mannes, Marya, "The Long Vigil," *Reporter*, December 19, 1963; and *Four Days: the historical record of the death of President Kennedy*, compiled by United Press International and *American Heritage Magazine* (New York, American Heritage, 1964).

5. ELDER

For the precedent-setting—and insufficiently recognized—work of the United Church of Christ in the field of minority programming see *Racial Justice in Broadcasting* (New York, United Church of Christ, 1970); also Barrett, Marvin (ed.), *Survey of Broadcast Journalism 1968-1969* (New York, Grosset & Dunlap, 1969).

The Adversary Culture

The adversary relationship between network divisions is especially well illuminated in Friendly, Fred W., *Due to Circumstances Beyond Our Control . . .* (New York, Random House, 1967) and on a continuing basis in the pages of *Columbia Journalism Review*, published quarterly; see its Spring 1964 issue for affiliate resistance to extended network news service. For Sevareid's comments on the "distribution of anxiety" see Sevareid, Eric, *This Is Eric Sevareid* (New York, McGraw-Hill 1964).

Daisy Girl

For interesting reflections on the 1964 television campaign see New York *Times*, October 21, 1964; *Reporter*, November 19, 1964; *Wall Street Journal*, January 15, 1965.

Paranoid Pictures

Instructions to writers for *Mission: Impossible* are quoted from the multigraphed *Writing "Mission Impossible"* (Hollywood, Geller, undated), issued to writers *ca.* 1966. For the comments by Robert Lewis Shayon see *Saturday Review*, November 19, 1966. Viewing patterns among the young are examined by Schramm, Wilbur, with Jack Lyle and Edwin Parker, in *Television in the Lives of Our Children* (Palo Alto, Stanford University Press, 1961).

Newsroom Uprising

The indispensable source is the previously mentioned *Due to Circumstances Beyond Our Control . . .* , by Fred W. Friendly. Other valuable sources: Arlen, Michael J., *Living Room War* (New York, Viking, 1969); MacNeil, Robert, *The People Machine* (New York, Harper & Row, 1968); Compton, Neil, "Consensus Television," *Commentary*, October 1965, and "Camping in the Wasteland," *Commentary*, January 1966; comments by Eric Sevareid quoted in *Congressional Record*, v. 112, pp. 14125-6; and *Columbia Journalism Review*, Spring 1966.

Guard That Image

Davie, Michael, *LBJ: a foreign observer's viewpoint* (New York, Ballantime, 1967) and Goldman, Eric F., *The Tragedy of Lyndon Johnson* (New York, Knopf, 1969) provide compelling close-ups of Johnson as broadcaster and image manager.

Fringes

See Innis, Harold A., *Empire and Communications* (Oxford, Clarendon Press, 1950) as a pioneer investigation of media monopolies and their relation to political power. See also Schiller, Herbert I., *Mass Com-*

munications and American Empire (New York, Kelley, 1969); and Greene, Felix, *A Curtain of Ignorance* (Garden City, N.Y., Doubleday, 1964). The uproar over *Inside North Vietnam* is discussed in *Saturday Review,* February 3, 1968. The Carnegie television recommendations are in *Public Television: a program for action* (New York, Bantam, 1967).

The Fortress

Brown, Les, *Television-the business behind the box* (New York, Harcourt Brace Jovanovich, 1971) provides a valuable industry close-up. See also the useful *Survey of Broadcast Journalism* series (1968-1969, 1969-1970, 1970-1971), a project of the Alfred I. Dupont-Columbia University awards and published by Grosset & Dunlap.

High Noon

The violent events of 1968 generated an extensive literature. Relevant to television developments are Mailer, Norman, *Miami and the Siege of Chicago* (New York, New American Library, 1968); Halberstam, David, *The Unfinished Odyssey of Robert F. Kennedy* (New York, Random House, 1969); Neufield, Jack, *Robert Kennedy: a memoir* (New York, Dutton, 1969); McGinniss, Joe, *The Selling of the President 1968* (New York, Trident, 1969); White, Theodore H., *The Making of the President 1968* (New York, Atheneum, 1969).

Cosmic Nielsen

Wilford, John Noble, *We Reach the Moon* (New York, Bantam, 1969), illustrated with photographs from the television screen, traces the evolution of the Apollo program. For the Shayon critique, see *Saturday Review,* August 9, 1969.

Conglomerate

Sampson, Anthony, *The Sovereign State of ITT* (New York, Stein & Day, 1973) reviews the controversy over the proposed ABC merger. For the various FCC opinions, including the 72-page dissent of Commissioner Nicholas Johnson, see FCC Docket No. 16828.

Relevance

For background on the Norman Lear programs, see especially *New York Times Magazine*, June 24, 1973. For the genesis of *Sesame Street* see Polsky, Richard M., *Getting to Sesame Street* (New York, Praeger, 1974). For a skeptical view see *Down Sesame Street* (New York, The Network Project, 1973).

Game Plans

Minow, Newton N., John Bartlow Martin, and Lee M. Mitchell, *Presidential Television* (New York, Basic Books, 1973) provides a fine survey of presidential uses of television. For the rise and fall of Vice President Agnew see Cohen, Richard M., and Jules Witcover, *A Heartbeat Away* (New York, Viking, 1974). For cogent analyses of network news operations see Epstein, Edward Jay, *News From Nowhere: television and the news* (New York, Random House, 1973), and the annual volumes edited by Marvin Barrett issued in conjunction with the Alfred I. Dupont-Columbia University awards.

Fiestas

For comments on *Roots* see Monaco, James, *Media Culture* (New York, Delta, 1978) and Sklar, Robert, *Prime-Time America* (New York, Oxford, 1980). The Bicentennial statements by Vincent T. Wasilewski and *Advertising Age* are quoted from "Advertising: 1776-1976," *Advertising Age*, April 19, 1976. On *The Ascent of Man* see Ledger, Marshall, "The Ascent of Adrian Malone," *New York Times Magazine*, March 15, 1981.

Demographics

For a more extensive discussion of the impact of demographic ratings see Barnouw, Erik, *The Sponsor: notes on a modern potentate* (New York, Oxford, 1978). See also *Where the Girls Are* (New York, CBS, 1970). The Nielsen publication *NTI in Action* gives an overview of Nielsen rating methods.

Squeaky Clean

The section is based mainly on Cowan, Geoffrey, *See No Evil* (New York, Simon & Schuster, 1978), a chronicle of the rise and fall of Family Time. For contemporary comment see Schrag, Peter, "TV's New Chastity Belt," *More*, August 1975. See *Emmy Magazine* (Los Angeles, Academy of Television Arts and Sciences) III, 3, Summer 1981, for a symposium on "Proliferation of Pressure Groups in Prime Time."

Voice From the West

For a review of the 1980 campaign see Harwood, Richard (ed.), *The Pursuit of the Presidency 1980* (New York, Berkley Books, 1980, in association with the Washington *Post*).

Winds of Doctrine

For enlightening comments on the new media technologies see especially Wicklein, John, *Electronic Nightmare: the new communications and freedom* (New York, Viking, 1981); also, Arlen, Michael J., "Talking Back," in *The Camera Age: essays on television* (New York, Farrar, Straus & Giroux, 1981). Various social issues are discussed in Joffe, Phyllis, "Cable and the Poor," *American Film*, October 1981; Schwartz, Tony, "The TV Pornographic Boom," *New York Times Magazine*, September 13, 1981; Gitlin, Todd, "Cabled Democracy," *Democracy*, October 1981.

6. PROGENY

For incipient struggles among new technologies see Wicklein, John, *Electronic Nightmare: the new communications and freedom* (New York, Viking, 1981), and special issues of *Channels* (New York) titled "1983 Field Guide to the Electronic Media" and "1984 Field Guide to the Electronic Media." For the rise of video see Boyle, Deirdre, *Subject to Change: guerrilla television revisited* (in process).

People Meters

The author is indebted to Couzens, Michael, "Invasion of the People Meters," *Channels*, June 1986; and to "Measuring the Audience," Summer 1988 issue of *Gannett Center Journal* (New York).

The Rise of the Laser

For the emergence of fiber optics and the laser-read videodisc see especially Brand, Stewart, *The Media Lab: inventing the future at M.I.T.* (New York, Penguin, 1988).

Mergermania

Key sources include Bagdikian, Ben H., *The Media Monopoly* (Boston, Beacon, 1983) and his "The Lords of the Global Village," special report in *The Nation*, June 12, 1989. Also Brown, Les, "Five Tumultuous Years," in 1987 guide to electronic media, *Channels;* Williams, Huntington (ed.), "The New Media Barons," Winter 1989 issue of *Gannett Center Journal.* For the submersion of the networks see Williams, Huntington, *Beyond Control: ABC and the fate of networks* (New York, Atheneum, 1989).

Product

Cable programming data are based on *TV Guide* 1988 issues. For *The Cosby Show* and other Carsey-Werner productions see *New York Times,* December 23, 1988. Quotations *re* the *Amerika* miniseries are from *New York Times*, Oct. 26, 1986; Jan. 5, 1987; Feb. 15, 1987. For the rise of "trash TV" see *Newsweek* and *Time* issues of Nov. 14, 1988. The troubles of documentarists vis-à-vis Reagan administration controls have been tellingly chronicled in *The Independent* (Association of Independent Video and Filmmakers, New York), issues of Nov. 1983, Aug./Sept. 1986, March 1988, March 1989, July 1989.

Twilight News

News management by Reagan White House is illuminated in Hertsgaard, Mark, *On Bended Knee: the press and the Reagan presidency* (New York, Farrar Straus Giroux, 1988); Schieffer, Bob, and Gates, Gary Paul, *The Acting President* (New York, Dutton, 1989); Wills, Garry, *Reagan's America: innocents abroad* (Garden City, N.Y., Doubleday, 1987).

Crossroads

For effects of U.S. television and associated institutions on electoral politics see Benjamin, Gerald (ed.), *The Communications Revolution in Politics* (New York, Academy of Political Science, 1982); Cobb, Jean, "The Power of the Purse," *Common Cause Magazine* (Washington, May/June issue 1988); and Stern, Philip M., *The Best Congress Money Can Buy* (New York, Pantheon, 1988).

INDEX